Reconstructing Development Theory

Reconstructing Development Theory

International Inequality, Institutional Reform and Social Emancipation

E.A. Brett
Development Studies Institute
London School of Economics

palgrave
macmillan

First published 2009 by
PALGRAVE MACMILLAN

Palgrave Macmillan in the UK is an imprint of Macmillan Publishers Limited, registered in England, company number 785998, of Houndmills, Basingstoke, Hampshire RG21 6XS.

Palgrave Macmillan in the US is a division of St Martin's Press LLC, 175 Fifth Avenue, New York, NY 10010.

Palgrave Macmillan is the global academic imprint of the above companies and has companies and representatives throughout the world.

Palgrave® and Macmillan® are registered trademarks in the United States, the United Kingdom, Europe and other countries.

ISBN-13: 978–0–230–22980–8 hardback
ISBN-13: 978–0–230–22981–5 paperback

This book is printed on paper suitable for recycling and made from fully managed and sustained forest sources. Logging, pulping and manufacturing processes are expected to conform to the environmental regulations of the country of origin.

A catalogue record for this book is available from the British Library.

A catalog record for this book is available from the Library of Congress.

10 9 8 7 6 5 4 3 2 1
18 17 16 15 14 13 12 11 10 09

Printed and bound in Great Britain by
CPI Antony Rowe, Chippenham and Eastbourne

For Daniel, Rebecca and Elliot
Stan and Spike

Contents

List of Figures and Tables

Figures

Tables

Preface

Against nature man can claim no right, but once society is established poverty immediately takes the form of a wrong done to one class by another. The important question of how poverty is to be abolished is one of the most disturbing problems which agitate modern society. (Hegel, 1821/1967: 277–8)

This book offers a synthetic review of a body of literature we now call 'development theory' that informs a rapidly expanding range of courses in institutes and departments of development studies across the world. Their graduates staff an increasingly important and sophisticated globalized enterprise that designs policy regimes and manages programmes and projects in what we will refer to as 'late developing countries' (LDCs), which have been managing transitions from colonialism or command planning for greater or shorter periods in the late 20th century. I use LDCs to refer to all third world countries, including successful ones like China.

'Latecomers' differ from 'first-comers' because they are still making their transitions to modernity, while the latter are already operating on the developmental frontier (Gerschenkron, 1965). The key role of the development community, and the academic community that informs it, is to support their attempt to transform the authority, incentive and accountability systems that govern their institutions and organizations, and therefore the principles that govern the political, economic, social and cultural systems that still operate in the second and third worlds. Their interventions are strongly influenced by theories based on the principles and practices that govern the institutional arrangements in first-comers, but what they do needs to be systematically modified to take account of the goals, capacities and endowments of the societies in which they operate. No one questions the existence or importance of this enterprise, or the scale and seriousness of their activities, since their work is central to all serious attempts to eliminate the problems of oppression, poverty, exclusion, instability and violence that disfigure the modern world. However, their diagnoses and policy prescriptions have always been heavily contested, and theorists and practitioners find it hard to distinguish between the assumptions and prescriptions that should guide courses in development theory as opposed to those in the orthodox social scientific disciplines to which they are closely related.

This book seeks to resolve some of these disagreements and provide an analytically coherent justification for our assumption that development studies already operates as 'an inherently multi-theoretical discipline' like political science (Dunleavy, 1991: 42), with a long and distinguished genealogy. It will do so by examining the causes and consequences of the tensions and disagreements between contending paradigms, look for underlying agreements in the work of the major theorists who lead the competing factions, and draw on all their critiques and prescriptions to reconstruct a policy-oriented approach to the specific problems of late development. We will identify some key issues in the rest of this Preface, and our formative assumptions and the structure of our argument in the Introduction.

A literature consciously concerned with problems of late development emerged after the war to address the economic problems confronted by 'new states' in the postcolonial world. These concerns differentiated it from orthodox neoclassical theorists who operated in industrialized and market-based societies, since these were still agrarian societies with repressed political and economic markets, traditional social systems, and embryonic capitalist classes. They therefore argued that these societies would need much higher levels of state intervention to manage their late transitions to market-based capitalism. This work in development economics was complemented by political scientists and public administration theorists who addressed the difficulties involved in building democratic states and modern bureaucracies, and by anthropologists and sociologists concerned with the tensions generated by the interaction between traditional and modern value and knowledge systems. Serious disagreements about how these processes should proceed existed between conservative and radical theorists from the beginning, but their influence over policy shifted dramatically in response to the success or failure of the policy regimes they supported.

Conservative 'modernization' theorists assumed that these transitions would be relatively rapid and painless as these societies imported western capital, technology and organizational systems to consolidate the political, economic and social institutions inherited from their former colonial masters, as Canada, New Zealand and Australia had done before them. Yet these processes rarely went according to plan – democratic rule gave way to authoritarianism, planned economies were destabilized by balance of payments and fiscal crises, and social cohesion was undermined by the inability to protect people from rapid and disruptive transfers of assets and increases in exclusion and insecurity.

Left- and right-wing corporatist theorists called for much higher levels of state intervention; some countries attempted to emulate Russia and China and make an immediate transition to state socialism and command planning, many more adopted left- or right-wing structuralist programmes by nationalizing the commanding heights of the economy and intensifying the controls they imposed on local and international markets.[1] Most of these experiments also failed, so structuralism gave way to neoliberal market-based programmes in the 1980s, managed by theorists who argued that the only way to overcome the problems of late development was to apply the orthodox models provided by the mainstream social science disciplines, while many third world theorists rejected the development project altogether. The ongoing crises that afflict many poor societies in Africa, Central America, Central Asia and elsewhere, as well as the deepening economic crisis in the north have now also undermined the neoliberal project.

These generalized failures confronted development theorists with a major crisis in the 1990s, when many practitioners believed that it had reached an impasse and did not represent:

> a body of knowledge with a coherent identity, or even coherent identities, as in competing schools of theory or paradigms. It no longer has pretensions of being, or becoming, a full-blown academic discipline. (Hoogvelt, 2001: xi)

Thus development studies has not been able to claim the status of a '"normal science" firmly based upon one or more past scientific achievements' (Kuhn, 1964: 10). Hence we can only validate our earlier claim that it should be given the status of a viable discipline if we can do two things – first, identify the concerns, analytical assumptions and empirical focus that differentiate development theory from the orthodox social sciences; and, second, subject the theoretical and empirical assertions of the competing factions within it to 'systematic rational enquiry' in order to establish the 'truth claims' of the competing paradigms (MacIntyre, 1998: 21).

First, many theorists in institutes of development studies simply use the models they learned in the mainstream disciplines to solve the problems they confront in LDCs. However, we will argue that this approach fails to address the most significant problems that are generating the ongoing crisis of blocked development. We believe that the classical modernization and dependency theorists, as well as many of the founding fathers of the modern social sciences clearly distinguished between the problems that confronted LDCs and the developed countries (DCs) that were already operating on the developmental frontier and of the corresponding need for a distinct body of policy theory to address them.

We will show that the crucial difference between their situations was the fact that the institutional and organizational arrangements that existed in DCs differed systematically from those that existed in LDCs, were strongly influenced by them, but did so on unequal terms. This has produced what Trotsky (1930/2000) called 'combined and uneven development', which has allowed the former to exercise significant political, military, economic and social influence over them, but not to simply reconstruct them in their own image. The tensions involved in these dynamic and evolutionary processes have created the conflicts and reversals that dominate so much of the third world, but also provided LDCs with access to new organizational and mechanical technologies, which is also allowing some of them, such as Taiwan and Malaysia, to achieve levels of welfare, autonomy and security comparable to those already existing in DCs.

The theorists who addressed these problems recognized that the orthodox disciplines did not provide them with all the resources they needed to do so, since they were not concerned with problems of institutional transitions, but with the challenges involved in maintaining existing systems in DCs. Yet the close links between the aspirations that existed in LDCs and the models and resources available in DCs meant that development theorists also needed to understand the principles that governed their systems and therefore the orthodox disciplines that informed their operation. This confronted them with two interdependent challenges – first, to understand the principles that govern liberal or social democratic institutional systems in the west; but then, second, to find ways of systematically modifying and extending them in order to overcome the obstacles created by attempts to manage the problems of transition generated by all attempts at structural change.

In the 18th and 19th centuries, what we now think of as liberal orthodoxy (itself initially a radical critique of the dominant feudal institutions of the day) only really matured after the completion of the Industrial Revolution in Britain. However, many leading theorists working in the 'new' states of Continental Europe and North America accepted the liberal model as a long-term goal, but called for far higher levels of state intervention to achieve it, as we will show. We also find that the structuralist and dependency theorists that emerged after the Second World War made extensive use of their findings as they attempted to build autonomous states, economies and social systems in the postcolonial world.

Thus, once we think of development studies as the body of theory concerned with the problems of structural institutional change in LDCs, we can constitute it as a distinct field of study and draw on the work of many of the greatest theorists in the social sciences who have consciously addressed comparable problems during earlier periods. This has already turned it into a discipline with deep historical roots, a complex literature, specific concerns, policy prescriptions, and increasingly complex modes of enquiry. So it already represents what MacIntyre (1998: 159) calls a major 'tradition of enquiry' or:

> the elaboration of a mode of social and moral life of which the intellectual enquiry ... [is] an integral part, and [where] the forms of that life were embodied with greater or lesser degrees of imperfection in social and political institutions which also draw their life from other sources.

Second, the paradigm disputes identified earlier stem from the fact that development theory does not exist to provide a static analysis of well-functioning institutional arrangements, but has to respond to the conflicts and insecurities generated by the integrated but uneven impact of capitalism on the modern world. Political, economic and social changes at one point have always had highly disruptive effects at many others, creating new opportunities for some people and threatening the livelihoods and identities of others. Capitalism has generated immense increases in output and welfare, but distributed them unequally between and within societies, including the DCs themselves where large disparities still exist. But it has also widened the gap between those that have completed their capitalist transitions, and the LDCs and least developed or late-late developers (LLDCs) that are still struggling to do so. The result has always been the serious and often violent conflicts between liberals, corporatists, democratic and authoritarian socialists, and ethnic or religious fundamentalists, which have not only manifested themselves in paradigm disputes, but also in wars within and between nations.

The most influential of these paradigms accepted that LDCs would have to replace their own 'traditional' institutions with 'modern' ones but disagreed violently about how to do so. Liberals argued that LDCs should make an immediate transition to market-based capitalist systems. Corporatists, or structuralists, argue that governments should subordinate markets to centralized social control, and radical dependency theorists that they should reject capitalism and make an immediate transition to socialism. The collapse of socialism in the 1980s and 90s turned capitalism into 'the only game in town' in the west (Desai, 2004: 303) and obliged most LDCs to treat western liberal democratic capitalist institutions as an image of their own futures. This has also created the unified global economic system that has intensified international interdependence and produced very uneven results. Managing these processes now dominates the work of the orthodox development community, but the tensions and failures that it has created has also produced a rapid growth in the influence of third world nationalists and Islamic fundamentalists. They claim that they should delink from both capitalism and socialism because they robbed people of different cultures of the opportunity 'to define the forms of their social life' and enslaved two thirds of the world 'to others' experiences and dreams' (Esteva, 1992: 9).

These conflicts have always generated unresolved normative, analytical and policy disputes in the discipline, but they do not justify a loss of faith in its intellectual agenda or achievements, since, as Kuhn (1964) shows, open experimentation in all the established disciplines constantly threatens established verities and sometimes leads to the replacement of one dominant paradigm by another. We would lose faith if none of these competing prescriptions ever succeeded, and if open debate between them failed to produce new syntheses that enabled us to reconcile some of their contradictory claims and produce better policy prescriptions. And, although we have emphasized the negatives thus far, we will also show that different varieties of development theory have played a critical role in removing many of the obstacles to progressive change in weaker societies – in Continental Europe, Japan and the former British Dominions in the 19th and early 20th centuries, and in the East Asian newly industrialized countries (NICs), China and Vietnam in the recent past. These societies have all used different kinds of non-liberal policy programmes to manage their successful early transitions and then, for the most part, adopted liberal ones once they had completed them.

Development studies, unlike mathematics or chemistry, has to deal with a conflict-ridden reality and produce future-oriented predictions and prescriptions that will constantly be undermined by unforeseen events. The fashionable orthodoxies of the day will always be threatened by dissolution, but they incorporate all the knowledge we have about how to proceed, and are constantly being criticized, corrected and improved as the development community responds to its successes and failures.

My own Marxist work in the 1970s and 80s was partially discredited by the failures of structuralism and the partial successes of market-based theories, but my general analysis of the political economy of uneven development and of capitalist crises is now being validated by the economic crisis that has ended the most recent boom.[2] We now recognize that both market- and state-led theories do provide us with valid, albeit partial insights into the nature of the development problem, and that the costs involved in rapid transitions from traditional to modern institutions do oblige us to take the culturalist claims of third world theorists far more seriously than before (see Allen, 2000). These claims and counterclaims are constantly being tested and refined through reflexive exchanges[3] between the academic theorists in the discipline, who are addressing these issues with greater seriousness than ever before, and an active community of development practitioners. They include local social, political and economic entrepreneurs or 'organic intellectuals', who are in fact influenced by changes in theoretical models without being aware of their existence, and local political, economic and social elites and the representatives of the donor community, who are not only directly influenced by these paradigm debates, but are conducting experiments with different solutions that also make an important contribution to changing them.

Thus the impasse identified by Hoogvelt and many others does represent a genuine theoretical crisis, since none of the paradigms that have dominated policy since the Second World War have been able to generate a hegemonic solution to the problem of uneven and blocked development. However, we believe that it is now possible to stand back from these conflicts and develop a more inclusive approach than before.

We will argue that these reflexive processes are now producing a new synthesis in the mainstream development community that we refer to here as 'liberal institutional pluralism', commonly referred to as the 'post-Washington consensus'.[4] This represents an important attempt to combine the valid insights and critiques of structuralist, neoliberal and traditionalist paradigms in order to respond to the limitations of both state and market-led programmes. This new agenda does offer practitioners a wider range of options than the agendas it is replacing, and is therefore playing a key role in reconstructing a viable basis for developmental interventions. However, we will also show that the 'liberal' version of this paradigm is generally failing to address the problems of the LDCs or LLDCs, because it does little more than transfer the 'third way' policy programmes, which have emerged in DCs to overcome the tensions generated by the application of one-sided neoliberal theories there, to LDCs and post-socialist countries. Practitioners will need these liberal models as they attempt to build or strengthen political, economic and civic institutions in transitional societies, but we will show that they have paid too little attention to the tensions and costs involved in making the changes they are asking for.

This suggests that we can only take the discipline forward by looking back to the classical traditions that did understand the theoretical implications of the analysis of late development, and its symbiotic relationship to the orthodox social science disciplines on which it has always drawn for images of alternative futures. This attempt to reconstruct development theory will therefore respond to these challenges in three stages. In Part I, we will provide an extended analysis of the methodological issues raised by all attempts to operationalize a theory of development as opposed to systems maintenance; in Part II, we will use new institutional theory to specify the principles that govern the currently hegemonic liberal pluralist project, and the way it is changing; and in Part III, we will use classic texts and recent research in development studies to address the political, economic and social problems associated with successful and unsuccessful attempts to manage emancipatory institutional transitions.

Notes

1   'Structuralism' refers to policy regimes that use centralized controls to overcome market failures that range from command planning to 'managed market' strategies, and take 'right-wing' or 'left-wing' forms, depending on whether controls are used to protect the interests of owners or workers. We contrast it with liberal theory, which emphasizes the role of 'analytically isolated "individuals" combined with a process of direct generalization from these facts' (Parsons, 1937/1968: 72).

2   That is my analysis of the inherent instability of the dollar-based international monetary system, and the way that unregulated international competiton forced banks to take unacceptable risks (Brett, 1983, 1985).

3   'Reflexivity' refers to processes where all 'social practices are constantly examined and reformed in the light of incoming information about those very practices, thus constantly altering their character' (Giddens, 1991: 90).

4   For a critical analysis, see Fine et al. (2003).

Acknowledgements

The book is based on 50 years of reading, research, teaching and personal observation in contexts dominated by the inequality, conflicts and attempted transitions that are the primary concern of development theory. My academic work has informed and been informed by my involvement in research and teaching, and participant observation as a member of political and social movements and consultancies in South Africa, the UK, Uganda, Somalia and Zimbabwe. I have witnessed many break-downs and failures, but also the popular struggles for democracy and social and economic reconstruction that then transformed Uganda and South Africa in the 1980s and 90s, and I have been part of the ongoing struggles over the search for 'third way' compromises in the west.

These experiences have generated more debts than I can possibly acknowledge. They draw on research supported by the South African Institute of Race Relations in 1960, The Rockefeller Foundation and the British Economic and Social Research Council in Uganda in the 1960s and 70s, and the Department for International Development for my recent work in Uganda, South Africa and Zimbabwe.

I have interviewed thousands of people, ranging from poor peasants, dispossessed labourers and former rebels, to heads of state and CEOs. My work has been challenged and enriched in exchanges with students and many colleagues in the universities where I have been fortunate enough to work over the years. But I owe a particular debt to colleagues who have been associated with this book over the past seven years. These include James Putzel at the Crisis States Research Centre; Andries Bezuidenhout, Sakhela Bulungu and Eddie Webster at the Sociology of Work Unit; Belinda Bozzoli, Steven Gelb, Shireen Hassim, Tom Lodge, Steven Louw and Noam Pines in the School of Humanities and Social Science at Witwatersrand University; and Sven Schwersensky at the Frederick Ebert Foundation in Zimbabwe. All my LSE colleagues have provided me with important insights – those associated with the Devel-opment Management Programme where I consolidated all these ideas – Tim Allen, Joe Beall, Jonathan DiJohn, Jean Paul Faguet, Lloyd Gruber, and Dennis Rodgers – and others in the Development Studies Programme – Stuart Corbridge, Tim Dyson, Tim Forsyth, John Harriss, Kate Meagher, Hugh Roberts, Ken Shadlin, and Robert Wade. I am also very grateful to David Lewis at LSE, Barbara Harriss-White at Oxford, Eddie Webster at Wits, Alejandro Gonzales Natal at Collegio Mexico,

Neera Chandhoke in Delhi, Philipp Lepenies in Frankfurt, Theo Mars and Colin Leys. Steven Kennedy, my publisher, has given me constant support and invaluable advice, and Amelia, my wife, edited the whole work, revealing hidden skills.

Most crucial of all is the debt I owe to my family who have tolerated the stresses associated with this enterprise for too long.

List of Abbreviations

CBO   community-based organization
DC   developed country
EOI   export-oriented industrialization
GATT General Agreement on Tariffs and Trade
IFI   international financial institution
IMF   International Monetary Fund
INGO international nongovernmental organization
ISI   import substituting industrialization
LDC   late developing country
LLDC late-late developing country
NGO   nongovernmental organization
NIC   newly industrializing country
NPM   new public management
OPM   old public management
PR   proportional representation
SO   solidaristic organization
SOE   state-owned enterprise
TNC   transnational corporation
WTO   World Trade Organization

Reconstructing Development Theory for the 21st Century

The crisis in development theory is a multiple one that is understood very differently by people with different ideological and theoretical perspectives. Most accept that the idea of development is directly linked to the changes 'towards those types of social, economic and political systems' created in Europe and the USA from the 17th century (Eisenstadt, 1966: 1),[1] but they often disagree over the objectives of these changes, their normative implications, and the way they should be managed. Modernization theorists like Eisenstadt saw this transition as a desirable, even inevitable process, but their views have always been challenged by a variety of radical voices, especially from the third world, that have rejected his equation of progress with western achievements, especially given the west's formal commitment to 'the principle of equality', and its continuing tendency 'to violate it in an extraordinarily systematic way' (Besis, 2003: 5). And even those who have accepted this view have disagreed about how it should be done, and especially about the relationship between conscious social intervention and free markets in managing these transitions. This has produced competing liberal and structuralist traditions that have sustained what Polanyi (1944/2001: 152) has called a 'double movement' in policy theory – an oscillation between an extension of markets across the world and subsequent counter-tendencies invoking state intervention to protect societies 'from the weaknesses and perils inherent in a self-regulating market system'.

All these competing paradigms are now confronting what MacIntyre (1998: 165) calls an epistemological crisis – a 'dissolution of [the] historically founded certitudes' on which their assumptions, their analytical categories and their predictions are based. Structuralism, understood in its most general sense as the range of theories that 'provide a reason for managing change by administrative action' (Little, 1982: 21), dominated theory and practice until the late 1970s, but was then discredited by economic and political failures in most of the countries that used it and was superseded by neoliberal market-based theories. However, they also failed to eliminate poverty, inequality, exclusion and violent conflict in many LDCs, and are clearly intensifying the environmental and financial crises that now dominate the international agenda. The result was a

1

double crisis in mainstream theory by the end of the 1990s that justified the radical critics who reject the whole exercise and see 'development' as 'a poisonous gift to the populations it set out to help' (Rahnema, 1997: 381).[2]

This crisis has therefore subjected the idea of development to

> the contempt of the generation that grew up during the great trau-matic collapse of the old concept of development ... [that] promised the constant progress of mankind rising in a straight line to a happier state. Contaminated with the stigma of disillusion, concepts like 'progress' and 'social development' seemed to have become unusable for research. (Elias, 2001: 175)

This book will show that this pessimism is not only misplaced, but counterproductive, since it fails to recognize that the idea of develop-ment is crucial to the survival of the global system as we know it, and that development theory is equally crucial for those who are still trying to discover 'how poverty is to be abolished' almost two centuries after Hegel posed the question in *The Philosophy of Right* (1821/1967). The rest of this Introduction will therefore identify the formative assump-tions and propositions that will underpin the rest of the text.

First, the claim that concepts such as 'progress' and 'development' and, indeed, their opposites like 'regression' or 'breakdown' are no longer relevant simply ignores the fact that

> they do not actually refer to obsolete, disappointing ideals but to simple observable facts [like the fact] that human knowledge of natural processes has progressed over the centuries, not least in the present one. (Elias, 2001: 175)

New technology is opening even remote places to new experiences and possibilities; political, social and economic institutions are being trans-formed by the liberal revolution; and concern about, and attempts to deal with, the problems of global inequality and poverty have never been greater. However, this produces disruption and regression, as well as progress, because creating new systems also destroys old ones, so development is never 'a harmless and peaceful process of growth, like that of organic life' (Hegel, 1822–30/1975: 127), but is an often violent and unequal struggle between competing ideologies, interests and nations, involving:

> great collisions between established and acknowledged duties, laws and rights on the one hand, and new possibilities which conflict with the existing system or violate it or even destroy its very foundations and continued existence, on the other. (Hegel, 1822–30/1975: 82)

Dramatic changes are occurring in DCs as well as LDCs that cannot be properly understood, even in the former, by using orthodox theories that explain how societies maintain existing systems rather than manage fundamental change, However, explanations that focus on equilibrium rather than change, as most orthodox theories do, are far less appropriate in LDCs that are restructuring their existing institutions and creating new ones, and must therefore be supplemented by developmental theories that focus on problems created by the need to transform rather than maintain existing systems.

Second, we do not assume that there is a single linear route to modernization based on western models that all societies are bound to follow, although we do accept, as Marx and Engels (1845–6/1974: 78) predicted, that the universalization of liberal democratic capitalism has

> produced world history for the first time, insofar as it [has] made all civilised nations and every individual member of them dependent for the satisfaction of their wants on the whole world, thus destroying the former exclusiveness of nations.

In Marx's day, only a small minority of people lived in independent 'civilized' nations, now all of them do or aspire to do so. Almost all these societies use or aspire to liberal democratic capitalistic institutions as the basis on which they manage their social relationships. These institutions originally emerged in the west and were then forcibly transferred across the globe by the dominant capitalist powers. However, the values and rules on which they are based have been adopted and adapted by indigenous social and political movements in LDCs and exercise a decisive influence on the way they construe their own futures. However, while these processes are all heavily conditioned by the rules set by the globalized system, we will also show why development must occur as

> path-dependent and historically contingent processes [that] are leading, not to convergence to a presumed unique 'Western' model, but to historically located and specific varieties of capitalism in each country. (Hodgson, 1999: 151)

Hence no two countries are likely to use the same combination of political, economic and social institutions to manage their transitions to modernity, but none can ignore the influence of the principles of freedom, equality, scientific objectivity and cooperative interdependence that originated in the western enlightenment project.

Third, much of the pessimism surrounding development theory stems from the failure of many of the attempts to implement its prescriptions in the LLDCs. However, we should not only judge a prescriptive policy paradigm by its immediate results in countries where the appropriate preconditions for its operation may not yet exist. Liberal theorists claim that modern institutions will increase freedom, equity, cooperative interdependence and prosperity, and point to the experience of the developed world to justify their claims. However, the fact that attempts to transfer them to LDCs have often failed does not deny the claims that can be made on behalf of democratic political systems, competitive economies or open civil societies. These institutions have only existed in their modern form over the past 250 years, and many of them were displaced by Fascism and command planning in parts of Europe during the interwar period. But this did not reduce the value of liberal institutions or the willingness of millions of people to risk their lives to defend them. It is indeed highly unlikely that LDCs will be able to make a shift to fully developed liberal institutions in a single giant stride, but this does not mean that they should be willing to accept anything less as their long-term goal.

Fourth, the fact that development theory is in a state of crisis has not threatened its role, but generated new challenges and opportunities. A theoretical crisis is not a breakdown but a situation in which recurrent failures have demonstrated that a particular paradigm can no longer achieve its original goals but must be systematically modified if it is to be reconstituted and put back to use. This is not a reason for despair, but a call for radical change that can lead to major discoveries and reformulations. According to Wolin (1960: 8, emphasis added):

> most of the great statements of political philosophy have been put forward in times of crisis: that is when political phenomena are less effectively integrated by institutional forms. Institutional breakdowns release phenomena, so to speak, causing political behavior and events to take on something of a random quality, and destroying the customary meanings that had been part of the old political world ... Although the task of political philosophy is greatly complicated in a period of disintegration ... [its theories] are evidence of a 'challenge and response' relationship between the disorder of the actual world and the role of the political philosopher as the encompasser of disorder. The range of possibilities appears infinite, for now the political philosopher is not confined to criticism and interpretation: he must *reconstruct* a shattered world of meanings and their accompanying institutional expressions: he must, in short, fashion a political cosmos out of political chaos.

We are clearly living in a period like this, in which development theorists and practitioners are producing important new syntheses that are helping to resolve at least some of the conflicts between competing paradigms of the past. This study will attempt to synthesize the most important of these shifts and use them to take the debate one step further.

Fifth, it will reject the adversarial, even nihilistic approaches that have dominated the debate since the 1960s. Many theorists have treated their role as a purely critical one, designed to 'deconstruct' the arguments used to justify the claims of everyone in authority by exposing their limitations, weaknesses and tendency to subordinate the weak to the demands of the strong.[3] Critical theory is certainly crucial to the maintenance of a civilized life, resistance to oppression, and the possibility of progress. However, it also has had regressive consequences when taken to extremes. Sometimes a one-sided commitment to a particular paradigm or subparadigm (like the varieties of Marxism contending for superiority during the 1970s) led to destructive attacks on the moral as well as the intellectual status of alternative positions. Sometimes theorists attacked particular institutional systems without providing viable alternatives, or utopian ones that ignore the complexity of the systems and the need for hierarchical controls to manage the competition for scarce resources in modern societies.[4]

Instead, this study is committed to reconstruction rather than deconstruction in two ways. First, it accepts that social transformations must operate within limits that are circumscribed by existing capacities, value systems or 'dispositions' and endowments, so that destroying old systems before the 'objective possibility'[5] of a new one has emerged will lead to breakdown rather than emancipation. Hence, we should not deconstruct systems of rule or thought unless we can identify better alternatives, nor treat

> scientific discussion as a process at law in which there is an accused and a public prosecutor whose professional duty it is to demonstrate that the accused is guilty and has to be put out of circulation. (Gramsci, 1971: 34–5)

Further it also recognizes that all the paradigms that have exerted a significant influence over events over the past 250 years have important positive and negative insights to offer. Thus freedom does depend on political and social as well as economic markets; peace and social justice depend on state intervention, while traditional value systems can increase the autonomy of local communities and protect the poor from destitution. Then again, the limitations of any of these paradigms are most clearly expressed in the work of their opponents. Liberals have produced the most convincing explanations for very real state failures, while structuralists have produced equally salient explanations for market failures. This study will therefore provide a positive synthesis based on the strengths rather than the weaknesses of the paradigms that have dominated the discipline since its inception.

Sixth, focusing on 'development' necessitates the use of institutional rather than individualistic theory for two reasons. First, although development does seek to maximize the freedoms, capabilities and entitlements of individuals (Sen, 1999), it can only do this by creating the appropriate *social* institutions – democratic states, competitive economies, and open civic organizations – that replace slavery, serfdom, patrimonialism or command planning, which repress personal freedom and choice. Hence, methodological individualism cannot be applied in societies where the institutions that allow people to think and behave as free individuals have yet to be created. According to Elias (2001: 141):

> This ego-ideal of the individual ... is something that has developed ... through social learning ... in conjunction with specific structural changes in social life ... [and] is part of a personality structure which only forms in conjunction with specific human situations, with societies having a particular structure. It is highly personal, yet at the same time society specific.[6]

Thus the individualistic assumptions that guide most of the orthodox social sciences cannot explain developmental changes because of 'the unreality of their fundamental empirical assumptions' (Leontief, 1966a: 93)[7] when applied to LDCs as opposed to DCs.

Second, this also means that the key difference between modern and pre-modern societies lies in the nature of their institutional arrangements – the rules and incentives, the dispositions and aptitudes – that govern the way in which people cooperate or compete with each other. These differ systematically and can be ranked in accordance with their capacity to maximize the achievement of clear normative criteria – personal autonomy, equity, efficiency, and free cooperative interdependence. In fact, 'development' or 'progress' has always related to the shift from less to more effective institutions – from slavery, feudalism and command planning to competitive capitalism and social democracy, from autocracy to democracy, from patriarchy to gender equality, and from theocracy to scientific rationality. We therefore treat development theory as an evolutionary theory of progressive institutional transformation.

Seventh, the prescriptive and policy-oriented nature of development theory also obliges us to use an interdisciplinary methodology to understand it, since 'political, economic and moral issues are inextricably connected at the base of every important issue of our time' (Brett, 1968: 49). As Lukacs (1971: 8) said:

> Only in [a] context which sees the isolated facts of social life as aspects of the historical process and integrates them in a *totality*, can knowledge of the facts hope to become knowledge of *reality*.

However, interdisciplinarity is inherently difficult, since, as Durkheim (1893/1964: 363) said: 'it is now impossible for the same man to practice a large number of sciences' so 'grand generalizations can only rest on a very summary view of things'. This book will nevertheless attempt to synthesize the literature addressing the political, economic and social implications of developmental change, and will not be able to address all the most significant texts in particular disciplines. However, as Durkheim also showed, 'the diversity of science disrupts the unity of science [so] a new science must be set up to re-establish it' by discovering the relationships between the various sciences and their continuity and 'summing up ... all their principles in a very small number of principles common to all' (p. 359). We therefore cannot claim to pay adequate attention to the most recent work in the mainstream disciplines, but do feel that this book represents a credible attempt to produce a synthesis of this kind.

Eighth, this approach enables us to treat the paradigm debate between structuralists, neoliberals and third world theorists as one over alternative institutional arrangements – those governed by collective state-enforced rules as opposed to market-based exchanges or soldaristic obligations. It also enables us to explain the powerful process of theoretical reconstruction that is now helping to resolve many of the disputes between structuralist and neoliberal paradigms by recognizing the need for institutional diversity, a shift that was acknowledged by the World Bank (1997: 18):

> Development – economic, social and sustainable – without an effective state is impossible ... an effective state – not a minimal one – is central to economic and social development, but more as partner and facilitator than as director. States should work to complement markets, not replace them.

This shift is producing a new synthetic paradigm that we call 'liberal institutional pluralism', which transcends many of the limitations of both structuralist and neoliberal theory. It does this by identifying the conditions under which hierarchical and solidaristic agencies should be used to counter the inevitable problems of market failure and enable societies to 'act, collectively, to improve their lot' (Leys, 1996: 3), as well as those where market-based or participatory political, economic and social processes should be used to enforce efficiency and accountability and guarantee autonomy and freedom. This model is in fact the basis of the 'post-Washington consensus' that now dominates development policy, and is designed to provide a comprehensive approach to the management of emancipatory change. We will identify the assumptions, the normative goals and the political, social and economic institutional arrangements that make up this model in Part II.

And finally, we will also argue that the liberal version of institutional pluralism is not a genuine theory of development but rather an important attempt to respond to the limits of the fundamentalist neoliberal theorists who rejected 'any dilution of the market-based system that they advocate' (Hodgson, 1999: 91), as we argued in the Preface. As a result, we devote the whole of Part III to a critical review of the limitations of orthodox liberal pluralism, and explore the immense difficulties involved in generating viable hybrid solutions that do indeed take account of local capacities, dispositions and needs, but retain a long-term commitment to the enlightenment 'conception of citizenship ... that there should be only one status of citizen (no estates or castes), so that everyone enjoys the same legal and political rights' (Barry, 2001: 7).

The argument

The book is divided into three parts. Part I addresses the methodological issues we have just identified; Part II sets out the theoretical assumptions and pluralistic policy models that dominate the orthodox liberal reform agenda that is now being applied across the third world; and Part III identifies the limitations of this agenda as a basis for developmental transitions, and draws on the insights of earlier classical traditions to explain the ongoing crisis in most LLDCs and the need to adopt second-best or hybrid alternatives to overcome them.

Part I

Chapter 1 explores the disagreements over the 'principles of rationality' or normative criteria that should guide development theory and practice, and why their models have often failed to produce their expected results. We outline the normative and analytical assumptions that separate the major traditions: positivists and methodological individualists who claim that development theory involves an illegitimate use of science to justify a normative and prescriptive enterprise; third world theorists who see it as the imposition of western values and achievements on their societies; right- and left-wing structuralists who claim that free-market solutions must block development; and neoliberals who argue that state planning must fail and call for a return to orthodox market-based theory. The chapter also argues that the generalized economic and political failures in most LLDCs had discredited all these models by the 1990s. Both structuralist and neoliberal policies were in crisis in the 1980s and many political systems were characterized by violence, corruption and authoritarianism. The result was a reversion to regressive theocratic, patriarchal or ethnic principles in many contexts that negated the liberal development project, but also generated intense and irreconcilable contradictions of their own.

We respond to these conflicting views in Chapter 2 by demonstrating that the idea of development plays a central role in the modern world, but has multiple meanings that generate different problems in different contexts. Development exists as a normative aspiration, is institutionalized in systems designed to facilitate progressive change, is embodied in conscious policy projects in LDCs, and operates as a set of teleological expectations about the future. It shows that its normative aspirations take the form of 'a universally valid notion of progress' (Barry, 2001: 4) based on the principles of equality embodied in the UN's *Universal Declaration of Human Rights* and other international covenants. These principles have now been institutionalized in the market- and science-based systems that operate in DCs, but are still reshaping institutions across the third world. Thus development has become an incremental but compulsory and spontaneous process in DCs, but is still a conscious and collective enterprise in LDCs where these open systems are still being created. We also show that the desire to give people in LDCs comparable opportunities to those in DCs, and the assumption that they will successfully demand similar political, economic and social rights, has turned the idea of development from a normative aspiration into a teleological expectation, thus confirming Kant's (1991a: 51) prediction that we can indeed produce 'a universal history of the world'.

We show in Chapter 3 that the limitations of orthodox liberal theory as a theory of development can be transcended by using 'evolutionary institutionalism' to explain the processes that produce structural change. Evolution is driven by unconscious selection in the natural world, but by human agency subject to unanticipated consequences in society. Social movements and the leaders and theorists they rely on struggle with other groups to maintain existing systems or replace them with new ones, but can rarely expect to achieve what they set out to do. The competition between social interests committed to contradictory systems like patrimonialism, Communism and liberal capitalism have dominated the modern era and have now created a world system in which liberal democratic capitalism has established a still incomplete dominance. This process of competitive evolutionary institutional change has eliminated many systems, and is still modifying all of them. The globalization of liberal capitalism has also globalized the liberal market theory that sustains it, but we will argue that it cannot be treated as the basis for an adequate theory of development.

Part II

Chapter 4 shows how the adversarial conflicts over state- versus market-led theory is now giving way to attempts to understand better ways of constructing symbiotic relationships based on organizational pluralism or diversity. It develops an interdisciplinary response to this problem by first identifying the advantages of market-based systems that do enable individuals to achieve their goals by entering into voluntary exchanges with others, and then identifies the many circumstances under which markets fail, producing a need for alternative hierarchical or solidaristic institutions in the form of strong states, hierarchical firms and civil society organizations.

Chapters 5 and 6 identify the functions that need to be performed by liberal states: to guarantee property rights and enforce contracts; regulate access to common property resources; manage externalities; and provide public goods and welfare services. Chapter 5 shows that the state must be able to force private individuals to obey its decisions, but must also be made accountable to them if it is not to abuse its power, through the operation of political markets in the form of regular elections. It notes that political authority has to be institutionalized at global and local as well as national levels, and describes the complex interactions between all three. It explores the strengths and weaknesses of democratic processes, and how state–economy relationships influence the options available to governments.

Chapter 6 examines the complex interactions between political and authority and bureaucratic apparatuses that should operate on the basis of 'relative autonomy'. Elected politicians are mandated to determine policy and monitor performance, and professional civil servants are recruited on the basis of their expertise to carry them out. It shows why state services were originally based on centralized hierarchies and permanent tenure, and are now being reformed through the introduction of results-oriented systems and market-based processes.

Chapter 7 uses Marxist and new institutional economic theory to explain why market failures, stemming from economies of scale and the transaction costs created by imperfect information and opportunistic behaviour, favour the growth of the large-scale hierarchical capitalist firms that dominate the global economy. It shows why the need to maximize efficiency and minimize costs generates different kinds of challenges and responses in different kinds of firms, and argues that the current shift to knowledge-based production systems is reducing the need for the oppressive hierarchies that dominated old mass-production systems, and producing new kinds of network-based authority systems in many contexts.

Chapter 8 considers the increasingly important political and economic role played by solidaristic organizations (SOs) – religions, associations, political parties and social movements, cooperatives, nongovernmental organizations (NGOs), families and networks – in modern societies. These organizations play an important economic and political as well as social role, but they operate in the private rather than public spheres, and those who run them are driven by affective and ethical needs rather than material self-interest. We show that their contributions are usually based on reciprocity rather than altruism, and that modern formal SOs demand skilled professional staff who have to be adequately compensated; need to create hierarchical organizations to ensure effective performance; and need to be subjected to open market-based accountability mechanisms to ensure that they make effective use of their resources.

Part III

Chapter 9 shows that the requirements of imported liberal systems generate serious conflicts with local values and capacities, and threaten groups that benefit from existing institutions. Societies often lack the values, skills and/or resources needed to manage these institutions, and this generates start-up problems that can produce crises or breakdowns. This suggests that orthodox liberal models need to be adapted to local circumstances, and that a distinctive body of development theory is needed to manage institutional transfers by generating hybrid solutions that incorporate elements of both local and imported institutions.

Chapter 10 contextualizes this problem by reviewing the policy regimes that have governed the developmental transitions that have taken place in the modern period, first in the north, and more recently in the south and east. These have all involved interventionist programmes that limited the operation of free political and economic markets during their early transitions to liberal democratic capitalism. We examine the conflictual processes generated by the attempts of northern countries to catch up with Britain in the 19th and early 20th century; those involved in the postcolonial and post-Communist world over the past 60 years; and those in modern LLDCs, using Uganda and Zimbabwe as case studies. We show that different kinds of structuralist programmes sometimes succeeded and sometimes failed, depending on local capacities and the external environments in which they operated.

Chapters 11 and 12 review the work of the classical theorists who examined the destabilizing consequences of the coexistence of western and local institutional systems. Chapter 11 shows that these 'dualistic' situations can generate antagonistic conflicts between contradictory value systems and power structures that can derail potentially progressive political, economic and social reforms, but also argues that these difficulties are unavoidable. Chapter 12 shows that 'pre-modern' institutions incorporate local values and skills that enable people to survive, often in contexts where new liberal initiatives have failed. It also shows that real changes do not emerge out of immediate shifts to modern institutions, but out of dialectical interactions between local institutions and modern ones, so practitioners should accept the need to facilitate transitions that may not measure up to the standards set by liberal theory, but are better than those they replace. These arguments raise important issues for ongoing programmes of political and economic reform.

We address these political issues in Chapter 13, by arguing that current programmes of democratic reform need not guarantee a transition to 'good governance'. Democracy requires values and skills that did not exist in pre-democratic systems, and competitive elections can intensify social conflict and produce populist policies and corruption in societies characterized by intense scarcity, low levels of trust, and weak political parties and pressure groups. Pre-modern systems used authoritarian regimes that often produced stagnation and decay, but also built strong capitalist states when their regimes recognized the need to adopt effective economic policies in order to maximize their own wealth and power. We show that authoritarian regimes are inherently unstable – successful ones in Europe and East Asia were democratized after completing their capitalist transitions; unsuccessful LLDCs now confront economic and political crises that have forced them to cede much of their authority to the donor community. Finally, we examine the political, administrative and economic consequences of this.

Chapter 14 revisits the classical debate over the economic consequences of the market failures created by late development. Structuralist theorists argue that economies that had yet to develop strong capitalist economies could not compete successfully with already developed ones, creating an 'infant industry' problem with significant economic and political effects. First, they could only 'catch up' with their competitors without imposing immense costs on their citizens by using protected markets and/or subsidized inputs. We show that recent import substituting versions of structuralism have generally failed but that new export-oriented versions have succeeded when managed by strong states. We then explore the political implications of the problem, showing that the need for 'rents' to build a new capitalist class explains the prevalence of often corrupt demands for political favours, and the absence of a consolidated capitalist and working class with the motivations and resources needed to maintain viable democratic states. We conclude with a discussion of the policy options available to practitioners in LLDCs with weak states and weak capitalist economies.

Notes

1   However, early modernizers in Western Europe looked back to the then more advanced civilizations of Greece, Rome and the Middle East for their organizational models and scientific achievements; many Islamists now look back to the caliphate.
2   The edited collections of Rahnema and Bawtree (1997) and Sachs (1992) contain some excellent relevant articles and seek to re-establish theocratic or traditional social systems that ignore the demands of modernity where they can 'live on their own terms' (Esteva, 1992: 20).
3   This represents a shift in my own approach, for example in Brett (1983).
4   Here I would include the critiques of third world theorists like Rahnema (1997) and Esteva (1992) and participatory and 'social movement' theorists like Bond and Manyanya (2002: 192), who imagine a world based on 'progressive politics and basic-needs development within formal and informal organisations – based in workforces, communities, women's and youth groups, environmental clubs and churches'.
5   This term has been appropriated from Lukacs (1971: 51). Bourdieu (1991: 53) talks of 'objective potentialities immediately inscribed in the present'.
6   Marx (1857–8/1972: 17, 65) argued that it is only 'bourgeois society, the society of free competition' that is constituted by a social network made up of 'individuals who remain indifferent to one another'.
7   Here Leontief is describing the basis for Kenyes' critique of neoclassical economics, but it applies even more strongly to development theory as a whole.

Part I

The Nature of Development Theory

Chapter 1

The Crisis in Development Theory

Paradigm conflicts and the developmental crisis

The fundamental assumptions and analytical models used in development studies are now heavily contested by theorists who adopt 'a variety of rival and contending conceptions of rationality', which cannot be reconciled because they cannot agree on the standards to be used 'by appeal to which defeat and victory can justly be claimed' (MacIntyre, 1998: 199). As a result, many theorists believe that development studies has ceased to make progress because:

> Its hitherto trusted methods of enquiry have become sterile. Conflicts over rival answers to key questions can no longer be settled rationally. Moreover ... the use of the methods of enquiry and the forms of argument, by means of which rational progress has been achieved so far, begins to have the effect of increasingly disclosing new inadequacies, hitherto unrecognised incoherences, and new problems for the solution of which there seem to be insufficient or no resources within the established fabric of belief ... This kind of dissolution of historically founded certainties is the mark of an epistemological crisis. (MacIntyre, 1998: 165)

Thus structuralist and neoliberal versions of development theory are based on a desire to universalize 'those types of social, economic and political systems that have developed' in the west, although they cannot agree on how this should be done.[1] But they both use science-based evidence to 'prove' that their prescriptive and transformatory models are superior to other systems and claim that their policies are based on a dispassionate analysis of 'the facts' and not on political ideology or subjective preferences. However, their claims are disputed by positivists who reject the use of normative values in scientific analysis, by methodological individualists who reject their emphasis on the need for structural transformation, and by postmodern and cultural relativists who reject their claim to universality. And as if this were not enough, the mainstream traditions not only deny these alternative principles, but also reject many of each other's formative assumptions.

17

Each of these paradigms has provided plausible critiques of the programmes promoted by their competitors, making it very difficult to resolve the crisis. Liberals attribute developmental failures to the rigidities and authoritarianism of the statist institutions created by structuralists; structuralists attribute them to the instability and exploitative nature of free markets; and third world critics to the imposition of western institutions on non-western societies. All of them have exercised a powerful political influence at different times and some have succeeded in some contexts, but none have been able to resolve the crisis of uneven development in the LLDCs in Africa, Central America and Central Asia that are our primary concern.

The credibility of a prescriptive policy-oriented paradigm depends on its logical coherence but also on the validity of its empirical assumptions and practical applicability (Frank, 1969: 21ff.). Unlike natural scientists, social scientists do not deal with inanimate objects or nonsentient beings, but with humans with different and sometimes conflicting interests, who build their own institutions on the basis of normative principles and conscious reflection. This makes it far more difficult for them to produce reliable explanations of what they are doing because the variable nature of their subject matter and the contestability of their assumptions and prescriptions all produce 'unanticipated consequences that may in retrospect be seen as decisive' (Kaplan, 1964: 60). Different paradigms give rise to different institutional systems that generate inequalities in power and wealth that are constantly challenged by contending political and economic forces. Thus paradigm shifts have inevitable ideological and political consequences, so attempts to substitute one for another not only raise issues of theoretical coherence, but of 'political agency' – the ability of practitioners to persuade powerful social groups to mobilize the resources required to overcome the resistance of their opponents and to develop the skills and discipline required to implement their programmes.

These problems are far more challenging for development theorists than their orthodox counterparts because development involves institutional 'transformations' – shifts from or to patrimonial, theocratic, statist or market-based systems. Orthodox liberal theory dominates DCs because most people there accept liberal institutions as a part of the natural order and think of themselves as free individuals with an equal right to participate as autonomous social agents in all aspects of political, economic and social life. But this is not yet the case in most LDCs, where existing institutions allocate great freedom to some 'individuals' and deny it to others. Thus liberal developmental transitions require changes in behaviour, value systems, understandings and endowments among both elites and people that threaten existing institutions and the wealth and power associated with them. This produces 'contending conceptions of rationality' that block agreements about goals and processes and generate resistance to the liberal project in new contexts and reversals in older ones. We examine these disagreements in this chapter, starting with some general points about the relationship between contending conceptions of rationality and show how different paradigms respond to these problems in the rest of this chapter, and then attempt to reconcile some of these disagreements in the rest of the book.

Science, agency and developmental transitions

We have just claimed that development theory is a prescriptive and political enterprise, yet its practitioners speak, like other social scientists, 'in the capacity of master of truth and justice', who should be heard, or who purport to make themselves heard, 'as the spokesman of the universal' (Foucault, 1980: 126). Thus we act as interlocutors who provide people with a general formulation of their own aspirations and how they could achieve them in a 'conscious elaborated form', rather than impose our own preferences onto them (Foucault, 1980). Yet we also operate in a modern world where people depend on 'specific' intellectuals with specialized expertise to overcome the complexities of every critical life problem – health, production, communication, social relationships. Their authority depends on an expertise that meets the rigorous requirements of the 'ordered procedures for the production, regulation, distribution, circulation and operation of statements' on which modern society's 'regimes of truth' depend, and are 'produced and transmitted under the control ... of a few great political and economic apparatuses' like reputable universities and research institutes (Foucault, 1980: 131–3). Hence solutions to the practical problems of daily life are now 'in large measure determined by the system of our technical achievements', and

> the assimilation of this technology into the practical life-world, bringing the technical control of particular areas within the reaches of the communication of acting men, really requires scientific reflection. The prescientific horizon of experience becomes infantile when it naively incorporates contact with the products of the most intensive rationality ... [Thus] in the political dimension at issue, the theoretical guidance of action must proceed from a scientifically explicated understanding of the world. (Habermas, 1971: 56–7)

This means not only that theorists provide people with a better understanding of their own situations than they can acquire unaided, but also that people cannot choose one paradigm rather than another without reference to the 'truth' of their claims.

This need for 'a scientifically explicated understanding of the world' is most urgent in contexts where people are involved in institutional change, and explains the critical role played by development theorists in managing the structuralist policies that dominated the first postcolonial period, and the neoliberal ones that replaced them. However, the crises that undermined both stemmed from the fact that successful change depends on 'agency' as well as expertise, that is, on the existence of actors with the motivation, skills and resources to put expert advice into practice. Theorists generally fail to ask who might be willing to implement their recommendations and simply refer to an indeterminate 'we', or community of 'practitioners' whom they expect to accept their scientific credentials and be able to persuade key decision-makers and social movements to implement their recommendations.

This is a presumptuous claim, but is normal practice among non-Marxist social scientists whose prescriptions are usually directed to society as a whole and not to particular social groups. However, this approach leads them to ignore key implications of the contradictory relationships that prevail between intellectuals, power-holders, and wider social and political movements. Theoretical prescriptions will only be taken up when they reflect the needs and goals of influential social groups. Marxist and other critical theorists recognize the fact that their prescriptions challenge existing power structures on behalf of subordinated groups, and place problems of agency at the centre of their analyses, but their analyses are now generally ignored in high-level seminars or official policy forums. However, the theoretical challenges created by these contested interactions between theory, agency and action constantly threaten the integrity of development theory as a whole.

Thus development theory is a policy-oriented discipline whose prescriptions rest on expertise, but are contested because of their normative, political, and practical consequences. Privileged access to science can make 'the expert' and not 'the people' the final arbiter of what should be done, and leave politicians with 'nothing but a fictitious decision-making power' (Habermas, 1971: 64), but using science to justify policy reform based on claims to truth and justice does not eliminate the resource transfers and conflicts they produce. The result is an inevitable tension between science and popular demands because

> the scientific control of natural and social processes – in a word technology – does not release men from action. Just as before, conflicts must be decided, interests realized, interpretations found – through both action and transactions structured by ordinary language. (Habermas, 1971: 56)

So even progressive policy changes will generate political crises unless they are based on viable compromises negotiated between competing groups.[2] Complex structures and processes have evolved in mature democracies to do this. They recognize that interventions must try to follow 'best practice', but also that change must take account of the need for social cohesion because it normally involves losers as well as winners. Here parties and social movements invoke theoretical paradigms to justify ideologically driven programmes that demonstrate their right to reallocate resources between groups and individuals, but they can only implement them by building majority coalitions. Winners can impose their will on losers and their electoral majorities oblige losers to recognize that they have the right to do so,[3] provided they can contest these results in later elections. Incorporating losers into representative bodies enables winners to maintain social cohesion by making concessions to losers through genuine negotiations designed to 'bring about an agreement that terminates in the intersubjective mutuality of reciprocal understanding, shared knowledge, mutual trust, and accord with one another' (Habermas, 1976: 3).

A dense community of sophisticated professionals has evolved in DCs to manage these processes in governments, firms, political parties, pressure groups and social movements that operate at the interface between science-based knowledge and the demands of the 'practical life-world'. They mediate conflicts and negotiate solutions that transcend the 'prescientific horizon of experience', while representing particular social constituencies and needs. They can make mutually acceptable compromises for many reasons. The open-ended nature of scientific knowledge allows competing yet potentially viable versions of 'best practice' to coexist and be used to justify competing claims, while open political and economic markets enable many interests to press their particular demands and achieve limited pay-offs that persuade them to stay in the game. The members or beneficiaries of these agencies are also well-enough informed to be able to make complex and critical judgements about the competing claims being pressed on their behalf.

Unfortunately, these processes and capacities only exist in most LDCs in an embryonic form. The technical knowledge that drives major structural transformations is largely imported, and the structural changes they are producing generate more losers than the incremental changes in DCs where losers are easier to compensate. These differences generate serious tensions between development theorists and practitioners and the elites and social and political movements who must accept their conception of 'truth and justice' if it is to be implemented, so they always risk 'not being followed, or only by very limited groups' in the societies they advise (Foucault: 1980: 130). They exercise a powerful influence, but their recommendations promote some interests and negate others.

Orthodox theorists speak to elites, but not necessarily to those who control political power, while critical theorists speak to subordinated groups who are commonly denied political or economic rights.

Development theorists operate as key players in the 'development community' – the decision-makers and their advisers in global agencies, corporations, and NGOs and their national counterparts. Their world-view is formed by the leading western universities and research centres that also train many of the most influential national and international practitioners to whom they speak. They form a community of 'specific' or 'technical intellectuals' (Gramsci, 1971: 347), whose authority depends on their access to western science, the weakness of local universities and research institutes, the fact that local organizations can rarely employ people with comparable skills, and because the donor community plays a critical political role in aid-dependent countries, as we will see in Chapter 13. This gives them a powerful influence over formal policy and management decisions, but it excludes them from the 'practical life-world' where most people actually live, undermining their ability to mobilize the support of the local social and political movements needed to ensure that their decisions will actually be implemented.

This gap between the development community and local 'organic' intellectuals has had serious practical and theoretical consequences, because it undermined the structuralist policy regimes adopted in the 1950s and 60s and their market-based alternatives in the 1980s and 90s. These models were successfully deployed in DCs where their claims were seriously debated and modified through ideological debates between social democratic political parties and trade unions, and conservative parties and business organizations. In LDCs, these debates were virtually confined to the research community and donor agencies, and shifts in policy regime emerged out of externally generated policy programmes that were treated as technical and apolitical interventions in order to preserve the illusion of sovereignty. They nevertheless produced major shifts in the distribution of assets, status and power, which led to widespread resistance, noncompliance and developmental failures.[4]

Critics attribute these failures to the use of western models and money to impose solutions on local people. Some have claimed that development theory has prevented poor people from thinking and acting for themselves, producing 'anti-developmental' results (Chambers, 1983: Ch. 1; Edwards, 1989: 78) and called for participatory processes that would enable them to 'plan, manage, control and assess' their own actions and become 'the agents of their own development' (Burkie, 1993: 205). Left-wing critics, local elites and organic intellectuals have argued that it has created a new form of neocolonialism that subjects local societies to external exploitation. Orthodox members of the development community have responded by reversing these claims and attribute the crisis to noncompliance with their technical prescriptions because of the prevalence of traditional values and corruption.

We cannot dismiss any of these criticisms, but attributing the theoretical crisis to any one of them also fails to address the challenges that confront them all. External advisers only play a dominant role in states that have failed to deal with their own problems – they advised the strong states in Asia, but local policy-makers adapted western theory to suit their own needs. The weakest states like Somalia and Sudan have been left to their own devices, but continue to decline, while successful reformers like Ghana and Uganda have close links with donors and their advisers and are making progress. Thus the key issue is not where advisers originate, but the way competing paradigms influence their recommendations and their subsequent impact on competing interests in local political and economic processes. We will review these contending claims in the rest of the chapter.

Positivism, atomistic individualism and cultural relativism

Positivists, methodological individualists, postmodernists and cultural relativists do not accept that scientific evidence based on a dispassionate analysis of the 'facts' can 'prove' that one policy regime will provide a better basis for emancipatory social change than another. They argue that facts are observable and measurable entities, but that values only exist as subjective preferences held by individuals that govern 'individual' behaviour but cannot be used as the basis for making normative judgements about the superiority or inferiority of 'social' systems, or the processes involved in 'emancipatory' social change. Hence:

> Where values are involved which are not facts which everyone must admit to be true or false, but which are 'subjective,' there is no rational means of getting another [person] to accept the [society's] end. An Indian mystic can tell an American business man that the things of this world to which he devotes his life – money and success – are pure illusion and that reality can only be approached by sitting under a tree and contemplating. It is unlikely he can prove this to the American's satisfaction. The only recourse in these cases is an appeal to the sentiments. Values are either accepted or rejected; they are not proved or disproved as facts are. (Parsons, 1937/1968: 277)[5]

They therefore argue that we must 'analyze our sociological models ... in terms of individuals, their attitudes, expectations, relations, etc – a postulate that may be called methodological individualism' (Popper, cited in Winch, 1970a: 11). This means that:

> all the facts necessary to the understanding of concrete social systems can be predicated on analytically isolated 'individuals' combined with a process of direct generalization from these facts, that is, those additional facts which the most general frame of reference makes necessary to the idea of a concrete system at all ... Hence the utilitarian position which has been defined by atomism in this sense as a principal criterion is inherently individualistic. (Parsons, 1937/1968: 72)

This tradition treats individual preferences, identities and capabilities as a matter of personal and therefore 'endogenous' choice, and adopts an abstract 'logico-deductive strategy' that assumes that 'at the basis of all social phenomena are specific actors striving for utility maximization' (Mouzelis, 1995: 40)[6] operating in efficient markets, ruling out the need for institutions and ideologies (North, 1995: 17). This turns development from a universalizable emancipatory process into a normative aspiration with the same status as any other, so that

> theories of progress, democracy, humanitarianism and the like ... [have] exactly the same status as those of karma and transmigration, as Catholic dogma or the mythology of the Eskimo. They are only pseudoscientific theories departing from the logico-scientific standard in respect both of formal precision and of the factual status of many of the entities involved. (Pareto, reported in Parsons, 1968: 274)

This implies that no 'objective social good can be defined independently of individual desires' (Arrow, 1963: 22), and confines theorists to analysis of the effects of market-based exchanges, which allocate resources through spontaneous individual choices without invoking 'interpersonal welfare comparisons' (Johnson, 1968: 85).[7] Here, 'institutions are unnecessary; ideas and ideologies don't matter; and efficient markets – both economic and political – characterize economies' (North, 1995: 17). Societies are seen as places where liberals treat *individuals* (unique, autonomous and self-oriented actors) and postcolonial theorists treat *communities* as 'the measure of all things'. Their only obligation is to maximize their own incommensurable preferences by interacting freely and, if need be, competitively with their fellows.[8] This, of course, negates the status of all collectively oriented development projects, since no planners 'are endowed with a superior wisdom which discloses to them a better range of beliefs and activities and which gives them authority to impose upon their subjects a quite different manner of life' (Oakeshott, 1971: 378).

These individualistic assumptions dominate the mainstream social sciences, but are also invoked, paradoxically and often unconsciously, by third world theorists, cultural relativists and postmodern theorists, who reject all 'metanarratives', deny all aprioristic notions of progress, and adopt relativistic positions that deny the ethical superiority of any one cultural system over any other. Thus, attempts to prove that preferring Fascism, theocracy, patriarchy or racism is worse than preferring freedom, scientific rationality or human equality does indeed rob 'peoples of different cultures of the opportunity to define the forms of their social life' and enslaves two-thirds of the world 'to others' experiences and dreams' (Esteva, 1992: 9).[9] These relativistic assumptions also pervade the work of participatory theorists, who claim that new scientific knowledge is determined by 'those who are powerful and dominant' in the west, is seen to be 'the only knowledge of any significance', and has marginalized the common-sense knowledge of local people who often provide them with better solutions to their problems (Chambers, 1983: 76). These theorists therefore reject the paradigms that have dominated 'the social science disciplines since the nineteenth century', because they have produced an 'elitist, oligarchical monopoly of knowledge' that is used 'to dominate nature and civilize diverse "backward" peoples', in favour of an approach that respects 'the types of knowledge that are built through daily experience and common sense' (Fals Borda, 1998: 157–9; see also Wignaraja, 1991).

While methodological individualists therefore reject development theory because of its commitment to a consciously managed collective project, cultural relativists and participatory theorists do so because they claim that the 'biases' that its practitioners 'carry with them from their training and cultural experiences' produce a community of practitioners who cannot understand local problems because these biases make it impossible for them to perceive the realities 'which shape the lives of real people', and prevent poor people from thinking and acting for themselves (Edwards, 1989: 78).

Development theory, western imperialism and cultural autonomy

This theoretical rejection of the universality of mainstream development theory is associated with a powerful critique of the role of the west in the rest of the world. Liberals and modernization theorists treat development as the processes involved in 'catching up' with and emulating the west through which rich nations diffuse 'knowledge, skills, organisation, values, technology and capital to a poor nation, until over time, its society, culture and personnel become variants of that which made the Atlantic community economically successful' (Nash, 1963: 5). Third world critics argue that this view seriously misrepresents the exploitative and asymmetrical nature of the relationship between the two, and many treat westernization as the cause of, rather than the solution to, their underdevelopment.

First, they note that the west did not go out to liberate, but to conquer and exploit local communities that they regarded as barbarians, whose rights were 'unequal to' their own and whose autonomy could be treated 'as only a formality' (Hegel, 1821/1967: 219). Hence foreign penetration began with the violent imposition of colonialism and used its dominance to affirm 'the supremacy of white values ... over the ways of life and of thought of the native ... that, in revenge, the native laughs in mockery when Western values are mentioned in front of him' (Fanon, 1967: 33). Thus the colonial and postcolonial western project that succeeded it were justified by evoking liberal principles that were then used to justify western supremacy and the subordination of the south. The result has been a fundamental contradiction between principles and practice through which 'the hegemonic position of the West has enabled it to erase the specificity of its experience and to theorise it as the only way towards universal progress, with itself as pioneer and guide' (Bessis, 2003: 140). They argue that buying into this project offers some LDCs possibilities that they would not otherwise have, but more often means that their industries are undermined by the superior power of western firms, their political autonomy by their dependence on western aid and protection, and their cultural heritage by the power of the western communications industry.

Second, they also argue that the individualism of the liberal project and the technocratic and collectivistic demands of structuralism undermine local values and practices in a variety of ways. Thus:

- anthropologists argue that local practices and values are as legitimate and rational and often more effective than imported ones (Chambers, 1983; Richards, 1985)
- radical nationalists argue that capitalism is based on imperialistic exploitation that creates inequality and exclusion, not freedom
- third world theorists call for a reversion to traditional ways of being
- religious and ethnic fundamentalists deny the principle of individual freedom and scientific autonomy altogether.

Their arguments differ but they all reject the link between progressive change and the diffusion of western models, and call for strategies that focus on 'local resources for local use in servicing local needs' (Thomas, 1974: 246) and on the need for local people to delink from the global system and return to a 'new commons' where they can 'live on their own terms' (Esteva, 1996: 20).

These traditions are treated as aberrations by the development community, but their influence has grown in response to the development crisis and, indeed, to the double standards and abuses of authority and power that characterize the relationships between the west, especially the USA under George W. Bush, and the rest of the third world. The resulting intensification of inequality and marginalization in the global system is 'not only ethically questionable but ... politically and socially unsustainable' (Castells, 2001: 67) and has often given rise to violent nationalist, ethnic or sectarian political and social movements that reject the very idea of freedom and progress itself. They are often dismissed as the expression of an irrational opposition to modernity, but they are actually an understandable and even inevitable response to the extent to which the failures of the postcolonial development project have marginalized poor people and communities and stripped them of their self-respect.

From right- or left-wing structuralism to neoliberalism

Both the structuralist and neoliberal traditions in development theory deny the legitimacy of these strategies of 'semi-autarchic socialist or traditionalistic development' because they assume that 'any significant national development of the productive forces' is virtually impossible without 'a close connection with the international division of labour' (Brenner, 1977: 92). However, they each attribute the crisis to each other's theoretical and practical policy failures, and make a systematic critique of them in order to assert their own hegemonic claims. These critiques represent the most substantial and systematic basis for our analysis of the crisis in mainstream theory and will therefore be the starting point for later attempts to resolve it.

Both left- and right-wing structuralists deny the liberal claim that free markets represent the best option that can be applied to all societies without reference to local circumstances or conditions. If orthodox theory could be used in this way, there would be no need for a distinct body of development theory, since all societies could maximize their welfare by adopting the institutional arrangements that the mainstream disciplines recommend. Hence classical development theorists argued that markets would not work effectively in LDCs until they had acquired the values, understandings and assets needed to support them, and that the absence of these conditions would generate political, economic and social weaknesses that would undermine attempts to build liberal capitalist institutions. Instead, they demanded systematic interventions by a modernizing elite that would capture the state and use it to build the new system. They usually accepted the need for an ultimate transition to liberal capitalism or modern socialism, but believed that this could only happen *after* these structural changes had been consolidated. Neoliberals responded by developing a systematic critique of state failures, and reasserting the classical principles of free-market theory.

The right-wing structuralist critique of liberal market theory

Right-wing mercantilism, structuralism or corporatism has its roots in pre-capitalist societies where markets were subordinated to state power. However, it took on its modern form in the early 19th century when Continental and American theorists called for state controls over trade, investment and sometimes personal freedom rather than the laissez faire advocated by liberals in Britain. Some treated liberalization as a long-term goal, but all of them claimed that controls would be necessary until these societies had 'caught up' with their developed counterparts. Their theories were used by many western governments in the 19th and early 20th centuries to justify authoritarianism at home and colonialism abroad, claiming that it was the only way to bring 'civilization' to local populations.[10] Structuralism was adopted by most postcolonial elites who built planned economies, governed by centralized bureaucracies and authoritarian political regimes. We refer to them as 'right-wing structuralists' or 'corporatists' because they used state controls over markets to build local capitalism rather than to protect workers from exploitation. Extreme versions like Nazism and Fascism rejected the liberal commitment to freedom. However, less extreme versions argued that premature liberalization in LDCs would lead to their 'universal subjection ... to the supremacy of the predominant manufacturing, commercial and naval power', but that once they had all achieved 'that stage of industrial development in which union with other nations equally well developed', market freedom could 'become possible and useful' (List, 1841/1904: 103).

The successful examples of this strategy – in 19th- and early 20th-century Continental Europe, in the postwar reconstruction programmes in Europe and Japan, and more recently in East Asia – produced 'cohesive capitalist states' that 'use state power to discipline their societies ... prioritize rapid industrialization as a national goal ... systematically discipline and repress labor, penetrate and control the rural society, and use economic nationalism as a tool of political mobilization' (Kohli, 2004: 381). Protectionism and state controls were used to build a national capitalist class, and more or less benevolent despotism was used to suppress the resistance and demands of the working class and other groups and strata whose interests were marginalized by the new system.

Modern liberal critics were able to ignore these successes (see Chang, 2002) because of the generalized crisis of structuralism in the

1970s. However, there were very different explanations for this in societies with strong as opposed to weak states. These conservative strategies worked well in the former, but here the successful creation of capitalist and working classes eventually led to successful demands for liberalization – as theorists like List had predicted. However, in the LLDCs in Africa and elsewhere, state capacity was so poor that structuralism encouraged rent-seeking, intensified conflict and inequality, and produced unsustainable fiscal, balance of payments and employment crises by the late 1960s, and political violence and breakdown in many others.

The left-wing structuralist or dependency critique of capitalism

Left-wing structuralists or socialists accepted the right-wing critique of free markets, but took this argument one step further by attributing the political oppression and economic inequalities that characterized these corporatist experiments to their 'capitalist' nature. They based their analysis on Marx's critique of capitalism as an exploitative system and on theories of imperialism derived from Hobson, Luxemburg, Lenin and Trotsky, who argued that capitalism subjected LDCs to super-exploitation that must perpetuate economic dependency and political decay.[11] Unlike Marx himself,[12] they believed that LDCs could make the transition to socialism before completing the process of capitalist development by nationalizing the means of production and creating a state-controlled planned economy. This analysis was used to justify the creation of socialist command economies in the Soviet Union, China and other third world countries, and for the state to impose far stronger controls over capitalists in social democracies in the west, and in nonrevolutionary LDCs in order to safeguard the working classes and peasantry from super-exploitation.

Up to the early 1970s, liberalism only existed as a dissenting view in development theory, and the major conflicts took place between right- and left-wing structuralists. Right-wing corporatism, embodied in modernization theory, was dominant until the 1960s, when there was a significant shift to the left, and the emergence of 'dependency' theorists who believed that it was 'impossible for the small dependent underdeveloped economy to achieve a basic transformation' by using 'some form or other of indigenous capitalism'. Hence, they argued that it was 'only on the basis of a planned socialist transformation that underdevelopment and poverty on a world scale ... [could] be overcome' (Thomas, 1974: 16).

This produced a number of socialist experiments in countries like Tanzania, Mozambique, Nicaragua under the Sandinistas, and Chile under Allende, but left-wing structuralism confronted even greater problems than right-wing structuralism, because of the inability of most new states to create the bureaucratic capacity needed to manage complex economic systems, and increase investment in industry and infrastructure while improving pro-poor services. Many treated the Soviet Union as a model, but ignored the enormous economic and political costs associated with forced industrialization. So the attempts to emulate this strategy in fragmented societies with weak states and limited economic endowments usually resulted in disaster. Austen (1987: 235), for example, shows why the socialist experiments in Tanzania and Ghana had 'been economic failures', while their state-led corporatist counterparts in Kenya and the Ivory Coast 'enjoyed relative economic success', although these last two countries also fell on hard times not much later.

The neoliberal critique of structuralism

The failures of left- and right-wing structuralism culminated in the shift to neoliberalism in Britain and the USA in the early 1980s and the collapse of Communism in 1989. This enabled neoliberal market-based programmes to displace statist social democracy in the west, as well as right- and left-wing structuralism in the south, and command planning in the east. Neoliberal theory had operated as a 'dissenting view' in development studies in the 1960s (Bauer, 1972), but moved centre stage in the 1980s with the World Bank's Berg Report, which attributed Africa's 'inferior performance in economic growth and poverty reduction' to 'inappropriate state dominated policies' that overloaded governments, distorted economic incentives, and generated unproductive monopoly rents (World Bank, 1981: 3; see also Bates, 1981; Lal, 1984). This turned neoliberalism into the dominant orthodoxy used to transform institutional systems across the world, and particularly in the second and third worlds that were obliged to adopt structural adjustment programmes managed by the international financial institutions (IFIs) based on the liberal Washington consensus (Williamson, 1990).

Left- and right-wing structuralism had used Keynesian theory to justify deficit financing in the state and Listean 'infant industry' arguments to justify protectionism and state ownership to provide basic services and build heavy industry. By the late 1970s, these policies had produced fiscal and balance of payments crises in all but the best managed East Asian states, justifying the liberal claim that only markets could set rational prices, enforce economic efficiency and generate fair rewards, using arguments that will be reviewed in Chapter 5. The new regimes responded to the crisis by calling for balanced budgets, trade and foreign exchange liberalization, the privatization of state-owned enterprises, and the removal of most of the licensing and planning controls that had been used to favour some kinds of investments and discourage others. Although these theorists saw themselves as creating new developmental programmes, their strategies were based on mainstream western liberal theory and consciously rejected the need for different policy regimes in LDCs than DCs, and therefore the need for a distinct discipline of development studies.

It was the sudden triumph of neoliberalism in the 1980s that led many structuralists to talk about the impasse in development studies,[13] but the new paradigm was soon confronted with many unanticipated problems because of the heavy demands it also imposed on weak states, its disruptive impact on employment and social security systems, the threat it posed to established interests and value systems, and its demand for complex new skills and attitudes. The result was economic, political and social crises in many societies that intensified those that predated the new reforms.[14] These economic failures were then attributed to state failures caused by corrupt and nonaccountable political systems, so 'good governance' – based on liberal demands for democracy, the rule of law, the separation of powers and administrative reform – was added to the conditions attached to structural adjustment programmes. This also ignored the problems associated with political transitions addressed by classical development theorists, since it assumed that orthodox western democratic institutions could simply be transferred to LDCs without taking account of their special circumstances.

Unfortunately, these reforms rarely succeeded because most governments 'refused to countenance real institutional reform', and often 'simply deceived ... [the IFIs], promising measures that they then failed to undertake or soon reversed' (van de Walle, 2001: 158). Elites manipulated elections and participatory processes, used state power to transfer assets to their families or cronies, and survived by accessing 'external resources to make good the deficiencies in their own rule' (Clapham, 1996: 21). Local communities continued to support theocratic, ethnic, patriarchal or hierarchical value systems rather than freedom, equality and scientific rationality. And donors sometimes used aid to further their own interests rather than those of their recipients, evaded accountability mechanisms, ignored noncompliance in client regimes, and protected their own producers while forcing LDCs to open their borders. The result was economic decline and growing inequality, exclusion and violence.[15] Thus the neoliberal project was also in crisis by the second half of the 1990s, since it, like structuralism, was not producing freedom, prosperity and justice but an 'acceleration of uneven development which ... translates into polarization, and the spread of misery among a growing number of people (Castells, 2000a: 352).

Conclusions

The impasse in development theory appeared to be insurmountable at the start of the 21st century because none of the dominant paradigms appeared to be able to map out a viable route to development in weak states. However, our concern in presenting this depressing analysis is to get rid of false optimism and to identify the most serious of the challenges that confront the discipline in order to identify an agenda for the rest of this book. These challenges are both analytical and practical, and raise three key questions that will be addressed in the chapters that follow:

1 Can we reconcile the demand for development – identified as the universalization of liberal or social democratic capitalistic institutions – with the social, political and economic autonomy of the communities that live in the weakest states in the third world?
2 Can we explain why the mainstream theories embodied in the orthodox social sciences need to be complemented by different kinds of policies in countries still involved in developmental transitions?
3 Can we suggest viable policy projects that will offer these countries the practical advice they need to complete the programmes that most of them have already begun?

The rest of Part I will take up the analytical and methodological problems identified in the first and second parts of this chapter in order to answer the first of these three questions. Part II will argue that the current crisis in orthodox neoliberalism is beginning to produce new pluralistic syntheses that are resolving some of the apparent contradictions between the use of state, for-profit and solidaristic institutions discussed in this chapter. Part III will identify the limitations of this new liberal pluralistic paradigm when it is applied in the particular conditions operating in LDCs and especially in LLDCs. Here we will return to many of the arguments presented by the classical developmental theorists, and consider new ways in which they can be combined with liberal theory to produce new and more effective solutions.

Notes

1 Coleman uses a similar phrase in his classic text (1960: 536).
2 This analysis draws heavily on the work of the Crisis States Programme at the London School of Economics.
3 I owe this point to Brian Barry.
4 For critical reviews of the nature of these 'depoliticized' processes, see Ferguson (1996) and Harriss (2002).
5 Here Parsons is paraphrasing Pareto.

6 Parsons and Marx provide the classic conservative and radical versions of anti-individualistic structuralist theory. In Parsonian theory, individual choices are seen as a function of the roles people occupy; in Marxism of their class positions.

7 We are ignoring the Marxist critique of capitalist markets here, although it will be addressed later.

8 According to Margaret Thatcher, 'there is no such thing as society, there are individual men and women and there are families' (cited in Slater and Tonkiss, 2001: 32).

9 For a powerful critique of these multiculturalist assumptions, see Barry (2001) and the responses in Kelly (2002).

10 Thus Hegel (1821/1967: 219) felt that 'civilized nations' were justified 'in regarding and treating as barbarians those who lag behind them ... and [treating] their autonomy only as a formality'; Mill (1859/1910: 73) argued that 'despotism is a legitimate mode of government in dealing with barbarians, provided the end be their improvement'; and Marx (1953/1973) saw British rule as the violent and exploitative, but nevertheless essential precondition for the development of India.

11 See Hobson (1902); Lenin (1916/1970); Luxemburg (1913/1963); Trotsky (1930/1977); and Mao Tse-tung (1939/1954).

12 Desai (2004) reviews of the ambiguous nature of Marx's critique of capitalism and imperialism.

13 For the 'crisis' debate, see Schuurman (1993), notably the chapter by Booth. Leys (1996) provides an excellent review.

14 'Growth outcomes were deeply disappointing and ... typically below the levels of the derided 1950s and 1960s. Poverty reduction made little headway ... the elimination of restrictions on domestic finance and on international capital flows resulted in huge global crises but did not succeed in enhancing [the] volume and efficiency of productive investment. [And] the transformation of Eastern bloc countries into capitalist market economies ... can only be described as an abject failure' (Fine et al., 2003: xv).

15 Many countries have experienced significant periods of violence, economic breakdown, or a failure to manage natural disasters over the past 15 years. They include Algeria, Burundi, Chad, Central African Republic, Congo Brazzaville, the Democratic Republic of the Congo, Eritrea, Ethiopia, Ivory Coast, Liberia, Malawi, Mozambique, Rwanda, Sierra Leone, Somalia, South Africa, Sudan, Uganda, Western Sahara, Zambia, Zimbabwe; Haiti, El Salvador, Guatemala, Nicaragua, Argentina, Colombia, Venezuela; Georgia, Bosnia, Serbia, Azerbaijan, Chechnya; Israel, Palestine, Iraq, Kurdistan, Afghanistan; Bihar and Kashmir in India, Nepal, Pakistan, Sri Lanka, Tibet, East Timor, Indonesia, and the Philippines. Some have resolved their problems, many have not. The global system is also now threatened by the environmental crisis, the fragility of the global monetary and credit system, and the threat of international terrorism.

Chapter 2

The Basic Assumptions of Development Theory

This chapter will respond to the disagreements identified in Chapter 1 by arguing that many of them can be transcended by using a comparative institutional theory, which assumes that social outcomes depend on the nature of the authority, incentive and accountability mechanisms that characterize different kinds of institutions and organizations, and that these are likely to operate very differently in DCs than in LDCs. We will show that the primary goal of the liberal market-based institutions in the former are designed to turn technological and organizational innovation into an automatic, even compulsory process; that those in pre-modern societies were generally designed to maintain existing arrangements and therefore discouraged change; and finally that the classical traditions in development theory emerged to deal with a distinct array of market failures which confront LDCs and not DCs because LDCs are still attempting to build modern institutions. These failures make it difficult for them to adopt orthodox policy solutions in the short run, and call for a variety of second-best alternatives that take account of local understandings, value systems and endowments.

The idea of development and structural change

The idea of development, and the possibility of social progress that it supports, has normative, prescriptive and teleological implications. Its supporters claim that:

- all societies could generate higher levels of freedom, cooperation, prosperity and justice than they already do
- these goals can only be achieved by creating democratic capitalist or socialist institutions
- these institutions must eventually be universalized because societies are composed of rational individuals who will recognize the benefits these systems offer and therefore create them.

This belief in the inevitability of progress is now under threat, as we have seen, but this has not reduced the optimism of an era that pervades both DCs and LDCs and exists as a generalized aspiration even among marginalized people in remote places.[1] The belief that progress could, should, and even must happen therefore dominates political, economic and social life across the modern world and justifies a social system that is more concerned with stimulating change than maintaining the status quo.

Thus the commitment to development is not just a set of normative aspirations, but depends on the institutionalization of organizational and cultural systems that 'routinize innovation' (Nelson and Winter, 1982: 133) by creating authority, incentive and accountability mechanisms that oblige agencies and their beneficiaries to meet ever-increasing performance targets at work, at school, on the sports field, and even in their social lives. In modern societies, governments should only be re-elected if they increase growth and improve services, firms only prosper if they provide cost-effective products, civic associations and NGOs only retain their members and donors if they serve them better than possible rivals, and spouses only stay together if they respect each others' needs and wishes. This was not the case in pre-modern societies whose institutions were designed to maintain stability rather than development by creating theocratic, despotic, monopolistic or patriarchal institutions that allowed elites to suppress innovation and criticism and obliged the subordinate strata to accept their lot. Modern people enjoy far greater freedom and prosperity but they also lead driven lives, because the demands their institutions impose on them no longer lie on their shoulders 'like a light cloak', but have 'become an iron cage' (Weber, 1976: 181).

The shift from institutions that enforce stability to those that institutionalize innovation has turned the idea of development from an 'aspiration' into a 'process', an 'enterprise' and an 'expectation':

- It operates as an *incremental process* when open systems exist whose rules and incentives facilitate autonomous but purposive exchanges between individuals or groups that generate continuous improvements in assets, capacities and entitlements, as liberal democratic capitalism does.
- It becomes an *enterprise* when individuals, groups, classes, large organizations or whole societies make conscious and collective decisions to shift from systems that block innovation and freedom to those that sustain it, an enterprise that has been organically linked to attempts to create modern capitalism or socialism.[2]
- It exists as an *expectation* when most people believe that their existing institutions, or those they are trying to build, can be relied on to generate constant improvements in their capacity to control nature and increase freedom and prosperity.

Theorists often focus exclusively on one or other of these aspects, but a coherent theory of development has to be able to explain the necessary relationships that have to operate between them all, and in our case, why these relationships generate different problems and demands in LDCs than DCs.

Development as a normative aspiration

'People are intentional and calculating animals who build history out of their pictures of the future' (Stinchcome, 1997: 387), but they can only do this when they have the knowledge and resources required to turn their dreams into reality. Most pre-modern societies were dominated by the struggle for survival, so the universalization of the idea of development is a modern phenomenon, since most past societies believed that their organizational and technological systems were natural and unchangeable, and sometimes retained them for centuries, even millennia. But a 'notion of progress' exists now that is seen to be universally valid and 'the key to the emancipation of human beings from oppression and exploitation ... everywhere' (Barry, 2001: 4). This idea rests on normative and technical assumptions – that freedom and equality are demonstrably preferable to coercion and dependence and most conducive to maximizing prosperity, and that socially and technologically replicable systems exist that will actually guarantee better outcomes wherever they are adopted. These normative assumptions play a central role in the social sciences as well, since:

> Social-scientific criticism proceeds from the assumption, theory or knowledge that a segment of the world under examination could be different from – and better than – what it is. Without an alternative, criticism loses its point. (Tilly, 1997e: 18)

The modern commitment to freedom and equal rights started to influence theory and policy in the 18th century when radical liberal theorists began to argue that simply allowing people the 'freedom to make public use of one's reason in all matters' would create an 'enlightenment' that would reform everyone's 'ways of thinking' (Kant, 1784/1991b: 55). The commitment to freedom necessarily entailed the principle of equal rights, because 'there should only be one status of citizen' who all have the same legal and political rights that 'should be assigned to individual citizens, with no special rights (or disabilities) accorded to some and not others on the basis of group membership' (Barry, 2001: 7).

More radical theorists then argued that 'substantive' freedom cannot only depend on formal legal entitlements, but also on 'the removal of the major sources of unfreedom: poverty as well as tyranny, poor economic opportunities as well as systematic social deprivation, neglect of public facilities as well as intolerance or overactivity of repressive states' (Sen, 1999: 3). These demands have necessary organizational consequences since they are incompatible with all institutions that allow one individual, class, religion or race to impose its will on others. Subsequent attempts to universalize these principles have turned 'history' into a developmental process in which societies have transformed their institutions from those that deny freedom to those that enforce it, and in doing so, extended the 'principle of freedom' from situations in which only 'one is free' to those where 'some are free', and ultimately to those where 'all men as such are free, and ... man is by nature free' (Hegel, 1822–30/1975: 54).

These processes have depended on a shift from institutions based on coercive hierarchies to those based on self-regulating markets whose role was 'insignificant up to recent times' (Polanyi, 1944/2001: 46). Markets are generally seen as purely economic institutions, but they also operate in political and social spheres in the form of multiparty democracy and free competition between individuals and associations in civil society. However, while the possibility of freedom depends on open systems, free competition can also create exclusion and inequality rather than freedom because it produces losers as well as winners. This requires conscious interventions to create social cohesion by protecting societies 'against the perils inherent in a self-regulating market system' (Polanyi, 1944/2001: 80), in the form of collective, coercive and hierarchical institutions that regulate market exchanges. Their activities can only be justified if they institutionalize the normative principles of equity and justice by demonstrating that the 'economic inequalities' they produce can be 'reasonably expected to be to everyone's advantage' (Rawls, 1973: 60). The need for regulation is accepted by conservatives and radicals, but its nature and extent has always been heavily contested.

These principles of freedom, equality and equity dominated liberal theory from the 18th century, but classical right- and left-wing development theorists also emphasized the need for economic growth based on a planned transition from low-technology agriculture to large-scale industry. Many practitioners now prioritize human rights and social provision over growth, but the need to increase output is as important as ever, since freedom is impossible without access to the technologies that have eliminated the tyranny of unassisted toil and facilitated higher and higher levels of communication and cooperative interdependence. Further, the possibility of growth and technical change also depends on individual autonomy and free competition, because it has only occurred where institutional arrangements exist that provide 'incentives to use factors of production more efficiently and direct resources into inventive and innovating activity' (North, 1981: 148). Liberal economists therefore treat the creation of secure individual property rights as the key to economic growth, and the freedom to experiment as the key to scientific and technological progress, because 'the only unfailing and permanent source of improvement is liberty, since by it there are as many possible independent centres of improvement as there are individuals' (Mill, 1859/1910: 128).[3]

Finally, although efficiency depends on market competition, the ultimate goal of development is not to maximize competition but large-scale cooperation. Modern individuals do not seek the freedom to grow their own food or build their own houses, but to perform specialized tasks in large organizations, and to enter into freely chosen social and economic exchanges with others across the world. However, doing this constantly forces them to subordinate their personal choices to the demands of the organizations they work for, that is, to the 'higher goals and integrations ... [derived] from the institutional setting' in which they operate (Simon, 1957: 101). As Marx (1858/1973: 84) said:

> Only in the eighteenth century, in 'civil society', do the various forms of social connectedness confront the individual as a mere means towards his private purposes, as external necessity. But the epoch which produces this standpoint, that of the isolated individual, is also precisely that of the hitherto most developed social (from this standpoint general) relations.

Thus markets do enable individuals to cooperate, even when they have no direct knowledge of what each other is doing, but the fact that markets also give rise to large-scale cooperation means that liberal theories that only focus on market-based individual exchanges have had to be complemented by institutional theories that explain the need for, and logic of, collective and/or hierarchical processes that govern collective behaviour in large private or public corporations or networks. The extent and nature of these processes is also a highly contested issue, but even liberal fundamentalists accept the need for institutionalized constraints to secure the benefits of reciprocal interdependence, while their structuralist opponents believe in personal autonomy, but argue that it must be grounded in a greater degree of obligatory mutual interdependence than liberals accept. What is crucial for this study, however, is the fact that the relationship between managed and market-based change processes operates very differently in first-comers than latecomers.

Incrementalism, planning and developmental transitions

The idea of progress now influences behaviour everywhere, but achieving it involves different processes in first-comers operating on the developmental frontier, than in latecomers that do not. This is because the possibility of progress depends on the existence of plausible 'pictures' of objectively possible futures that people could create by modifying what they actually do. First-comers cannot access tried-and-tested systems that already operate more effectively than their own, so they imagine better alternatives and then attempt to create them through risky experiments with unpredictable outcomes. However, once a country or region has actually created a more effective system than its neighbours, it becomes what Hegel (1822–30/1975: 60, 145) calls a 'world-historical nation' and its institutions and practices can be used as 'a template for the reconstruction of other states' (Tilly, 1997c: 149). Thus latecomers in the west used the British model to create their own capitalist revolutions in the 19th century, and, once capitalism had emerged fully 'in one and only one part of the world', the 'rest' were transformed using western models (Hobsbawm, 1976: 160). This sometimes took the form of voluntary imitation, more often it involved 'the direct, sustained organization of others in global regimes of control' (Geyer and Bright, 2000: 61).

The existence of late and uneven development therefore means that LDCs need not reinvent the wheel, but can draw on the accumulated knowledge of humanity in order to expedite their early transitions. This transforms development from a spontaneous process into a conscious and collective enterprise. This gives development theorists a different agenda from orthodox ones because it generates possibilities and constraints that the latter, who focus exclusively on the problems of DCs, do not have to address. Thus the critical issue at stake here is whether the intellectual heritage that underpins western institutions is indeed 'valid of itself, independently of its origin', and 'identically transferable' without reference to local conditions or cultures (Jaspers, 1963: 72).

This study will in fact argue that these conditions mean that no society can hope to transform itself through mere imitation, but also that none have ever done so without learning from best practice elsewhere and 'adapting' it to suit its own needs and capacities. This need not produce dependent development as nationalist critics claim, nor does it assume that the existence of western templates enables planners to think that they 'already know the answers' and turn development into 'a technical engineering problem that his answers will solve', as neoliberal critics assume (Easterly, 2006: 5). This generates a complex and ambiguous relationship between orthodox and development theory that will be addressed throughout this book; what concerns us is that the nature and implications of the use of conscious planning as opposed to markets in development management are often conflated with those involved in its use in the first world itself. These confusions have had a major influence on policy debates between structuralists and neoliberals in LDCs, so we must revisit them here before we can proceed further.

Orthodox liberals, and neoclassical economists in particular, argue that unanticipated consequences ensure that our 'pictures of the future are always wrong' (Stinchcombe, 1997: 387), making attempts to plan large-scale social transformations futile and often dangerous. They therefore claim that progressive change can only emerge incrementally in response to spontaneous exchanges between free individuals operating in competitive markets, that the 'central control of all economic activity' must lead to totalitarianism and inefficiency (Hayek, 1944/1994: xxxii),[4] so that 'the right plan is to have no plan' (Easterly, 2006: 5). However, these 'spontaneous' processes also generate long-term structural changes in the institutional arrangements that have transformed the modern world. In market societies, the fate of a new process or product depends on the number of people willing to adopt it. Most innovations usually only have minor effects, but they do produce structural changes when all these 'small changes consistently occur in a given direction' (Brett, 1969: 66). Here, continuous innovation leads to cumulative changes that 'generate novelty and change in problem solutions' followed by self-generated feedbacks with unpredictable outcomes that never replicate the original model but produce 'generic change by altering the environment's structure by infusing it with novelty' (Dopfer, 2005: 28, 30).

When sequences of this kind mature, societies have to make fundamental institutional transformations to accommodate them. The first Industrial Revolution in Britain emerged out of incremental processes that eventually created a new bourgeoisie and the shift from an aristocratic to a liberal state system by the late 19th century (Hobsbawm, 1969). The consequent growth of an organized working class then led to a shift to a corporatist social democratic state by the end of the 1940s (Thompson, 1968). The growth of automation and the transformation of communications in the 20th century virtually eliminated the mass working class and facilitated the liberal revival in the 1980s. The ongoing revolution in information technology in the 21st century and the emergence of a knowledge-based economic system are now having equally significant consequences by transforming the hierarchical authority relationships that characterized classical capitalism, as Hodgson shows (1999: 210ff.).

This liberal model depends on the existence of individual freedom, formally equal rights and voluntary exchange, which rules out the possibility of consciously managed social change and therefore ignores any attempt to question the nature or justice of existing institutional arrangements, or the distribution of wealth and power on which they rest. Instead, liberals assume that equitable market-based systems already exist that enable autonomous individuals to maximize their own interests, while satisfying other people's needs, and thus 'assume away all organisational considerations' (Moe, 1984: 739). However, western socialists used Marx's critique of the inherently exploitative nature of capitalism to argue that the existing institutions and practices in even the most advanced societies must generate exploitation, imperialism and even barbarism, unless they were replaced by 'a definite plan' based on 'the conscious will of the masses' (Luxemburg, 1918/1972: 195). Thus the institutional changes that transformed the developed world were also shaped by the outcome of the clash between 'two fundamentally different and irreconcilable attitudes' – a belief in individualism that attributes progress to the voluntary 'efforts of individual men' who have combined 'to produce our civilization' and use this understanding 'to derive the power to create conditions favorable to further growth', and, on the other hand, 'collectivism which aims at conscious direction of all forces of society' (Hayek, 1944/1994: xxxii).

The inequalities and instability that characterized early capitalist development in most DCs, as well as two world wars and depressions in the first half of the 20th century, enabled political movements committed to interventionism to capture state power across most of the world. They attempted to protect society from the 'weaknesses and perils' of 'self-governing markets' (Polanyi, 1944/2001: 152) by regulating or even eliminating competition, and redistributing resources between classes, regions and/or communities. Thus structuralist governments dominated most of the 20th century, although the nature of their methods and goals depended on the social composition of the political movements that introduced them in different contexts. Left-wing versions based on Marxist and neo-Marxist theory produced authoritarian state socialism in the command economies, and social democratic 'mixed economies' in Western Europe. Authoritarian right-wing versions were adopted in Fascist states in Germany, Japan, Italy, Spain and Portugal, and later in authoritarian states like South Korea and Taiwan, where working-class political movements were defeated and state controls were used to build corporatist capitalist societies rather than socialism or social democracy. The defeat of the major Fascist powers meant that left-wing structuralism rather than liberalism dominated DCs in the third quarter of the 20th century, when most advanced societies believed that 'basic equality' could not be created and preserved without 'invading the freedom of the competitive market ... [so] our modern system is frankly a Socialist system ... [but one where] the market still functions – within limits' (Marshall, 1964: 71).

Yet these struggles occurred in very different environments from those that prevailed in LDCs, because they had already built more or less successful liberal capitalist economies before they began their structuralist experiments. Thus their attempts to create new regulatory regimes, public enterprises and welfare systems occurred when their states had already acquired a powerful capacity to tax, enforce the law and deliver effective services. All of them had to create new systems and called on Marxist, Leninist, Fabian and/or Keynesian theory to do so, but had to build their command or mixed economies by creating new structures where 'learning-by-doing' was probably as important as the theoretical models they used to guide and justify their actions. When structuralism collapsed in the 1980s, conservative parties could return to the liberal orthodoxies that had dominated policy in the 'world-historical nations' – Britain in the 19th and the USA in the 20th centuries.[5]

Thus liberal optimists assumed that the end of the cold war marked 'the end of history', since 'liberal democracy remains the only coherent political aspiration that spans different regions and cultures around the globe' and free markets 'have succeeded in producing unprecedented levels of material prosperity, both in industrially developed countries and in ... the impoverished Third World' (Fukuyama, 1992: xiii). This turned market theory, once seen as a 'dissenting view' (Bauer, 1972), into the dominant orthodoxy and the intellectual basis for the unity of the new 'cosmopolitical' liberal democratic capitalist global system, managed at the global level by the IFIs.[6] Neoliberals claimed that this justified their long-standing critique of interventionism and that this 'demise' of development economics would be 'conducive to the health of both the economics and economies of developing countries' (Lal, 1996: 36).

This validated Marx's (1846/1974: 78) prediction that capitalism would produce 'world history for the first time, insofar as it made all civilised nations and every individual member of them dependent for the satisfaction of their wants on the whole world, thus destroying the natural exclusiveness of nations'. But, while Fukuyama treats this shift as the end of history, Marx (1858/1973: 162) believed that capitalism was the most progressive system yet invented, but still so coercive and unstable that once people had used it to create 'the conditions of their social life', they would be unable to begin, 'on the basis of these conditions, to live it', without making a further step to libertarian socialism. However, the influence of the new paradigm was so pervasive in the 1980s and 90s that the development community did not attempt to modify it to meet local conditions, but simply used IFI-managed structural adjustment programmes to transfer it to the great majority of LDCs that were unable to manage their economic crises.

Managing transitions: structuralism, markets and dualistic development

The theoretical and political debate over policy agendas in LDCs has closely paralleled those between liberals and structuralists in DCs, but it has always had different implications for countries seeking to design new futures using any of the models based on what seemed to be successful practice in DCs. The existence of these models reinforced the claims of classical modernization theorists who argued that they enabled latecomers to adopt policy regimes that involved higher levels of centralized guidance and control than those applied to DCs, whose 'coerciveness and comprehensiveness' would be proportional to their levels of backwardness (Gerschenkron, 1962/1976: 90).[7] This was true for conservatives as well as socialists – authoritarian right-wing governments used force to create what Kohli (2004: 10) calls 'cohesive capitalist states' based on a 'close alliance with producer or capitalist groups' and 'a tight control over labor'. Left-wing governments believed that a planned economy based on Soviet or social democratic models was 'an essential, indeed indispensable condition for the attainment of economic and social progress in undeveloped countries', but that its primary objective should be to shift the balance of power from the capitalist elite to the subordinated classes (Baran, 1962: 261).

However, both right- and left-wing policy programmes were heavily influenced by the practices that dominated the DCs with which they had the strongest political links. Thus, Communist regimes depended on technical advice from the Soviet Union; reforming socialist regimes depended on advisers from social democratic European societies; and conservative regimes on advice from the USA. In the 1980s and 90s, they were replaced by neoliberal IFI-sponsored economists trained in the leading universities in the USA and Western Europe. As a result, both structuralist and liberal practitioners failed to take full account of the demanding conditions on which the success of their programmes depended. The postcolonial structuralist programmes depended on the existence of strong state apparatuses, economies and human and social capital, but were entrusted to authoritarian governments with weak bureaucracies and often embryonic capitalist classes. Similar problems undermined most neoliberal experiments because they imposed excessive demands on weak states and capitalist classes, and assumed that conscious planning could be replaced by spontaneous exchanges in societies where the markets and the 'free' individuals needed to sustain them had been systematically suppressed during the structuralist period.

Thus these programmes confronted an inherent contradiction – political democracy and liberal capitalism had to be *created through* conscious state-managed programmes mainly operationalized in structural adjustment programmes designed to build the institutional arrangements prescribed by the liberal model.[8] The result was a developmental enterprise that was just as interventionist and disruptive as structuralism, although one that created very different relationships between the groups that controlled political, economic and social organizations.

Many structuralists and neoliberals also failed to acknowledge the political and social implications of their prescriptions that could only be operationalized by governments. All attempts to implement major institutional transformations threaten existing rule systems, social and economic practices and the allocation of wealth and power. Thus development theory has never simply operated 'within the parameters of an unquestioned capitalist world order', but as 'a field of critical enquiry about the contemporary dynamics of that order itself, with imperative policy implications for the survival of civilized and decent life, and not just in the ex-colonial countries' (Leys, 1996: 43). The real significance of the paradigm debates between structuralists and neoliberals stems from the fact that they inevitably generate struggles between political movements committed to different kinds of capitalism on the one hand, and socialism on the other. Thus the success or failure of one model or another ultimately depends on its ability to persuade emerging groups in existing societies to mobilize the skills and resources needed to operationalize the new system, and to maintain the political support and coercive capacity needed to overcome the resistance of those with a vested interest in the existing order.[9]

Hence, the 'implementability' of any paradigm is strongly path dependent because it depends on existing levels of economic, political and social development that vary dramatically from one context to another. Creating democratic states, rational bureaucracies, capitalist firms and strong civic organizations imposes heavy costs on all societies, and particularly heavy ones on formerly despotic state-controlled societies trying to do so for the first time. Democracy is closely linked to economic systems that separated political and economic power (Friedman, 1962) and only highly productive societies have access to the surpluses needed to build strong states and civic institutions and create the 'market friendly environment' which liberals see as 'the ultimate goal of institutional reform in poor countries' (Clague, 1997a: 369). All LDCs have a long history of capitalist penetration and modern state formation, but they vary enormously from place to place, with serious implications for all attempts to build democratic capitalist institutions in most LDCs, and especially in the LLDCs in Africa, Central America and Central Asia with pitifully weak state capacity and embryonic capitalist classes.

All this suggests that development theorists and practitioners cannot ignore the achievements of the developed world, but also cannot expect to adopt them in a mechanical way. Hence they confront a major paradox – they know that LDCs need to import better practices from DCs, but they also have to accept that these models are unlikely to be identically transferable to new environments where the necessary preconditions do not exist. Thus 'different strategies ... [are needed] in different circumstances', because 'the requirements of start-up and breakthrough economies are not the same as those of front-runners and cruisers' (Landes, 1999: 391).

Both theorists and practitioners therefore have to carry a double burden – they need a comprehensive understanding of the orthodox disciplines that are used to manage policy programmes in DCs, but they also need an equally comprehensive understanding of the modifications they will have to make when they attempt to operationalize them in new environments. Institutional transfers will only succeed when they are 'not an imitative and dependent activity ... [but] a creative process which must ultimately result in new social forms and autonomous modes of thought' (Brett, 1973: 16). Thus latecomers do depend on external models, but they cannot travel the same road in a linear way, because the spontaneous processes that generated institutional change in first-comers cannot be repeated in latecomers, because they can make systematic use of the knowledge provided by their predecessors, and because their plans will always be 'distorted' by the demands and limitations emanating from local social and cultural systems.

However, some development theorists do claim that the same solutions can be applied in LDCs as DCs. Thus neoliberal theorists ignore local differences, and assume that even 'uneducated private agents' in LDCs will respond to market signals 'much as neoclassical theory would predict' (Lal, 1996: 30). This implies that all that is needed to create functioning markets is to change the formal rules governing property rights and contract enforcement. And some dependency theorists like Frank (1969: 62) also claimed that LDCs could make an immediate transition to socialism because 'the entire social fabric of the underdeveloped countries has long since been penetrated and transformed by, and integrated into, the world embracing [capitalist] system of which it is an integral part'. However, the recent failures of both structuralist and neoliberal projects now oblige us to return to the early dualistic analyses of classical modernization and Marxist theorists who accepted that pre-modern local institutions had been influenced by modern ones for centuries, but nevertheless continued to coexist with them and block or distort attempts to replace them with standardized western models.

Different traditions have drawn different conclusions from this claim. Classical modernization and Marxist theorists recognized that dualism obliges societies to modify their policy agendas during early developmental transitions, but assume that local institutions will disappear once the transition to modernity is completed. Radical dependency theorists argued that the exploitative nature of capitalism was responsible for the survival of regressive traditional systems, so that 'the modernity of one sector is a function of the backwardness of the other' (Laclau, 1971: 31). And multiculturalists have seen traditional cultures and institutions as the basis for successful 'revolts against colonialism' by 'dissident elites' who use 'place-bound traditions … [as] weapons against the European civilization' (Sachs, 1992: 111–12). In our view, all these competing views are partially valid, and will be used to provide us with the insights needed to develop a new synthesis in Part III.

Teleology, linearity and hybridity in development theory

The power exerted over modern society by the idea of development depends on a generalized expectation that a necessary and therefore teleological relationship exists between rationally designed institutions and the inevitability of progressive social change.[10] Thus development theorists not only identify a set of universal normative goals, but also make strong predictive claims about the likelihood of achieving them. The most optimistic teleologists not only claim that these ends will be achieved if their proposals are adopted, but also that all societies must inevitably do so because once better institutions have been created somewhere, rational individuals will soon adopt them everywhere else. This optimism has never been universally shared, but it has dominated western thought since the Enlightenment in the 18th century, when Kant (1784/1991b: 51) argued that:

> A philosophical attempt to work out a universal history of the world in accordance with a plan of nature aimed at a perfect civil union of mankind must be regarded as possible and even capable of furthering the purpose of nature itself.

He recognized that attempting to 'write a history according to an idea of how world events must develop if they are to conform to certain rational ends' raised many problems, but he still predicted that this 'cosmopolitan goal' would ultimately be achieved through social experimentation that would produce 'a regular process of improvement in the political constitutions of our continent (which will probably legislate eventually for all other continents)' (Kant, 1784/1991b: 52–3). Many economists still assume that if people are allowed to experiment in competitive markets, the efforts 'of every individual to better his own condition' will be so powerful 'that it alone, and without any assistance, is not only capable of carrying on the society to wealth and prosperity, but of surmounting a hundred impertinent obstructions with which the folly of human laws too often encumbers its operations' (Smith, 1776/1991: 479). And socialists have also claimed that 'the natural laws of capitalist production' must work 'with iron necessity towards inevitable results' (Marx, 1867/1974: 19), producing 'world history for the first time' and making all nations 'dependent for the satisfaction of their wants on the whole world, thus destroying the former exclusiveness of nations' (Marx and Engels, 1845–6/1974: 78), and, having done so, produce an equally inevitable transition to socialism involving 'the expropriation of a few usurpers by the mass of the people' (Marx, 1867/1974: 715).

These predictions are particularly significant for latecomers, so modernization theorists assumed that the same processes would transform 'traditional' societies into modern capitalist or socialist democracies, turning development into a 'normal condition'

> when the old blocks and resistances to steady growth are finally overcome. The forces making for economic progress, which yielded limited bursts and enclaves of modern activity, expand and come to dominate the society ... Compound interest becomes built, as it were, into its habits and institutional structure. (Rostow, 1971: 7)

However, devastating failures and reversals in the weakest LLDCs have seriously undermined these teleological claims. Liberals attributed them to the failure of structuralism in the 1980s and 90s, but the subsequent failure of many liberalization programmes has led critics to question the whole development project, as we saw in Chapter 1. Liberals attribute these failures to the continued existence of dysfunctional local values and institutions that block progressive change 'unless the reformers know how to solve the conflict and are able to do so' (Eggertsson, 2005: 30). Dependency theorists blame the capitalist system itself, arguing that 'within a capitalist world economy, all states cannot "develop" simultaneously by definition, since the system functions by virtue of having unequal core and peripheral regions' (Wallerstein, 1998: 286). These breakdowns have also raised serious doubts about the normative claims of the individualistic market-based societies to which everyone is supposed to aspire, and more especially about the assumption that latecomers can transform themselves by replicating the experiences of their now developed predecessors. Hence most theorists rejected the teleological claims of classical modernization and Marxist theory in the 1980s and 90s, claiming that LDCs could not and/or should not follow a linear path to liberal capitalism or socialism, thus generating the crisis in development that is the starting point of this study.

Now these criticisms cannot simply be dismissed, but they also seriously underestimate the achievements of the increasingly globalized modernization process that began with the scientific revolution in the 18th century by substituting the authority of scientific experimentation for a notion of an unchanging truth that carried an authority 'coeval with the institution of God' (Foucault, 1970: 34). The end of the cold war, the elimination of trade barriers, rapid technological change, widespread democratization and rapid growth in some of the largest LDCs have actually confirmed Kant and Smith's optimism and Marx's claim that capitalism must transform and unify the world, although not (yet) his claim that it would then produce a subsequent transition to socialism. This does not mean that a more complex and desirable future will unfold organically out of a less complex present, but it does mean that new understandings, practices and technologies have indeed evolved in first-comers and been adopted in latecomers, the most successful (and largest of which) are now growing at an unprecedented speed by adopting modified versions of 'best practice' from DCs. This is clearly changing the global system in ways that tend to confirm rather than deny the teleological claims of classical liberals, Marxist and modernization theorists.

The universalization of liberal democratic capitalism over the past 25 years and the immense improvements in productivity generated by the scientific revolution have created a world in which the more fortunate of us assume that we can expect our societies to overcome the worst threats that we still confront. The intensifying environmental crisis represents the greatest challenge to these assumptions to emerge since the start of the modern era, but it is also clear that it can only be addressed by strengthening modern science and using democratic institutions to mobilize the support needed to force governments and producers to take the drastic action needed to avert an impending catastrophe.

Further, the changes in local, national and global institutions that are beginning to create Kant's 'civil union of mankind' have not simply emerged out of academic texts, but have been generated by the demands of formerly marginalized groups – colonized societies, oppressed workers in authoritarian capitalist and command economies, subordinated women and many others. Their increasingly successful attempts to transform the terms on which they deal with those in authority over them also confirm the optimistic assumptions about the human capacity for rationality and socially oriented collective action that lie at the heart of the enlightenment project. No society has yet been able to fully develop 'the kind of political and social institutions that favour the achievement of ... material progress and general enrichment', but the enlightenment project 'nevertheless highlights the direction of history' (Landes, 1999: 217–18).

However, although these progressive changes have transformed billions of lives in DCs and the more successful LDCs, they have not reached billions more still living in poverty in LLDCs in Africa, Central America, Central Asia and the Middle East, and many still trapped in poverty in Latin America, China and South Asia. The fact that development is possible, even probable, does not guarantee that it will occur everywhere or rule out the possibility of major reversals in places where it had already occurred. Societies can lose their capacity to organize themselves effectively as Rome did when it succumbed to the barbarians, and liberal Germany did when it succumbed to their modern equivalents in the 1930s, and as modern capitalist society will do unless it can reduce its demands on the planet and control the systemic crises that periodically disrupt its operation.

Conclusions

The fact that global inequalities are still increasing and institutional change is still generating serious conflicts and disjunctures that block progress in many countries demands a critical review of current orthodoxies, but also justifies the existence of a theory of development that addresses those problems that orthodox theorists working in DCs can afford to ignore. We have shown that the idea of development is complex and heavily contested, yet is central to our ability to believe that the normative and practical threats created by these inequalities will eventually be overcome. The paradigms that have been deployed to solve these problems are in a state of crisis, but we will not resolve these problems through another round of critiques and deconstruction. Instead we need to re-evaluate the goals, analytical models and prescriptions that have succeeded in the past, but are not meeting contemporary challenges. We believe that these 'particular and partial standpoints' can be reconstructed through 'progress in [a theoretical] enquiry' (MacIntyre, 1998: 207), thus allowing new and more effective agendas to emerge.

Societies attempting to overcome poverty, ignorance and disease have always used models derived from societies that have already demonstrated their ability to do so. These attempts have been criticized by nationalists, but those who refuse to learn the lessons that first-comers offer to late-comers deny themselves access to the accumulated knowledge of humankind. Development practitioners are therefore partially attempting to reconstruct their own institutions using templates borrowed from first-comers. However, we will also show that their attempts to do this cannot be treated as a purely technical process for two reasons:

1 The models of 'best practice' in DCs are heavily contested, as we have seen, and constantly evolving in response to new political, economic and environmental crises, so choosing one or another – neoliberalism, liberal pluralism or structuralism – has major political implications.

2 The institutional changes resulting from attempts to implement any of them will have highly disruptive effects in LDCs. Their histories have in fact left them with a legacy of 'uncivic vicious circles that have trapped ... [them] in backwardness' for millennia (Putnam,

1993: 184). To escape these traps, they must find ways of getting their pasts out of their futures by adopting policies and processes that will be very different from those that exist in countries that have already completed their transitions.

And any attempt to address these issues demands three things:

1 A clear statement of the theoretical principles that enable us to argue that development theory can justify its claim to science.
2 An outline of the liberal model that dominates development discourse in the current era.
3 A systematic review of the contextual and historical factors that differentiate LDCs from DCs, which therefore call for different kinds of short-term solutions than those specified in the orthodox model.

We will address the first issue in Chapter 3 and the other two in Parts II and III.

Notes

1 Development was a real aspiration but seen as an unobtainable goal among the poor people I interviewed in the remotest parts of postwar Uganda in the 1980s and 90s.
2 This distinction between development as a 'process' and an 'enterprise' is derived from Cowan and Shenton (1996: viii–ix), who use the term 'doctrine' to refer to activities based on 'an intention to develop'.
3 Hegel (1821/1967: 72) notes how the Catholic Inquisition forced Galileo to 'abjure, dam, and execrate with my whole heart and true belief the absurd, false and heretical doctrine of the motion of the earth [around the sun]', thereby denying the principles of 'freedom of thought and science based on self-conscious, objective rationality'.
4 The quotation is from the Preface to the 1956 edition.
5 Although the USA confined its liberalism to the domestic economy, it was protectionist up to the Second World War, has never given up agricualtural subsidies, and rapidly reverted to interventionism to defend its banking system in 2008.
6 For the historical background, see, in particular, Horsefield (1969), Keynes (1943/1969) and Brett (1983, 1985). The term 'cosmopolitical' is taken from List (1841/1904: 98), which he contrasts with a 'true political or national economy'.
7 This study provides us with the classic formulation of the economic consequences of backwardness and being a 'latecomer' and its implications for different approaches to policy.
8 And notably in Afghanistan and Iraq over the past five years. Even Hayek (1955/1964: 84) acknowledges that liberal institutions emerged first in England 'as a by-product of a struggle for power rather than as the result of deliberate aim', and that 'its institutions and traditions [then] became the model for the civilized world'.
9 Parsons (1951/1964: 497ff.) shows how 'vested interests' resist change that threatens 'established ways'. Tilly (1997a: Chs 1–3) provides a useful formulation of the nature of the processes involved in this kind of change.
10 According to MacIntyre (1998: 182), 'the *telos/finis* of any type of systemic activity ... [is to] that end internal to the activity of that specific kind, for the sake of which and in the direction of which activity of that kind is carried forward'.

Chapter 3

Evolutionary Institutional Change and Developmental Transitions

A theory of development has to address several interdependent issues:

- the implications of structural change in LDCs rather than incremental change in DCs
- the demand for progressive change based on open systems and equal rights, and not just for change itself
- the relationship between conscious management and the spontaneous operation of market forces
- the need for processes and incentives that might persuade major social groups committed to different systems to recognize the need to change their institutions and in so doing solve the problems involved in emancipatory social transformations.

We also saw in Chapter 1 that:

- methodological positivists and individualists deny the possibility of value-driven theory and managed social change
- cultural relativists reject its implicit or explicit demand for a shift to western institutions
- corporatists and Communists are committed to systems based on centralized controls rather than free political and economic markets.

We can only reconstruct the development project by addressing these conflicting claims, since they seem to involve

> systematic and apparently ineliminable disagreements between the protagonists of rival moral points of view, each of whom claims rational justification for their own standpoint and none of whom seems able – except by their own standards – to rebut the claims of their rivals. (MacIntyre, 1998: 2002)

We will begin that reconstruction process here by first advancing a theory based on comparative and evolutionary institutionalism, and then by showing how it can help to transcend many of these disagreements.

51

Agency, institutional change and developmental transitions

Institutions are systems of rules and practices 'that structure social interactions in particular ways', imposing constraints on behaviour, and generating incentives and sanctions that must apply to all 'the members of the relevant community' (Knight, 1992: 2). Orthodox liberal theorists operate in societies that have already adopted market-based systems that 'meet a society's functional needs', and therefore 'persist because they continue to satisfy [its] needs' (Knight, 1992: 4). This allows them to focus on the 'functional prerequisites' that enable societies 'to constitute a persistent order [rather than disintegrate] or to undergo an orderly process of developmental change' (Parsons, 1951/1964: 27) and to assume that the world can be 'reasonably viewed as in equilibrium' (North 1990: 19). However, this reliance 'on equilibrium analysis, even in its more flexible forms leaves ... [them] largely blind to phenomena associated with historical change' (Nelson and Winter, 1982: 8) as well as conflict and exploitation.

Development theorists focus on societies where different institutional systems coexist, some of whose rules do *not* adequately satisfy people's needs because they are based on perverse incentives and oppressive power structures. Segmentary, patrimonial, slave, feudal, patriarchal, caste, Fascist or Communist systems produce servitude and/or stagnation, so individual and social rationality diverge, power can be abused for private gain, and regressive institutions survive because they serve the interests of dominant elites or conservative social groups. Since functionalist methodologies are designed to constitute 'a persistent social order', they must exclude criticism and change, and consign people to perpetual servitude in oppressive societies, so development must demand an ability to reform existing institutions by generating new incentive and accountability mechanisms that oblige people to behave in more appropriate ways.

Theorists need to understand how such institutions maintain themselves in order to respond effectively to the problems they generate, but also why their rules perpetuate dysfunctional and/or unjust outcomes that social groups may want to subvert or replace by shifting from one institutional type to another. It is 'the development of these contradictions that impels society forward and starts the process of the supersession of the old society by the new one' (Mao Tse-tung, 1937/1954: 16), for example by producing shifts from feudalism or slavery to capitalism, dictatorship to democracy, patriarchy to gender equality, theocracy to religious pluralism. Development theorists therefore deal with societies characterized by irreconcilable conflicts of interest and the need for structural change that cannot be understood using the static and functionalist assumptions of orthodoxy, but only by developing a theory 'that makes theoretical statements about the historicity of [social] phenomena' (Dopfer, 2005: 16) in order to explain why structural change occurs and what needs to be done if it is to take progressive and not regressive forms.

Social interactions and the personalities of the people involved in them are shaped by the nature of the institutionalized rules and routines that have to exist 'to meet that society's needs', but many different types of institution have coexisted in the modern world that have produced very different outcomes for different groups in each society, and for whole societies based on one type rather than another. This multiplicity of institutional types has major theoretical implications, because each type deploys different rules and routines whose effects can only be understood by using different analytical models. Thus, orthodox political scientists only derived their generalizations from 'a limited sector of man's experience with politics – the modern, complex, primarily Western states', and were unaware

> of how special and peculiar are the political forms and processes that he does study, since he is not aware of the composition of the total universe, of the range of complexity, and the kinds and frequencies of patterns to be found in it. The capacity to identify the peculiar properties of a particular species of politics, and the conditions with which it is associated, is dependent upon the variety of contrasting species with which one can compare it. (Almond, 1960: 10)

This is equally true of economic and social 'forms and processes' and the economic and sociological theories used to deal with them. Neoclassical market theory cannot explain the operation of the command economy in North Korea, nor can liberal democratic theory explain the subordination of women in theocratic Afghanistan. What is needed is specialized models that identify the distinctive principles that enable them to function, and that differentiate them from the institutional types being used in other societies to solve similar problems.

Now, treating the social universe as a system composed of a variety of interdependent and sometimes contradictory institutional arrangements obliges us to recognize that the processes that determine people's life chances and drive institutional change are the outcome of how the rules that govern their particular social systems oblige them to behave, and how this influences the way their society interacts with other types of society in the global system. Individuals or social groups make choices that influence these outcomes, but they are tightly constrained by their non-chosen positions in particular institutional systems that offer them different opportunities and rewards. This has several crucial empirical and therefore theoretical consequences:

1 Individuals who occupy a position in one institutional system rather than another – for example a serf on a feudal estate, as opposed to a software engineer at IBM – will earn unequal rewards and will form different judgements about the justice of the rules that govern their own situation in comparison with those that operate in other societies.

2 The fate of these individuals will not only depend on the position they occupy within their own social order, but also on the ability of their societies to compete with other societies for scarce resources. Their gains or losses will then be determined by the relative strength of each of their institutional arrangements, so the coexistence of unequal systems, such as feudalism, slavery, Communism, artisanal or peasant production, and capitalism will generate stresses in the weaker systems and the possibility of structural change.

3 The competitive nature of these processes means that people living in less efficient societies cannot simply ignore what happens elsewhere but will have to reform their own institutions – states, armies, firms and educational systems – if they wish to resist external threats.

4 This need to reform their institutions will force them to transcend the limits of their individual capacities and preferences because their ability to do so will depend on the effectiveness of the social processes that condition their behaviour. They will therefore have to respond to these challenges by developing collective solutions to their problems.

5 This need to create better institutions will force them to look for tried-and-tested models that have already proved their worth in more successful societies, and to acquire the skills and value systems needed to operate them, which they must 'necessarily' accept because they are not just a matter of political ideology or subjective individual preference.[1]

6 To do this effectively, they will need to develop a conscious understanding of the nature of their own institutions, those they are attempting to resist or emulate, and the whole system and their location in it.

These six challenges confront every LDC and the theorists who speak for them. Identifying them as we have done here enables us to show why the paradigm disagreements in development studies are best understood as debates over the relative merits of competing institutional arrangements:

- liberals support market-based systems
- socialists believe in collectivism
- cultural relativists and nationalist want a return to one or other kind of pre-modern system.

These claims, and the conflicts between them, are not primarily governed by academic debates but by the historically generated institutional requirements of a differentiated and asymmetrical global system, and the varied and contradictory demands that it imposes on its members and the opportunities or threats it offers them. Our social world is populated by a single species that is endowed with the same capacity for rational thought and action, a world whose members constantly attempt to better their lot by devising new solutions to their problems, and by looking to other societies for better ways of doing so.

However, their ability to do this not only depends on their access to new ideas, but also on the historically generated capacities and limitations embedded in their own situation and the way these constrain or facilitate their ability to compete or cooperate with other societies. Thus, they 'make their own history, but they do not make it as they please; they do not make it under circumstances chosen by themselves, but under circumstances directly encountered, given and transmitted from the past' (Marx, 1852/1968: 96). Competing paradigms are actually attempts to understand, manage and justify competing institutional systems; in the final analysis, the 'truth' of their competing claims depends on their ability to persuade people to adopt them and defend them by making them work in changed circumstances.

Now these issues cannot be addressed using the positivistic, individualistic and equilibrium assumptions of orthodox liberal theory, because they depend on 'logico deductive theorizing ... [that cannot] take into account "emergence", history and context' (Mouzelis, 1995: 5). They also cannot be fully addressed by cultural relativists, because they fail to recognize the extent to which the weaknesses of some kinds of institutions – for example patriarchy, patrimonialism or theocracy – perpetuate exploitation inside societies and destroy their ability to resist the threats posed by stronger external systems. History has always involved violent and unequal competition between different kinds of social systems producing 'new possibilities which conflict with the existing system or violate it or even destroy its very foundations and continued existence' (Hegel, 1822–30/1975: 82). The transformative and contradictory nature of such transitions therefore demands a theory that recognizes the normative, collective, conscious and conflictual nature of transformative change, and the problems involved in understanding the relationship between social 'agency' and freedom on the one hand, and the necessities imposed by historically determined institutional arrangements and the incessant clash between them on the other.

We therefore need to develop a theory of 'comparative evolutionary institutionalism' to explain the processes of 'institutional origination, adoption and retention', where new structures emerge that must disturb 'the prevailing coordinate relations, and constitute a potential source of de-coordination' (Dopfer, 2005: 48). This depends 'upon a theory of instituted coordination and order', not 'upon the often related notion of equilibrium', and can therefore offer us 'a non-equilibrium account of why the world changes', which emphasizes its 'structural dimensions' that 'provide the natural framework in which to analyse the ever-changing relative importance of firms, industries, regions and nations' (Metcalf, 2005: 392).[2]

The following analysis has much in common with evolutionary biology, since we argue that historically driven changes in biological species and ecologies are directly comparable to those taking place within particular social institutional set-ups, and in the distribution of institutional types across the globe. However, social processes differ from biological ones in two key respects:

1 They are played out over decades or centuries rather than millennia.
2 They are influenced but not determined by the conscious decisions made by individuals and collectivities of a species with a unique capacity for rational and value-driven thought and self-organization.

The implications of the relationship that evolutionary theory posits between conscious agency, the structural requirements of existing systems, and the often destructive effects of zero-sum conflicts are highly complex and have always been actively contested on normative, theoretical and empirical grounds. Nevertheless, we will argue that evolutionary principles offer social scientists a 'natural framework' for the analysis of how the coexistence of different but interacting institutional types constrain or facilitate the freedom or 'agency' of individuals, communities and/or societies, and how their conscious responses can generate developmental transformations or breakdowns in response. We will set out these principles in the next section, and respond to some of these criticisms in the one that follows.

An evolutionary approach to developmental transformations

Evolutionary theory in biology and the social sciences uses the effects of competition within and between species or social systems to explain both stability and transformation in the natural and social worlds. Biologists treat the survival of existing species and the emergence of new ones as a function of the ability of the members with the best adapted genes within a particular species to outcompete others, and, by doing so, to improve the capacities of the species as a whole and therefore its ability to outcompete other species. These processes are driven by self-interest rather than altruism (Dawkins, 1989), and exclude the possibility of conscious agency since outcomes depend on 'natural selection', which 'does not see ahead, does not plan consequences, has no purpose in view' (Dawkins, 1988: 21), yet can still produce 'living results' in the natural world that are so 'complex and beautiful' that most people have believed that they must have been designed by an all-knowing deity (Dawkins, 1988: Ch. 1).

This process was described by Darwin as the 'survival of the fittest', because the 'struggle for life' ensures that any 'variations' that are 'in any degree profitable to the individuals of a species' will help to preserve them and 'be inherited by their offspring', thus improving 'each creature in relation to its conditions', and inevitably leading 'to the gradual advancement of the greatest number of living beings throughout the world' (Darwin, 1859/1872: 76–7, 151). Darwin also recognized that the fittest only survive by eliminating the unfit where resources are scarce, because 'if any one species does not become modified and improved in a corresponding degree with its competitors, it will be exterminated' (p. 125). This process has not only eliminated the mammoth and the dodo, but also feudalism and slavery, and, in all probability, statist Communism as well. This suggests that 'the wellsprings of human freedom' do not just lie in 'the aspirations of classes about to take power, but even more in the dying wail of a class over whom the wave of progress is about to roll' (Moore, 1967: 505).

This image of nonequilibrating competition is central to evolutionary theory in biology and the social sciences. 'Ideas of competition and struggle in the writings of Smith and Malthus strongly influenced Darwin, while his work has exerted a powerful influence over subsequent generations of economists' (Hodgson, 2005: 105). It has been embedded (although not always fully articulated) in many varieties of development theory, and is compatible with 'the Austrian notion of the open-ended historical development of market economies' in economics, (Metcalf, 2005: 400) and with Marxist theories of historical materialism,[3] and also provides 'a natural-scientific basis for the class-struggle in history' (Marx, 1862/1977: 525). However, social scientific theorists cannot confine themselves to biological analogies, because biologists deal with the effects of competition between physically distinct species made up of individuals that cannot make conscious individual or collective decisions about how to change their futures, whereas social science deals with people who constantly make such choices about how to achieve their normative goals. These competitive natural and social processes operate on two different levels, first in interactions that occur within particular systems and influence 'the internal unfolding of entities', and, second, in interactions between systems resulting in the 'adaptation of populations of entities under a guiding process of competitive selection' (Metcalf, 2005: 391).

Now modern evolutionary economists focus on the processes generating changes within single systems, and usually with changes in DCs where competitive market-based processes already dominate the institutional landscape.[4] Their work transcends the equilibrium assumptions of neoclassical theory, and shows how the 'organizational traits' that characterize particular kinds of firms not only influence their capacity for competitive survival but also ensure that more successful traits are diffused to others 'by imitation' (Witt, 2005: 344). Austrian School theorists like Hayek (1955/1964) operated within this framework by attributing both order and innovation to 'spontaneous interactions' between firms in market societies, and Schumpeter (1943: 83) attributed the emergence of the giant modern corporation to 'an evolutionary process ... of industrial mutation that constantly revolutionizes the economic structure from within', through a 'process of creative destruction'.

However, focusing on changes within societies where markets already exist tells us little about behaviour in societies where they do not, or about the effects of the interactions between market- and non-market-based societies. Yet these are central to the developmental project that is ultimately concerned with the 'processes that generate variations in the pool characteristics in the population by adding or subtracting competing entities or by altering the characteristics of existing entities' (Metcalf, 2005: 395). Thus, while most evolutionary economists are concerned with structural changes within societies, development theory is ultimately concerned with the combined effects of competition within and between different kinds of institutional systems.

Evolutionary theory explains changes in populations with three defining characteristics:

1 *variation* – between their members 'with respect to at least one characteristic with selective significance'
2 *heredity* (or retention) – which presuppose the existence of mechanisms that 'ensure continuity over time in the form and behaviour of the entities in the population'
3 *selection* – which assumes that 'the characteristics of some entities are better adapted to prevailing evolutionary pressures and, consequently, these entities increase in numerical significance relative to less well-adapted entities' (Metcalf, 2005: 394).

The 'entities' that concern us are the differentiated, interactive and changing array of political, economic and social institutions that have existed during the past 500 years:

- *variation* depends on their use of differentiated authority, incentive systems and accountability mechanisms to generate and allocate resources
- *heredity* depends on people's tendency to retain the inherited values, understandings and endowments that sustain each system
- *selection* depends on the extent to which their differing authority, incentive and accountability systems – slavery, feudalism, theocracy, patrimonialism, statism, capitalism – enable their members to compete successfully with others in the world system.

Change can be generated by exogenous or endogenous shocks, changes in the domestic or external environment, or internal 'mutations' stemming from contingent historical events, such as political realignments that produce sudden shifts in social relations, demands and/or capacities. The pre-modern world was made up of many relatively autarchic systems where high communication costs enabled them to retain some degree of continuity over time. Development can therefore be understood as a function of the way in which rapid increases in asymmetrical interactions with corporatist or capitalist systems have eliminated, marginalized or restructured them over time.

This approach enables us to treat change as a five-stage process:

1 change begins when a population of institutional systems exists that is characterized by *variation* and potential instability
2 this is destabilized by an internal *mutation* or an external shock
3 which generates *adaptations* in response to the pressures of competitive *selection*
4 and produces new *structures* and a new distribution of systems
5 which are then subject to *retention*, provided the new arrivals can mobilize the powers needed to maintain themselves over time.[5]

Dopfer (2005: 16) conceives of this sequence as 'an evolutionary regime', and 'evolution' as a process involving 'one or more transitions from one regime to another'.[6]

This model undoubtedly provides us with a more realistic and complex version of the social, political and economic processes that have restructured the world system over the past 400 years than we can glean from currently dominant liberal theories, or indeed from the other major traditions involved in the paradigm debate. When we look back at these – liberalism, right- and left-wing structuralism, modernization and cultural relativism and critical dependency theory, and at the debates between them – we discover that these evolutionary principles not only enable us to identify some of their key weaknesses, but also the contribution they can make to the reconstruction of a viable synthesis.

Positivism, methodological individualism and evolutionary change

The methodological assumptions of orthodox liberal theory clash with those used in an evolutionary approach to development in three key ways:

1 they are positivistic and not emancipatory
2 they are individualistic and not collectivistic
3 they focus on static equilibriums rather than structural change, and the role of conflict in generating it.

How does evolutionary theory justify these differences?

Orthodox liberal theorists and most natural scientists argue that science cannot be used to validate a theory of emancipation, because it can only produce statements 'of belief in what is the case', and cannot advocate 'what ought to be the case' (Dawkins, 1989: 3), as we saw in Chapter 1. The natural sciences originally attempted to create 'a coherent, logical, necessary system of ideas' to explain 'every element of our experience' through the operation of invariant laws, and assumed that concerns about the social world 'associated to the idea of democracy which emphasizes human freedom, creativity and responsibility ... choice and, therefore, the concept of value' could not be subjected to the same kind of logico-deductive theorizing but only operate under the guise of humanism (Prigogine, 2005: 62).

However, Prigogine claims that recent developments in 'non-equilibrium physics and chemistry' can be used to restore 'the idea of value' to the natural sciences and 'overcome the Cartesian duality' between them and the social sciences (p. 64). We believe that evolutionary institutionalism enables and even obliges development theorists to address 'the concept of value' by shifting from a static version of methodological individualism to a theory that focuses on the relationship between the agency of individuals and groups, and the institutional frameworks that structure them.

We saw in Chapter 1 that positivistic theories are inherently individualistic, and assume that 'all the facts necessary to the understanding of concrete social systems can be predicated on analytically isolated "individuals" combined with a process of direct generalization from these facts' (Parsons, 1937/1968: 72). This enables theorists to treat atomized individuals, driven by values that only exist as 'endogenous' personal preferences, as the primary source of social action. This therefore deinstitutionalizes these processes and delegitimates attempts to make normative judgements about the rules that enable elites to impose particular preferences and patterns of behaviour onto them. It also excludes the use of normative criteria to compare the performance of one institutional system with another. Cultural relativists also reject normative judgements of this kind, and agree with positivists in rejecting both the conservative Parsonian and radical Marxist versions of structuralism that see individual choices as a function of their institutional roles or their class positions. Treating individual values and choices as facts in the way that natural scientists treat the behaviour of atoms or microbes therefore ignores the fact that they are institutionally constructed, since:

> This ego-ideal of the individual ... is something that has developed ... through social learning ... in conjunction with specific structural changes in social life ... [and] is part of a personality structure which only forms in conjunction with specific human situations, with societies having a particular structure. It is highly personal, yet at the same time society specific. (Elias, 2001: 141)[7]

Thus attributing social action and change to the choices of 'autonomous' individuals or communities can only generate partially valid results because:

> The relation of individual and society that can be observed in the twentieth century in industrial nation states, that embrace more than a million and perhaps more than 100 million people, the personality structures and the whole group-formation at this stage, cannot be used as an experimental model with the aid of which universal statements about human personality structures, social forms, or the relation of individual and society can be even tentatively made or tested. (Elias, 2001: 172–3)

This may be appropriate for societies where 'the personality structure' and individual conscience connected with these principles have already been effectively institutionalized and 'are taken completely for granted' (Elias, 2001: 179), but not in LDCs where they have not. Liberal capitalism is the only system where this is even partially true, so liberal theorists can assume that individuals are already free, and that fundamental conflicts over goals, processes and the role of science itself have already been resolved. This allows them to focus on technical evaluations of means rather than ends, and confine their role to the measurement of what Weber (1922/1968) calls the 'formal rationality' of the decisions that individuals make by evaluating their effectiveness in achieving a given set of socially chosen goals, where 'action is based on "goal-oriented" rational calculation with the technically most adequate available methods'.[8] This eliminates the need to address structural problems stemming from competing 'value systems' that produce competing 'social needs and objective states of consciousness … [and] the directions of emancipation and regression' (Habermas, 1971: 64).

Hence a positivistic social science based on methodological individualism is only possible in market-based societies. Positivists, like biologists operating in what remains of the natural world not yet restructured by human intervention, can therefore ignore the role of conscious design in structural change. However, when they do this, they ignore the fact that the possibility of free individual choice in human society is a recent outcome of conscious institutional transformations driven by normative objectives, with freedom to choose pre-eminent among them. In fact, Darwin (1859/1872: 34, 76) used the idea of natural selection, which dominates evolutionary biology, in order to distinguish the processes based on competitive selection in nature from those where 'man's [conscious] powers of selection' have produced massive transformations in the distribution and nature of species through 'adaptation, not indeed to the animal or plant's own good, but to man's use or fancy'.

To argue that we need to recognize the role of values in creating the facts that we confront in the social and physical worlds does not rule out the need for a rigorous and objective scientific analysis of those facts and the way they are transforming those worlds. In fact, market-based models provide indispensable information about how people do behave and should behave in developed societies where most individuals have actually internalized the rational and self-interested patterns of behaviour demanded by market-based systems.[9] Hence positivistic individualism in its neoclassical or Austrian form is not a general but a specific theoretical framework for the analysis of market societies whose recent creation involved major conflicts with groups committed to institutions designed to suppress freedom rather than facilitate it. However, this process has yet to be completed in most LDCs, since premodern institutions still perpetuate relationships of personal or economic dependence based on the superior authority of husbands, the community, the church or the party. Thus treating these societies as though their populations were already able to act as free individuals systematically misrepresents their situations and options, because it assumes 'as actually in existence a state of things which has yet to come into existence' (List, 1841/1904: 102).

So development theorists cannot just make 'objective' technical judgements about whether 'individuals' or 'communities' are choosing the best means to achieve their own preferences, because their preferences are exogenous, not endogenous[10] and are institutionally constructed in ways that can oblige them to make choices they do not prefer. Hence they, and the theorists who interpret their situations to them, need to address problems of 'substantive rationality' and identify 'criteria of ultimate ends, whether they be ethical, political, utilitarian, hedonistic, feudal ... egalitarian or whatever', and find ways to measure the results of action 'however formally rational ... against these scales of value rationality or substantive goal rationality' (Weber, 1922/1968: 85–6). Evolutionary institutionalism therefore demands a 'process-sociological approach' that recognizes the effects of 'changes in human groups and the corresponding changes in the personality structures of individual people, when making universal statements about human beings' (Elias, 2001: 173).

Liberal theory does provide a viable and indispensable understanding of the institutional prerequisites and consequences of liberal capitalism, and of the normative, technical and empirical problems that groups in pre-capitalist societies must solve if they wish to adopt it. Thus societies that are still creating these institutions have to use liberal theory to identify the 'socially necessary' changes in institutional rules and routines that everyone will have to accept if they are to create what they will experience as a new kind of social system designed to maximize freedom, equity and productivity. However, the nature of these constraints and the institutions needed to operationalize them are not self-evident, since 'what is right for the individual is not necessarily right for society', so this creates 'both an opening and a need for a *science* of morals' (Ayer, 1948: 249, emphasis added), which involves the 'transition from factual to value statements, indicatives to imperatives' that positivists believe to be 'logically inadmissible' (Bhaskar, 1979: 69).[11] It is this that justifies the scientific claims of liberal development theory, and has both cultural and substantive implications.

Creating new institutions involves 'conscious management', since people have to acquire new understandings and value systems, and be persuaded or forced to renounce their old ones, thus generating major conflicts and possible reversals. This also contradicts the equilibrium and Pareto optimal assumptions of neoliberal market theory, which treat 'the state of competition' as 'a structural property defining a state of rest in a particular market context, usually characterized in terms of the number of identical competing firms', thus excluding the analysis of problems of structural inequality and zero-sum competition (Metcalf, 2005: 399). However, these processes can be understood using evolutionary theory, with its clear recognition that the survival of the fittest forces the less fit to adapt, face elimination or suppress the competitive process altogether – as entrenched elites have tried to do across the ages.

These evolutionary arguments implicitly validate liberal democratic capitalism by treating its ability to eliminate most of its competitors, like feudalism and Communism, as proof that market reforms are a necessary prerequisite for development in pre-capitalist societies, as the donors who introduced the liberal structural adjustment programmes in the 1980s and 90s claimed. The fact that market theory rests on normative assumptions and has disruptive social consequences neither proves nor disproves its claim to offer LDCs the best solution to their problems. Instead, it obliges us to develop a rigorous analysis of the changes in values, authority systems, incentives and sanctions that introducing markets must involve, to find ways of accurately measuring the costs of doing this, identify the groups that are likely to benefit or lose from them, and find ways of overcoming the transitional problems that reforms must create.

The stability and efficacy of liberal institutions depend on their ability to create rules, aptitudes, incentive and accountability systems that not only maximize productivity, but also generate an equitable allocation of resources and benefits. We will describe the systems and relationships that need to be created for these purposes in Part II. But these systems have also often failed – in the developed world in the first two-thirds of the 20th century, and in LDCs virtually everywhere. Thus, while liberalism appears to have won the battle for survival over the past 30 years, it lost many earlier contests with Fascism, Communism, democratic socialism and corporatism, since 'it was prewar liberal economics that lost the battle after 1914', and planning in 'a mixed economy' that won it (Desai, 2004: ix). These strategies were based on a systematic critique of possessive individualism that sustained the socialist and corporatist political movements that dominated theory and practice in the postwar period in both DCs and LDCs until the end of the 1970s. We will outline its methodological assumptions below, and its institutional and historical consequences in Part III.

Corporate capitalism, extended cooperation and uneven development

Liberal individualists assume that any person should be free to pursue a 'course of his own' and not subjected to decisions by central planners (Oakeshott, 1971: 377), but ignore the fact that capitalist markets do not constantly recreate systems based on 'identical competing firms' (Metcalf, 2005: 399), but ones dominated by large hierarchical corporations – state bureaucracies, multinational firms and global civic institutions. Modern people prefer to see themselves as autonomous individuals, but depend on these large-scale organizations that are 'the fundamental phenomena of modern political, social and economic life' (Wolin, 1960: 423). They use complex incentive and accountability mechanisms and top-down authority systems to ensure that the 'human rationality' of their workers is subordinated to the 'higher goals and integrations ... [derived] from the institutional setting in which ... [they] operate and by which ... [they are] moulded' (Simon, 1957: 101). They use hierarchical systems to exploit economies of scale that generate processes of competitive selection, which have enabled them to eliminate smaller firms, pay higher wages, and charge lower prices, making them 'the most powerful engines of ... progress' (Schumpeter, 1943: 106; Brett, 1983, Ch. 3).

The result is large-scale cooperation, but also glaring inequalities in organizational capacity, power and wealth that are not accidental, but are inherent 'characteristics of real markets' (White, 1993a: 4–5) because they are designed to maximize 'cooperative interdependence' rather than atomistic individualism. A few pre-modern societies like the Roman or Egyptian Empires could coordinate the activities of millions of people; they had to use brutal sanctions to enforce compliance but were also able to dominate those who failed to achieve comparable levels of control. Liberal market systems do not, in the last analysis, eliminate the need for hierarchical systems, but what they claim to do is minimize the coercion they require, and so produce results that are seen to be fair and therefore just, as we will see in Part II.

The implications of the shift from competitive to oligopolistic capitalism have dominated academic and ideological conflicts about the relationship between individual agency and institutional structure since the 19th century, in both orthodox and development theory. Methodological individualism ignores the issues generated by the problems of planning, discipline and interorganizational coordination that confront managers and whole societies that depend on their ability to run large organizations. At the micro-level, we encounter parallel universes, with individualism dominating the academic social sciences, and functionalist versions of institutional theory dominating management and business schools, which teach managers how to create incentive systems that will persuade workers to accept the 'higher goals and integrations' of their organizations.

Their work coexists with that of radical theorists and social activists who use critical theory to attack their authoritarian and exploitative nature, and teach workers how to create solidaristic organizations to resist them. At the macro-level, we find that the need to manage relationships between large organizational systems means that a realistic view of democracy has to accept that it is 'inherently impossible' for 'all members or citizens' to play an active and continuous role in the decision-making process, and that it actually depends on 'the conflict of organized groups competing for support' (Lipset, 1962: 34, 36). 'Individuals' intervene in these processes in many different and complex ways that we will examine in later chapters, but modern societies as 'systems' cannot simply depend on 'spontaneous interactions' but on systematically managed exchanges at the level of individual firms, nations and the global system, which impose 'necessary' constraints on individual freedom and depend on complex systems of law, communications, education and much else.

These requirements have serious consequences for LDCs that have yet to create these capacities, and therefore for development theory. Complex systems cannot use traditional value systems designed to run small and relatively static societies dominated by face-to-face relationships, while competitive selection marginalizes small-scale societies that fail to adopt their principles. Command over large-scale organizations allowed DCs to impose colonialism onto latecomers, and still explains the structural inequalities between societies that have already made these shifts and those that have not, and the continuing conflict between 'modern' and 'traditional' sectors within each country. Here, organizations based on legal rational principles coexist with informal microenterprises, and informal social security and service systems, producing what Trotsky (1930/1977: 278) called 'combined and uneven development':

> Unevenness, the most general law of the historic process, reveals itself most sharply and complexly in the destiny of the backward countries. Under the whip of external necessity their backward culture is compelled to make leaps. From the universal law of unevenness thus derives another law ... [what] we may call the law of combined development – by which we mean a drawing together of the different stages of the journey, a combining of the separate steps, an amalgam of archaic with more contemporary forms. Without this law ... it is impossible to understand the history of Russia, and indeed of any country of the second, third, or tenth rank.

Combined and uneven development generates unavoidable tensions that manifest themselves in many complex ways, for example:

- in 'infant industry' problems where weak local firms have to compete with strong foreign ones
- in unemployment and exclusion when capital-intensive products displace labour-intensive ones
- in 'corruption' generated by patrimonial value systems within bureaucracies
- in ethnic or fundamentalist political and social movements that reject liberal democracy
- in the problem of institutional dualism or multiplicity more generally.

These inequalities and contradictions constantly threaten the economic, political and social autonomy of LDCs but also present them with major opportunities.

Many Asian states have appropriated the knowledge required to create modern organizations and transformed themselves at unprecedented speed. However, developmental transitions always come at a heavy price because they involve major transformations in value systems, organizational capacities and technologies. The gap has narrowed in the success stories but is widening in the LLDCs. Classical development theorists recognized the need to understand the implications of the coevolution of modern and pre-modern institutions in LDCs, but modern liberals do not and cultural relativists underestimate the ambiguous and inescapable nature of the pressures that external models inevitably impose on local ones. We will address these issues in the next section, and the wider problem in Part III.

Evolutionary theory, cultural relativism and dualistic development

Evolutionary theory was discredited by crude modernization arguments that justified colonialism and racism by treating historical change as the outcome of the processes of natural selection, which allowed social systems run by supposedly superior races to eliminate those run by inferior ones. Yet its assumption that competitive selection based on spontaneous interactions between genetically equal individuals in free markets, rather than conscious intervention, generates 'best practice' still represents the key justification for liberal theory. Thus neoliberals are the true inheritors of the Darwinian tradition,[12] but their individualistic and static methodological assumptions lead them to ignore the destabilizing consequences of the 'elimination' of the unfit that markets generate.

However, the fact that competitive selection has destructive and destabilising consequences does not allow us to ignore its effects. Societies that attempt to retain old or create new systems that fail to achieve the necessary standards have been marginalized by their competitors, as feudalism was at the end of the Middle Ages, and Communism has been in the Soviet Union. Cultural pluralists assume that local societies can avoid these challenges by building 'forms of friendship and solidarity' that will be able to interact in order to stop the evil forces of the 'global village' from destroying the last 'good people' who are struggling to protect themselves from them by 'replacing outdated paradigms like the nation-state as the protector of the people ... progress and development ... [and] scarcity – as the basis of modern economy' (Rahnema, 1997: 400). But the dominance of global capitalism now means that there is nowhere left where such people can safely go.

Thus, evolutionary theory forces us to recognize that competitive selection has real effects and imposes many necessary choices on societies that wish to protect themselves from its effects, but we also saw that it recognizes that systems are not infinitely malleable but subject to heredity or retention, based on the resilience of existing cultural values, capacities and endowments. These shape institutional arrangements and performance, are deeply engrained in social systems and only change slowly and unevenly, so development does not just involve the elimination of worse by better institutions, but far more ambiguous processes where new hybrids emerge out of the competition between those attempting to create new systems and those trying to retain old ones. This has three important methodological consequences:

1 Institutional variety problematizes the relationship between the models that people as opposed to theorists use to understand their own actions (also see Brett, 1973: 5ff.). Methodological individualism based on the assumption that all societies consist of autonomous and fully informed individuals tells us little about those societies that deny the equality, and even the humanity, of others – unbelievers, women, inferior races, castes or classes. These societies therefore reject liberal institutions, and proscribe the social scientific enterprise that sustains them, which demands 'standards of decent treatment that ... [are] the birthright of all human beings, standards to which all states should be held internationally accountable' (Barry, 2001: 5). Hence, institutional multiplicity produces fundamental disagreements about principles 'that appear to be intractable and not susceptible to rational resolution' (MacIntyre, 1998: 203) and threatens the universalization of the liberal development project.

2 Formal institutional changes based on the introduction of new rules will not eliminate these problems because the assumption that liberalization will automatically turn people into good democrats, socially responsible entrepreneurs or liberated husbands is clearly untenable. However, the existence of entrenched values and practices does not justify authoritarianism, serfdom, slavery or the subordination of women. Liberals ignore these conflicts by assuming that individuals are already free, or can be easily be liberated by changing the rules. Cultural relativists expose the authoritarian and often counterproductive implications of liberal or structuralist interventions that demonized 'traditional practices', but they also ignore their often regressive effects, and assume that they can coexist with modern ones. Their rejection of the idea of a unified system of human values can also legitimate claims that irreconcilable differences exist between 'civilizations' that make it impossible 'to shift societies from one civilization to another' (Huntingdon, 1997: 28), and thus threaten the possibility of global cooperation and coexistence.

3 Local communities cannot evade competitive selection, but they can respond to it creatively by acquiring new skills and capacities. Their existing institutions must constrain what they are allowed to think and do, but new threats force them to develop new stratagems by learning from more successful neighbours. Thus, MacIntyre (1998) shows that disputes over the 'truth claims' of competing knowledge systems cannot be deflected by appealing to pure relativism because they depend on the substantive circumstances under which each system operates, and on the ability of local communities to respond to the challenges they have to confront when external threats to their world-views produce 'persistent and intractable problems' that cannot be resolved within the limitations of their own conceptual frameworks (MacIntyre, 1998: 218). These can only be resolved when some local people can transcend their limitations and 'learn what it would be like to think, feel and act from ... some alternative and rival standpoint, acquiring in so doing an ability to understand his or her own tradition in the perspective afforded by that rival' (p. 219)[13] and modify their values accordingly. Local cultures have responded like this to the destructive effects of capitalism for centuries, with results that we will deal with in Part III. The result is a world of asymmetrical juxtapositions that can produce dissonance and dependence, but also one in which 'adequate resources' can sometimes be found to overcome these disagreements (p. 220). Indeed, development theory has always existed to do exactly that.

Evolutionary transformations, science and the politics of development

Evolutionary theory therefore treats development as a dialectical process driven by the social energy generated by competition within and between incompatible types of institutional system. Its insights enable us to re-evaluate some of the competing claims made by liberals, structuralists and cultural relativists who commonly present the choice between central planning, spontaneous individual exchanges and human agency, between social stability and revolutionary change, or between modernity and traditionalism as contradictory dichotomies.

Structure, agency and consciousness in institutional change

Biologists can treat structural change within and between species as an unconscious process generated by competitive selection, and survivability as the sole criterion for fitness, because the ability to capture prey or avoid predation is what separates the fit from the unfit. However, institutional evolution is more complex because people consciously construct, maintain and/or reconstruct their institutions; and the kinds of institutions they have constructed partially determine the kinds of consciousnesses they unconsciously acquire. Thus, when they 'change the institutional framework', they 'can be certain to change the way economic life evolves' (Metcalf, 2005: 392). This has crucial implications for the long-standing debate between conservatives and radicals about the relationship between agency and structure, freedom and necessity and especially about the role of conscious design in institutional reform.

The evolutionary emphasis on the role of inherited understandings and dispositions in institutional retention confirms conservative claims that social systems cannot be fully understood by their members and only survive because of the unconscious responses that combine and adjust 'the knowledge of successive generations and millions of people living simultaneously' (Hayek, 1955/1964: 91). Hence they cannot be easily restructured by individuals or political movements in accordance with imported blueprints in either liberal or pre-modern systems. Yet market systems exist in modern societies because they recognize that 'a state without the means of some change is without the means of its own conservation' (Burke, 1790/1803: 59) and allow, indeed impose, continuous but incremental innovation; whereas patrimonial, theocratic, patriarchal or commandist ones attempt to block the adoption of new knowledge, new processes and new social relations. However, this does not guarantee stability, because external ideas and demands transmitted through war, trade, technology and knowledge transfers often turn 'encounters into chaos ... [which] renders dialogue impossible, and obscures (and also deepens) injustice' (Halpern, 1971: 15). Images of better systems, the disintegrating effects of long-term relationships with more powerful societies[14] or conquest can generate internal demands for change from local elites or emerging or oppressed social groups, or force the society to accede to the demands of conquerors or benefactors.

These external threats and opportunities force social groups to rethink and redesign existing institutions and practices, although their solutions are always based on imperfect information and have unanticipated consequences. However, they demand conscious and collective responses to what are social, not individual problems that transcend the limits of inherited traditions by introducing radical reforms, such as the current shift to market systems or to socialism in the 20th century. To do this successfully, existing elites or their opponents must develop a conscious understanding of the limits and benefits of their existing traditions, and 'technically viable' alternative policy programmes that will enable them to create 'the political and economic means to assert the revolutionary project against its enemies, not only in the moment of its inception but also in the course of its growth and transformation' (Wolf, 1971: 4).

Competing values, inequality, political conflict and scientific theory

Tigers pay little attention to normative principles when they kill other tigers or deer, but norms, and the political struggles to enforce them, dominate processes of institutional change, since 'justice is the first value of institutions' (Rawls, 1973: 3). Thus elites, their opponents and the social theorists they rely on use normative criteria to measure the achievements of their own and other people's systems, and to mobilize support for, or resistance to, them. Patrimonialism, slavery, caste systems, feudalism, theocracy, Fascism, colonialism, Communism and capitalism have all depended on different systems of 'interconnected moral and legal norms, the order and stability of which ... [were] maintained by the political order' (Fortes and Evans-Pritchard, 1940/1970: 20). These norms are therefore endogenous, differ systematically from system to system, and are socially enforced. However, they are not necessarily accepted with the same grace by everyone, since they allocate wealth and power to some people and poverty and servitude to others.

People's location in society and their knowledge of other systems that might offer them a better deal determine their willingness to support or change existing rules. 'Stable poverty ... [where] individuals are not exposed to the possibilities of change breeds, if anything, conservatism' (Lipset, 1963: 63), but even highly marginalized communities now have unprecedented access to information, suffer from greatly increased 'polarization in the distribution of wealth ... intra-country income inequality', and a 'substantial growth of poverty and misery' (Castells, 2000b: 82). This can lead quiescent groups to reassess the justice of their situations and poses 'problems of might and right, of human freedom and coercion, of relevance and purpose' that can lead to 'protest and revolt, confrontation and revolution' (Wolf, 1971: 2). Successful resistance may then lead to structural rather than incremental changes in institutional arrangements that will usually depend on imported models and value systems.[15] These will involve attempts to find ways to enable a wider range of groups to benefit from the normal operation of the society's institutions, therefore creating higher levels of justice than prevailed before (see Marx and Engels, 1845–6/1974: 66). However, they will only succeed if they produce technically sustainable solutions that recognize the necessary 'interdependence between values that proceed from interest situations and techniques that can be utilized for the satisfaction of value-oriented needs', which therefore produce a 'critical interaction' between 'the expert and the politician' (Habermas, 1971: 66).

Coercion can enable systems to survive for long periods, but it cannot legitimate them, since justice is not simply the will of the stronger. Thus, institutional models, and the paradigms that articulate them, must be able to substantiate their normative claim to provide the poor as well as the rich with a better set of possibilities than any other. Conservatives emphasize the moral claims of stability, authority and virtue, and radicals those of equity and autonomy, but all institutional systems, and liberalism in particular, can only legitimate themselves by proving that they can satisfy such goals more effectively than any others, and thus persuade social groups to accept the costs of creating or sustaining them.

Theory, practice and developmental failures

The ultimate fate of any institutional paradigm depends on its efficacy in practice, but we cannot simply reject the liberal or structuralist projects, as many critics do, because they fail in particular contexts. Their performance depends on their normative goals and technical adequacy, but also on the characteristics of the societies using them – their human and social capital, cultural values, assets and endowments, levels of inequality and fragmentation, and the ability of their social movements to mobilize the political support needed to overcome resistance to them. The authority of modern capitalist and corporatist projects exists because they allowed the societies that first institutionalized them to increase their military and economic power to the point where they could rule 'over the others', thus giving their models 'world-historical significance' (Hegel, 1822–30/1975: 60). Liberalism was validated by British and then American successes, and structuralism by the successes of Europe and North America in the 19th century, the postwar reconstruction in Western Europe and Japan after 1947, and in East Asia more recently. Managed liberalization is also producing gains in China and India and in African states like South Africa, Uganda and Mozambique.

These successes have turned these models into blueprints for change in LDCs, but they do not guarantee success in contexts where new institutions coexist with the old, and where people lack the appropriate skills, values and assets. This generates political and social resistance that can only be overcome by mobilizing the necessary support from potential winners, demobilizing opposition by compensating losers, and providing the resources needed to build new assets and skills. Where this does not happen, new models will be ignored and practitioners will attribute failures to noncompliance. However, noncompliance always has real political roots, in that it stems from the contradictory demands that institutional transitions impose on different groups and will only disappear when those who stand to benefit have acquired the skills and power needed to push the new agenda through.

Capitalism emerged within feudal society, generated a contradiction between the 'direct producers and their feudal overlords', and triumphed when the capitalist class was able to seize state power (Dobb, 1976: 166).[16] The nationalist revolt against colonialism occurred after a new petty bourgeoisie had emerged whose economic and political demands were blocked by the colonial state acting on behalf of expatriate interests (Brett, 1973: 305ff.). Marxists assumed that the proletariat created by capitalism would produce a socialist revolution, but capitalism responded by adopting social democratic reforms that incorporated the working class without threatening the system's basic arrangements (Crosland, 1956; Dahrendorf, 1959; Bernstein, 1961/1989). The current liberal revolution in the third world is driven by a dominant international capitalist class associated with a new domestic bourgeoisie that has emerged in the postcolonial period,[17] and has yet to be effectively challenged by political movements that offer the poor a viable alternative. Oppression has led to 'everyday forms of resistance', such as crime, shirking, smuggling or tax evasion, which reduce social productivity and can produce 'crises of appropriation that threaten the state' (Scott, 1997: 313–18),[18] but the crisis of socialism has created a political vacuum that has driven many poor people into the hands of regressive ethnonationalist or sectarian movements.

Conclusions

The fact that these conflicts have often sidelined effective institutional reform and generated incoherence, failures and breakdowns does not justify a shift from general theory to pragmatism or ethnomethodological micro-action studies.[19] The reasons for these failures have to be sought in a rigorous analysis of the relationship between the demands being made by the structuralist and liberal models that are introduced at the macro-level, and the opportunities and constraints that real people confront as a result of their particular location in the contradictory institutional systems that they have inherited and which partially shape their understandings and values.

Thus paradigm failures alone do not discredit development theory but are the primary justification for its role as a distinct intellectual tradition. Orthodox theory focuses on societies that have already overcome most of these problems; it makes a crucial contribution to development theory because it provides the models that most LDCs are trying to implement, but it fails to provide practitioners with solutions that recognize the special needs, values and capacities of people in societies that would like to have the benefits generated by modern institutions, but cannot expect to achieve them in a single giant stride. Development theory exists to build bridges between orthodoxy that deals with modern systems and the theories that govern the pre-modern systems that are changing in response to the dialectical processes generated by competitive selection by producing new hybrids that are creating new possibilities and trajectories.

Theorists must take responsibility for policy failures, but policy failures, in contexts where they have been undermined by the contradictory and disruptive effects of institutional multiplicity and competitive selection, do not discredit the liberal or structuralist paradigms that have worked well in many others. The obstacles to their adoption cannot be ignored, but societies that refuse to adopt modern institutions, and the technologies associated with them, do so at their peril. However, treating these models as one-size-fits-all blueprints is also a recipe for disaster. In a postcolonial era, these models cannot be 'imposed' on local societies but have to be 'adapted' to local needs, values and capacities, however 'irrational', authoritarian or counterproductive they might appear to be.

The commitment to democracy, freedom, equity and efficiency that drives liberal and socialist theories embedded in liberal institutions provides societies with the organizational models needed for emancipatory change, and attempts to create these institutions are not simply an external imposition, but are strongly supported by progressive local movements that often pay a heavy price for doing so. Failing to build democracy, competitive firms and redistributive welfare systems will perpetuate the authoritarianism, monopolies and exclusion that continue to impoverish most LLDCs. We will therefore look at the way in which neoliberal and structuralist fundamentalism is giving way to new pluralistic syntheses in Part II, and at the challenges to orthodoxy posed by the disruptive effects of combined, competitive and uneven development in Part III.

Notes

1   This formulation of the relationship between 'necessity' and 'freedom' is derived from Hegel (1821/1967).
2   Metcalf is referring to economic theory here, but we believe that the same principles can be applied to development theory in general. We will have to ignore many of the heavily contested issues within evolutionary theory itself – they are rigorously examined in Dopfer (2005).
3   Marx (1862/1977: 525) claimed: 'Darwin's book is very important and serves me as a natural-scientific basis for the class struggle in history.' The concept of comparative histori-

cal institutionalism invoked here owes a great deal to Marxist theories of historical material-ism, but attempts to transcend its one-sided emphasis on the primacy of economic causation.

4   This is true of Dopfer's (2005) seminal collection on which much of this analysis depends.

5   This formulation is adapted from Dopfer (2005: 15).

6   This formulation is taken from Dopfer (2005). He places most emphasis on the role of internal mutations; we have added the effect of external shocks, since most developmental transitions stem from contact with more powerful systems.

7   Marx (1858/1972: 17, 65–6) argued that it is only 'bourgeois society, the society of free competition' which has been constituted by a social network made up of 'individuals who remain indifferent to one another'.

8   Modern development economics now focuses almost exclusively on developing mathe-matically based econometric techniques to make calculations of this kind, thus excluding the 'existence of time irreversability, structural change and true uncertainty in historical processes', which are the primary concern of development theorists (Foster, 2005: 370).

9   Such activities 'may be extremely useful for the macroeconomist who wants to explain why, for instance, when the state raises corporation taxes entrepreneurs tend to disinvest, or why, in a perfectly competitive market, an increase in the demand of [sic] a commodity raises its price and vice versa' (Mouzelis, 1995: 29).

10 I owe this point to Samuel Bowles.

11 Bhaskar himself rejects this view.

12 According to Marx (1862/1977: 526): 'It is remarkable how Darwin recognizes among beasts and plants his English society with its division of labour, competition, opening up of new markets, "inventions", and the Malthusian "struggle for existence".'

13 MacIntyre (1998: 219) continues: 'The analogy here is with the ability of an anthropolo-gist to learn not only how to inhabit an alternative and very different culture, but also how to view her or his own culture from that alien perspective.'

14 As capitalism did in 'disintegrating China's social economy' by destroying its pre-modern economic systems, accelerating the development of a 'commodity economy', thus initiat-ing revolutionary social change (Mao Tse-tung, 1939/1954: 77).

15 As Gramsci (1971: 182) put it: 'An ideology, coming into existence in a more developed country, is diffused in less developed countries, cutting across the local play of combinations.'

16 For an analysis of the nature of this process in France, see Tilly (1997a).

17 For analyses of the relationship between statism and the growth of capitalism, see Kohli (2004) and Khan and Sundaram (2000); for an account of the emergence of a new capital-ist class 'from below', see MacGaffey (1987).

18 For an African case, see Bunker (1985).

19 For a discussion, see Booth (1993: 58ff.)

PART II

The Institutional Arrangements of Liberal Democratic Capitalism

Chapter 4

Market Societies, Open Systems and Institutional Pluralism

From paradigm conflicts to liberal institutional pluralism

We showed in Part I that the challenges of late development impose a dual task on the theorists whose primary concern is the fate of the poorest rather than the richest societies in the world. On the one hand, LDCs need to access the models of best practice that already exist in DCs in order to redesign their own futures, on the other, they need to find their own ways of overcoming the tensions they generate when they attempt to transfer these models to their own societies. Thus a comprehensive review of development theory needs to start by outlining the assumptions and prescriptions that not only dominate policy and practice in DCs, but also guide the liberal reform programmes now being institutionalized in most LDCs.

However, we also showed that the conflicts generated by the development process in both DCs and LDCs have produced intense disagreements over the nature of the institutional arrangements that would maximize freedom, growth and cooperative interdependence. The most significant of these produced the 'paradigm disputes' between liberals and structuralists outlined in Chapter 1 that were directly linked to the major ideological and political struggles of the era. These struggles produced many experiments with more or less authoritarian versions of corporatism, socialism and liberal capitalism, all of which have confronted crises that have now culminated in a search for new ways of relating state, market and solidaristic institutions in more flexible and productive ways. These experiments are also taking place in LDCs and are producing very uneven results, which will be examined in detail in Part III. We can only evaluate the likely outcome of these experiments by setting out the analytical and empirical assumptions of the new institutional theories that sustain them.

Radical structuralists and liberals as well as socialists and capitalists treated state and market-based institutions as incompatible opposites, but in the real world, extreme versions of corporatism or laissez faire produced political and economic crises. The result was the use of markets to overcome the rigidities created by command planning, and

social and political interventions to protect society from the consequences of free competition:

> To allow the market mechanism to be the sole director of the fate of
> human beings and their natural environment, indeed even of the amount
> and use of purchasing power, would result in the demolition of society ...
> Robbed of the protective covering of cultural institutions, human beings
> would perish from the effects of social exposure; they would die as the
> victims of acute social dislocation. (Polanyi, 1944/2001: 76)

The result has been a wide range of experiments with synthetic policy
regimes, such as the 'third way' strategies of 'New Labour' in Britain,
and the 'post-Washington consensus' in the donor community, where:

> the virtues of the market and its opposition to the state are replaced
> by a balance between the two; the perfection of the market gives way
> to emphasis on informationally led market imperfections that can be
> corrected; and the treatment of the non-economic as if ... [it was]
> economic gives way to a more rounded understanding of the forma-
> tion of, and the interaction between, market and non-market institu-
> tions. (Fine et al., 2003: 10)[1]

These shifts have led to innovations in institutional theory in economics,
political science, public management and sociology that recognize the
need to build complementary relationships between economic markets,
democratic states, public and private bureaucracies, and solidaristic civic
associations and community-based organizations.[2] These changes have
originated within particular disciplines, but their focus on structural
constraints imposed by institutional systems rather than individual choices
is generating interdisciplinary analyses of the 'condition of the institutional environment', which includes 'constitutions, laws, property rights',
and 'taboos, customs, traditions' (Williamson, 2000: 92–7). Recognizing
the need for pluralistic solutions based on institutional diversity generates
an evolutionary process that produces new syntheses, which combine
different kinds of organizations – governments, firms and civic institutions – in creative ways that solve 'specific provision and production
problems in a particular economic, technological and cultural setting'
(Ostrom et al., 1993: 230). This has now sidelined earlier conflicts
between socialists and conservatives. They still have different agendas,
but these no longer produce 'ideological' conflicts over fundamentals, but
increasingly technical debates over the use of alternative organizational
models – state bureaucracies, for-profit or non-profit firms, solidaristic
organizations (SOs), surrogate markets or participatory processes – to
solve particular problems in particular kinds of contexts.

Yet this new pluralism is not simply based on an eclectic combination of organizational forms, but is dominated by liberal theory that treats markets as the best solution to coordination problems, and then asks 'what conditions will cause some of these market mechanisms to fail and be replaced' by organizational alternatives, that is, bureaucratic hierarchies or reciprocal solidarities (Ouchi, 1980: 133).[3] We have therefore called it 'liberal institutional pluralism', because it assumes that 'the individual is where the behavioural assumptions originate' (Williamson, 2000: 96) and follows a 'choice theoretic approach' that attempts to integrate 'individual choices with the constraints that institutions impose on choice sets' (North, 1990: 5).

Now, prioritizing markets in this way does not mean that exchanges based on individual attempts to maximize their short-term material gains actually dominate our lives. Instead, the need for cooperation, trust and long-term security means that we usually work in hierarchical private or public agencies, find love and personal security in affective families and networks, and meet our physical, cultural, religious and political needs through solidaristic clubs, churches, and social and political movements. Combining markets with hierarchies and solidarities is producing many experiments with new forms of social provision in DCs and in LDCs, based on the assumption that 'varied experience with traditional and innovative modes of service delivery clearly shows that no single solution fits all services in all countries' (World Bank, 2004: 12). Thus, hierarchical or solidaristic private and public organizations will not disappear in DCs or LDCs as liberal capitalism evolves, so institutional pluralism is not an optional choice, but a necessary consequence of the way it operates as a total system.

However, while pluralism requires organizational diversity, it also insists that all agencies must use authority, accountability and incentive mechanisms that give citizens real control over the agencies that serve them, and agents the autonomy and rewards needed to properly exercise their professional and managerial skills. Different kinds of organizations combine authority, incentive and accountability systems in different ways, and have to be understood as systems of structured reciprocal relationships rather than atomistic exchanges. This obliges us to treat 'free organizations' rather than the 'free individual' as our analytical starting point. This also provides us with the basis for a macro- and microanalytical approach to problems of organizational performance,[4] and helps us to understand 'the costs and benefits of inter-organizational cooperation' (Alter and Hage, 1993: 32). We will identify the key features of this approach here, and deal with its macroanalytical aspects in the rest of this chapter and with its microanalytical implications in the rest of Part II.

Different types of organization use different authority systems to coordinate joint activities and enforce compliance, different methods to extract payments from their consumers, and different accountability mechanisms to 'ensure a desired level and type of performance' (Paul, 1992: 1047). Authority systems can be based on hierarchy, markets, or negotiated agreements; access to resources on coercive extraction, competitive exchange or reciprocal altruism; and accountability on giving consumers the right to 'exit' and find an alternative supplier, or through the expression of 'voice' in participatory or representative processes (Hirschmann, 1970):

- *States* use 'voice' to negotiate policy agreements, hierarchical bureaucracies to execute decisions, compulsion to collect taxes, and democratic competition to guarantee accountability to citizens.
- *Firms* use hierarchy to coordinate collective action, and competitive markets to generate resources that also create accountability because they enable customers to go elsewhere.
- *Large solidaristic organizations* also use hierarchy to coordinate action and decisions that are sometimes democratic and sometimes not, they depend heavily on ethical or affective rewards to generate support, but also employ paid labour, and they need to perform effectively or they will lose the loyalty of their members.

Markets, hierarchies and solidarities are therefore combined in different ways in different sectors to meet the different challenges they confront.[5]

Institutional theorists treat exchanges between managers, workers and consumers as relationships between 'principals' and 'agents' where 'one individual [the principal] depends on the action of another [the agent]' (Pratt and Zeckhauser, 1985: 2). These relationships are complex since they involve a range of 'stakeholders' who depend on the organization to satisfy some of their needs, but relate to it in different ways. Inside the organization, the manager is the principal and the worker the agent, while outside it, the organization is the agent and those who use its services or products are the principals.

Liberal institutional theorists assume that agency relationships should be 'structured so as to enable principals to exert an appropriate influence over the actions of agents' (Pratt and Zeckhauser, 1985: 2–3), by prescribing 'payoff rules' so that 'before the agent chooses the action, the principal determines a rule that specifies a fee to be paid to the agent as a function of the principal's observation of the results of the action' (Arrow, 1991: 37). Principals should be free to choose the best agent and monitor their actions, but theorists know that 'problems of inducement and enforcement' are common when agents have monopoly power or can conceal information from principals. However, they also claim that the fact that principals and agents do generally succeed in coordinating their activities to achieve common purposes has produced organizational forms that generally 'perform reasonably well' (Pratt and Zeckhauser, 1985: 2–5; see also Jensen and Meckling, 1976: 308–10).

Principals can only exercise an 'appropriate influence' over their agents in governments, firms or families where the appropriate governance structures actually exist and enable stakeholders to impose 'credible commitments on each other' (Williamson, 1987: 45–8). This requires open systems and adequate levels of human, social and economic capital, or else agents will be able to 'capture organizations and engage in rent seeking' (Paul, 1992: 1067), by extracting payments that exceed the real value of what they produce, or by forcibly stopping them from going elsewhere. In fact, 'capture' rather than accountability to principals is the dominant feature of many pre-modern institutions, since their authority systems create political, economic and/or social monopolies that enable agents to turn their people into subjects rather than citizens or principals. Liberal agency theory ignores this problem by assuming that competitive markets already exist, so it actually constitutes an ideal typical description of how institutions should operate, not how they always do. However, agency theory does enable us to identify the processes that should be introduced to punish agents and agencies 'for actions that yield an unsustainable investment', and to create positive incentives that 'motivate the individual to generate net benefits rather than net costs for all' (Ostrom et al., 1993: 8–9).[6] We will look at the processes needed to do this in this part, and at the problems of perverse incentives, 'capture' and noncompliance in Part III.

The structural and normative implications of institutional pluralism

Pluralistic societies need to coordinate the exchanges between different kinds of autonomous organizations to produce total social systems by creating mechanisms 'by which the extremely varied potentialities of "human nature" become integrated in such a way as to dovetail into a single integrated system capable of meeting the situational exigencies with which the society and its members are faced' (Parsons, 1954: 230). Earlier societies were also pluralistic, but large-scale cooperation was only sporadic 'in ancient times, in the middle ages, and in modern colonies' that 'dovetailed' humans into large-scale integrated systems through 'relations of domination and servitude', not voluntary cooperation (Marx, 1867/1974: 316).

However, modern societies are not only highly integrated, but are run by actors whose 'highly specialist knowledge' gives them 'control of the work process', turning them into virtually autonomous agents (Hodgson, 1999: 209), so these societies depend on intra- and interorganizational relationships based on 'autonomous interdependence' rather than simple coexistence or coercion – what Durkheim called 'organic solidarity'. Here, autonomy gives each person or agency 'an integrity which they lack in less developed systems' that insulates them from direct control by other agencies, protecting them from domination by the special interests 'of particular social groups' (Huntington, 1968: 20); while interdependence allows each agency – government, firm, civic association or family – to exchange specialized services for equally specialized products from all the rest. Hence:

> each one depends as much more strictly on society as labour is more divided; and on the other [hand] the activity of each is as much more personal as it is more specialized ... Here the individuality of all grows at the same time as that of its parts. Society becomes more capable of collective movement, at the same time that each of its elements has more freedom of movement. (Durkheim, 1893/1964: 131)

Here everyone must respect each other's rights, but compete with them for scarce resources, creating problems of control and coordination at the level of society as a whole:

> For organic solidarity to exist, it is not enough that there be a system of organs necessary to one another, which in a general way feel solid, but it is also necessary that the way in which they should come together ... be predetermined. Otherwise, at every moment new conflicts would have to be equilibrated, for the conditions of equilibrium can be discovered only through groupings in the course of which one part treats the other as an adversary as much as an auxiliary. (Durkheim, 1893/1964: 365)

This creates normative and practical problems – it requires an overarching ethical order in which each agency 'has rights in so far as ... [it] has duties, and duties in so far as ... [it] has rights' (Hegel, 1821/1967: 109), and a division of labour based on incentive and accountability systems that provide each agency with resources while obliging it to supply the rest with its own products in exchange.

Within these general limits, liberal pluralism generates unique ensembles of historically created institutions and organizations in each society because it allows them to use a diverse range of specialized agencies to structure social interactions. These need to be designed to take account of their particular capacities and value systems, and to meet the different needs and characteristics of particular services and consumers. Marx (1847/1968: 80ff.) called these ensembles their 'social relations of production', and Bourdieu (1992: 52ff.) their 'habitus'. They generate people's social and cultural identities, and their 'agency' or capacity to 'act and bring about change' in response to their 'own values and objectives' (Sen, 1999: 19). Here, autonomous interdependence should maximize innovation and efficiency as well as interorganizational competition, while permitting the coexistence of different, even contradictory motivational and normative principles. It also obliges individuals to depend on a variety of organizational types, and therefore to assume 'a plurality of roles' that generate conflicting demands and expectations.

We can produce a typology of major organizational types that operate or have operated in modern and pre-modern societies by using three key criteria (Table 4.1):

1 the nature of their authority systems or their use of hierarchical, market or solidaristic control mechanisms
2 their function or role in satisfying political, economic or social needs
3 the spatial level at which they operate – local, national or global.

These organizations can also interact on the basis of coexistence, command, competition, or voluntary coordination.[7] These variables generate many institutional alternatives, since states can use centralized hierarchies, open market competition, or solidaristic collectivism, and operate at every level from global to local, and so can economic and solidaristic organizations. Combining these possibilities produces 27 organizational types, identified in Table 4.2.

Modern societies still incorporate many authoritarian, ascriptive or theocratic institutions (Parsons, 1951/1964: 167ff.; Almond, 1960: 23ff.), but modernization has led to ongoing shifts to autonomous markets or solidaristic agencies and from national to either global or local organizations.[8] Managing large-scale open societies demands effective internal mechanisms for the allocation of authority and resources and for conflict resolution within particular organizations (governments, firms, associations or families) and sectors (polities, economies and civil societies), and also intra-organizational mechanisms that allow them to compete or cooperate on an autonomous basis. We address the normative implications of these changes next, and structural ones in the rest of Part II.

Table 4.1 *Dimensions of organizational differentiation*

Organizational function	Governance	Production	Meeting affective and ethical needs
Authority and incentive system	Hierarchy	Market competition	Solidaristic cooperation
Scale of operation	Global	National	Local

Table 4.2 *A typology of alternative organizational forms*

	State agencies	Economic agencies	Civic agencies
Hierarchical global	A colonial empire	A transnational corporation	The Catholic Church
Hierarchical national	A state bureaucracy	A national company	An authoritarian political party
Hierarchical local	A local warlord	A local firm	A local sect
Representative or market-based global	United Nations (UN)	World Trade Organization (WTO)	Fédération Internationale de Football Association (FIFA)
Representative or market-based national	A democratic national state	A national market economy	The Football Association (FA) (England)
Representative or market-based local	A democratic local council	A local formal or informal market	Manchester United Football Club
Solidaristic global	An anarchical world order	The International Co-operative Alliance	Rotary International
Solidaristic national	A libertarian socialist state	A national cooperative network	A national professional association
Solidaristic local	A local kinship-based community	A cooperative firm	A community-based organization

The prevalence of impersonal and competitive exchanges in large-scale societies increases the 'incentives for non-compliance' (Knight, 1992: 181), and therefore the need to formalize and institutionalize the rules and values required for extended cooperation by creating a 'public conception of justice' (Rawls, 1973: 5)[9] and mutual payment systems that meet the needs of agencies as independent units, which oblige winners to at least partially compensate losers. This only occurs where everyone recognizes the 'legitimacy' of these contradictory motivational 'patterns' (Parsons, 1951/1964: 280–2), which is why institutional pluralism has profound normative implications for societies as totalities, which Rawls (1973: 4–5) addresses by formulating two principles of justice:

1 Just societies should be governed by inclusive market-based institutions and the principle of 'equal citizenship', whose rules make 'no arbitrary distinctions ... between persons ... and ... [which] determine a proper balance between competing claims' (Rawls, 1973: 4–5). Access to benefits should depend on open and competitive processes when possible, but when hierarchical bureaucracies or

solidaristic associations are required, they should also be made accountable through the creation of what we will call 'second-order markets' – democratic elections for governments, international competition for oligopolistic firms, and free contracting between partners, members, supporters or donors in SOs. This will not be possible where authoritarian states or monopolistic firms use their power to subvert competitive processes, religions block free scientific investigation, or the marriage laws stop abused partners from divorcing their spouses, so a defining feature of 'liberal' pluralism is its generalized commitment to market-based accountability systems that allow people to choose better options or exit from those that no longer benefit them.

2 'Social and economic inequalities' must be 'reasonably expected to be to everyone's advantage', and produce 'a distribution of wealth' that 'need not be equal ... [but] must be to everyone's advantage, and at the same time, positions of authority and offices of command must be accessible to all' (Rawls, 1973: 60–1). Perfect markets do in fact meet these conditions, but we will soon see why real markets need to be supplemented by credible and compulsory systems of redistribution and restitution in order to ensure that they actually do so. This condition is more demanding than the first because all institutional arrangements – planning or markets, despotism or democracy, theocracy or religious toleration, patriarchy or gender equality – alter substantive allocations of political, economic or social resources and thus everyone's 'capabilities and entitlements'.[10]

This approach to liberal pluralism therefore obliges us not only to specify the principles that structure and legitimate market-based social systems, but also to identify the factors that should govern hierarchical or solidaristic institutions in the state, the economy and civil society that emerge when markets fail. We will deal with the first issue in the next section, and the general problems generated by problems of market failure in the one that follows. In Part III, we will show that it is the additional problems of market failure generated by problems of underdevelopment that create problems of transition and the need for different kinds of relationships between hierarchies, markets and solidarity in LDCs.

The benefits, costs and social consequences of market-based systems

Liberal theorists argue that fully competitive markets provide the best solution to resource allocation problems, because they maximize freedom, efficiency, equity and autonomous interdependence by giving individuals the right to choose and therefore to 'be an autonomous source of action' (Durkheim, 1893/1964: 403). They accept that perfect competition is an unrealizable ideal, but argue that societies that come closest to operationalizing it will perform better than those that do not. We will examine these claims now and then the problems of market failure and the need for state and solidaristic alternatives.

The pure theory of competitive markets

In perfectly competitive markets, autonomous, fully informed, self-interested individuals with secure property rights voluntarily exchange their own goods and services for those produced by others in transactions that are 'uncontrolled either by the mandate of the law or by the meddling of any public functionary' (Mill, 1848/1900: 575). The voluntary nature of these transactions excludes the need for hierarchy and the possibility of exploitation, perfect information enables participants to make rational choices about the use of their own assets and to avoid being cheated by others, and free access to all markets eliminates monopolies and minimizes costs and prices. All exchanges are completed on the spot, so they create no lasting social obligations because both parties 'surrender and acquire property, and ... both remain property owners even in the act of surrender' (Hegel, 1821/1967: 242–3). This deinstitutionalizes social relationships and reduces 'all that goes by the name of "society", or social structure, to individual actions ... in more extreme formulations ... society has no reality at all' (Slater and Tonkiss, 2001: 32).[11] Market systems generate many benefits, which we now outline.

Markets maximize freedom

Markets maximize freedom by allowing individuals, not political or social elites, to make value judgements about individual preferences, using a relativistic morality designed to 'give as many people as possible as much as possible of whatever it is they want' (Ayer, 1948: 256). They operate as though 'there are no values in the objective sense, only subjective valuations' (Myrdal, 1953: 13; Brett, 1969: 52), so absolute judgements only apply to 'means, not ends; [so] a regressive society is one which places [political or economic] limits upon free entry into the market' (Brett, 1969: 54). Market societies are therefore inhabited by atomized individuals whose only obligation is to maximize their own interests and recognize everyone else's right to maximize theirs.

This need to satisfy individual rather than collective preferences has practical as well as normative implications because it eliminates the 'success indicator problem' that centrally planned economies cannot resolve (Nove, 1983: 74). Economic efficiency depends on the ability to minimize costs but also to satisfy consumer demand by producing goods of the right quantity, quality and variety. Planners who attempt to do this for whole societies have to specify each of these requirements for every firm, product and input:

> The same number of tonnes, meters, pairs can be of very different use-values and fulfil widely different needs. In any event, quality is a concept frequently inseparable from use; thus a dress or a machine can be fully in accord with technological standards, but still not be suitable for a particular wearer or factory process. How can this problem be overcome if plans are the order of superior authority ... and not those placed by the users? (Nove, 1983: 74)

It is equally difficult to make appropriate judgements about the value of particular kinds of work, for example that of social workers, pop stars, and bakers, or a painting by Picasso and a local amateur. The only alternative to centralized allocations is to allow 'horizontal' relationships between supplier and customer, but this 'is a market solution' (Nove, 1983: 75).

Markets maximize economic efficiency

Markets maximize economic efficiency by producing rational prices, strong incentives, technological innovation, and by coordinating exchanges between autonomous firms (see Hayek, 1944/1994, 1955/1964). Only firms can set prices because planners cannot acquire the necessary information about the cost of capital, labour, inputs and the processes that put them together. Average prices of inputs may be known at any point in time, but efficient firms pay less for them than weak ones, and incur much lower costs of production. Competition forces all firms to try to achieve best practice, and this maximizes technological and organizational innovation and imposes a pervasive downward pressure on costs and profits that planners cannot replicate. When demand exceeds supply, low-cost firms make superprofits, increasing investment in the sector; and when supply exceeds demand, the fittest firms make below-average profits and the unfit are eliminated to produce the evolutionary processes of 'creative destruction' described in Chapter 3. According to Schumpeter (1964: 66):

> What dominates the picture of capitalistic life and is more than anything else responsible for our impression of a prevalence of decreasing cost, causing disequilibria, cut-throat competition and so on, is innovation, the intrusion into the system of new production functions which incessantly shift existing cost curves.

Innovation eliminates inefficient firms and marginalizes all economic systems where traditional cultures block scientific progress or use the state to protect inefficient firms from the need for innovation.[12] Hence, competition encourages freedom and also imposes more effective disciplines on managers and workers than systems that allow their actions to be governed by tradition in pre-modern societies, or by political controls in command economies.

These decentralized competitive processes maximize the efficiency and complexity of market systems by solving the otherwise impossible information problems created by the need to coordinate supply and demand nationally and globally. Thus, Leontief (1966b: 237–8) compared the market to an 'impersonal, automatic ... miraculous computer' constantly solving an immense range of input–output problems too complex for even planners to comprehend. The calculations needed to coordinate the constantly changing input–output relationships generated by a modern economy are so immense that no 'single person or board' could acquire all the necessary information to make them, so decentralization is 'imperative', and firms must be 'free to adjust their activities to the facts that only they can know' so they can 'bring about a mutual adjustment of their respective plans' (Hayek, 1944/1994: 55–6). Only they can do this 'by watching the movement of comparatively few prices', which in turn depends on a 'division of knowledge between individuals whose separate efforts are co-ordinated by the impersonal mechanism for transmitting the relevant information known by us as the price mechanism' (p. 56).

Markets should maximize equity

Markets should maximize equity as well as efficiency because of 'Say's law', which recognizes that 'supply creates its own demand'. Producing any commodity will generate an expenditure on wages, inputs and profits equivalent to its value that will reappear as the correct amount of demand needed to use all the available commodities and labour.[13] Hence, 'flexible prices and wage rates can restore commodity, money and labor markets to equilibria which are consistent with full employment' (Rima, 1978: 433). Unemployment will reduce wages and increase profits and investment until the demand for labour exceeds the supply, and this will increase wages and reduce profits and employment until equilibrium is restored. Levels of employment will vary in response to changes in business cycles and technology, but will always move towards full employment unless states or trade unions distort markets by imposing controls over wages, labour conditions or profits, or print money to increase demand. This is not just true at the national, but also at the global level, because international free trade should allow all countries to produce and export the goods in which they have a comparative advantage and import the rest (Krugman, 1997; Bhagwhati, 2002). Capital will move from places where labour is scarce and costly to those where it is abundant and cheap, and labour in the opposite direction, eventually equalizing costs, wages and productivity, and maximizing 'world income' (Johnson, 1968: 88). This suggests that uneven development is not caused by market forces but by the constraints on the free movement of goods, capital and labour imposed by protectionist states; a claim we will challenge later.

Liberals reject the Marxist claim that capitalist labour processes generate exploitation where free labour markets exist, because such markets allow workers to choose whether to work for wages or themselves. This implies that they must be better off when they choose to sell their labour rather than work for themselves, however low the wage might be. This also allows them to ignore the existence of hierarchy within the firm, and to see firms as 'in some sense an instrumentality of individuals rather than as an autonomous entity' (Nelson and Winter 1982: 54). Hence, 'bad jobs at bad wages are better than no jobs at all ... [so] as long as you have no alternative to industrialization based on low wages, to oppose it means you are willing to deny desperately poor people the best chance they have of progress' (Krugman, n.d.). Attempts by governments or ethical campaigners to raise wages or working conditions above market-determined levels will therefore hurt labour as well as capital by increasing costs and reducing profits, investment and employment.[14]

Full employment and wage levels therefore depend on 'the proportion between the number of the labouring population, and the capital or other funds devoted to the purchase of labour', so that 'it is impossible that population should increase at its utmost rate without lowering wages' (Mill, 1848/1900: 211). Thus controls may benefit workers who already have jobs, but will reduce the incentive to invest and punish the unemployed, creating structural unemployment that will be intensified by rapid population growth.

Markets extend social cooperation

Markets extend the scope and scale of social cooperation even though their basic rules assume that people should only cooperate in order to maximize their own interests and exit from any relationship if they can do better elsewhere. Despite this, markets have created high levels of cooperative interdependence by connecting consumers with suppliers from across the world, creating large-scale firms that coordinate the activities of thousands of people, as well as long-term and extended networks between firms and individuals that depend on using each other's inputs, markets, knowledge and capital. Thus, paradoxically, competitive markets increase the need for coordination and cooperation in contexts where firms that benefit from economies of scale or the use of extended networks can outcompete their smaller or less well-connected rivals (Brett, 2000a).

The growing power and reach of transnational firms produced a major critique of their role by radical theorists in the 1960s and 70s, who argued that their market power enabled them to administer prices, erect barriers to entry for new firms, allow managers to take control away from shareholders, and evade state regulation through international transfer pricing.[15] Neoclassical theorists ignore these problems, as we saw in Chapter 3, but Schumpeter (1943) provided the seminal defence of the role of large-scale firms regulated by oligopolistic competition. He accepted that competitive markets produce centralization and concentration through processes of 'creative destruction'. But he argued that scale could reduce production costs and foster innovation, and that competition between a few large firms was more demanding than when it took place between many small, technologically constrained ones. Schumpeter (1943: 99, 102) also showed that even 'a single seller' could only retain its position provided 'he does not behave like a monopolist', and that 'a monopoly position is in general no cushion to sleep on. As it can be gained, so it can be retained only by alertness and energy.'[16] Thus, oligopolistic competition should generate higher output and lower prices than perfect competition, although it could also lead to greater inequality, as we will see in the next section. This theory of oligopolistic competition not only enables institutional economists to reject the radical critique of international firms, but also has important effects on the internal processes that structure the relationships between capital and labour, which we discuss in Chapter 7.

Market failures, political regulation and social provision

The pure theory of market systems operates under neoclassical assumptions where fully informed individuals with secure property rights exchange goods and services in a world where there are diminishing returns to scale and no barriers to entry. This analytical model has been subjected to rigorous criticism for two centuries and survived, so we cannot take issue with its logical coherence. But what does concern us is the fact that the actual effects of real markets also depend on the realism of their behavioural and social assumptions and that they can generate hierarchy, structural inequality and crises, not freedom, and 'even' as opposed to 'uneven' development, where their assumptions do not hold. Many liberal theorists accept that all their assumptions only hold in exceptional circumstances,[17] and that 'the existence of externalities in production and consumption and increasing returns to scale in production, or either of them, will rule out the existence of perfectly competitive markets ... provid[ing] a prima facie case for government intervention' (Lal, 1996: 31).

This contradiction between assumptions and reality has major institutional implications. Centralized regulation and enforcement would not be needed if everyone was indeed fully informed and trustworthy, since they would automatically respect all property rights and honour all contracts.[18] However, people do make well-intentioned mistakes and fail to meet their obligations, some even cheat or steal. Thus, they 'are subjected to bounded rationality ... and are given to opportunism ... [or] self-seeking with guile' (Williamson, 1987: 30), which can produce malfeasance and contractual failures that need to be regulated or adjudicated by modern states. Further, in the real world, increasing, not diminishing, returns to scale often enable large firms to wipe out small ones, producing uneven rather than even development, unemployment and crises (Brett, 1983: Chs 3 and 4). The existence of opportunism, imperfect information and scale economies then generate four kinds of market failure relating to enforcement, excludability, externalities, and uneven development, and a corresponding need for a formalized system of enforceable law, adjudication, retribution and redistribution, and a set of non-market institutions to provide them.

Enforcement

Markets do not allocate most key resources in semi-subsistence economies, but they do in modern market societies where their operation generates high levels of social interdependence and determines everyone's relative income and status:[19]

> In the course of the actual attainment of selfish ends ... there is formed a system of complete interdependence, wherein the livelihood, happiness, and legal status of one man is interwoven with the livelihood, happiness, and legal rights of all. On this system, individual happiness etc. depend, and only in this connected system are they actualised and secured. (Hegel, 1821/1967: 123)[20]

Thus, shifting from self-sufficiency or command planning to markets increases freedom, but produces far-reaching normative and structural change by creating a specialized division of labour, universal interdependence, and the need to meet the high standards imposed by competition.

Cooperative interdependence based on market competition also generates zero-sum conflicts, since 'any two men ... [who] desire the same thing ... become enemies', so uncontrolled competition can lead to 'a warre ... of every man against every man' (Hobbes, 1651/1968: 184–5). Thus market societies only survive when losers as well as winners are obliged to accept the results of free competition, even when it threatens the survival of individuals, firms, nations or regions. The disruptive effects of competition were once controlled by the coercive imposition of a unified system of rules and values, but in market societies, everyone has the right to unite for any purpose and compete with everyone else. This generates high 'contestation costs'[21] that produce conflict and breakdown and threaten 'the human and natural components of the social fabric' (Polanyi, 1944/2001: 156), unless they are effectively managed, producing what Parsons (1951/1964: 36–7) calls 'the problem of order':

> The problem of order, and thus of the nature of the integration of stable systems of social integration, that is, of social structure, thus focuses on the integration of the motivation of actors with the normative cultural standards which integrate the action system, in our context impersonally. These standards are ... patterns of value-orientation, and as such are a particularly crucial part of the cultural tradition of the social system.

Modern societies, as Spencer (1850/1971: 194) recognized, have created 'the extremest mutual dependence' but also assume that 'each individual must have the opportunity to do whatever his desires prompt'. But he also saw that this created a potential contradiction between private and collective demands that would only be resolved when a new kind of person had emerged 'whose private requirements coincide with public ones ... who, in spontaneously fulfilling his own nature, incidentally performs the functions of a social unit; and yet is only enabled so to fulfil his own nature, by all others doing the like' (p. 194). Where most people have acquired the necessary dispositions, the processes that 'integrate' societies operate virtually unseen, being embedded in 'concrete personal relations and structures (or "networks") of such relations' in day-to-day interactions (Granovetter, 1992: 60). Here, rules operate as though everyone has freely chosen to obey them, but the understandings and dispositions that allow this to happen exist 'not as freedom but as necessity, since it is by compulsion that the particular rises to the form of universality and seeks and gains its stability in that form' (Hegel, 1821/1967: 124). Once these 'necessary' conditions exist, individual freedom can be taken for granted, but it still depends on the existence of socially and collectively generated obligations because, as Hegel (p. 282) also said, 'when we walk the streets at night in safety ... we do not reflect on just how this is due solely to the working of special institutions'. Thus state regulation is not a source of illegitimate constraint but the basis for 'liberty itself' (Durkheim, 1893/1964: 386).

This does not discredit the market model, but it does explain the need for the external enforcement of a system of law that 'cannot be founded on the basis of the power and freedom of the people', because 'the power and freedom of the people ... [must find] its stability in the law', and in the existence of a constitution that creates coercive power rather than simply delimiting it (Fine, 2001: 128).[22] According to Foucault (1980: 119):

> defining the effects of power as [no more than] repression ... [is to ignore] the fact that it doesn't only weigh on us as a force that says no, but that it traverses and produces things, it induces pleasure, forms knowledge, produces discourse. It needs to be considered as a productive network which runs through the whole social body, much more than as a negative function whose function is repression.

Thus all market societies need coercive states, although the strength and nature of the sanctions they need to use will depend on the extent to which people have voluntarily accepted the necessary obligations that market societies demand. This cultural shift has gone a long way in many DCs, but has much further to go in LDCs, as we will see in Part III.

Excludability

Market exchanges depend on 'excludability', since producers cannot finance their activities unless they can oblige consumers to pay for their products. And the only way they can do so without resorting to force themselves is to create a state that will stop others from invading their property rights and oblige them to pay for the products they receive. This is also why states have to use compulsory taxation to finance many 'open access' services like policing, money, roads or street lighting, and to regulate open access resources like the air, sea, forest reserves or common pastures where exclusion is difficult or impossible. The former are generally goods with low subtractability, 'where consumption by one beneficiary does not reduce availability of the good to others' (Picciotto, 1997: 349). The latter are common resources like fisheries or common pastures, which 'lack excludability while possessing subtractability' (p. 348), where users will be tempted to increase consumption 'without limit – in a world that is limited', producing what Hardin (1968: 1244) called the 'tragedy of the commons'. It is impossible to use free markets to limit the use of these open access resources, so some form of collective management by governments or communities is needed to overcome free-rider problems and maintain the natural and social conditions on which civilized life depends (Ostrom, 1990: 3).

Externalities

Closely related to the excludability problem, negative or positive externalities emerge where producers can transfer some of their costs of production to outsiders, or enable outsiders to exploit resources they have produced without paying for them. Negative externalities would include carbon emissions or chemical wastes dumped into the atmosphere or a river; positive externalities include the formula for a drug that was costly to invent but could be reproduced by a competitor at negligible cost. Negative externalities require state intervention to force polluters to limit their waste or clean it up; positive ones require enforceable patent laws that protect their intellectual property rights (Coase, 1960).

Uneven development

Economies of scale undermine the stability of competitive processes because larger firms increase their ability to eliminate smaller ones as they grow, and this creates barriers to entry and corresponding tendencies to monopoly and the concentration of production in the hands of a limited range of firms or geographic regions.[23] These effects create natural monopolies where high set-up and low marginal costs generate impenetrable barriers to entry – as with roads, railways, or piped water systems – that could be exploited to make excessive profits or provide services to the poor. These services were often provided by state-owned enterprises (SOEs), or, when privatized, are now subjected to state regulation. However, scale economies can also stem from technological change, the lower costs of advertising, research or the credit enjoyed by large firms, or the 'clustering' of interdependent firms in particular regions or nations. Indeed, the crucial difference between neoclassical and Marxist theory is that the former assumes diminishing returns to scale, and the latter that 'the normal case of modern industry ... [involves] an increasing productivity of labour and the operation of a larger quantity of means of production by fewer labourers' (Marx, 1894/1972: 58). The way this leads to structural unemployment and uneven development is set out in *Capital* (Marx, 1967/1974: vol. 1, Ch. 25).

This generates two additional kinds of market failure – the need for hierarchical firms, which will be addressed in Chapter 6, and the need for state intervention to deal with the problems of uneven development by regulating competitive processes and redistributing resources from winners to losers, which we address here.

State intervention and viable market systems

Scale economies have produced the immense increases in output that have transformed the modern world, but also the structural crises that have threatened its stability and the inequalities that threaten the legitimacy of its capitalist institutions (Wade, 2004). The 'creative destruction' of obsolete technologies has threatened the economic survival of individuals and groups, and concentrated immense wealth at some points in the system, and endemic poverty at others. Sometimes this stems from inappropriate state intervention, such as the maintenance of an overvalued exchange rate, but it also occurs because established firms, nations and regions can use their historically based advantages to defeat potential challenges from new ones. This has trade and industrial policy implications for LDCs that will be explored in Part III, but also generates exclusion and instability in DCs, where markets cannot guarantee the disabled, the old and the undereducated a living wage, and flexible labour markets, trade cycles and technical change put everyone's income at risk. This has normative, structural and therefore political consequences.

The legitimacy of markets cannot be separated from the substantive outcomes of market competition, because losers will reject them unless they produce 'compensating benefits for everyone, and especially for the least advantaged members of society' (Rawls, 1973: 14–15). MacPherson (1962) shows that Hobbes 'saw, accurately, that in a possessive market society all values and entitlements are in fact established by the operation of the market', and that this implies that 'all morality tends to be the morality of the market'. Such societies therefore 'establish rights by facts ... [because] every man's entitlements are determined by the actual competitive relationship between the powers of individuals'. Thus, only if the outcome of these market-based allocations is 'accepted as justice by all members of the society' will there be 'a sufficient basis for rational obligation, binding on all men to an authority which could maintain and enforce the market system', and an obligation on 'all rational men ... to accept the market concept of justice as the only one' (MacPherson, 1962: 78).

However, when uncontrolled competition produces uneven development, an excluded stratum will emerge that will reject market morality because their 'poverty leaves them more or less deprived of all the advantages of society, of the opportunity of acquiring skill or education of any kind, as well as of the administration of justice, the public health services, and often even of the consolations of religion' (Hegel, 1821/1967: 149). The need to overcome these problems has produced the modern welfare state that uses its capacity to tax the rich in order to protect the poor from the potentially destructive effects of market competition by insuring them against unemployment, and enabling even the poor to receive an adequate supply of what are referred to as 'merit goods'. These are services that are seen to be essential to the maintenance of a decent life – education, health, housing and social protection.

The potentially destructive effects of competition also help to explain problems of imperfect information and the need to enforce contracts because it makes it impossible to accurately predict outcomes, while losers will be unable to meet their obligations.

Conservatives and radicals, liberals and structuralists agree over the need for state intervention, but disagree over the goals, methods and levels of provision. Their disagreements have produced experiments with regulatory policy regimes that allocate governments different levels of power over private firms, manifested in what Polanyi (1944/2001: 79–80) referred to as 'a double movement' – 'the extension of the market organization ... all over the face of the globe', associated with a powerful countermovement by society to protect itself from its disruptive effects. We outlined these theoretical debates in Chapter 1, and will examine historical processes in Chapter 10. What concerns us next is the way different economic policy regimes structure the relationships between states, firms and civil society.

The political implications of economic regulation

State regulation is essential but generates inevitable contradictions because competition will be disrupted when governments control market access, set prices and/or favour some firms at the expense of others. While liberals believe that interventions should be primarily designed to facilitate market competition, structuralists use them to change market outcomes by redistributing resources, protecting domestic producers, allocating monopoly privileges to favoured enterprises and creating SOEs. Laissez faire dominated theory up to the late 1920s, but depressions and wars produced a generalized shift to structuralism in the middle years of the 20th century. Right-wing corporatists used state power to subordinate labour to capital in South Korea (Kohli, 2004), and left-wing social democrats used it to protect workers' rights and guarantee access to safety nets and merit goods in Labour Britain (Crosland, 1956). The structuralist crises of the 1970s and 80s produced a return to laissez faire that has now evolved into a search for new pluralistic syntheses that will overcome the difficulties generated by these competing policy experiments.

The need for state regulation in the most liberal capitalist states therefore challenges the neoclassical assumption that markets will not only generate efficiency and full employment but also depoliticize the relationship between firms, workers and the state. This is because the instability and inequalities in wealth and power that markets generate can increase levels of personal insecurity that losers will try to challenge, and the property rights that the state is expected to protect will include the great fortunes of small elites. Thus:

> in reality civil society and the State are one and the same, [so] it must be made clear that laissez faire too is a form of state 'regulation', introduced and maintained by legislation and coercive means. It is a deliberate policy, conscious of its own ends and not the spontaneous, automatic expression of economic facts. Consequently, laissez faire liberalism is a political programme, designed to change the economic programme of the State itself – in other words the distribution of national income. (Gramsci, 1971: 159–60)

The normative claims and political legitimacy of laissez faire therefore depend on its ability to deliver full employment and/or an adequate level of social protection to those excluded from the market. Orthodox economists have agued that it can be relied on to do this, provided that states do not interfere with the market mechanism, and they attributed crises to inappropriate state policies.[24] However, their critics attribute crises to the nature of the capitalist system itself, and argue that the demand for regulation is in fact a response to its inherent instability (Polanyi, 1944/2001, Ch. 12; Brett, 1983, Ch. 4). The interwar depressions were used to justify command planning in the Soviet Union and Fascist Europe, while Keynesian theory facilitated a crucial compromise between statist and market theories in the stronger democracies. It attributed unemployment to the vicious circles generated by the lack of appropriate incentives to invest during economic downturns, and called for state intervention to expand demand until full employment had been restored (Keynes, 1936/1973). Right-wing Keynesians limited this to tax cuts and deficit spending, while social democrats used it to build interventionist states based on redistributive taxation to encourage industry and employment and finance welfare systems, and combined it with state ownership and managed trade based on protectionist theory (Brett, 1985; Desai, 2004).

Left Keynesianism significantly reduced the autonomy of the business class, but rescued capitalism from the serious threats it confronted in the 1930s by restoring full employment without eliminating private property rights and markets. Keynes himself argued that once the state had established the right balance between output and employment:

> there is no objection to be raised against the classical analysis of the manner in which private self-interest will determine what in particu-

lar is produced, in what proportions the factors of production will be combined to produce it, and how the value of the final product will be distributed between them ... Thus, apart from the necessity of central controls to bring about an adjustment between the propensity to consume and the inducement to invest, there is no more reason to socialise economic life than there was before. (Keynes, 1936/1973: 378–9)

The effect of this compromise was to turn policy negotiations into a tripartite corporatist debate between 'leaders of key labour, business and state organizations to resolve major political issues in exchange for the enhancement of the corporate interests' (Held, 1987: 206), but it also politicized the operation of labour and commodity markets and had serious structural consequences.

Keynesian theory emerged in a world dominated by depressions and falling prices where underemployed capital coexisted with unemployed labour.[25] Keynes (1936/1973: 289) knew that increasing deficit spending and/or wages would only increase investment and output, rather than prices, where there was surplus labour or capital, and that doing so once full employment existed would produce inflation and not growth, just as orthodox theory claimed. During the postwar era, the policy community ignored this insight and invoked Keynesian theory to justify expansionary policies during even short-term economic recessions. Full employment, high wages and growing public spending were combined with low inflation in the most successful economies during the postwar boom, sustained by productivity gains created by transferring labour from agriculture to industry, and introducing new technologies financed by the USA (Brett, 1985: Chs 5 and 6). But once these easy productivity gains were no longer available, when postwar reconstruction had been completed, the combination of deficit spending and full employment produced inflation, fiscal and balance of payments crises, and falling profit rates that eventually destabilized the social democratic compromise, discredited Keynesian theory, and opened the way for a return to neoclassical orthodoxy.[26]

Here governments could either tighten wage controls, state spending and imports, or allow markets to do this for them. Making these choices generated intense political conflicts, but most governments eventually chose the latter course, in part because trade and monetary liberalization had made it increasingly difficult for them to protect high-cost domestic producers from international competition. The result was a return to laissez faire, using public spending cuts to weaken demand, and removing subsidies and protection to increase competition in domestic markets. This bankrupted uncompetitive firms and increased unemployment and the power of capital over labour. These reforms dominated the structural adjustment programmes introduced by the IFIs across the third world and post-Communist countries from the early 1980s. They were much less influential in Continental Europe and East Asia, but they were also forced to respond to falling profits and rising unemployment and fiscal deficits. However, while Keynes's ideas were marginalized during the boom years by the neoliberal ascendancy, they are being invoked again now to deal with the deflationary consequences of the current global economic crisis.

The shift from structuralism to liberalism changed the nature and role of the state as well as economic policy, since it significantly reduced the range of policy options that governments could deploy to deal with problems of uneven development and social marginalization. They could no longer:

- use deficit spending or impose high taxes on the rich to redistribute resources to the poor and reduce inequalities
- use tariffs, controlled exchange rates, licences or subsidies to protect jobs or wages from local or international competition
- use loss-making state enterprises to alter relationships between workers and mangers
- invest in new industries
- guarantee the poor access to merit goods like water, housing or energy.

This has led to a significant redistribution of income from poor to rich, the emergence of an increasingly marginalized underclass, often operating in the informal economy, and an equally comprehensive marginalization of socialism as a viable political creed. However, it has now also produced yet another capitalist crisis comparable to that which disrupted the global system in the 1930s. This has already produced a reversion to Keynesian policies and yet another return to structuralism, confirming Polanyi's claim (1944/2201: 155) that economic liberals confronted with a crisis were bound to turn against laissez faire and choose 'as any antiliberal would have done, the so-called collectivist methods of regulation and restriction'. We briefly examine the implications of this change below.

Conclusions

The analysis in this chapter that has examined the institutional implications of current attempts to build social systems using pluralistic institutional arrangements based on a variety of authority systems, incentives and accountability mechanisms does not claim to provide new blueprints for the solution of developmental crises. However, it does provide the basis for a transition from the adversarial conflicts between liberal or structuralist fundamentalists that produced one-sided solutions that often led to serious failures. It provides a rigorous basis for the analysis of the benefits and costs of market solutions, and the political and social interventions that are potentially available to deal with the particular kinds of challenges confronted by particular kinds of societies. It tells us that the hegemonic status of modern liberal institutions does not depend on neoliberal market theory because it ignores problems of market failure and assumes that interventionist states must always fail. Instead, it tells us that viable liberal institutions depend on an ability to systematically combine political, economic and social markets with strong bureaucratic apparatuses, appropriate systems of cultural values, and collectively managed political and civic institutions.

These agencies need to provide their managers with appropriate levels of authority and rewards, but also oblige them to meet universalistic ethical obligations and maximize their technical effectiveness, rather than operate on the basis of pure self-interest. These arrangements also need to redistribute enough resources from winners to losers to promote social cohesion by protecting the poor from the destructive effects of uncontrolled competition. These principles have already been institutionalized in most DCs, although only after the massive conflicts and many failures that led to Communist and Fascist revolutions in the east and west. These agreements are still accompanied by an intense debate over the levels of redistribution required in the north, and over the nature of the organizational systems needed to achieve them, and are again being threatened by the serious economic crisis generated by neoliberal governments that failed to subject their financial institutions to effective regulation. These ideological debates are associated with important reforms in institutional theory, which is attempting to design political, economic and social organizations that will address these contradictory problems more successfully than existing ones. These include new forms of public management and alternative kinds of for-profit or non-profit private agencies. These innovations will be discussed in the rest of Part II, and the way in which they are being used as models in LDCs, which confront far more serious problems of market failure than those described here, will be addressed in Part III.

Notes

1 For a concise summary, see Stiglitz (2008).
2 Key contributions in economics would include Schumpeter, Coase, Williamson, North, Hirschmann and Stiglitz; in management theory, Chandler, Hood, Vincent Ostrom and Tullock; in the sociology of organizational life, Parsons, Elinor Ostrom, Olson and Granovetter. The classical foundations for this approach were created by Hegel, List, Marx, Durkheim and Weber.

3   Ouchi uses the term 'clan' to refer to solidaristic organizations.

4   The idea comes from Williamson (1987: 1).

5   Further texts include Brett (1993); Harriss-White (2003); Hood (1991); Kanter (1972); Manning (2002); Streek and Smitter (1991); and White (1993a).

6   See also Clarke and Wilson (1961: 130) and Brett (1993: 276).

7   I have excluded cooperation here. All organizations exist to manage cooperation but do so using processes that involve qualitatively different levels of hierarchy as opposed to autonomy in coordinating joint activities.

8   The role of 'traditional' institutions in developmental transitions will be addressed in Part III.

9   'Just as ancient peoples needed, above all, a common faith to live by, so we need justice, and we can be sure that this need will become ever more exacting if, as every facet presages, the conditions dominating social evolution remain the same' (Durkheim, 1893/1964: 388).

10 Sen (1999: 56) fails to recognize the demanding implications of this principle, when he claims that 'Rawlsian justice has serious flaws, if substantive individual freedoms [or capabilities] are taken to be important'.

11 According to Margaret Thatcher: 'There is no such thing as society, there are individual men and women and there are families' (Slater and Tonkiss, 2001: 32).

12 See Lipsey et al. (2005) for an account of the role of scientific tolerance in economic development, and Nove (1983: 176–8) for a theoretical account and Dudintsev (1957) for a fictional account of the obstacles to innovation in command economies.

13 Keynes (1936/1973: 23–6) shows why 'Say's law, that the aggregate demand price of output as a whole is equal to its aggregate supply price for all volumes of output, is equivalent to the proposition that there is no obstacle to full employment'.

14 'By giving more to each person employed, they limit the power of giving employment to numbers; and however excellent their moral effect, they do little good economically, unless the pauperism of those who are shut out, leads indirectly to a readjustment by means of an increased restraint on population' (Mill, 1848/1900: 244).

15 See Lenin (1916/1970); see also Bain (1962); Berle and Means (1932); Blair (1972); Brett (1983); Eaton and Lipsey (1978); Holland (1976); Murray (1981); Sweezy (1970); and Vaitsos (1974).

16 IBM had a virtual monopoly in computer production in the 1970s, but lost it after the invention of microprocessors.

17 Thus, Haberler (1961: 18) argued that the assumptions justifying liberal trade theory 'are so restrictive and so unrepresentative of actual reality the theory can be said to prove the opposite of what it seems to purport to say – namely, that there is no chance whatsoever that factor prices will ever be equalized by free commodity trade'; and Keynes (1936/1973: 378) argued that the 'tacit assumptions' of classical economic theory 'are seldom if ever satisfied ... [so] that it cannot solve the economic problems of the actual world'.

18 Economists assume that individuals do 'not buy more than they can pay for, they do not embezzle funds, they do not rob banks' (Diamond, cited in Williamson, 1987: 49).

19 Polanyi's work provides a seminal analysis of the consequences of the transition from pre-market to market societies.

20 The editor notes that these passages are influenced by Adam Smith's belief that 'a country best attains commercial prosperity ... if it leaves individual entrepreneurs as far as possible free to pursue their own selfish aims' (p. 354)

21 I owe this point to Jonathan Di John.

22 Fine's (2001: 127–8) argument is based on Arendt's understanding of the modern state.

23 For a detailed analysis, see Brett (1983: Chs 3 and 4).

24 For example, Friedman and Schwartz (1963) attribute the Great Depression of the 1930s in the USA to state failures.

25 'Except during the war, I doubt if we have any recent experience of a boom so strong that it led to full employment' (Keynes, 1936/1973: 322).

26 See Glyn and Sutcliffe (1972), Bacon and Eltis (1978), and Brett (1985, Ch. 6).

Chapter 5

State Regulation, Democratic Politics and Accountable Governance

> If he lives amongst others of his own species, man is an animal who needs a master. For he certainly abuses his freedom in relation to others of his own kind. (Kant, 1784/1991a: 46)

Rulers can rule in many different ways:

- In segmentary societies, rules have been enforced by households, kinship networks, clans or religious leaders, rather than hierarchical states (Almond, 1960: 11–12).
- In traditional empires, rulers had absolute power and bureaucratic appointments were based on patronage (Eisenstadt, 1963).
- In modern totalitarian states, 'illiberal political systems ... annihilate all boundaries between the state, civil society and individual personality' (Fine, 2001: 107).
- In liberal societies, however, rulers should enable citizens to achieve their own goals and oblige them to respect the right of others to do the same.

Thus political development involves a transition from political systems based on command and control to cooperation and consent. This has structural and spatial implications – it requires authority systems that not only facilitate autonomous interdependence between people and organizations, but also operate at national, global and local levels. Liberal states do this by designing institutions that subject citizens and rulers to the rule of law, make them accountable through democratic markets, and oblige them to respect the autonomy of private producers and their own officials. In this chapter, we look at the constitutional rules, economic policy regimes, and party systems that have evolved to deal with this problem, and at public management systems in Chapter 6.

Political authority, organizational autonomy and complex interdependence

Political authority in modern states rests on the principle of national sovereignty that vests the supreme authority within the territory of the state ... [creating a] political world ... [consisting of] a number of states that within their respective territories ... [are], legally speaking, completely independent of each other recognizing no secular authority above themselves. (Morgenthau, 1954: 250)

This idea has been evolving since the 17th century, when it was used by rulers to justify absolute control over their own citizens and their right to subject other states to their will. However, resistance to oppression by citizens and the costs of international conflict have led to major structural changes in the way it has been institutionalized, both within states and in interstate relationships.

Law, institutionalized autonomy and political authority

Liberal political theory exists to find ways of reconciling the need for state sovereignty with people's right to freedom. Thus North (1981: 24) notes that:

The economies of scale associated with devising a system of law, justice, and defence are the basic underlying source of civilization: and the creation of the state in the millennia following the first economic revolution was the necessary condition for all subsequent economic development.

But he also shows that rulers have particular needs and interests, and will turn states into 'the agency of a group or class' that 'extracts income from the rest', and a 'source of man-made economic decline' (1981: 21–2) unless they are constrained by enforceable rules.

This means that 'in contrast with the spheres of private rights and private welfare (the family and civil society), the state is from one point of view an external necessity and their higher authority: its nature is such that their laws and interests are subordinate to it and dependent on it'. But it also means that if states are to promote freedom not servitude, rulers should not exploit their people, but recognize that the objectives of the state are 'immanent within' those of their citizens, 'and its strength lies in the unity of its own universal end and with the particular interest of individuals, in the fact that individuals have duties to the state in proportion as they have rights against it' (Hegel, 1821/1967: 161).

Attempts to create rule-governed systems began in pre-democratic societies, but liberal states emerged where pressure from economic elites obliged rulers to recognize that 'no man shall be compelled to do things to which the law does not oblige him, nor forced to abstain from things which the law permits' (Montesquieu, 1748, cited in Held, 1987: 57). However, laws can institutionalize injustice as well as justice, and they only constrain behaviour when they are effectively enforced, so their effectiveness and legitimacy require autonomous institutions, where representatives of the people can make rules and monitor their implementation, judges can settle disputes, and incorruptible officials can enforce them. Thus modern states are tripartite structures, comprising:

- an executive that writes and enforces laws and implements policy
- a legislature where elected representatives use 'voice' to make or modify laws and monitor and sanction rulers
- an independent judiciary and enforcement agencies that adjudicate disputes between citizens and between citizens and rulers.

All sectors are interdependent, but their effective functioning depends on the separation of powers, since each must be autonomous in order to

> so modify the sovereignty as that it may be sufficiently neutral between different parts of the Society to control one part from invading the rights of another, and at the same time sufficiently controlled itself, from setting up an interest adverse to that of the entire Society. (Madison, cited in Keohane, 2000: 113)

Liberal states originally existed to defend borders and safeguard private property rights, but modern pluralism allocates governments extensive regulatory and service delivery responsibilities, as we know. This problematizes relationships between the political and administrative arms of the executive, because control over armies and police, taxation, property rights, and access to state services threatens the integrity of political systems, and because politicians can use these resources to:

- disable democratic processes by buying political support or punishing political opponents
- distort market processes by enforcing inappropriate economic policies
- undermine the professional autonomy of officials by politicizing the management of state services.

We will take up these issues later, but must first address the spatial dimensions of the governance problem, since claims to sovereignty raise complex questions about the balance between institutions of national, global and local governance.

Nation-states, complex interdependence and global governance

Sovereignty was once invoked to justify the right of rulers to colonize weaker states and adopt beggar-thy-neighbour economic policies as well as to control policy in their own territories. This culminated in world wars that convinced many people that outlawing war 'is the only reasonable alternative to suicide' (Laski, 1938: 587), and produced a general recognition that the 'basic rule of coexistence within the state system' needs to be based on a 'conception of sovereignty' that reflects 'equality and reciprocity', and creates the possibility of complex interdependence' (Keohane, 2000: 113; Bull, 1977: 34–7). The result has been a serious attempt to shift from a world system based on mutual deterrence and economic protectionism to one that would universalize the principle of national self-determination, encourage economic interdependence and guarantee 'perpetual peace'. These principles have both domestic and external implications, as Kant recognized in the 18th century. He argued that 'a state of peace' among nations 'must be formally instituted, for a suspension of hostilities is not in itself a guarantee of peace', and that the viability of the guarantees exchanged between states must depend on both already living 'in a lawful state', so that:

> all men who can at all influence one another must adhere to some kind of civil constitution ... [that] will conform to one of the three following types:
>
> (1) a constitution based on the *civil right* of individuals within a nation ...
> (2) a constitution based on the *international right* of states in their relationships with one another ...
> (3) a constitution based on *cosmopolitan right*, insofar as individuals and states, coexisting in an eternal relationship of mutual influences, may be regarded as citizens of a universal state of mankind ...
>
> This classification with respect to the idea of perpetual peace *is not arbitrary, but necessary* [emphases added]. For if even one of the parties were able to influence the others physically and yet itself remained in a state of nature, there would be a risk of war, which is precisely the aim of the above articles to prevent. (Kant, 1991b: 98–9)

The United Nations (UN), the International Court of Justice, and the international financial institutions (IFIs) were set up after the Second Word War in an attempt to create a structure of global governance that would impose real, although limited constraints on the exercise of political and economic sovereignty by nation-states.

Political sovereignty and the UN system

The UN system is expected to balance the right to self-determination with the need to oblige states to refrain from actions that could threaten international peace. Article 2 of the UN Charter places the major emphasis on the former, since it stops it from intervening in 'matters which are essentially within the domestic jurisdiction of the state'. However, its agencies have implicitly recognized that peace depends on all societies living in 'a lawful state' by persuading almost all nations to acknowledge the general framework of liberal principles embodied in various charters of human, political, economic and social rights, and General Assembly resolutions. Taking these obligations seriously would have a profound influence on internal systems of governance as well as external relationships, and create conditions under which 'justice and respect for treaties and international law can be maintained', but they are not binding and are often treated as no more than 'a collection of pious phrases' (Allen, 2006: 4–7). However, the UN also set up the Security Council and gave it 'the power to take decisions which Member States are obligated under the Charter to carry out' (www.un.org), and to take military action if necessary to deal with international threats to peace. The UN was also given the right and the financial support to create many implementing agencies needed to provide services crucial to the welfare of the international system, such as health, fisheries, refugees and economic development, many of whose mandates overlap with those of the IFIs and national donor agencies.

The UN plays a key role in sustaining peace and promoting liberal constitutional principles, but its prioritization of national sovereignty and its dependence on the goodwill of the great powers heavily constrains its ability to do so. Charters and General Assembly resolutions have moral authority but are not binding, while UN agencies have far less leverage over host governments than do the IFIs, as we will see. Security Council decisions are enforceable, but its ability to act is heavily constrained by both its rules and political factors. Its five permanent members can each veto any decision, so action was virtually impossible during the cold war and 'appalling governments' could 'act without any expectation that they would be prosecuted for their barbaric behaviour' (Allen, 2006: 7–8). And its lack of a monopoly of force or the power to tax means that it can only act when the major powers allow it to do so. Thus, they can ignore its decisions with impunity, and it can only ever impose its decisions on weak states that cannot resist its interventions.

So the UN system has not institutionalized a viable system of international rights that enforces generally agreed moral obligations on strong as well as weak states. This means that its prescriptions can be ignored by powerful states, for example the USA and the UK when they invaded Iraq in 2002, or by states like Israel with powerful friends. UN agencies have often failed but the UN system has not created effective representative institutions that subject them to strong democratic accountability.

These weaknesses, however, should not be allowed to obscure the UN's very real achievements. Its conventions have been signed by most governments so they have a moral authority that can be invoked by opposition groups when they campaign for political, economic and social rights; agreement on the Security Council can occasionally be reached and give legal authority to international interventions like the 1991 Iraq War. Decisions to flout Security Council resolutions can be clearly labelled as unlawful and impose political costs on governments that do so, as the US and UK governments eventually discovered. UN decisions clarify the obligations of states involved in negotiations that do not involve serious conflicts of interest, as do decisions of the International Court of Justice, whose judgements are requested and therefore usually respected by interested parties.[1] Further, its agencies represent the only constitutional basis for multilateral intervention in crisis situations of all kinds, so they avoid the political problems associated with external interventions by individual states.

Thus complex interdependence is indeed increasing the need for a transition to a strong global system that will eventually be based on 'cosmopolitan right', which enables 'individuals and states' to coexist 'in an eternal relationship of mutual influences' so they 'may be regarded as citizens of a universal state of mankind' (Kant, 1991b: 98–9). The UN is the only viable basis for such a transition; completing it will depend on the ability of the international society to consolidate and extend its current attempts to create a world system governed by legally constituted right rather than force.

Economic sovereignty, regulatory regimes and global financial institutions

Complex international interdependence also demands economic rules that enable states to operate in domestic and foreign markets without threatening the survival of their neighbours. This was problematic when protectionist policies based on managed exchange rates, tariffs and quotas, and subsidies to national producers were 'the normal practice of the world' (Emmanuel, 1972: xiv), so postwar attempts to institutionalize 'cosmopolitan right' have involved an attempt to institutionalize free trade. We will examine the structural implications of this shift here, and its origins and consequences in Chapter 10.

States can choose to specify the terms on which goods, money and labour cross their borders, to determine whether foreign producers will be allowed to operate on their territory, and whether to give producers subsidies and/or monopolies or delegate these decisions to free markets. When international economic policy regimes change these rules – for example by reducing tariffs or allowing states to devalue their currencies – they benefit some firms and economies and threaten others, and therefore have crucial political and economic implications. These arrangements are no longer negotiated bilaterally, but operate through a rule-based system managed by the International Monetary Fund (IMF), the World Bank and the World Trade Organization (WTO), which are based on a general commitment to trade and financial liberalization, and now incorporate almost all states.

Poor countries have generally called for protection from foreign competition, and will only willingly remain in an open system if it leads to even rather than uneven development, because 'there is an incompatibility between the extraordinary performance of one or more members in a system and the maintenance of a voluntary rule-based order' (Hager, 1980: 12). When they believe that strong countries are profiting at their expense, and they cannot maintain a balance of payments equilibrium, mutuality can give way to conflict and the beggar-thy-neighbour policies of the 1930s. Liberalizing the postwar economic order has facilitated a large growth in international trade and financial flows. However, it has been heavily contested, threatened by periodic economic crises, is still incomplete, and is associated with growing inequalities between the richest and poorest societies and people (Wade, 2004).[2] We will consider some of the reasons for this in Chapter 10, and the conflicts that had to be resolved and the compromises that have been needed to establish and sustain the IMF and World Bank, which were created at the Bretton Woods Conference in 1944 to manage monetary policy and lend to weak economies, and the General Agreement on Tariffs and Trade (GATT, the forerunner of the WTO), set up in 1947 to manage trade negotiations.

At the end of the Second World War, strong economies, initially only the USA, wanted to facilitate an open market-based system, while weaker ones (the rest of the world) believed that they would only be able to rebuild or create new industries if they could limit access to their markets and/or be given access to enough external financial support to enable them to do so. The IFIs that were created to manage the relationships between these countries had to find ways of overcoming the contradictory demands of both sides. They did this by getting all players to accept a transition to an open international economic order as a long-term goal, but allowed the weaker economies to maintain protectionist policies in the short run.

Thus the IMF and World Bank now create the rules that specify the terms on which states control relationships between their own and foreign currencies, and access financial support when they confront balance of payments or fiscal crises. Countries were initially expected to maintain fixed exchange rates, and the weaker ones were permitted to impose direct controls over access to foreign currencies. From the 1970s, exchange rates were increasingly determined by market conditions, and most countries have now made their currencies fully convertible so that private agents can buy and sell domestic and foreign currencies at market prices. Under earlier systems, governments could manipulate access to foreign currencies and were expected to maintain fixed exchange rates that gave them considerable control over access to domestic and foreign markets and enabled them to meet their own foreign exchange needs, whereas under current arrangements, access to foreign currency and exchange rates are set by the market. These changes have been associated with the liberalization of international trade in response to a series of negotiations carried out by the GATT and the WTO. As a result, weak economies cannot reintroduce the protectionist policies that virtually all weaker countries used to manage their transitions to industrialization.

The liberals involved in setting up the IFIs believed that open markets would normally generate long-term balance of payments and fiscal stability, while the structuralists believed that weak countries could only give up protectionism if they were given access to public funds in a crisis. The IFIs were therefore given limited budgets that they could use to give countries short-term balance of payments and budgetary support when they confronted a 'fundamental' balance of payments disequilibrium, provided they did not revert to protectionism. This facility was rarely used during the boom years after the war when protectionist policies still prevailed, but had to be used to deal with the oil crisis in the late 1970s, and with many crises that have occurred since the start of the neoliberal revolution.[3] These interventions – formerly called 'structural adjustment programmes' and now called 'poverty reduction programmes' – have involved explicit policy conditionalities. They, together with the many rounds of tariff reductions negotiated by GATT and the WTO since 1948, have given the IFIs a crucial role in managing the generalized transition from structuralism to liberalization that has taken place across the world since the 1980s, as we will see in Part III. We conclude here by emphasizing three points:

1   The IFIs are not supposed to interfere in the 'political' affairs of member states, but accepting their rules, and the policy conditionality attached to their aid, significantly constrains the policy options available to all states. These constraints are complemented for many states by membership in regional organizations like the EU and the North American Free Trade Area (NAFTA). Membership is volun-

tary, but noncompliance is so costly that all but a few countries have had to join (Gruber, 2000), reducing, for better or worse, their government's ability to exercise 'supreme authority within the territory of the state'. We will examine some of the implications of aid dependency in LLDCs in Part III.

2 All states operate under the same rules, but the IMF and the World Bank can only intervene directly when economic crises force states to go to them for support. The deficit countries tried to introduce rules that also imposed sanctions on countries that ran chronic surpluses that imposed deflationary pressures on the world economy. They inserted the 'scarce currency clause' into the IMF Articles of Agreement, while the Havana Charter (1948) for the proposed International Trade Organization allowed them to discriminate against their imports. However, the scarce currency clause has never been used, and the Havana Charter was vetoed by the US Congress because it was too interventionist (Brett, 1985: 261). The result is an asymmetrical system that fails to meet Rawls' second condition for justice described in Chapter 4.

3 The system gives the USA special privileges and responsibilities because the US dollar became the currency used to finance global transactions. This has allowed it to live beyond its means by running chronic balance of payments and fiscal deficits, and avoiding the fiscal and economic disciplines imposed on all other states. US deficits have had an expansionary impact on the world economy by providing markets for foreign producers, but have now left the USA with immense international debts, which are threatening the value of the dollar and therefore most countries' reserve assets, thus threatening the viability of the global economy. The contradictory nature of these arrangements has been clearly exposed by the global credit crisis in 2008, and led to widespread demands for a fundamental reform of the Bretton Woods system.

Below the nation state: decentralization and devolution

The sovereignty of national governments is not only constrained by international agreements, but also by the devolution of political authority to local agents whose legitimacy is based on local elections and not delegated to them by the central government. The powers and autonomy of local governments vary. In confederal systems like the EU, member states have greater authority than the central authority. In strong federal states like the USA, the authority of local states is constitutionally guaranteed – they may control more services than the central government and have independent taxing powers. In unitary states, local authorities can exercise important powers, but their decisions can be reversed by the centre and they often depend on discretionary grants from the national treasury.

There are three key justifications for decentralization:

1 It should improve democratic accountability by allowing local electorates to exercise closer control over local politicians than is often possible over their national representatives.
2 It should improve the management of local services by making local officials directly accountable to local politicians and civic organizations.
3 It can help to overcome ethnic or sectarian divisions by allowing minority communities to control political decisions in their home territories.

Its ability to achieve these goals cannot be taken for granted, however, but depends on contingent contextual variables – the powers and degree of political autonomy devolved to local governments, the resources at their disposal, and especially the adequacy of local democratic processes and the intensity of the conflicting interests they are expected to resolve.

Central governments have always had to delegate some authority to local bureaucratic structures, but devolution involves an obligation to cede control over many activities to local politicians who may oppose their policies. Support for federalism is based on the success of the strong countries that pioneered the system – the USA, Switzerland, Canada and Australia. Their successes were undoubtedly linked to their constitutional arrangements, but also to the strength of the social, economic and political capital that existed in these wealthy countries. Decentralization of various kinds has been a crucial part of postwar constitutional reforms especially in LDCs attempting to consolidate their democratic transitions. Performance in poor and fragmented countries has been far more uneven, since local governments can also be captured by incompetent or predatory elites, undermined by ethnic or sectarian conflict, or by the incompetence of poorly qualified and paid local officials. Local autonomy can also intensify inequalities between wealthy regions that have more resources at their disposal and are likely to use them more effectively than poor ones.[4]

However, successful or not, decentralization does reduce the capacity of central governments to enforce unilateral policy decisions on local communities. It obliges them to enter into negotiated settlements with local authorities that may be controlled by opposition parties with an independent political mandate to implement policy programmes that central government reject. The result can be serious conflict and inefficient outcomes, but the overall process is yet another manifestation of the ongoing shift from unitary to pluralistic ways of managing interorganizational relationships in modern states.

State power, political markets and democratic accountability

Democratic accountability is the primary means of limiting the monopoly power exercised by national governments. Before the First World War, liberal democracy only existed in a minority of western states, but has now been extended to most former colonies, military dictatorships and command economies. Democracy exists to solve the 'problem of order', identified in Chapter 4, by creating a system that enables rulers to oblige citizens to obey the law, and citizens to oblige rulers to use their authority to satisfy social needs rather than their own. Citizens confront a single government, so they depend on 'voice' rather than 'exit' to make their needs known. This creates two problems:

1 They can rarely use voice on their own behalf, but must rely on their representatives to speak for them, because 'every free individual … [cannot be given] a share in debating and deciding political affairs of individual concern' (Hegel, 1801/1964: 159).
2 Voices that are not backed by the possibility of exit can be ignored, so their representatives should be obliged to compete for the right to represent them in regular but rare political contests.

Support for democratic governance is almost universal, but so is distrust of elected politicians who are often seen as hypocritical, partial, driven by populist pressures rather than rational analysis, and, in the worst cases, opportunistic or corrupt. This pessimism may be justified, but it takes little account of the intrinsic difficulties involved in managing modern states, or the obligations that enforcing democratic accountability on their representatives should impose on citizens. These difficulties stem from four problems:

1 The limitations intrinsic to the operation of political as opposed to economic markets.
2 The economic constraints that limit the scope for political action.
3 The problems involved in managing the social and political organizations that compete for power and represent interests.
4 The tensions involved in the relationships between politicians and the officials who produce public services.

We will address the first three of these issues here, and the fourth in Chapter 6.

The strengths and weaknesses of liberal democracy

Democratic states use what can be called 'second-order markets' to manage the problem of order. In primary or spot markets, consumers can exit to an alternative supplier at will, and each agent's choices have a negligible effect on everyone else's options. However, governments operate as a single supplier and are allowed to enforce the law and execute their own policy agenda once they have captured power. They nevertheless have to allocate scarce resources between competing interests, so even well-intentioned rulers must disadvantage some groups and generate inequality and conflict. Authoritarian rulers do not need to answer directly to their subjects for what they do, but democracy obliges them to do so by having to compete for power with opposition movements on a regular basis. Thus democracy does not threaten the state's right to use force, or eliminate conflicts of interest or unpopular decisions, but it should oblige governments to maximize efficiency, minimize inequalities, and find acceptable compromises between contending interests. Its ability to do this, however, is heavily constrained by problems of *political* market failures generated by conflicting preferences, oligopolistic competition and resource constraints.

Rational choice theory demonstrates that individuals have such diverse needs that governments cannot translate 'the preferences of rational individuals into a coherent group preference', so there has to be 'a tradeoff between social rationality and the concentration of power' in political life (Shepsle and Bonchek, 1997: 67).[5] Elections usually make it possible for 'winners' to take all the benefits so that supporters of minority parties are 'either unrepresented or misrepresented' (Mill, 1861/1910: 259), so regimes can often discriminate against losers with impunity, while ruling parties cannot even satisfy all their own supporters because they have multiple and competing interests. However, the legitimacy of the political system depends on their willingness to take account of the wider national interest, although democratic processes can disappoint even groups with direct access to power, and systematically exclude significant economic, ethnic or sectarian minorities.

These difficulties are compounded by the oligopolistic nature of democratic markets. Perfectly competitive markets need multiple suppliers, but elections cannot involve more than a handful of credible contenders because they have to aggregate community-wide interests and transform them into policy programmes that claim majority support, thus often excluding minority interests (Downs, 1957). Voters gravitate to potentially electable parties that often make promises to competing groups in order to win support that they cannot fulfil once they are elected. They can only do this because contracts between politicians and electors are incomplete and difficult to enforce – promises are imprecise, enforcement will depend on unanticipated eventualities, citizens have very little information about the quality of state performance, and governments can manage economic resources and the media to retain power. Citizens can only choose between a few policy packages, everyone has to accept the winning package, governments that default on their promises can only be removed at long intervals, and the opposition might be even less effective.

Hence democratic markets cannot give everyone what they want, but only produce second-best or even least-worst solutions based on untidy and usually contingent compromises (Shepsle and Bonchek, 1997: 77–81). Serious liberals recognize these problems, and radicals are even more critical of pluralistic or 'bourgeois' democracy, arguing that custom and the media systematically exclude many issues from political debate (Bachrach and Baratz: 1962). Marxists argue that the economic power disposed of by the capitalist class allows them to

> enjoy a massive preponderance in society, in the political systems, and in the determination of the state's policies and actions ... [so] political equality, save in formal terms, is impossible in ... advanced capitalism ... [and] economic life cannot be separated from political life. (Miliband, 1973: 237)

This explains why politicians and electoral processes are often distrusted, why Fascist and Communist regimes emerged during the interwar period, and why neoliberals demand privatization now. However, we also saw in Chapter 4 that state intervention is an inescapable necessity, so even though democracy cannot offer everyone what they want, it does create an arena where competing groups – both 'dominant' and 'dominated' classes – can be represented and struggle for control, and elect regimes that can impose at least some 'short-term material sacrifices on the dominant classes' (Poulantzas, 1980: 184). This, as Poulantzas (p. 140) argued, meant that democratic capitalist states could not simply be seen as agents of the capitalist class, but as arenas where the 'material compromises' needed to maintain the long-term coherence of the whole system could be agreed and enforced.[6]

The effectiveness of these processes then depends on two crucial variables that will be addressed next:

1 The ability of rulers to maintain a balance between popular demands and economic constraints needed to sustain their capitalist economies.
2 The quality of the social and political movements and media and research agencies in civil society that enable people to enforce their constitutional rights.

Politics, economics and state sovereignty

Rulers are not only constrained by democratic competition but also by the need to maintain a strong economy, since governments need strong profitable firms in order to guarantee livelihoods and their tax revenues. We saw in Chapter 4 that firms also need a strong state for protection, regulation and to provide essential services, although not one that rewards or punishes individual firms, so their role should be to provide public goods, create a 'level playing field' and referee the game. The separation of political and economic authority also means that capitalists should not be able to control elections and dictate to rulers, and rulers should not use their power to allocate subsidies, jobs or contracts to buy political support (Friedman, 1962).

Thus the relationships between state and private for-profit agencies should be based on relative autonomy and complex interdependence rather than simple coexistence (Poulantzas, 1980). However, sustaining reciprocal independence is a contradictory and conflictual process because state policies must influence the ability of capitalists to invest, and the investment decisions they make will increase or diminish support for the regime. Social democratic regimes responded to this contradiction by adopting the structuralist programmes that prevailed until the 1970s, and neoliberals returned to laissez faire in the 1980s and 90s. We will look at the way public sector management is changing as governments attempt to reconcile these contradictory demands in Chapter 6, and in Part III. What concerns us here is the nature of the economic and therefore political constraints that managing the economy imposes on governments.

Governments have the power to transfer economic resources from one group or activity to another, but the policies they can use to do so differ fundamentally in structuralist as opposed to market-based systems. However, their success or failure not only depends on the policy regimes they choose, but how well they manage them. Some countries, like Germany, Japan, South Korea and Taiwan, used structuralism very effectively; many others did not. The former succeeded because they allocated resources and managed political demands in ways that not only allowed capitalists to prosper, but also forced them to maximize their efficiency; the latter adopted populist or predatory policies that suppressed investment and led to economic decline. These differences depended on the ability of governments to deny the short-term and often contradictory demands of special interest groups, even those they relied on for political support (Kohli, 2004). The need to ensure that firms can make adequate profits presents governments, especially those representing subordinate classes, with their greatest political challenge because using taxes or protection to transfer resources to new firms or to the poor will penalize profitable firms. Once this drives their profits below sustainable levels, investment, output, exports, employment and taxation will fall and this will threaten livelihoods, public services and political support.[7]

This means that rulers confront a budget constraint that is as or even more powerful than the democratic constraint, which can force them to pay more attention to the demand for higher profits than for higher wages or pro-poor public services. Thus the political influence of business does not just depend on the ability of capitalists to buy politicians or votes (although they often do), but on the structural demands of the relationship between the state and an economy based on private ownership and market competition. This relationship can involve levels of state intervention ranging from mixed economies based on structuralism to well-regulated laissez faire, but all governments along this continuum have to respect the economic needs of private or public sector firms. Where they try to 'buy' political support from 'special interests' in ways that undermine the incentive to invest, they 'do great damage to economic efficiency' (Olson, 1997: 46), and, in the worst cases, produce vicious circles and cumulative processes of political and economic decline, which we will describe in Chapter 10.

These links between economic and political processes are often ignored by liberal political theorists and are used by Marxists to demonstrate that workers can never have comparable rights to capitalists in 'bourgeois' democracies.[8] Regimes that tried to transfer real control and assets from capital to labour did indeed confront economic crises induced by a falling rate of profit and had to nationalize assets and protect boundaries to sustain employment and output.[9] However, statist regimes also had to ration resources and enforce economic discipline and faced problems of collective action that led to rigidities, authoritarianism and the economic crises that produced the neoliberal revolution in the 1980s and 90s. Thus Marxist theorists are right to claim that 'bourgeois states' have to respect the needs of capital, but they have yet to produce a system that combines freedom with economic discipline any better. What liberal democratic capitalism does do is oblige governments to negotiate complex compromises between capital and labour, create autonomous state bureaucracies, and oblige firms to look for less authoritarian ways of managing their authority systems, which we will examine in Chapters 6 and 7.

Budget and foreign exchange constraints also limit the autonomy of autocratic rulers or 'stationary bandits' (Olson, 1997: Ch. 3). They may use their power to expropriate as much of the economic surplus as they can, but Olson shows that rational autocrats should recognize that economic growth will increase their ability to tax and maintain compliance, and should therefore allow producers to retain at least enough resources to sustain or increase their output. Pre-modern history suggests that many autocratic rulers did not behave like this, turning the 'ten millennia' after the 'creation of settled agriculture' into a saga 'of war and butchery ... enslavement and mass murder' (North, 1981: 24). But Olson's formulation does explain many 'periods of economic progress under strong autocrats', such as those that have managed the recent economic miracles in East Asia (Olson, 1997: 50). Further, autocratic regimes that ignore the need to control their economic demands also confront serious political threats generated by long-term economic decline, fiscal and foreign exchange constraints, and resistance from disaffected groups, with consequences we will explore in Part III.

Parties, party systems and democratic accountability

Introducing competitive political markets is a precondition for demo-cratic rule, but their operation demands strong, representative and autonomous parties that organize 'mass publics' and compete for power (Sartori, 1976), and civic associations or 'pressure groups' that organize limited interest groups that influence and monitor what policy-makers do (Bentley, 1908; Trueman, 1951). They exist in most societies, but their efficacy depends on the amount of 'political capital' that political and social activists have invested in building and maintaining them. Their capacity is also closely linked to levels of development since 'only long-stable societies have dense and powerful networks of organizations for collective action' (Olson 1997: 47). Sustaining viable relationships between party systems, pressure groups and governments always involves major political challenges because of the tension between the representa-tiveness and governability of political systems identified earlier. We will show how this problem affects democratic transitions in Chapter 12, internal party and group organization in Chapter 8, and the relation-ships between party systems, pressure groups and rulers here.

Democratic accountability depends on the effectiveness of party systems – on the existence of more than one party that can make a credi-ble bid for power or operate as an informed critic of and potential alter-native to the existing regime. Systems vary and include cases where one party has dominated power for decades, where two or three parties have alternated in power at national or local level, and where many parties have only minority support and have to form coalition governments. Their operation also depends on the constitutional rules that balance the need for representativeness and governability by enforcing different rela-tionships between rulers, legislators, parties and voters. Too much repre-sentativeness can produce unstable minority coalitions or 'gridlock', and too little can exclude important social groups and/or facilitate authoritar-ian or opportunistic rule (Duverger, 1954; Sartori, 1976).

Representativeness depends on the range of parties operating in any system, and the leverage that supporters and elected legislators exercise over governments. In parliamentary systems, regimes are selected from the party or party coalition with majority support, and are removed if they lose it; in presidential systems, the head of state is directly elected and cannot be removed even if they lose majority support. The former produces strong government when the ruling party or parties have a majority, but instability when minority parties cannot form stable coalitions; in the latter, presidents also depend on parties for support, retain power when they do not have a majority but find it hard to govern (Foweraker, 1998). In plurality-based voting systems, candidates represent geographic constituencies and win office if they obtain a simple majority. Here the need for an overall majority reduces the number of parties, but underrepresents minority interests. With proportional representation (PR), seats are allocated in direct relation to their votes, producing more parties and a fairer representation of interests.

Competition is far from perfect in all these systems, as is the ability of citizens, as principals, to control the governments that should serve as their agents. Firms need only satisfy the specialized needs of their own customers, but parties have to represent all the diverse and often competing interests of the mass publics they represent. Parties differentiate themselves from each other by appealing to particular kinds of publics united by class interest or ethnic or sectarian identity. In fragmented societies, especially with PR, many minority parties based on ideological, ethnic and/or sectarian identities can coexist and be forced into uneasy governing coalitions that often cannot reach agreements and sustain coherent policy programmes. In less fragmented societies, two or three dominant parties attempt to create 'an encompassing interest' on the centre ground by building coalitions between many groups. Pluralist theorists argue that this will benefit society as a whole (see Olson, 1997: 45ff.), but it internalizes rather than eliminates conflicts of interest, often producing factional conflicts inside parties that leaders manage by producing often unstable and inconsistent compromises.[10]

Ruling parties or coalitions cannot keep all their promises because of the constraints imposed by constitutional rules, international agreements, economic exigencies, bureaucratic limitations, and the impossibility of satisfying multiple and conflicting demands with scarce resources. Opposition parties confront fewer reality checks, and exploit the resulting disappointments by making promises that will be equally difficult to keep should they win power. Democratic governance is therefore an inherently imperfect process, which often generates unrealistic expectations about the effects of participation, and equally unreasonable disappointments at the inability of governments to satisfy every need. These limitations can only be overcome where citizens develop realistic expectations, are willing to accept the compromises needed to resolve inevitable conflicts of interest, and to invest time and energy into the organizations that mediate, however imperfectly, the relationships between citizens and rulers.

These include pressure groups as well as political parties, since the constraints imposed by oligopolistic competition are eased by the role of civic associations that do not compete for power but represent the political interests of different groups. We will look at the factors that influence their structures and effectiveness in Chapter 8. Here we will only make three points about their role in mediating relationships between citizens, parties and rulers:

1 Pressure group systems require rules that guarantee the 'absolute freedom of opinion and sentiment on all subjects ... liberty of expressing and publishing opinions ... [and] the liberty of combination among individuals ... for any purpose not involving harm to others' (Mill, 1859/1910: 75).
2 Democracy depends on the capacity of organizations without a directly political role, like families, religions and clubs, to create the 'social capital' needed to sustain social solidarity and discipline in open political systems (Putnam, 1993). It also requires an independent and responsible media and research community to subject policies to rigorous analysis that is not driven by populist demands or special interest groups.
3 We should therefore treat the democratic process as 'a two-stage ... game':

   In the first stage, politicians compete in elections for control rights over political institutions, public resources and the right to make ... policy. The second stage consists of a number of single issue subgames in which civic and private actors lobby elected officials for policies that favour them. There are as many sub-games as there are distinct policy questions. (Faguet, 2002: 212)

Thus associations also compete with each other for access, and their ability to be heard depends on their relationship with the regime in power, their social status, economic resources, access to the media, or ability to mobilize public support.[11] Governments cannot satisfy everyone, but they can build close links with a wide range of civic actors with competing demands in order to produce compromises all of them will accept.

Conclusions

This chapter has emphasized the serious problems that elected governments confront as they try to reconcile competing demands for scarce
resources with economic and social discipline, and the limits imposed
on their autonomy by their obligations to global and local political
agencies. These have produced long periods of unstable or ineffective
governance in DCs as well as LDCs[12] that have been eased (but not
eliminated) by allowing rulers to enforce decisions between elections
even when they have lost majority support, and by giving leaders a
powerful influence over their own parties, as we will see in Chapter 8.[13]
This has often produced uneasy compromises, widespread distrust in
politicians, shifting loyalties and changes of regime. But these problems
are inevitable, given the logical impossibility of creating governance
systems that can please all citizens all of the time. Authoritarian ideolo-
gists use these inconsistencies to justify the need for benevolent dictatorship. This may or may not produce strong government, but it also allows
the state to be captured by special interests and used to marginalize
minority or even majority groups.

The competitive processes that govern democratic markets are therefore inherently imperfect, but, given our failure to invent anything better,
they still represent a best rather than second-best solution because they
allow all interests to organize and speak. However, these processes will
fail unless societies can overcome 'the asymmetrical dilemma' implicit in
the neoclassical model of the state by persuading enough individuals not
to use a 'purely individualistic calculus of benefits and costs' and accept
their collective obligations rather than free-ride (North, 1981: 45–6). In
fact, as North points out, people often operate collectively even 'when
there is no evident benefit to counter the substantial costs' involved
(p. 46). Thus the effectiveness of democratic markets ultimately depends
on the substantive capacity of societies to persuade individuals to forego
their short-term material interests. We will consider the implications of
this problem in DCs in Chapter 8, and in LDCs in Part III.

Notes

1 Personal communication from Professor Rosalind Higgins, chief justice, International
   Court of Justice.
2 For a detailed case, see Brett (1983, 1985). I am now less critical of liberalization but still
   believe that national and global political interventions are needed to overcome uneven
   development, and that the dollar-based monetary order is unsustainable in the long term –
   a view that has been strongly reinforced by the current global financial crisis, partially
   caused by the chronic fiscal and balance of payments deficits in the USA. Bhagwhati (2002)
   and Krugman (1997) provide accessible and authoritative defences of free-trade theory;
   and Chang (2002) provides an important reassertion of the structuralist case.

3   These include the debt crisis in Latin America in the 1980s and in Africa and many other weak states in the 1980s and 90s; the crisis in Asia and the former Soviet Union in the late 1990s; and now the financial crisis precipitated by irresponsible lending and especially the collapse of the subprime mortgage market in the USA.

4   See Putnam's (1993) comparison of north and south Italy and Faguet's (2002) of two Bolivian municipalities.

5   Shepsle and Bonchek are invoking Arrow's (1963) claim that it is impossible to produce agreed outcomes for groups composed of individuals with differently ordered preferences using an individualistic calculus.

6   This is a loose interpretation of Poulantzas's formulation of Marxist state theory that has close affinities with elitist theories of democracy (see Poulantzas, 1980: Part 2; Held, 1987: Part II).

7   For a detailed case study of this process in postwar Britain, see Brett (1985, Ch. 6).

8   For a recent study, see Jessop (2003); for the 1970s debate, see Poulantzas (1978); and Holloway and Picciotto (1978).

9   For a review, see Held (1987: 113–39, 205–14).

10 Harris (1972: 256) demonstrates that the contradictory or 'muddled' policy agenda of the British Conservative Party was a function of its existence as a 'coalition' that had to permit 'the expression in elliptical form of contradictory interests without precipitating open conflict within the party'. The Labour Party leadership found it equally difficult to reconcile the ideological demands of Left and Right, and the needs of trade unions and constituency parties (participant observation).

11 Key texts include Bentley (1908); Trueman (1951); Key (1952); and Finer (1958).

12 In Italy and Germany before the war, in France under the Third and Fourth Republics, and in contemporary Italy.

13 According to Rousseau (cited in Held, 1987: 75), once 'Members [of Parliament] are elected, the [English] people is enslaved; it is nothing'.

Chapter 6

Politics, Bureaucracy and Hierarchy in Public Management Systems[1]

Democracy, bureaucracy and good governance

The problematic nature of the relationship between representativeness and governability identified in Chapter 5 manifests itself in its starkest form in the uneasy relationship between citizens, their representatives, and rulers on the one hand and permanent officials on the other. Rulers are expected to implement the policy package chosen by the electorate, and use paid and mostly permanent officials to do so. These relationships, however, should not be dominated by either politicians or bureaucrats, but be based on reciprocity and relative autonomy. As Weber (1922/1968: 1404) said, 'independent decision-making and imaginative organizational capabilities ... are usually also demanded of the bureaucrat', but politicians play the dominant role because they have to generate the authority and support needed to justify and enforce policies and take 'personal responsibility' for doing so.

Politicians should identify policies, raise the taxes to finance them, mobilize the political support and negotiate the compromises needed to sustain them, and monitor and discipline the officials who implement them. Yet they should not impose their own individual or partisan preference on officials, or interfere with their science-based decisions, but allow them to respect the law and exercise 'the power of technical control over nature' and over 'human behaviour' needed to provide effective services (Habermas, 1971: 56; see also Brett, 1988; Moe, 1995: 130–1). Yet politicians also have to take responsibility for success or failure, and this gives them the final say over what their officials do and how well they do it.

Thus democracy 'cannot be consolidated without an effective instrument at its disposal', so 'mass democracy and the development of ... the modern bureaucracy went hand in hand' (Suleiman, 2003: 6–7). By the end of the 19th century, an 'orthodox' model for the public provision of universal and collective services had emerged, involving centralized control, top-down management and monopoly powers whose principles were authoritatively specified by Weber (1922/1968). This enabled rulers to deliver standardized services to millions of clients, was the

124

primary mechanism for the implementation of right- and left-wing structuralism, and dominated public management systems in the 19th and most of the 20th century. It was then subjected to intensive criticism by neoliberal theorists in the 1970s and 80s, who

> give remarkably little recognition to either work or organization. Not long ago, commentators pontificated about the Age of Organization and agonized about being trapped in Weber's iron cage. Organization was The Solution to every problem; it brought peace, prosperity and progress. Now there are just the State and the Market. (Mars, 1992: 23)

Their critique of hierarchical state-led systems has produced a partial, ongoing and heavily contested transition from Weberian orthodoxy to market-based new public management (NPM) systems. How valid were these criticisms, and how effectively is public management responding to 'the great orthodoxies of today'?

Private and public bureaucracies have similar hierarchical structures, but operate very differently because they have to meet different demands and are governed by different incentive and accountability mechanisms. Firms have limited objectives, autonomous control over their management systems and procedures, respond directly to market forces, and use profits to measure their success or failure. Public agencies are bound by law, provide open access resources using compulsory taxation, and are controlled by politicians with broad and often open-ended agendas, and only indirectly by market competition, as we saw in Chapter 5 (Bower, 1977). Thus firms have to maximize efficiency, but 'political actors ... are typically not concerned with efficiency in the usual economic sense, and the political systems clearly do not weed out the inefficient. The actors and the systems are very different; presumably, their organizations are very different too' (Moe, 1995: 119).

The rules and practices of modern states have been dominated by the Weberian model but few if any of them meet these exacting demands in full because the relationship between democratic accountability and bureaucratic autonomy is an inherently contradictory one. Legal constraints stop state agents from abusing their power, but also give them less room for manoeuvre than their private sector counterparts. Bureaucratic autonomy enables officials to solve technical problems, but also limits the ability of citizens to control what they do, and can also depoliticize 'the mass of the population' and produce a 'bureaucratized exercise of power ... [that] has its counterpart in a public realm confined to spectacles and acclamation' (Habermas, 1971: 75). Thus even in well-managed states, officials often resist change, encourage free-riding, create coercive hierarchies and protect political and administrative incompetence and even corruption (Banfield, 1975). Schaffer (1969: 190–1) shows that 'the bureaucratic model is not really an efficiency or "output' model", but emphasizes 'repetition and reiteration rather than ... innovation', and institutional maintenance, 'come what may', producing 'a sacrifice of output to maintenance functions'.

However, this does not discredit the orthodox theoretical model, because its role is not to describe reality but to guide practice. It asserts that the closer societies come to meeting its demands, the better off they will be, but it does not deny the difficulties involved in doing so.[2] There is overwhelming empirical evidence to support this claim. According to Weber (1922/1968: 971), 'in the continental states power at the beginning of the modern period ... accumulated in the hands of those princes who most relentlessly took the course of administrative bureaucratisation'. Schaffer (1969: 191) also shows that:

> Bureaucracy is a style which maintains the possibilities of scale, of scattered but continuous relationships, of accepting a degree of coincidence, inconvenience and the unexpected into the running of affairs. It allows for the expert but inner directed, the non-arbitrary, and the authority of supervision as a right of appeal. The rules are both formalised and accepted in practice. That provides stability. Behaviour is expert and therefore reliable and also impersonal. The style is, then, instrumental: but not necessarily for programme achievement. That was the main positive advantage of the Weber model and also of those Western and later nineteenth-century reforms which, as it happens, coincided with the model, like changes in recruitment, function and parliamentary appropriations.

Thus the limitations inherent in public management systems do not justify the intensity of the 'relentless attacks on and denigration of the state', as well as 'the state's chief instrument – the bureaucracy' that have taken place since the 1970s (Suleiman, 2003: 2). Some of these weaknesses are embedded in the nature of public management itself, and some are generated by the contradictory nature of interactions between interest groups, party systems and governability identified in Chapter 5. Some stem from contextually determined failures to meet the political or administrative requirements of the model itself, notably in LDCs, as we will see in Part III. Others have emerged because existing structures cannot meet the demands of changing economic circumstances and new social groups – the main reason for the current crisis in public management systems and theory – and ongoing shifts from 'old' to 'new' forms public management – the issue that concerns us here.

These problems are often ignored or misunderstood in orthodox theory because political science deals with the role of 'politicians, constituents and their voting behavior', and pays little attention to the processes and struggles that impact on the exercise of public authority and the structure of the public bureaucracies needed to enforce it (Moe, 1995: 130, 121). Public administration traditionally 'rested on the premise that administration is simply the carrying out of public duties by others'. It has recognized the artificiality of 'the presumed separation of administration from policy and politics', but has found it hard to offer 'a fully satisfactory substitute' (Mosher, 1978: 9). In actuality, modern states depend on the existence of political/administrative systems that consist of

> a two-tiered hierarchy: one tier is the internal hierarchy of the agency, the other is the political control structure linking it to politicians and groups ... [This consists of an] extended hierarchy of public authority that begins at the top with politicians and interest groups and moves down through bureaucratic leaders to the lowest reaches of the organization. (Moe, 1995: 122)

These two tiers are not separate, but 'constitute a single control structure for ensuring that the agency acts in the best interests of its creators' (p. 150). Theory tells us how these relationships should operate. Why is it so difficult to arrange this in practice?

The political economy of bureaucratic reform

Moe (1995: 122) shows that bureaucratic structure is not only determined by technical considerations, but also by attempts by particular interests, and the politicians who represent them, to 'create an agency with a desirable mandate, but also to design a structure for ensuring that the agency subsequently does what its creators want it to do'. These agencies can be designed to enable the poor to use state power to provide them with welfare services by taxing the rich; they can also be designed to stop the state from doing so. Thus bureaucratic structure is unavoidably political and will be politically contested:

> Structure cannot somehow be taken out of politics, divorced from the necessities of compromise, and designed according to technical requirements and efficiency. Interest groups and politicians know that there is no meaningful distinction between policy and structure. Structural choices have all sorts of important consequences for the content and direction of policy, and, because this is so, choices about structure are implicitly choices about policy. (Moe, 1995: 127)

Administration and the laws under which it operates in authoritarian states are 'nothing but a technical instrument for the execution of certain political objectives' (Neumann, 1937/1957: 61). Rameses II built immense monuments, Stalin collectivized agriculture, and Hitler carried out the Holocaust by creating bureaucratic apparatuses that were able and willing to obey the commands that they issued. The bourgeoisie in early liberal capitalist states were able to create rules that stopped politicians from interfering with their property rights and ensured 'that the official business of public administration be discharged precisely, unambiguously, continuously and with as much speed as possible' (Weber, 1922/1968: 974). Later, they and the new working classes expanded the state's role to provide infrastructure, protect markets, promote industrialization and maintain full employment by nationalizing a wide range of public utilities and basic industries, and to provide comprehensive welfare services. The 'non-interfering liberal state ... disappeared from view', there was general agreement on 'the merits of a "mixed economy"', and the 'state's budgets increased to a high permanent level in peacetime and went on increasing' until the 1980s (Desai, 2004: 218). These processes were guided by theory, but driven by the demands of competing political interests, and each set of structural solutions generated new political conflicts over levels of hierarchy and the relationships between political authority and bureaucratic discretion.

The liberal demand for the separation between political and bureaucratic authority is driven by the need for hierarchy to achieve practical goals by maximizing technical expertise and control, and minimizing the opportunism and informational asymmetries that might lead to goal displacement and/or inefficiency. These threats also exist in private firms, as we know, but the risks are particularly large in the public sector because states not only regulate all economic and social processes, but politicians and officials can also 'impose their decisions on everyone else' (Moe, 1995: 120):

> All of the monopoly power of a bureaucracy derives from the monopoly power of the government that finances its services ... Some of the monopoly power of the government will be appropriated by a bureau, depending on the structure of the bureaucracy and the review process. (Niskanen, 1975: 629)

Politicians and officials could therefore use their monopoly powers to enrich themselves, favour supporters or cronies, politicize technical decisions, or use taxes to sustain unproductive activities. Authoritarian systems facilitate this kind of behaviour; democratic accountability and the separation of political and administrative power were designed to control it. In Britain, the Northcote-Trevelyan Report in 1854 eventually led to the 'abandonment of patronage' and recruitment and promotions based on 'open competitive examinations'; in the USA, where Woodrow Wilson claimed that only the 'separation of the political sphere, where policy derives, from the administrative sphere, where policies are administered, could address many evils of the spoils system', this occurred at the end of the 19th century (Hughes, 1994: 27, 33).

Depoliticization required systems where most officials had permanent tenure and their activities were protected by official secrets acts, appointments and promotions were vested in independent boards,[3] and salaries were based on seniority, not performance. The key objective was 'the continuous and inexorable application of legal norms', where officials could not question their orders and it was 'clear in every instance who gives orders to whom, and with respect to what, so the possibility of negotiation, interpretation, or consultation is eliminated' (Offe, 1985: 301). This produced process- rather than output-oriented systems which then conflicted with the demands of interventionist states promoting industrialization and welfare services, where 'the fulfilment of concrete tasks' was the primary criterion for judging administrative performance, and efficiency was no longer defined as 'following the rules', but as the 'causing of effects' (Offe, 1985: 305). Hence:

> the incongruity between the internal modes of operation and external functional demands on the state administration have their basis in the quality of the socio-economic environment, rather than in 'deficient' bureaucracies. The environment binds the state administration to specific modes of operation, yet simultaneously makes claims on its performance which cannot be satisfied by these same modes of operation. (Offe, 1985: 303)

Thus the depoliticized and process-oriented structures created during the liberal period generated inflexibility, conservatism and rigidity that created serious tensions during the transition from liberalism to structuralism. However, the uneasy political coalition between capitalist and working-class interests committed to state intervention also produced a real expansion in state capacity and new forms of administration designed to circumvent the limitations imposed by national state bureaucracies. Central ministries did expand, and were complemented by local governments, independent boards and agencies, and semi-autonomous nationalized industries.[4] These agencies expanded the state's ability to 'create effects', but they retained hierarchical and depoliticized structures, which, given the limitations of democratic markets, gave wide discretion to ministers and senior officials who protected the state machinery 'from the dangerous influence of the masses' (Leys, 1983: 234). In Britain, these processes vested state authority in the hands of an 'administrative class' selected from elite schools and universities, and the heads of other state agencies were 'co-opted or appointed by secret processes which are informal and, it appears, subjective and arbitrary' (Leys, 1983: 267). In the USA, a fragmented political system, combined with powerfully organized interest groups and anti-statist ideologies, generates a process where:

> Opposing groups are dedicated to crippling the bureaucracy and gaining control over its decisions, and they will pressure for fragmented authority, labyrinthine procedures, mechanisms of political intervention, and other structures that subvert the bureaucracy's performance and open it up to attack. In the politics of structural choice, the inevitability of compromise means that agencies will be burdened with structures fully intended to cause their failure. (Moe, 1995: 138)

The Weberian model exercised a profound, but varied influence over the state apparatuses that were used to manage the expansion in public services in DCs until the 1970s, although the nature of the actual structures that emerged was a function of local political struggles and bureaucratic traditions (see Suleiman, 2003: 128ff.). However, the fiscal crisis of the structuralist state, referred to in Chapter 4, the costs and rigidities of the model itself, and a generalized political and theoretical shift from collective to individualistic ideologies produced a systematic attack on the orthodox model by liberal and radical theorists that paved the way for a new round of structural reforms. This took 'the organizational issue into hitherto unknown territory' where the questions 'were as unprecedented as the answers ... because the organization of work has to change in sympathy with the great orthodoxies of today, liberal individualism, representative democracy and free market economics' (Mars, 1992: 23; see also Ostrom, 1974; Hood, 1991).

The most damaging attack on Weberian bureaucracy was provided by liberal economists who began to apply individualistic rational choice theory to state institutions in the 1960s and 70s, by challenging the assumption that officials were fully committed to public service goals and subject to effective political oversight.[5] Orthodox theorists had previously attributed bureaucratic failures to inappropriate structures and limited expertise, and therefore focused on improvements in processes and technical competence, assuming that 'proper value orientations could be inculcated into public administration through professionalism, itself a value of a sort to be achieved by training, education, and the redesign of administrative arrangements and procedures' (Siffin, 1957: 8–9). Officials themselves liked to see 'administration as a technical process', based on 'management science' that justified official claims 'to the status of a "profession"' (Mars, 1974: 346).

New public management (NPM) theorists, however, shifted the emphasis from expertise and processes to incentives and therefore motivation, arguing that officials were also subject to opportunism and imperfect information, thus challenging the assumption that they invariably carried out 'the orders of ... [their] superiors who act for the whole organisation in reaching policy decisions' (Buchanan, 1987: 2; Tullock, 1987). Downs (1967: 83) assumed that officials were primarily committed to maximizing their own interests 'even when acting in a purely official capacity' and that this led them to block effective external control by distorting information and by discretionary behaviour in policy implementation, and in the search for new policy solutions (Downs, 1967: 77–8; Dunleavy, 1991: 147–54). In the 1970s, Niskanen (1975) applied this analysis to the relationships between bureau heads and their political masters, arguing that the primary concern of officials was to maximize budgets rather than outputs, and of legislators to maximizing their chances of re-election, rather than exercising effective controls over officials. He then produced a model showing that public sector budgets must be unnecessarily high, and reinforced his claim by citing studies that showed that public bureaus are 'significantly less efficient than profit-seeking firms in supplying the same output' (p. 635), and 'governmental utilities are more capital intensive than private utilities' (p. 639). Niskanen (1975: 627) attributed this failure to the inherent weaknesses of democratic accountability:

> The monitoring function ... is a public good within a legislature; the benefits of monitoring accrue to the whole population as a function of their tax costs. This creates a substantial 'free-rider' problem internal to legislatures and the expectation that monitoring activities will be under-supplied.

And, further, that 'individual citizens ... face a similar and much more massive free-rider problem in monitoring the performance of their representatives' (p. 628).

This analysis was based on 'right-wing suspicions of liberal democracy', and 'has formed the core of a coherent and influential new right theory of the state' (Dunleavy, 1991: 5). However, the hierarchical nature and depoliticization of orthodox state structures led to an equally damning critique from the Left. These theorists believed that democracy only offered people 'a particularly exiguous form of accountability (periodic voting) which has been used to distance them from the polity' (Ranson and Stewart, 1994: 235). They acknowledged that the welfare state did generate some real benefits for the poor but that the need for tight rationing and centralized controls meant that

they 'experience the state not as "our" state but as an oppressive institution' (London Edinburgh Weekend Return Group, 1980: 53). According to Mandel (1992: 161):

> municipal, state, para-state, and public sector administrators ... act
> in direct contradiction with the interests of the mass membership of
> the working-class movement, tending more and more to turn an
> indifferent face to the people they are supposed to serve. They
> thereby discredit the very idea of social services and public owner-
> ship of the means of production, which appears to at least part of
> the working class as a remote domain of wasteful bureaucratic
> machines, not fundamentally different from private corporations
> geared to profit.

By the end of the 1960s, radical theorists no longer looked to the state
to liberate the working class, but took the benefits provided by its
welfare services for granted, and focused on the need to 'smash the
bourgeois state' because it could only provide 'bits of social welfare, the
proverbial crumbs from the rich man's table, easily given or taken away
at his discretion' (Rowbotham et al., 1979: 17).

Thus both left- and right-wing theorists ignored the achievements
of orthodox state systems, and emphasized the democratic deficits,
rigidity and hierarchy inherent in the Weberian model. Their solutions
were, of course, radically different. NPM theorists asked for results-
based incentives, market-driven services that put consumers rather
than politicians and bureaucrats in command.[6] The libertarian Left
rejected capitalist ownership, market competition and hierarchical
structures and called for a 'political anti-bureaucratic revolution' that
would enable 'the producers ... to be the real masters of the major
means of production and exchange' (Mandel, 1992: 196). Two
contrasting solutions emerged – market-based NPM on the one hand
and participatory theory on the other. We will deal with the former
here and the latter in Chapter 8.

NPM dominated neoliberal attempts to reconstruct state structures
generated by the crisis of the interventionist social democratic state.
They began in the 1980s in the UK, Australia, New Zealand and the
USA and were then widely taken up, and have became the new orthodoxy for development administration as well, as we will see later (Suleiman, 2003). While they were introduced by the New Right, the left-wing
critique also allowed them to be adopted by social democratic parties
looking for a 'third way', so 'radical business-emulating reforms' were
promoted 'both by the Left and the Right', although the former
confronted greater opposition from their traditional supporters (Suleiman, 2003: 142–3).

Hood (1991: 4–5) shows that the new model rejected the 19th-century controls designed to depoliticize bureaucracy and maximize honesty, stability and security in seven ways. It called for:

- greater managerial responsibility
- explicit measurement of performance
- a focus on results, not procedures
- disaggregation of centralized structures
- private sector personnel practices
- greater discipline and cost-effectiveness
- competition within and between agencies (see also Ranson and Stewart, 1994: 13–16).

Actual adoption varied, for political, contextual or technical reasons, but a general shift has occurred, from the orthodox 'monocratic' model to a variety of pluralistic solutions that used markets to increase accountability, and performance-based managerial practices to improve responsiveness and cost-effectiveness.

The World Bank's *World Development Report 2004* (World Bank, 2004: Chs 3 and 6) produced a useful analytical framework to address this issue (Figure 6.1). It saw accountability as the key problem, and distinguished between services that could be directly marketed and those that could not. In the former, accountability could be enforced through market competition, thus creating a 'short route' that did not require direct political supervision; in the latter, it would require a 'long' democratic route where citizens had to depend on elected policy-makers to do

Figure 6.1 *Alternative routes to accountability*

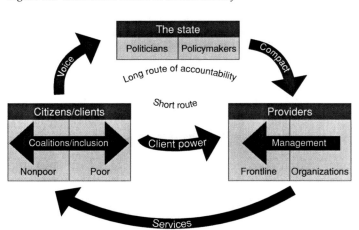

Source: World Bank, 2004: 49

the job for them, providing eight alternative mechanisms for doing this that depended on different kinds of market and political failure:

> Clients may seek to hold service providers accountable for perform-ance in two ways. Client power connecting clients and providers is the direct, 'short' route of accountability. When such client power is weak or not possible to use, clients must use voice and politics in their role as citizens to hold politicians accountable – and politicians/ policymakers must in turn use the compact to do the same with providers. The combination of the two is the roundabout 'long' route of accountability. (World Bank, 2004: 48)[7]

The 'short route' solutions that emerged in DCs like Britain were designed to reform the state agencies that had been created to deal with the different kinds of market failures identified in Chapter 4. In the structuralist era, centralized state agencies, often with monopoly powers, were set up to run industries that produced marketed products and utilities that constituted natural monopolies, as well as agencies that provided merit goods like health, housing and education. Different kinds of markets were created to meet these different challenges:

1 Many industries like coal, steel and armaments had been national-ized in the past to achieve political goals like security, employment or national self-sufficiency or to eliminate the possibility of monopoly pricing in companies with dominant positions in domestic markets. These companies were privatized by neoliberal regimes anxious to reduce wage rates, restrictive practices and state subsidies. They believed that globalization imposed competitive pressures on even the largest domestic producers.
2 Major public utilities like water, power and communications had been nationalized because they were seen as natural monopolies producing essential goods, so that public control was needed to guar-antee access, reduce prices and allow cross-subsidization. They were also privatized, but were subjected to state regulation to overcome the threat of monopoly power and to guarantee access. Where possi-ble, companies were split into smaller units to encourage compet-ition, as with telecommunications, electricity supply and railways.
3 Many services had been nationalized to provide free or heavily subsi-dized access to merit goods like health, education or public housing. Their staffs had guaranteed salaries and tenure, and had been allo-cated monopoly powers that gave their clients little choice and virtu-ally no exit option. These could not be fully privatized, but internal 'quasi-markets' were introduced in state schools, university depart-ments and hospitals, which guaranteed access to all clients, but tied

rewards to the ability of suppliers to compete for business. Privatization was taken even further in many cases by 'contracting out' services to for-profit or non-profit agencies or by creating public–private partnerships – generally involving subsidized or free access and political regulation of quality and prices (see LeGrand and Robinson, 1984).

These shifts were complemented by attempts to strengthen 'long route' procedures by reducing the rigidities and waste associated with orthodox bureaucracy by shifting from process- to results-oriented systems, reducing job security and seniority, introducing merit-based payments and promotions, and mechanisms for the measurement, monitoring and evaluation of performance and outputs. Agencies were expected to specify and meet targets, measure progress against baseline data using clear performance indicators, and give politicians and 'customers' access to published results as well as to internal processes formerly protected by official secrets acts (for a review, see Suleiman, 2003: Chs 6 and 7). And, given the need to strengthen political accountability, they also called for the devolution of as many services as possible to local governments ('subsidiarity'), on the assumption that they would be more responsive to local needs.

The benefits and risks of new public management

The jury is still out on the efficacy of the NPM revolution, but we can address some of the normative, technical and measurement issues raised by the new approach that relate to both ends and means – to the goals that states pursue and the nature and impact of the structures created to achieve them.[8] Private agencies pursue their own limited objectives and choose their own management systems, but the public domain depends on 'public discourse leading to collective choice based on public consent', and has an 'unbounded' obligation to respond to the demands and meet the needs of 'the whole of the community' (Ranson and Stewart, 1994: 88).

Public sector reforms should increase growth, equity, autonomy and cooperative interdependence by maximizing output, fairness and organizational resilience, and the opportunities for public discourse and learning, accountability and consent (Hood, 1994: 11ff.; Ranson and Stewart, 1994: Ch. 4). Most observers accept all these goals, but in different measure. Old public management (OPM), based on Weberian principles, emphasized fairness, reliability, honesty and universal access; NPM the need for 'freedom rather than equality, individualism rather than community, efficiency rather than justice, and competition rather than cooperation' (Ranson and Stewart, 1994: 48). NPM began as a 'new right theory of the state', based on 'a subtly skewed' model of democratic processes 'fostered by the overwhelming predominance of new right and neo-conservative thinking amongst exponents of public choice theory' (Dunleavy, 1991: 5).

However, the choice between NPM and OPM does not depend on ideology alone, because the relationships between goals, structures and agency performance are complex, contingent and contradictory, and the structures created to achieve them will always impose constraints that will favour some goals and some citizens at the expense of others. We believe that NPM is not 'intrinsically tied to right-wing political values', but that, as Duleavy (1991: 5–7) argues, public choice theory could, with some changes in premises and assumptions, also be used to 'contest key elements of new right and pluralist thinking based upon public choice methods', and 'lead to conclusions sympathetic to democratic socialist positions in practical politics'.

Personal observation as a consumer and provider of public services, and as a political activist, suggests that NPM reforms have generated gains and losses in productivity and equity. Inefficient structures can only be replaced when the objective conditions required to create better ones are available, otherwise unrealistic expectations and the assumption that the grass must be greener on the other side of the fence lead us to jettison one structure only to find that the grass is actually browner on the other side. Strong societies cannot achieve all the goals they desire all of the time, while weak ones can hardly achieve any of them any of the time. We can only decide whether we have overestimated the weaknesses of OPM and underestimated the costs of NPM by re-examining the public choice critique of OPM and the implications of the prescriptions of its rival.

OPM relied on process-oriented systems to reduce the risks of political 'interference' as well as political and official malfeasance that had afflicted earlier systems, and used hierarchical and science-based systems that also produced major gains where democratic processes worked reasonably well. Opponents took these benefits for granted, and used questionable assumptions to criticize them. Thus Margolis (1975: 647ff.) notes that Niskanen's budget maximization assumption ignored differences between agencies and officials that often led many of them to perform well for professional or ethical reasons; Niskanen used a political model that ignored the role of the executive and civic groups in improving the quality of state performance (p. 651ff.); and Margolis questioned Niskanen's exclusive emphasis on soft budget constraints, and noted that underspending on important services could be as serious a problem as overspending and waste (p. 657).[9] Soft budget constraints can exist in favoured agencies like the US military, and were once sustained by Keynesian theories of deficit spending, but taxpayer revolts and fiscal crises mean that they are now the exception, not the rule.

Political failures, oppressive and non-accountable hierarchies, bureaucratic opportunism and waste do exist and undermine the legitimacy and efficacy of state agencies, but as Margolis (1975: 656) also says, this is true in 'some situations, false in others', so he is 'not persuaded ... [by Niskanen's] arguments and therefore prescriptions'. Suleiman (2003: 86–7) also shows that citizens are less dissatisfied with governance in DCs than critics assume, and that 'in most countries people have more confidence in the civil service than in labor unions, the press, and, more often than not, big companies'. Thus poor performance under OPM cannot be treated as a pure function of organizational design, but will be contingent on the quality of political parties, pressure groups, media and representative institutions, and on the extent to which bureaucratic structures have been designed to deliver services rather than block them. Hence, an evaluation of its effects must transcend sweeping generalizations and show how different circumstances and different kinds of reforms are likely to affect performance.

We will consider these problems in societies with effectively functioning democratic processes here, and then address the complex issues generated by democratic and bureaucratic failures in weak states in Part III. To do this, we will first consider the risks and benefits associated with 'short route' market-based reforms and 'long route' political solutions outlined earlier – full privatization, regulated privatization, subcontracting and the use of quasi-markets; and then look at the effects of results-oriented management into traditional bureaucracies.

The critical problems generated by NPM do not relate to the privatization of fully marketable products, but to regulated privatizations, subcontracting and the introduction of quasi-markets to supply natural monopolies, open access or merit goods. These raise at least three potential problems:

1 Privatization increases managerial autonomy and the pressure to perform, because even monopolistic firms have to compete for their customers' disposable incomes. However, they could still abuse their monopoly positions, and rely on state subsidies or controls in order to guarantee access to essential or merit goods. Thus their efficiency continues to depend on effective state regulation and support, both to stop them from abusing their monopoly power and to enable them to set prices and terms of service that guarantee access to the poor when they are given tax-based subsidies. Effective regulation also depends on the strength of the political processes that neoliberals deeply distrust, since democratic deficits will enable them to be captured by vested interests (Paul, 1992). Thus neoliberals place political and official opportunism at the centre of their critique of OPM, but then promote solutions that depend on the existence of 'a

culture of public service honesty', a culture that their own reforms could easily undermine (Hood, 1991: 16).

2 Subcontracting the production of monopoly or merit goods to private suppliers will only succeed where such suppliers already exist, which may be true in DCs, but was much less certain in the east and is especially problematic in LDCs.[10] Further, providers have to be selected by politicians, and they confront problems of 'adverse selection' stemming from imperfect information and the possibility of opportunism and corruption. This makes it hard to identify good suppliers ex ante, or to punish ex post contract failures that can only be identified after the damage has been done. These systems can work well but also depend on the pre-existence of effective democracy and public service honesty.

3 Using quasi-markets for merit goods in sectors like health and education, or within individual agencies like universities, can also generate perverse results. Competition works in private markets because it enforces efficiency and meets effective demand by eliminating bad performers and rewarding good ones for expanding production until it meets effective demand. Quasi-markets may impose greater pressures on agencies by allowing consumer choice and publishing performance evaluations. However, governments find it hard to close poorly performing schools and hospitals, or to raise the extra budgets needed to upgrade them or build new ones. In the absence of effective mechanisms that facilitate both entry and exit, competition can produce vicious circles because poor performers lose out to good ones, receive fewer resources, and produce worse rather than better services. The result is intense conflict for access to the limited supply of 'good' providers, unavoidable injustices, and unrealizable political demands on governments.

Attempts to shift from process- to results-oriented management also raise difficult issues. OPM used 'fixed salaries, rules of procedure, permanence of tenure, restraints on the power of line managers, clear lines of division between public and private sectors', and an elitist form of democratic accountability to 'ensure honesty and neutrality in the public service' (Hood, 1991: 16). These, properly supervised, reduced the risks of politicized decision-making, as well as opportunism and corruption, but increased costs by constraining the ability of politicians to implement new programmes,[11] the ability of officials to exercise their professional discretion, and by creating a culture of secrecy that could also conceal skiving, waste or corruption. NPM introduces results and performance-based systems designed to reduce costs and strengthen incentives to overcome these weaknesses, but can only do so where two difficult problems can be resolved:

1   The new system increases the authority of politicians over bureau-
    crats and therefore ignores the possibility that they will abuse their
    powers, returning us to the problematic issue of the effectiveness of
    democratic processes.[12]
2   It also assumes that politicians and voters can make reliable judge-
    ments about the quality of official performance, which raises serious
    problems of measurement, monitoring and evaluation. Public agencies
    have diffuse and contradictory goals, so their outputs are correspond-
    ingly difficult to measure and evaluate. This requires reliable baseline
    information against which to measure results, and performance indica-
    tors that accurately reflect all the outcomes of the relevant activity and
    do not impose excessive reporting costs on agents. These conditions are
    difficult to meet. Indicators are often misleading and can distort
    performance, arm's-length evaluation is difficult to guarantee, agents
    can conceal poor performance, and statistics can be manipulated.

Thus, while few people want to revert to old-style procedures, serious
questions still need to be answered about the viability of the ongoing
shift to NPM:

> Broadly, NPM assumes a culture of public service honesty as given.
> Its recipes to some degree removed devices instituted to ensure
> honesty and neutrality in the public service in the past ... The extent
> to which NPM is likely to induce corrosion in terms of such tradi-
> tional values remains to be tested [especially] in many Third World
> countries and perhaps Eastern Europe too will be particularly inter-
> esting to observe ...

> [Thus] whether the emphasis on cost-cutting, contracting-out,
> compartmentalizing and top-slicing is compatible with a safety
> culture in the front line needs to be tested. The new breed of organi-
> sationally created disasters over the past 15 years or so, of which
> some dramatic examples have occurred in the UK, suggest that the
> issue at least needs investigating. (Hood, 1991: 16)

Conclusions

Orthodox bureaucracies have provided the indispensable basis for the
provision of large-scale infrastructure and mass welfare services in the
modern state. However, the problems of rigidity, compartmentaliza-
tion, hierarchy, goal displacement and inertia identified by their critics
like Crozier (1967) are very real and cannot be ignored. NPM has
responded to these problems by introducing results- rather than

process-oriented systems into state apparatuses, and devolving many functions to for-profit and non-profit agencies partially regulated by quasi- or surrogate markets.

This has taken the principle of organizational pluralism into the heart of the state apparatus itself. Governments that subcontract services to private agencies are no longer able simply to give orders, or even to stand 'above society and ... "steer" it', but have to enter into relationships in which they can only operate as 'first among equals' (Kickert et al., 1997: 3). The significance of these changes can be exaggerated, especially in LDCs where centralized bureaucracies are still the norm, but Kickert et al. are right to emphasize the importance of an ongoing shift from centralized and monopolistic state agencies to 'policy networks' involving 'public, semi-public, and private actors participating in certain policy fields' (p. 1).

At its best, in states with high levels of social and human capital, these systems hold out the promise of a far less hierarchical world in which policy-making and implementation will be about cooperation or non-cooperation between interdependent agencies with different and often conflicting rationalities, interests and strategies. Policy processes will not take the form of the implementation of ex ante formulated goals, but of a consultative process in which actors exchange information about problems, preferences and means, and trade off goals and resources (Kickert et al., 1997: 9). These processes are emerging in many modern states, and their effects are also exerting a powerful influence on the operation of hierarchies in modern firms, as we will see in the next chapter.

However, we have also seen that reforms based on NPM also confront the problems of political or bureaucratic opportunism and/or incompetence that can characterize OPM; indeed, they may well also take honesty in the public sector as a given, and fail to recognize that its reforms 'could produce corrosion in those values' (Hood, 1991: 16). This review does not suggest that we should return to the old system, although it does suggest that its benefits should be taken far more seriously than has been the case in the recent past. However, it also suggests that effective reforms have to be tailored to meet the needs of different services and contexts, and that all solutions will only succeed where they are able to overcome the political problems generated by scarcity and incompatible demands by creating collective forms of organizational capacity that transcend the limits of methodological individualism.

Notes

1   I am indebted to Theo Mars for many of the ideas and readings that have informed this chapter.

2   Weber's model of 'rational bureaucracy' is often treated as if it were an inadequate account of how real systems actually operate, but he fully understood the difficulties involved in creating a viable relationship between a democratized political authority and a technical-legal-rational bureaucracy, as the appendix to *Economy and Society* shows (1922/1968: 1381–6). Suleiman (2003: 128–30) shows that convergence with the Weberian model was 'only partially realized' in the DCs, but that it nevertheless provided the normative framework for the 'comparison of bureaucracies' and subsequent reforms.

3   The USA is a partial exception to this rule (Moe, 1995: 143–6).

4   The demands of a war economy and then for postwar reconstruction produced a major expansion in state powers and capacity everywhere. For a description written in postwar Britain, see Harrison (1960: Chs 6 and 7) and Brett (1985: Ch. 6).

5   See especially Downs (1967); Tullock (1965, 1987); Niskanen (1971, 1973, 1975); and Banfield (1975).

6   See Dunleavy (1991), Hood (1991) and Suleiman (2003) for accounts of the politics associated with the transition to NPM.

7   The analysis focused on development problems, but is equally relevant to DCs; an equally rigorous analysis is provided by Paul (1992). Suleiman (2003) reviews the way in which these reforms have been adopted in DCs.

8   Suleiman (2003) provides us with a critical overview of the results.

9   For an excellent extended analysis of the limits and strengths of NPM, see Dunleavy (1991, Part II).

10 A rigorous evaluation of the perfomance of private foreign contractors in postwar reconstruction in Iraq and Afghanistan would make interesting reading.

11 Personal communication, Robin Murray, chief economic adviser, Greater London Council, 1982–6. See also Crosland (1956).

12 Suleiman (2003: Chs 9 and 10) provides an extended review of the consequences of politicization under NPM.

Chapter 7

Hierarchy, Quasi-markets and Solidarity in Capitalist Firms

Past disagreements over the consequences of capitalist development have focused on two key issues: the role of markets in allocating resources and restructuring social and organizational systems; and the nature of the relationships between owners or managers and workers in capitalist firms. We dealt with markets in Chapter 4, and now ask why capitalist firms set up authority systems that use different degrees of coercion or consent to coordinate the activities of their workers. This issue has, of course, always been central to the debate between capitalists and socialists in both DCs and LDCs. The former treat hierarchy as inescapable and argue that market competition makes it impossible for capitalists to exploit their workers or customers; the latter argue that their market power not only enables large firms to exploit their workers, but also to collude with western states in subordinating or even under-developing the third world. The collapse of statist socialism has now marginalized the radical Marxist critique of capitalism, and changes in technologies and management systems are altering the authority systems within modern firms. We will examine the general implications of these changes for theories of the firm in this chapter, and the role of capitalist firms in development in Chapter 14.

Capitalist societies are dominated by large-scale hierarchical firms that exploit economies of scale in production, research, credit and marketing, and have replaced 'the invisible hand of market mechanisms ... in coordinating flows and allocating resources' with 'the visible hand of managerial direction' (Chandler, 1980/1990: 95). The exercise of 'rational' bureaucratic authority involves pyramidal hierarchies divided into horizontal strata, where orders should flow from top to bottom, and accountability and information should flow from bottom to top. Higher strata direct lower ones, monitor and reward or sanction their performance, and are responsible for the organization's overall performance and its ability to generate the resources it needs. Vertical or 'monocratic' control is combined with merit-based appointments, full-time employment and an agreed set of rules specifying both rights and responsibilities (Weber, 1968; Jaques, 1990a, 1990b). And, as Williamson (1987: 270) says:

Hierarchy is ubiquitous in all organizations of any size. This holds not merely within the private-for-profit sector but among nonprofits and government bureaus as well. It likewise holds across national boundaries and is independent of political systems. In short inveighing against hierarchy is rhetoric; both the logic of efficiency and the historical evidence disclose that non-hierarchical modes are mainly of ephemeral duration.

However, hierarchical control can take many different forms. It can be associated with public, private or social ownership, with centralized, decentralized or participatory authority systems, and deploy very different levels of coercion or consent to solve collective action problems. Capitalist firms have always been dominated by hierarchy, but have also experimented with many innovations designed to reduce the coerciveness of traditional authority relationships. We will show how institutional economists operating within an individualistic paradigm explain the need for top-down management systems, and then examine the factors that are finding solutions that reduce managerial discretion.

Imperfect information, opportunism and hierarchy in capitalist firms

The need for hierarchy is generally attributed to the existence of scale and technological complexity, but workers could self-organize any production process if they were fully committed to the success of the joint enterprise, understood its technological requirements, and found it easy to make collective decisions. Neoclassical theorists assume that this is so and treat firms as 'an instrumentality of individuals' (Nelson and Winter, 1982: 54). Here, forms of cooperation would quickly emerge that would enable 'the members of the organisation ... [to] achieve their own goals best by directing their efforts towards the success of the enterprise' (McGregor, 1990: 369). But if they lack the necessary knowledge and/or are unwilling to place the collective interest ahead of their own, they will only cooperate successfully 'under external coercion and control' (p. 359). Most firms operate at some point between these two extremes, but most institutional theory starts from a weaker or stronger version of what McGregor calls 'theory X' – the assumption that workers treat work as a disutility and lack the knowledge and motivations required for successful self-organization (see also Bowles, 1985). Here voluntary exchange or solidarity fails, and hierarchy emerges to reduce the costs of transacting agreements generated by problems of opportunism and bounded rationality.

Coase (1937: 391) introduced the idea of 'transaction costs' into the theory of the firm by showing that the costs of constantly renegotiating day-to-day contracts between many workers could be significantly reduced if firms shifted to long-term standardized contracts by paying an agreed wage in exchange for a commitment to 'obey the directions of the entrepreneur within certain limits'. He said little about the nature of these costs, but his successors have since attributed them to problems of opportunism, stemming from the existence of individual self-interest, and informational inequalities. Here hierarchy exists to oblige workers to subordinate their personal goals to those of the organization, and solve the technical and organizational problems involved in complex production processes.

Buchanan and Tullock (1962: 98–9) showed that self-interested individuals involved in cooperative decision-making would find it difficult to reconcile individual and collective interests, even where each 'could expect to be "better off" or at least "no worse off" as a result of the decision'. This is because each 'will seek to secure the maximum gains possible for himself while keeping the net gains to his partners in the agreement to the minimum' and therefore try to 'conceal his own true preferences from the others in order to secure a greater share of the "surplus" expected to be created from the choice being carried out'. Buchanan and Tullock therefore argued that the 'costs of consent' involved in bargaining would reduce the social product and everyone's benefits, and that these could be eliminated if everyone agreed to transfer control 'to a single individual and to abide by the choices that he makes for the whole group':

> Under such conditions the delegation of all effective decision-making power to a single decision-maker, and an accompanying hierarchy, may appear perfectly rational. *If some means can be taken to ensure that the dictator will, in fact, remain 'benevolent', the argument becomes even stronger.* (Buchanan and Tulloch, 1962: 99–100, emphases added)

Alcain and Demsetz (1972) then argued that an incentive system based on the separation between profits and wages that characterizes the capitalist labour relationship virtually guarantees benevolent despotism and productive efficiency, rather than exploitation as Marx claimed. Workers able to monitor each other's performance could run their own firms, but the costs of doing so would be so great that they would all benefit by transferring control over the labour process and ownership of the final product to a capitalist in exchange for a guaranteed wage. This gave owners a powerful interest in enforcing discipline and minimizing costs, because their income is a function of the difference between costs and the value of the product. This system generates conflicts of interest over the relative shares of wages and profits, but both parties depend on the success of the whole enterprise, and the existence of a free labour market allows workers to exit so that owners cannot exploit them, only assign them tasks 'at a price that must be acceptable to both parties' (Alchian and Demsetz, 1972: 777).

Williamson (1987) then introduced problems of scale, time and opportunism into this analysis, by showing that large-scale production processes depend on long-term cooperation between agents that involve investments in costly assets that are tailored to specific purposes. The results of these investments and the relative costs and benefits of each agent cannot be known in advance, making it impossible for them to generate complete ex ante contracts about their distribution. Where expectations fail, relationships between agents will be threatened and require new ex post agreements where agreements cannot be guaranteed unless the parties have absolute trust in each other. The possibility that either party will cheat, fail to perform adequately or withdraw is a function of the level of bounded rationality and opportunism involved in the transaction. Where these are high, vertically integrated firms will emerge that internalize all the relevant activities so that 'adaptations can be made in a sequential way without the need to consult, complete, or revise interfirm agreements', and 'market contracting gives way to bilateral contracting, which in turn is supplanted by unified contracting (internal organization) as asset specificity progressively deepens' (Williamson, 1987: 78).

These costs of reaching agreements and balancing effort and rewards in complex production processes are compounded by their dependence on the rare and costly expertise needed to control complex machinery and organizational systems, and on the privileged knowledge confined to managers, about the relationship between individual decisions and the long-term needs of the organization as a whole (Jaques, 1990a). Hence, bureaucratic control 'means fundamentally domination through knowledge', which includes 'technical knowledge' and 'the knowledge growing out of experience in the service' (Weber, 1922/1968: 225).

Taylor (1912/1990: 204–6), the father of 'scientific management', claimed that authority imposed four duties on managers:

1 to centralize and systematize the 'traditional knowledge' formerly embedded in the heads and physical skills of the workmen, and then apply them to the whole enterprise
2 to organize the 'scientific selection and then the progressive development of the workmen', so they could do 'the most interesting and most profitable' work they were capable of
3 to bring 'the science and the scientifically selected and trained workmen together' to ensure that they actually adopt best practice

4　to increase greatly the day-to-day responsibilities of management so that 'every workman's acts are dovetailed in between corresponding acts of the management'.

He showed that scientific management could even generate large productivity gains in processes as simple as shovelling coal by ensuring that all workers adopt the best methods and are given the best equipment. He also claimed that it was managers, who were unwilling to assume these extra responsibilities, rather than workers, who were likely to gain from improvements in productivity, who were most resistant to his methods.

The need to manage transaction costs and maximize the value of scarce and costly expertise explain the success of hierarchical systems and the limited role of participatory decision-making in organizational systems. On the other hand, they also imply that managers should build positive relationships with workers, and involve those who do have relevant expertise in decision-making. Thus institutional economists have a pessimistic view of human nature, but one that makes it possible to explain why large-scale, multiunit, joint stock companies, using hierarchical management systems based on professional managers rather than private owners, 'changed the nature of capitalism' in the 20th century (Chandler, 1980/1990: 97ff.). Henry Ford used 'Taylorism' to revolutionize industrial systems in the early 20th century, and even paid his workers twice the market wage in order to guarantee compliance (Miller, 1992: 67ff.). The resulting increases in productivity led to massive improvements in living standards and working conditions that undermined the Marxist theory of exploitation in the countries that fully adopted them. Indeed, hierarchy was adopted with the greatest enthusiasm in the Soviet Union where Lenin himself accepted that 'it was a "mere anarchist dream" to hold that "all administration," all "subordination" could be disposed of' (cited in Wolin, 1960: 426).

From command to consent: reforming hierarchical management systems

Hierarchy is 'the only way to structure unified working systems with hundreds, thousands or tens of thousands of employees', because it enables organizations to

> add real value to work as it moves through the organization, to identify and nail down accountability at each stage of the value adding process, to place people with the necessary competence at each organizational layer, and to build a general consensus and acceptance of the managerial structure that achieves these ends. (Jaques, 1990a: 129)

Hierarchical theorists therefore attribute the need for centralized command to ignorance and opportunism in the workforce, but this varies dramatically in the real world where it depends on the levels of human and social capital and technology, and the quality and justice of the incentive systems that exist in each society. The coercive capitalism that Marx described in 19th-century England was associated with a semi-literate working class, chronic unemployment, immense inequality, and the imposition of repetitive and alienating labour processes. An open frontier, full employment and limited supplies of labour produced far lower levels of coercion and class conflict in the USA. In all DCs:

- universal education, higher social capital and better regulation have now increased knowledge and integrity
- full employment, the welfare state and unionization have altered the balance of power in labour's favour
- automation has virtually eliminated the industrial proletariat that was expected to socialize the capitalist system (Gorz, 1982).

These changes have not eliminated hierarchy, but they have led to changes in organizational design based on pluralistic solutions that combine hierarchy with markets and solidaristic solutions in a variety of ways.

We also know that the excessively centralized command structures will be dysfunctional, rigid, and constrain flexibility, experimentation, innovation and reform (Crozier, 1967; Dias and Vaughan, 2006), and encourage opportunism, increase the need for surveillance, and intensify alienation and class conflict. Thus hierarchy may be inescapable, but its efficacy will depend on organizations' ability to minimize these costs by balancing the centralized controls needed to guarantee effective performance with appropriate rewards, sanctions and degrees of discretion for the actors involved at each level. Organizations need to oblige many people to forgo alternative objectives if they are to deliver a joint product, but they use incentives involving qualitatively different levels of coercion or consent to do so.

Different levels of coercion or consent are associated with different institutional arrangements:

- enforced compliance with slavery or serfdom
- the exchange of equivalents with wage labour
- entrepreneurship or professionalism with autonomous contracting
- voluntary contributions with solidarity.

Each form of control is likely to produce a different kind of cooperation, with passive or calculated compliance at one end, and creative or active cooperation at the other (Table 7.1). Slaves only do what they can

Table 7.1 *Incentive systems and forms of cooperation*

Incentive system	Force	Intrinsic	Material	Reciprocal/ethical
Type of actor	Slave/serf	Entrepreneur/professional	Wage labourer	Volunteer/partner
Type of cooperation	Passive	Creative	Calculated	Active

be forced to do, wage workers only do what they are paid to do, professionals and entrepreneurs do as much as they are given the opportunity to do, and volunteers do what they have a calling to do. The greater the commitment and skills, the lower the levels of command and control required to achieve organizational goals. Hierarchy may be needed to create clear lines of responsibility, but soft management and creative cooperation rather than enforced or calculated compliance will often produce the best results.

These alternative forms of cooperation can be articulated by using three different authority and incentive systems – market exchange, central command, and solidaristic cooperation (Ouchi, 1980). Choosing between them depends on the extent to which the actors share common goals and can measure and guarantee effective performance:

- *Markets* involve voluntary contracting and mutual self-interest, where everyone can maximize their own goals but cannot 'exploit' each other because contributions are easy to measure and exit options exist.
- *Centralized command* emerges where actors do not share the organization's goals so they have commonly been forced to cooperate, but will only contribute effectively where they agree to obey a higher authority that can fairly measure, compensate and enforce their performance, and that 'has the legitimate authority to provide this mediation' (Ouchi, 1980: 130).
- *Solidarity* is possible where actors share the organization's goals so their rewards are partially determined by the intrinsic value of what they do, so they need not be accurately measured, but based on 'non-performance related criteria that are relatively inexpensive to determine' (Ouchi, 1980: 131).

These relationships are formalized in Table 7.2.

Table 7.2 *Goals, rewards and organizational structure*

	Market	Bureaucracy	Solidarity
Commonality of purpose	Low	Moderate	High
Ease of performance evaluation	Easy	Moderate	Hard

Source: Based on Ouchi, 1980

Now, particular kinds of firms will be dominated by particular kinds of contracts, but those of any size will make use of all three modes to manage their internal and external transactions:

- spot or long-term market contracts to buy or sell labour or commodities when they can guarantee quality and price
- hierarchy to facilitate cooperation and overcome deficits of information or integrity
- ethical or affective motivations when non-material incentives exist and performance is difficult to measure and compensate in money.

And managers and workers have mixed motives too:

- the need to satisfy selfish goals
- a willingness to accept or contest higher authority
- a normative commitment to at least some aspect of the joint enterprise.

Effective organizational design depends on the ability to combine these alternatives in different proportions that take account of the technological demands of the activity and the sociological features of the environment. This challenge raises two major sets of issues that relate to the role of financial or other material incentives, and institutional reforms designed to create authority systems that elicit active and creative participation rather than passive or calculated compliance.[1]

Material rewards are not the only way to generate compliance, but their level and how they are administered will always be critical to performance, since they determine status inside the organization and life chances outside it. Etzioni, for example, found that a group of American workers chose to leave jobs that offered them greater satisfaction and take 'frustrating assembly-line jobs basically because ... [they] offered higher and more secure income' (cited in Williamson, 1987: 269). And Kanter's (1972) work on utopian communities shows that lower than average wages require an exceptional ideological commitment and some insulation from 'normal' society. Where the value of actual contributions can be accurately measured, piecework or commission-based payments can be tied directly to output, but this is difficult in team production. Hence salaries are usually standardized by grade, and increments and pensions tied to years of service to reward fidelity and retain experience, and the possibility of bonuses and promotion used to reward effort and excellence. However, while financial rewards are central to motivation, their level is strongly determined by the state of the labour market, the need to control costs and the strength or weakness of labour unions. Thus managers can often do little to alter wage rates, but can often improve performance by using non-material incentives and better responsibility systems.

Non-material incentives are often linked to the degree of autonomy and discretion that higher management is willing to cede to lower levels. This, in turn, depends on the level of knowledge and commitment that exists in the firm, and the creation of authority structures based on creative cooperation rather than command. Authoritarian 'Fordist' hierarchies disempower and deskill workers. This was certainly the case in commandist forms of capitalism where 'the particular organisation of work' resulted in alienated types of labour processes (Bowles, 1985: 32),[2] and in Soviet factories where the need to 'fulfil plan orders received from above' also created a 'command relationship between the manager and his subordinates' (Nove, 1983: 82).

However, these coercive systems only work well with standardized production processes, they also impose heavy supervision costs, reduce the worker's willingness and ability to make a positive input into the activity, and generate the class antagonisms that were used to justify socialist demands for the elimination of private ownership. Many capitalist firms have now discovered that higher levels of human capital in their workforces and the technological changes that have eliminated most repetitive manufacturing process enable them to flatten their hierarchies, and devolve higher levels of discretion to lower levels. This, combined with rising wages and the creation of joint stock companies that are partially owned by the workers' pension and insurance funds, has significantly reduced class conflict in many contexts. These apparently technical changes have therefore had profound political as well as economic consequences.

The key mechanisms that have been used to generate higher levels of creative and voluntary commitment in firms are associated with shifts from centralized command to long-term quasi-market relationships that enable all the agents involved to create a 'mutual reliance relation' (Williamson, 1987: 190). These arrangements encourage entrepreneurialism, and depend on different variables, notably the ability to measure the market value of each contractor's contribution to the joint enterprise and reward it appropriately, and on levels of trust that are 'an essential ingredient' in long-term relationships, 'given the possibility of opportunistic behaviour' (Lorenz, 1991: 186). These forms can be classified by the degree of control sacrificed by a potentially dominant actor, and have involved the use of participatory management systems, shifts from vertical integration to multidivisionalization, franchising, long-term contracting and partnerships, the creation of networks of independent firms, and cooperative or worker-managed firms.

Kanter (1985) showed that firms that allowed lower level managers to participate in decision-making and encouraged horizontal as well as vertical communication systems performed better than those that did not. Multidivisional (M-form) firms devolve responsibility for managing specialized aspects of the production process to lower levels inside large-scale firms, because 'multidivisionalization, assuming that the M-form is feasible, serves as a check against the bureaucratic distortions that appear in the unitary (U-form) of enterprise' (Williamson, 1987: 95, 1975). The franchising systems used by Coca-Cola and McDonald's are possible where the franchisor develops a production system, controls the technology, marketing, credit and inputs, but cedes ownership and control over day-to-day production of the final product to local owners. Where firms can build stable long-term relationships with trusted suppliers, they can subcontract a wider and wider range of activities to them, while retaining control over the operation as a whole (Semmler, 1989; Womack et al., 1990; Alter and Hague, 1993). Even lower levels of hierarchy prevail in contexts where a range of specialized firms with a clear knowledge of each other's capacities and trustworthiness create long-term or short-term partnerships that increase scale, spread risks and increase autonomy (Piore and Sable, 1984; Lorenz, 1991; Granovetter, 1992). Long-term informal subcontracting also emerges to overcome the rigidities created by centralized planning, as in the Soviet Union, where it produced illegal 'horizontal links between enterprises, a network of personal relationships, supply agents ... and also corrupt practices' (Nove, 1983: 78). In all these cases, managed markets emerge that enable firms to devolve authority to lower level units, while still achieving economies of scale.

The introduction of controlled markets is possible where production can be broken into discrete activities and accurately rewarded, as when producers can use market prices as a basis for contracts with independent suppliers. But this is impossible in many forms of team production where work is cooperative, the value of individual contributions cannot be accurately measured, and the levels of performance are determined by the skills provided by the workers rather than the supervisors. According to a senior Japanese manager, in complex modern industries, firms 'based on Taylor's principles ... will lose ... because the intelligence of a few technocrats ... has become totally inadequate to face the challenges [of competition]. Only the intellects of all employees can permit a company to live with the ups and downs and all the requirements of the new environment.'[3] So Japanese firms like Toyota overcome bounded rationality by building highly skilled teams, and overcome opportunism by building solidaristic groups – what Ouchi called 'clans' – by persuading workers to develop a strong normative commitment to the firm rather than a purely instrumental one.

The Japanese firms that succeeded in doing this did not need to tie rewards directly to performance and still got better results than companies that did not (Ouchi, 1980).[4] The ability of firms to actually do this depends in turn on the nature of working practices. In industry, Japanese firms pioneered joint and 'lean production' systems that reduced levels of hierarchy and increased the worker's discretion (Womack et al., 1990).[5] Their superiority displaced their British rivals who operated an adversarial system based on 'inadequate institutions' and perverse incentives (Turner et al., 1967). These tendencies towards devolution are most pronounced in knowledge-based industries 'composed largely of specialists who direct and discipline their own performance through organized feedback from colleagues and customers' (Drucker, 1990: 200; Hodgson, 1999: Part III). Here workers with professional skills gain strong positive benefits from being allowed to exercise their talents, and are often willing to accept lower rewards in order to be allowed to do so.

However, the libertarian alternative to capitalism has always been cooperative ownership, following principles formulated by John Stuart Mill in the late 19th century. He argued that increasingly educated workers would reject the dependence forced on them by the wages system, and that:

> The form of association which ... must be expected to in the end predominate, is not that which can exist between a capitalist as chief, and workpeople without a voice in the management, but the association of the labourers themselves on terms of equality, collectively owning the capital with which they carry on their operations and working under managers elected and removable by themselves. (Mill, 1848/1900: 465)

Mill believed that the greater efficiency of worker-owned firms whose workers would 'do the utmost instead of the least possible in exchange for their remuneration' (p. 475) would enable them to outcompete their capitalist rivals. This would produce a peaceful transition to socialism without the need to expropriate private owners or eliminate the benefits of market competition that was essential because 'monopoly, in all its forms, is the taxation of the industrious for the supporters of indolence, if not of plunder' (p. 477).

Experiments with different kinds of cooperative management systems have used different forms of collective ownership in different kinds of enterprises. These have included agricultural cooperatives, retail and wholesale marketing, mutual funds and solidaristic microcredit agencies, financial services, the management of common property resources (Ostrom, 1990), industrial enterprises (Bradley and Gelb, 1983), and law and accounting firms. Their results have been uneven and have yet to justify Mill's optimism for technical, organizational and contextual reasons.[6] They have sometimes worked well, but mainly in DCs among the highly educated, such as Scandinavian and Japanese farmers running marketing cooperatives, and professional partnerships between lawyers, accountants and doctors. However, similar attempts in LDCs have often failed because comparable skills did not yet exist. In fact, optimists like Mill ignored the problems of opportunism, imperfect information, and the coordination costs outlined above, so relatively few cooperatives have competed success-fully with capitalist firms (Putterman, 1986: 19; Brett, 1996).

However, they have sometimes survived because of monopoly powers or subsidies granted by the state:

- in Yugoslavia, for example, where 'socialist markets' were encour-aged and large-scale private firms suppressed (Vanek, 1973)
- in agricultural cooperatives in Israel (Zusman, 1988) and China (Nolan, 1988)
- in agricultural marketing cooperatives in Africa (Brett, 1970, 1992/3; Young et al., 1981)
- in solidaristic microcredit schemes (Jain, 1995; Reinke, 1998; Islam and Jackson, 2001).

Yet protecting them from competition has often imposed heavy costs on consumers, and encouraged opportunism and waste, as Mill predicted when he argued that cooperatives should be subjected to the same competitive pressures as capitalist firms.[7] Retail and financial coopera-tives played a key role in improving working-class access in the 19th and early 20th century in Britain and other DCs, but their role has now been marginalized by more efficient private banks and retail chains.

Conclusions

While full-scale collective ownership has lost ground over the past 25 years, the demand for more autonomy and devolution in firms is stronger than ever, manifesting itself in the management reforms outlined earlier, which have generated an immense literature; the latest versions are promoted at business schools and exported to LDCs by highly paid consultants. Different models have all succeeded in the hands of compe-tent managers, and where workers have the appropriate levels of skill and commitment. Transferring them to LDCs that lack these capacities will always be a risky business, although this does not mean that old-style hierarchies will necessarily work better than decentralized systems, as we will see in Part III.

Notes

1   See Williamson (1987: Chs 9 and 10) for an excellent review of the literature.
2   For the Marxist analysis of these relationships, see Braverman (1971); Gintis (1976); and
    Roemer (1979). Taylor himself claimed that 'it would be possible to train an intelligent

gorilla so as to become a more efficient pig-iron handler that any man could be' (cited in Gramsci, 1971: 302).

3   Konosuke Matsushita, founder of the Matsushita Electric Industrial Co., cited in Hodgson (1999: 179).

4   There is evidence to suggest that individuals in work groups prefer payment systems that do not generate large inequaltiies in return (Deutsch, 1985).

5   At Honda, workers 'are given the responsibility and autonomy to change anything in their work area or production process ... I'm not talking just about an equipment process, but synchronization of equipment and associates to achieve high efficiency' (Larry Jutte, vice president, Honda of America, cited in Vasilash, 1997).

6   See, for example, Bonin et al. (1993); Bowles and Gintis (1996); Bradley and Gelb (1983); Brett (1996a); Jensen and Meckling (1979); Kanter (1972); Putterman (1987); Vanek (1975); and Williamson (1987).

7   'To be protected against competition is to be protected in idleness in mental dullness; to be saved the necessity of being active and as intelligent as other people; and if it is also to be protected against being underbid for employment by a less highly paid class of labourers, this is only where old custom or local and partial monopoly has placed some particular class of artisans in a privileged position as regards the rest' (Mill, 1848/1900: 477).

Chapter 8

Incentives and Accountability in Solidaristic Organizations

Solidaristic organizations and institutional pluralism

The role and influence of voluntary or solidaristic organizations (SOs) is growing in DCs and LDCs. Their role and structures differ dramatically in different institutional systems since SOs include:

- nuclear families and global religions
- radical and conservative political and social movements
- democratic modern associations and ascriptive or theocratic traditional ones
- small local community-based organizations (CBOs) and international NGOs (INGOs)
- large and small cooperatives competing in the market economy.

Pre-modern societies were dominated by 'traditional' solidaristic agencies like families, kinship networks, clans and religions, based on ascriptive authority systems that combined social, economic and political functions. Fascist or Communist regimes subordinated most civic agencies to the state or party, but illegal groups, networks and social movements survived that opposed the status quo. Liberal conservatives and social democrats recognized their value and respected their autonomy, but did not treat them as key players in state-building or service provision.

However, theorists now give them a key role in building the trust needed to sustain political and economic systems (Putnam, 1993; Fukuyama, 1995), and in providing many services that could be provided by state or for-profit agencies. In the USA, 'non-profit but non-governmental institutions … include the majority of America's hospitals, a very large part of the schools, and an even larger percentage of colleges and universities', and half of the adult population 'are estimated to work in the third sector', mostly as unpaid volunteers. They therefore constitute a 'third sector' governed by 'a counterculture, different and separate from both the governmental and the business sectors and their respective values and cultures' (Drucker, 1990: 189, 191). They are especially important in the USA, but operate everywhere, often because their supporters believe that they provide an ethically superior alternative to state or for-profit organizations. They constitute the 'social' as opposed to the political and economic spheres in modern differentiated societies, where the level of social capital can be treated as a function of their density, resources, unity and capabilities (Putnam, 1993: Ch. 6).

The role of SOs as opposed to state or for-profit organizations has been influenced by long-standing and often adversarial debates between libertarians, statist socialists or corporatists and market-oriented liberals. Libertarians believe that only self-managed SOs can provide the real freedom implicit in 'the radical humanist message of the enlightenment' and a superior alternative to 'industrial capitalism', which they rejected as a 'new and unanticipated system of injustice', and to 'authoritarian' socialism, which they rejected because it depended on the coercive 'intervention of the State in social life' (Chomsky, 1970: x–xi). Radical libertarians marginalized themselves in the 19th and 20th centuries by calling for unfettered freedom and a violent revolt against the 'tyranny' of all states, private property and markets (see Guerin, 1970). However, serious libertarians did not oppose organization per se, but the coercive hierarchies and inequalities generated by state agencies and for-profit firms in corporatist, social democratic or liberal capitalist states. According to Voline, a Russian anarchist:

> Of course, say the anarchists, society must be organized. However, the new organization ... must be established freely, socially, and above all, from below. The principle of organization must not issue from a center created in advance to capture the whole and impose itself on it but, on the contrary, it must come from all sides to create nodes of coordination, natural centers to serve all these points. (cited in Guerin, 1970: 43)

These once marginalized ideas are now increasingly influential among modern communitarian theorists who support freedom and cooperative interdependence, but reject authoritarian state socialism and believe that the atomistic individualism espoused by radical neoliberals poses a threat to social responsibility and cohesion (Etzioni, 1994). They are still espoused by radical supporters of the 'new social movements' who see them as the basis for democratic resistance to power structures in capitalist states.[1] They see the growth of this sector as a vindication of the vision of the early anarchists like Kropotkin who believed that:

> In a [free] society, the voluntary associations which already now begin to cover all the fields of human activity would take a still greater extension so as to substitute themselves for the State in all its functions.

They would represent an interwoven network, composed of an infinite variety of groups and federations of all sizes and degrees, local, regional, national and international ... for all possible purposes: production, consumption, and exchange, communications, sanitary arrangements, education, defence of the territory, and so on; and [also] for the satisfaction of an ever-increasing number of scientific, artistic, literary and sociable needs. (Kropotikin, 1910/1971: 229)

These views have now been adapted by the mainstream development community, who believe that SOs must play an increasingly important role as one of the 'three primary institutional sectors of human society' (Korten, 1989: 15) in pluralistic modern systems that prioritize what Habermas calls 'communicative action' rather than centralized command.[2]

SOs are therefore being actively promoted in DCs and LDCs by theorists and practitioners who believe that they use participatory authority systems that maximize autonomy and cooperative interdependence, and that their dependence on affective or ethical motivations enables them to attract voluntary labour and therefore minimize costs, and ensures that their paid staff will work harder, with greater integrity and for less than those in private firms or state agencies. However, they do not always use participatory management systems nor promote what libertarians would see as progressive programmes. If we are to develop a balanced view of their potential, we need to look more closely at the different functions they perform, the different authority, incentive and accountability mechanisms they use, and the way they interact with state and for-profit agencies.

Functions and authority in solidaristic organizations

SOs share many common characteristics. Unlike state agencies, they are voluntary, private, and respond to the needs and demands of particularistic groups, and unlike for-profit firms, their members are driven by affective, ethical or cultural rather than material goals, and by incentives based on reciprocal exchange rather than individual self-interest. They depend on voluntary contributions of labour, money or social support based on affective, ethical or social commitment rather than pure material gain and short-term individual self-interest, or legal obligation based on the coercive authority of the state. Contributions sometimes depend on 'altruism', where people are rewarded by what they give rather than receive, but more usually on 'reciprocity' involving mutually beneficial exchange. Yet their functions have indeed covered 'all the fields of human activity', as Kropotikin predicted, and they also have very different goals, and use different authority, incentive and accountability mechanisms, so no single analytical framework exists comparable to those used in political science or economics to account for their operation:

- Families and kinship networks meet people's affective needs but can also operate as small businesses and sources of credit, social insurance and political or economic preferment.
- Religions enable people to meet their spiritual needs but have also run hospitals, schools, charities and businesses, and sponsored political parties.
- Informal networks, social movements and formal associations enable particular kinds of people – such as Muslims or Catholics, peasants, workers or industrialists – to achieve common goals and also act as 'pressure groups' representing their political interests (Bentley, 1908; Trueman, 1951), some of which support, while others resist, the established social order.
- Political parties aggregate the demands of all social groups and compete for state power.
- People's militias, vigilante groups and rebel armies can play very different roles – they can defend the state or local communities, police neighbourhoods or wage civil wars, while criminal gangs rob the poor as well as the rich, and produce and supply illegal commodities (Rodgers, 2006).
- Clubs and societies enable members to engage in a wide range of leisure activities.
- Cooperatives sell goods and services in the market, but are based on mutual ownership and democratic control rather than individual ownership and self-interest.
- Charities support marginalized groups and worthy causes, and provide essential services on a non-commercial basis, some operating as national or international NGOs managing million-dollar development programmes.

Libertarians assume that SOs use participatory decision-making processes and recognize the need for toleration and pluralism, but this is not always so. Traditional SOs like patriarchal families, chieftaincies and religions are hierarchical, not democratic, use ascriptive and/or theocratic systems of legitimation, and have used draconian sanctions to enforce their rules.[3] Authoritarian states used 'official' trade unions, mother's unions, youth movements and cultural associations to incorporate their citizens into a totalitarian social order – here 'all forms of representation were suppressed except that of the totalitarian movement itself: representation was not overcome, it was monopolised' (Fine,

2001: 115). Modern SOs do use democratic authority systems, but difficult issues arise about their effectiveness and the strength of their accountability mechanisms when compared with those imposed on elected politicians or competitive firms, as we will see in the next section (Brett, 1993, 1996b, 2003).

SOs can support reactionary as well as progressive causes, since they exist to promote every possible kind of interest, ranging from environment protection to the promotion of racial supremacy. A dense and encompassing system of groups and strong political parties is certainly crucial to the success of the democratic process, so democracy and institutional pluralism depend on people's 'freedom to unite for any purpose not involving harm to others', even where we may think their activities to be 'foolish, perverse or wrong' (Mill, 1859/1910: 75). However, particular SOs do not exist to promote freedom and social cohesion but to enable their members to maximize their own access to scarce resources. Thus they have to exclude 'outsiders' as well as incorporate 'insiders', and have a 'dark side' when they are used to promote racist, sectarian or sexist values and reactionary causes (Putzel, 1997). So their activities can promote freedom and cohesion in some contexts and intensify conflict, violence and subordination in others. Their tendency to do one or the other therefore depends on the interests they represent, the incentive and accountability mechanisms they use, and the nature of the wider framework of general rules that govern their relationships with the state and for-profit sectors. We will look at the role of 'traditional' organizations in Chapters 11 and 12, and at the operation of modern SOs next.

Incentives, accountability and efficiency in solidaristic organizations

Societies can use state, for-profit or SOs to provide the same services, so we need to be clear about the criteria that should be used to decide between them. Protagonists claim that using SOs will promote freedom, empower communities, minimize costs and maximize effectiveness. However, they will only do this if they are able to reward effective performance, punish opportunism and incompetence, and meet the needs of their beneficiaries rather than impose their own priorities on them. Libertarians assume that altruism or a sense of ethical obligation will make people work harder for less in SOs than they would in state agencies or private firms, that they will use participatory management systems that guarantee 'bottom-up' control, and will operate in an open environment that guarantees freedom of entry and exit. However, this need not be so, since SOs can fail because of well-intentioned incompetence, opportunism or malfeasance, be governed by self-perpetuating cliques, and abuse monopoly privileges. State agencies and private firms are controlled through democratic elections and market competition. What comparable mechanisms exist in the third sector?

Reciprocal rewards and rational calculation in solidaristic organizations[4]

SOs survive because the world is full of mothers, believers, political and social activists, volunteers and community leaders motivated by love or ethical commitment that lead them to do much more for their children, churches, causes, clubs or community than they would in exchange for a profit, a wage, a ministerial office, or a bribe. This 'other-oriented' behaviour is especially useful in pre-capitalist contexts where state agencies are underresourced or corrupt, but is also indispensable in DCs in the form of 'housework' in families and donations of labour and money to informal and formal SOs. Thus Drucker (1990: 191) claims that 'volunteers put in the equivalent of seven and a half million full-time work years' in the US that would cost $150bn a year if it had to be paid. Small SOs can depend entirely on voluntary labour, but larger ones need professional workers, and rely on donations that allow them to pay wages that cannot deviate too far from the norm unless there is exceptional ideological commitment and some insulation from 'normal' society (Kanter, 1972).

Thus affective and ethical orientations enable us to explain 'behavior in which calculated self-interest is not the motivating factor', where people are willing 'to engage in immense sacrifice with no evident possible gain', and to participate 'in voluntary organizations where the individual returns are small or negligible' (North, 1981: 11), accepting lower incomes and greater risks and discomfort than comparable workers in states or private firms.[5] This is because they obtain an intrinsic reward from what they do,[6] so labour becomes a utility not a disutility. This undermines the use of a 'reward or penalty system' that is usually 'stated in terms of monetary payments' because, as Arrow (1985: 50) argues, 'there is a whole world of rewards and penalties that take social rather than monetary forms' (see also Bowles, 1985). These conditions appear to eliminate the need to minimize the costs of participation, since the actors gain positive benefits from their contributions, and the need for hierarchy and accountability that operate in state and for-profit agencies, since they should rule out opportunism and malfeasance (Brett, 1993: 281ff.). However, both assumptions need to be looked at carefully.

Assuming that contributions to SOs are based on altruism makes it easy to ignore the possibility that they are not being used efficiently, but using excessive inputs generates opportunity costs by denying their use to produce something else. Second, it also makes it easy to underestimate the rewards that providers legitimately expect to gain from the contributions they make. In fact, they are rarely motivated by altruism, defined rigorously as behaviour that 'increases another entity's welfare at the expense of their own' (Dawkins, 1989: 4). Instead, they contribute to SOs in order to meet their own affective or ethical needs rather than material gains and will stop doing so if the returns are too low. Thus rational choices are just as prevalent in the voluntary as the state and for-profit sectors, and can best be understood as driven by reciprocity, which depends on an exchange of favours – of love and affection, or the ability of the organization to actually promote the ethical goals of its members or supporters – rather than selfless giving. Thus, as Lester (2000: 39) shows:

> There need be no particular problem with allowing that people can have interests that embrace promoting (or destroying, come to that) the interests of others. Of course, it will some times be useful for economic analysis to distinguish what kinds of self-interests are in operation; but there is no need to think that the altruistic kinds (ideology, charity, and so on) are ipso facto beyond economic analysis.

Mothers, priests or charity workers may indeed be rewarded by their sense of achievement in enhancing the capacities and spiritual or economic welfare of their beneficiaries, but they also lose out when their efforts fail to produce the desired result. So basing contributions to SOs on the existence of an 'unconditional' willingness to sacrifice personal interests to serve others makes it impossible to develop a plausible theory of the incentives and accountability mechanisms in the sector.[7] People will contribute to a relationship, an organization or a cause for as long as it continues to meet their needs, and withdraw support when it fails. This proposition gives rise to a theory of reciprocal altruism, which

> predicts: 1) A will help B (nonkin) if, in A's view, the probability of reciprocation by B times the probable benefit of this reciprocation equals or exceeds the initial cost to A ... 2) failure to reciprocate evokes moralistic aggression; 3) nonreciprocation will rise at the end of a period of association: and 4) nonreciprocators will have fewer allies. (McGuire and Troisi, 1997: 25)

Reciprocity can take specific or generalized forms. The former involves 'a simultaneous exchange of items of equivalent value'; the latter 'a continuing relationship that is at any given time unrequited or imbalanced, but is 'usually characterized by ... short-term altruism and long-term self-interest', where 'I help you out now in the (possibly vague, uncertain and uncalculating) expectation that you will help me out in the future' (Taylor, cited in Putnam, 1993: 172). These exchanges can be between individuals, between people and organizations, or they can operate at the social level, where 'norms of generalized reciprocity' are a key component of social capital because they ensure that people do favours to others because they can expect similar favours from someone else, and thus 'restrain opportunism and resolve problems of collective action' (Putnam, 1993: 172).

These norms and expectations can be formally specified in contracts through which marriages, religions, associations and political parties are constituted. They also operate informally in friendship or other networks where their purpose in generating mutual obligations will be systematically concealed where 'elective relations of reciprocity' have to depend on 'the sincere fiction of disinterested exchange' (Bourdieu, 1992: 112). Thus social advantage cannot be openly paid for in the political economy of gift economies where it depends on a reputation for generosity and right conduct. Here gifts are made to gain affection, influence or power, but would be polluted if they were seen as self-interested payment for social, economic or political advantage. Hence the viability of these transactions depends on an 'institutionally organized and guaranteed misrecognition that is the basis of the gift exchange' that can also conceal relationships of structural inequality and set up 'durable relations of reciprocity – and domination' (Bourdieu, 1992: 112).

Thus people operate in SOs to serve their own interests and contribute to others, and can gain status, power and wealth from what they do. Members of political parties can be elected to parliament or the presidency, managers of NGOs control large budgets, and leadership or membership of influential associations can bestow high social status and useful professional or business contacts. This does not negate the value of what they do, but it does oblige us to ask realistic questions about the incentives, dispositions and accountability mechanisms that should ensure that agencies perform in a cost-effective way, and are not subverted by opportunism, malfeasance or incompetence. The likelihood that they will do so, just as with state and for-profit agencies, depends on the nature of their internal authority mechanisms, the external processes that govern their access to resources, and the terms on which they provide services and their external relationships. These processes operate in very different ways in modern families, networks, social and political movements and associations, NGOs and cooperative firms.

Variations on a theme: democracy, hierarchy and accountability in SOs

Traditional SOs have had monopoly powers, used hierarchical authority systems and perpetuated structural inequality; modern ones operate as democratic systems that should create powerful links between activists and beneficiaries, and, in doing so, create the social capital essential for the survival of open societies. However, this is easier said than done. People join SOs because they provide a framework that enables them to achieve collective goals, but members will have different agendas and need to compete for the scarce resources at the organization's disposal. Organizations therefore need 'governance structures' with decision-making processes that enable them to arrive at generally acceptable compromises, allocate the rewards and sanctions needed to secure adequate contributions and effort from members or workers, and ensure that they are managed by people with the appropriate knowledge and skills. These processes, like those in state and for-profit agencies, also generate transaction costs stemming from opportunism, malfeasance and/or imperfect or asymmetrical information.[8] They assume many different forms in SOs depending on circumstances – scale, cultural expectations, levels of human and social capital and inequality in communities, goals and tasks, access to resources, and relationships with supporters or beneficiaries. We will conclude this chapter by looking at three different organizational types – families; social and political movements and associations; and non-profit charities and NGOs.

Families and households

Families depend on face-to-face relationships, affection and mutuality, but also have to create a viable division of labour and equitable authority systems. These generate high transaction costs because of the conflicting interests of husbands, wives and children.[9] This problem was originally solved through the patriarchal assumption that 'the father ought to command' for 'reasons which lie in nature', since 'the authority ought not to be equally divided' and that 'in every division of opinion there must be one preponderant voice to decide' (Rousseau, 1758/1973: 118). Theorists generally ignored the resulting structural inequalities, or assumed that families operated as open and mutual organizations. Thus Samuelson (1956: 10) saw the family as an egalitarian and consensual unit that recognized 'the deservingness or ethical worths of the consumption levels of each of the members'; and Becker (1981) assumed that membership was freely chosen by both partners, but the father was the ultimate decision-maker who would promote everyone's best interests out of altruism.

However, the idea that a 'family ruled over and provided for by father, suckled and nurtured by mother' was 'inherent in the natural order' (Greer, 1971: 219) was rejected by feminists, who claimed that it was actually 'founded on the open or concealed slavery of the wife' (Engels, cited in Greer, 1971: 220). In DCs, this 'natural order' perpetrated inequality despite a formal commitment to gender equality because it was based on deep-seated cultural dispositions and manifested in asymmetrical property rights and access to work and other resources (Mill, 1869/1985). The nature of the family was more effectively conceptualized by Sen (2006) as an arena of 'cooperative conflict':

> Women and men have both congruent and conflicting interests affecting family living. Because of the extensive areas of congruence of interest, decision-making in the family tends to take the form of the pursuit of cooperation, with some agreed solution, usually implicit, of the conflicting aspects. Each of the parties has much to lose if cooperation were to break down, and yet there are various alternative 'cooperative solutions,' each of which is better for both the parties than no cooperation at all, but which respectively give different, possibly extremely different, relative gains to the two parties ... [where] the more powerful party can obtain more favourable divisions of the family's overall benefits and chores.

Sen (1990) also recognizes that the division of advantages in families will be influenced by broader social norms and the rules that allocate property rights and access to external resources. His analysis is complemented by Folbre's (1994) work on intrahousehold allocations that shows that the norms allocating unpaid caring roles to women systematically disadvantaged them; and by Pollak's (1985) application of transaction cost theory to the dynamics of family-based governance structures and the processes that create 'marriage-specific capital' that lead partners to chose to remain in a particular marriage.

The contingent and context-dependent nature of the status of women in family systems has subsequently been demonstrated by the profound although still incomplete revolution in gender relations generated by the feminist campaign against institutionalized patriarchy over the past 40 years. This has given women easier access to exit through divorce, and fairer but not yet equal control over property and access to work. These achievements have yet to be replicated in most LDCs, but are being actively promoted by local women's movements, and are central to the agenda of the development community.

Parties, social movements and membership-based associations

Parties, social movements and membership-based associations play a key role in democratic and economic processes by representing the political and economic interests of their members and supporters and providing them with services, so 'virtually all serious observers understand that liberal political and economic institutions depend on a healthy and dynamic civil society for their vitality' (Fukuyama, 1995: 4). However, their ability to perform these roles is heavily constrained by incentive problems generated by the allocation of costs and benefits, and by management issues related to the adequacy of their representative structures.

The costs of SOs are mainly carried by leaders and activists who provide beneficiaries with services they need not pay for because they are public goods, which, 'if provided to anyone, go to everyone in … [the] group' (Olson, 1982: 19, 1965). This creates a potential 'free-rider problem' since rational individuals may well fail to contribute to these costs. No SOs would exist if this were always so, but Olson's analysis does force us to recognize the asymmetric distribution of effort and rewards that sustain them, and to identify the 'special arrangements or circumstances' that are needed to respond to it.

SOs emerge where groups need to respond to threats or opportunities that demand a collective response – to resist an oppressive regime (Brett, 1995a), bargain collectively for better wages, or protect the planet. They are run by leaders and activists with exceptional commitment, capabilities and resources who work on behalf of the wider group. Survival depends on an ability to combine 'three fundamental elements' effectively:

- a leadership 'with the powers of innovation' and 'centralisation'
- a mass of supporters willing to meet some of their costs
- an 'intermediate element, which articulates the first element with the second and maintains contact between them' (Gramsci, 1971: 152–3).[10]

The enterprise should play a key role in the social life and identity of the leaders and activists, providing them with status, contacts, friendships and a sense of ethical achievement from their work; and supporters can join formally, make donations and attend occasional meetings, while other beneficiaries free-ride on their efforts. Support and contributions increase during crises, but most beneficiaries will lack the time and/or expertise to play an active part in all the groups that influence their daily lives. Indeed, many theorists have argued that 'excessive participation' would threaten organizational and political stability and saw nonparticipation as an indicator of trust in leaderships (Held, 1987: 189–90).

Thus free-riding concentrates the control of SOs in the hands of active elites, and ensures that generalized participation only occurs where groups are small, direct benefits are large and communities are homogeneous (Olson, 1982: Ch. 2; Hardin, 1982).[11] Hence most rational members do free-ride, but SOs nevertheless survive where they provide active minorities with enough ethical and affective rewards, and where enough beneficiaries accept a formal obligation to provide the donations needed to create a 'bureaucratic administration', as Weber claimed (1922/1968: 123). This appears to threaten democratic theory because it seems to 'impose limited roles upon individuals' (Held, 1987: 145), but it can in fact be reconciled with liberal pluralism where two demanding contextual conditions can be met – first, that a broad array of representative organizations do exist, and, second, that their leaders do actually represent the interests of their beneficiaries rather than their own.

First, individuals have multiple interests that need to be represented, but can usually only participate actively in one or two of the SOs that they depend on to do this. The ability of any society to satisfy their needs therefore depends on the emergence of norms of 'generalized reciprocity' – or social capital – that allow all the necessary organizations to exist because the contributions that individuals make to one are reciprocated by comparable contributions made to others by their fellow citizens (Putnam, 1993: 182–3). Societies vary dramatically in this regard, as Putnam's contrasting studies of north and south Italy show, but most DCs have created a wide array of SOs that support social, political, economic, professional, religious, cultural or leisure-based activities. However, these systems do not guarantee equitable return. Thus:

- wealthy groups with enough skills, leisure and incomes are best served
- groups representing poor and marginalized groups have sometimes been built by activists willing to endure immense personal costs, as Thompson's (1968) study of the 'making' of the English working class shows
- many poor communities have not been able to create autonomous organizations to represent their own interests, but have had to rely on existing religions or ethnic associations to do so for them (Meagher, 2006).

These propositions have important implications for development theory, which will be addressed in more detail in Part III.

Second, minority control threatens democratic principles by creating what Michels (1911/1962) described in his classic study of political parties as the 'iron law of oligarchy'. He argued that the leadership's personal charisma and command over information and resources in nominally democratic left-wing political organizations allowed it to exert a decisive influence over policies and resource allocation, and even to impose policies that were 'at variance with the original objectives of the organisations and the interests and attitudes of their members' (Lipset, 1962: 32). These tendencies dominated avowedly 'vanguard' Communist parties, but critics used them to explain failures to implement radical policies by their nominally democratic socialist counterparts as well (Miliband, 1973; Coates, 1975).

Yet these claims should be treated with care, since Michels' assumption that elites must follow 'a logic of self-interest, of exploiting the masses to maintain or extend their own privilege and power' need not hold (Lipset, 1962: 34). Leaders and activists do invest more in, and gain more from, organizations than their beneficiaries, have 'interests which are somewhat at variance with those of the people they represent' (Lipset, 1962: 34), and can 'capture' control and use it to promote their own views or 'appropriate service benefits and to engage in rent-seeking' (Paul, 1992: 1047).

However, these discrepancies, and the ability of organized minorities to capture power within organizations, are often the outcome of genuine attempts to promote a particular vision of the collective interest rather than purely selfish interests. Furthermore:

- *leaders* who negotiate agreements with outside agencies usually have to make compromises that activists dislike
- *activists* are often more radical than rank-and-file supporters, so leaders who have to generate widespread support have to resist them
- *supporters* usually depend on leaders to make policies for them because they lack the knowledge, time and energy to make them for themselves.

Thus, organizational capture is a real danger that cannot be overcome by generalized participation where people 'plan, manage, control and assess the individual and collective actions they themselves decide upon' (Burkie, 1993: 205), so avoiding it depends instead on the effectiveness of 'the system of representation' that specifies the terms on which leaders, activists and supporters relate to each other (Lipset, 1962: 35).

We also saw that effective representation requires the elimination of legal barriers to the formation of competing organizations and democratic constitutions that enable participants to exit if they are dissatisfied, and policy-making processes that enable all the stakeholders to use voice to arrive at agreed compromises (Hirschmann, 1970). However, these processes usually work imperfectly because large organizations often provide monopoly services for their constituents and free-riding confines the exercise of voice to appointed officials and self-selected groups of activists. Well-managed organizations rarely engage in active debate and heavily contested elections; these are more likely to be associated with high levels of factional conflict and organizational crises.[12]

Yet SOs cannot always insulate themselves from external pressures in democratic societies. They lose members and subscriptions if they fail to deliver, and dissatisfied factions can exit and set up competing organizations; activists ensure that a wide range of collective interests are represented and use voice in well-managed organizations to reach acceptable compromises; and sleeping members often wake up and raise their voices when their interests are directly threatened. The relationship between exit and voice in enforcing accountability and producing viable solutions is highly complex, and depends on many different organizational characteristics and the nature of the services they provide, as we have seen. These and possible ways of improving accountability are comprehensively addressed in Paul's (1992) exploration of the use of exit and voice by beneficiaries to defend themselves from the negative effects of organizational capture by dominant elites. His analysis focuses on public sector providers, but provides us with a systematic analysis of the conditions that create weak or strong exit or voice (Paul, 1992: 1052, Figure 3), and a comprehensive list of reforms designed to overcome the tendencies to oligarchy that exist when either or both are very weak, many of which could also be applied to SOs (pp. 1058ff.).

Non-profit organizations and NGOs

Charities and non-profit suppliers of merit goods, like health, education or housing, to beneficiaries have existed for centuries, and range in size from global to local. They are created by enthusiasts or organizations like churches, and based on voluntary labour or donations from members. Large modern NGOs are

> not membership based, governed, or financed ... [but] guided and driven by staff, self-appointed Boards, or very small numbers of formal members, and the driving force for their work emerges generally from a religious or ethical base – their values. (Kilby, 2006: 952)[13]

The role of NGOs is expanding because neoliberals prefer them to state agencies since they are private, not public; and socialists prefer them to private firms because they maximize ethical goals, not profits. Supporters claim that NGOs:

- strengthen democracy
- empower beneficiaries

- provide cost-effective services
- operate in hostile environments where states have failed and firms cannot make profits.

Detractors believe that NGOs:

- undermine a state's capacity
- are not accountable to beneficiaries
- are often inefficient
- respond to the demands of donors rather than local communities.

Empirical evidence can be found to substantiate both sets of claims since extraordinarily impressive and wasteful NGO projects exist in many contexts.[14] The most successful NGOs mobilize large numbers of highly committed workers, volunteers and donors, but also control large budgets. Thus here, as elsewhere, we cannot 'assume that power will be deployed in a responsible manner' but must 'assume the opportunity for abuse' (Spiro, 2002: 162), in the absence of effective accountability mechanisms. How effective are the mechanisms that operate in the NGO sector?

Interactions between NGOs and their stakeholders generate far more complex, contradictory and ambiguous accountability problems than those between states and firms that are governed by competitive economic and political markets. These problems relate to the criteria against which performance should be judged, the rights and resources of different stakeholders – staff, trustees, beneficiaries, donors or states – and especially the degree of 'leverage' that each should be able to exercise over agencies. Accountability involves 'internal' and 'upward' accountability between professional staff and trustees, and 'external' and 'horizontal' accountability to beneficiaries, donors or states (Brett, 1993: 291ff.; Ebrahim, 2003: 814–15). What, then, are the most difficult issues involved in managing these relationships.[15]

NGO managers are legally obliged to report to trustees who should be 'motivated by "felt responsibility" as expressed through individual action and organizational mission' (Ebrahim, 2003: 814). Trustees should be trustworthy because they obtain ethical rather than financial rewards, and should have a strong interest in controlling opportunism and/or inefficiency in their organizations. Since their agencies are mission driven and privately resourced, they do not have to satisfy a broad range of interests, like political parties, but only those of their supporters or beneficiaries; indeed, the right of NGOs to promote oppositional causes is based directly on the liberal commitment to freedom of association and democratic principles (Kingsbury, 2002). An effective relationship between managers and trustees depends on the adequacy of the reporting and auditing tools, and the decision-making processes that operate in the organization (Ebrahim, 2003; Kilby, 2006).

However, a voluntary commitment to the mission needs to be supplemented by pressures from external stakeholders. Trustees and managers may suffer personal disappointments when projects fail, but 'the strength of accountability' can only be measured by 'the degree of "rectification" or change' that their external stakeholders can impose on agencies when they fail, but, as Kilby (2006: 954, 952) argues, 'there is no clearly defined path by which ... [NGOs] can be held to account by ... [their beneficiaries] who have little power in the relationship' (see also Brett, 1993: 276–8). Beneficiaries are generally poor and dependent on the agency, and cannot vote them out of office or exit to another supplier if they are dissatisfied. Many NGOs are committed to downward accountability and have developed demanding ways of enforcing it, as Kilby and Ebrahim both show, but this depends on their own goodwill, which produces an 'accountability gap' that is the major weakness of the sector (Kilby, 2006: 952; Brett, 1993: 292–3).

Legally enforced accountability by home governments, or host governments in the case of INGOs, is also weak, since democratic theory insists that all groups should have a right to organize, so state controls are generally confined to enforcing formal reporting and accounting procedures (Kingsbury, 2002). This is especially true in LDCs where INGOs come bearing gifts that local governments cannot afford to turn down, although they do resent and resist the tendency for donors to support them rather than state agencies (Brett, 1993: 295–6).

In the end, it is only donors and supporters who can impose real sanctions on NGOs because they can exit when they are dissatisfied, and sometimes use voice as well. These pressures differ in different kinds of agencies. Those that depend on parent organizations like ecumenical NGOs are likely to be actively scrutinized by their trustees and the members who fund them. INGOs supported by the general public have great autonomy because their donors are obliged to take the agency's claims on trust and will support them unless a major scandal reaches the media. Perhaps the most demanding relationship is that between INGOs and governments and multilateral donors that use them as subcontractors to manage large projects, especially in weak states. Small private donors cannot negotiate changes to projects or monitor what INGOs do but large public donors can. In fact, many of the largest NGOs depend on official aid funding, must compete for contracts with their peers, negotiate programmes with officials, and allow their performance to be formally monitored and evaluated by donors (see Brett, 1993: 291–8).

These relationships, and notably those between INGOs and state donors, raise many contested issues. First, they are criticized for disempowering beneficiaries since they transfer decision-making power to donors and/or NGOs who act on their behalf. However, given the 'high cost of voice' and lack of exit facing the poor, they can play a positive, albeit constrained role as 'voice surrogates' that could 'mobilize or organize the local public' to demand better services (Paul, 1992: 1055). INGOs also, in fact, play a key advocacy role in development policy-making in DCs, where these issues rarely feature in broader political debates. Again, monitoring by donors is costly, the performance indicators used to evaluate outcomes can distort or undervalue outcomes, and NGOs can manipulate their results and manage visiting missions. Equally, excessive dependence on state support can drive NGOs into inappropriate projects driven by the political or economic interests of donors.

These issues are a cause for concern, but they do not undermine the role of NGOs as a whole. Choosing to use state, firms or NGOs to provide particular services depends on relative rather than absolute judgements. What is at issue is not whether NGOs meet some ideal standard, but whether they offer better prospects than local states with limited capacity, or for-profit contractors that may be less accountable to the poor or charge much higher fees. Keohane (2002) also shows that the need for strong accountability is also not an absolute value, but should depend 'on the power of the entity being held accountable'. Thus very powerful organizations 'such as a major multinational corporation or a state ... may be able to ignore many sanctions', but this would not be true of 'a weak NGO'. Hence, Keohane (2002: 478–9) argues that their work should indeed 'be scrutinized and their frequent lack of accountability criticized', but 'they should be held externally accountable chiefly through peer and reputational accountability'. Here again, effective choices between state, for-profit and solidaristic agencies to achieve particular purposes will have to depend on contextual and contingent variables, and not simply on abstract theoretical principles.

Conclusions

The 'third sector' agencies examined here, together with the cooperative firms described in Chapter 6, depend on affective and ethical values. They offer libertarians a route to a non-capitalist future, and are treated as one possible institutional option by institutional pluralists. We have questioned some of the more optimistic libertarian claims by showing that SOs depend on reciprocal rewards rather than pure altruism, that large agencies use hierarchical structures that can be captured by elites and subverted by opportunism, bounded rationality and antagonistic conflict. We argued that they also need to be subjected to effective accountability mechanisms based on realistic forms of exit and voice, and it is these that distinguish modern from traditional SOs that were dominated by theocratic or ascriptive elites. We then examined the principles governing three major subgroups within the sector – families, membership-based organizations and NGOs – looking at the different principles that governed their internal and external relationships in order to provide some guidance about how they should be better organized and used.

Notes

1 See, for example, *Social Research* (1985); Wignaraja (1991); Fals Borda (1992); and Foweraker (1995).
2 That is, voluntary negotiations designed to achieve an 'intersubjective mutuality of reciprocal understanding, shared knowledge, mutual trust, and accord with one another' (Habermas, 1979: 3).
3 These are going out of fashion, but still exist. Burning at the stake is no longer legal in Europe, but stoning for adultery is still allowed in some cultures.
4 I am indebted to insights and readings provided by Jamie Ward of Sussex University here.
5 Local and international NGO workers worked throughout the warzone in Uganda in the 1980s and 90s, when UN personnel were forbidden from doing so on security grounds, but nevertheless received their salaries and allowances in full.
6 As Ella Fitzgerald sings: 'I want to be happy, but I won't be happy till I make you happy too.'
7 'Properly speaking, altruism is an absurdity. Women are self-sacrificing in direct proportion to their incapacity to offer anything but this sacrifice' (Greer, 1971: 151).
8 This generalization is based on long-term personal observation and experience of a diverse range of SOs in DCs and LDCs.
9 See Pollak (1985) for a complex analysis of the role of transaction costs and governance structures in families.
10 Gramsci (1971: 153) is referring to political parties here, but his analysis has general application. He attributes the key role to the leadership – 'an actually existing army is destroyed if it loses its generals, while the existence of a united group of generals who agree among themselves and have common aims soon creates an army, even where none exists'.
11 This is so in common pool resource organizations that are crucial to livelihoods, whose members can monitor each other's behaviour and exclude those who break the rules (Wade, 1988; Ostrom, 1990).
12 These observations are confirmed by long-term participant observation in the British Labour Party.
13 They should be distinguished from CBOs run by and serving their own members since they operate on the democratic principles dealt with in the last section (Uphof, 1995).
14 I encountered both during fieldwork in Uganda (see Brett, 1996a; Allen, 1996).
15 See Ebrahim (2003); Edwards and Hulme (1995); Keohane (2002); Kilby (2006); Kingsbury (2002); Lewis (1999); and Spiro (2002).

Explaining Blocked Development

Chapter 9

Competing Models and Developmental Transitions

Back to the future: from liberal pluralism to development theory

Classical theorists saw development as a process through which traditional societies shifted from pre-modern institutions of various kinds to capitalism or socialism; their successors now treat it as a shift to the pluralistic institutions described in Part II. This new consensus represents no more (and no less) than a summation of the 'third way' programmes that have emerged to address the crisis in both structuralist and neoliberal programmes in the west, turning the old conflicts between Left and Right into a far less adversarial debate over the use of different kinds of state, for-profit or non-profit agencies to maximize autonomy, growth and solidarity in new and creative ways. These models are promoting new forms of state regulations and relationships with private agencies in the north whose outcomes are still a matter for debate. What concerns us, however, is that the most successful East Asian NICs have not used the liberal versions of this model to manage their developmental transitions, and these liberal programmes have often failed in the weakest LDCs. This is because the values, understandings and endowments needed to sustain liberal institutions still coexist and conflict with others associated with their recent past that distort and/or block liberal transitions in LDCs.

This does not discredit the normative or technical claims of the liberal project, since progressive movements in DCs and LDCs are committed to democracy, open systems, gender equality and free scientific enquiry (Schuurman, 1993: 27). It provides mainstream practitioners with a broader range of options than either structuralism or neoliberalism, but it does not provide us with a comprehensive theory of development that enables us to understand the processes involved in making transitions from pre-market to market-based societies, set out in Part II. But it does mean that while LDCs look to DCs for models, their ability to adopt democratic constitutions, merit-based bureaucracies, competitive markets, an open civil society and science-based authority systems is heavily constrained by their historical legacies because they question the terms on which people relate to each other and to other societies, producing transformations that now 'engulf people whom their past culture has neither prepared for nor disposed towards it' (Jaspers, 1963: 72).

This discrepancy between the demands of the orthodox model and the objective possibilities that constrain local societies enables us to explain many aspects of the crisis in development theory described in Chapter 1. It does not suggest that we should halt ongoing attempts to create participatory citizenship, political and economic freedom and personal autonomy in societies where they were formerly suppressed, but it does explain why it generates serious conflicts with groups still committed to patrimonial, theocratic, patriarchal, racist and commandist institutional arrangements. The pluralistic 'post-Washington consensus' is rooted in methodological individualism, and presupposes the existence of the social, economic and political capital needed to sustain liberal institutions. Thus it ignores the insights of classical development theorists who recognized that market failures in LDCs stem from their attempts to build rather than maintain liberal institutions and the social and human capital needed to sustain them, and are therefore far more serious than those which liberal pluralism is designed to address in DCs, described in Part II.

Pluralists now ask LDCs to make an immediate shift from authoritarianism to democracy, from state-led economies to markets and private enterprise, and from traditional or collective cultural systems to individualism and rational science. Most classical theorists accepted these changes as a long-term goal, but believed that dualistic value systems, weak states, non-functioning markets and limited endowments meant that LDCs needed to use far higher levels of centralization and collective control to achieve them in the short term. Thus, it is hardly surprising that liberal policies have often failed in the weakest states, while the most successful transitions have taken place in authoritarian 'cohesive capitalist states' rather than socialist or liberal democratic ones. This, as Kohli (2004) says, 'raises serious normative dilemmas'. These states use 'power well in some areas but also curtail the important urge of the many to participate politically and to control their own destinies'. Hence:

> It is important to resist the temptation to embrace growth-producing right-wing authoritarianisms, it is also important to distance oneself from the fantasy that all good things can be had together, that democracy, equality, free-markets, and rapid economic growth can all be achieved simultaneously in the contemporary developing world. Not only is there no evidence for this in the contemporary developing world, but it also represents a poor reading of how development proceeded in the west. (Kohli, 2004: 421–2)

Structuralists have been susceptible to the first temptation, liberals to the second. Our final task, therefore, is to expose the limitations of the current pluralistic orthodoxy, and to suggest the need for a far more open-ended approach, involving a search for hybrid solutions based on second-best compromises between the 'good things', described in Part II, and the varied value systems, goals and capacities of local communities. Liberal institutions were only consolidated in the west after long and often bloody conflicts. Classical development theorists argued that dualistic value systems, structural inequalities and limited human and physical capital in late developers ruled out a transition to democracy and free trade during early transitions in the poorest LDCs until they had created the human, social and physical capital needed to sustain them.

They therefore adopted structuralist programmes that succeeded in states with strong regimes, and failed where they were weak.[1] They operated differently in different periods and societies, but always involved complex and disruptive relationships between imported models and external agents and agencies and local ones, and relied on what we now think of as 'development' theorists to understand and find solutions to these problems that orthodox theorists could afford to ignore.

In Part I, we defined development as a long-term process of managed institutional change involving shifts from oppressive institutional arrangements like slavery, feudalism, theocracy and command planning to open systems based on free markets and rational scientific experimentation. But recognizing the contradictory nature of these processes, as we have done here, explains why these shifts will always be contested and will not generate a linear transition to liberal pluralism. Thus, addressing these problems of transition takes us far beyond the narrowly focused and technical attempts to analyse and evaluate the liberal projects and programmes that now dominate the work of modern development economists. Instead, it obliges us to re-evaluate the whole debate about the new liberal consensus representing the 'end of history'. Institutional change transforms social relations and possibilities for personal autonomy and interdependence, and therefore creates or blocks the conditions for the 'penetration and transformation of secular life by the principle of freedom' (Hegel, 1822–30/1975: 54). Attempting to extend the possibility of autonomous interdependence from the few to the many has always been heavily contested. It is going on, with very uneven results, in most LDCs and transitional economies where institutional reform and the models used to direct it do not just raise technical issues, but involve the great historical conflicts between classes, religions, ethnicities, nationalities and genders that produced the institutional arrangements of 'modern bourgeois society' (Marx and Engels, 1848/1968: 35–6).

Part III will look systematically at the social, political and economic factors that differentiate LDCs from DCs, which produce the complex and highly differentiated outcomes that we see in the success stories like China and Malaysia, the disastrous failures like Somalia and the Democratic Republic of the Congo, and in the great majority of LDCs that operate somewhere in between.

Formal models, objective possibilities and social change

Theorists use five variables to measure the effectiveness of the different kinds of models or 'politico-economic set-ups' (Wiles, 1962: 2) that they use to guide social change in LDCs:

- the levels of personal autonomy or dependence that characterize social relationships
- the degree of democracy or autocracy that characterizes the state–society relationship
- the strength of the state's capacity to deliver services
- the existence of economic markets as opposed to centralized command
- the extent to which enterprises are privately or socially owned.[2]

Sociologists usually focus on the first, political scientists on the next two, and economists on the last two, but development theorists have to address the methodological, practical and normative problems generated by the relationship between them all. Doing this raises three problems.

First, it raises complicated questions about the links between particular kinds of political, economic and social institutions and developmental outcomes. Theorists often assume that institutional types must be combined in consistent ways:

- democracy with individualism, free markets and capitalism
- autocracy with collectivistic values and command economies
- strong states with interventionism
- weak states with laissez faire

but these relationships are not consistent in real societies. Autocratic and democratic states have sometimes relied on collective value systems and used competitive or controlled markets, and capitalist or collective ownership. And both interventionist and liberal economies depend on the existence of strong state capacity, and both have sometimes succeeded in creating it and sometimes failed.

Further, real societies never fully comply with the ideal typical models, but occupy intermediate positions along the continuums that stretch between democracy and autocracy, markets and command:

- democracies need to constrain popular rights
- autocracies need to retain the support of key social groups
- markets require political regulation and often include state and socially owned enterprises
- planned and command economies usually contain formal or informal markets.

Thus Wiles (1962: 19) showed that 'there has never been such a thing as capitalist [full] F[ree] M[arket] and Yugoslav socialism might at one time have approached FM more nearly than, say, French capitalism'; while Neumann (1942: 24) stated that Nazi Germany was 'a monopolistic economy and a command economy ... a private capitalist economy regimented by a totalitarian state'.[3] So models are never operationalized in their pure form, which produces 'considerable uncertainty with regard to exact outcomes and causal mechanisms' (Silverberg and Verspagen, 2005: 532).

Second, the conflicts and organizational challenges generated by attempts to shift from one model to another also explain why 'the sense of precision offered by the mainstream models is to some extent illusory' (Silverberg and Verspagen, 2005: 530). Institutional reform involves conflicts over transfers of wealth and power whose outcomes are not only influenced by the characteristics of new rules, but also by the ability of influential social groups to implement or resist them. These contextual factors determine the objective possibilities for social change by creating 'the transition paths available and the tasks different countries face when they begin their struggles to develop consolidated democracies' (Linz and Stepan, 1996: 55). The contrasting results of democratic reforms – West Germany in the 1940s, Russia in the 1990s, and Iraq and Afghanistan in the 2000s – confirm the validity of this proposition.

Third, institutional change generates conflicts over normative goals. Liberals assume that all good things – personal autonomy, democracy, meritocratic bureaucracy, free markets and secure property rights – can and should go together. However, Fascists, racists and theocrats deny that they are actually good things, and structuralists deny that they can all be achieved together in transitional societies lacking the necessary values, endowments and social groups committed to liberal reform. They believe that asking for too much too soon can generate normative conflicts and impose impossible pressures on insecure regimes, while liberals and socialists believe that asking for too little can reinforce the authority of regressive elites.

We raised many of these issues in Part I, and Part III will now show how the complexity of these relationships between theoretical models and social change influences the problems involved in managing emancipatory transitions to modernity. The contingent nature of the relationship between social realities and prescriptive models does not mean that we can ignore their role in guiding historical processes, but it does suggest that practitioners should be wary of premature attempts to impose pure versions of particular paradigms on all societies. Few models have survived the rigorous tests imposed by scientific debate and/or the even more demanding tests of history. Liberalism was marginalized by various forms of authoritarian corporatism and socialism during most of the 20th century because it failed to resolve serious political and economic crises, while authoritarian corporatism or socialism dominated most LDCs until the late 20th century but also generated political and economic problems it could not resolve. The triumph of liberal democratic capitalism appears to have resolved the debate between Marx and Engels (1848/1968) and Mill in 1848 when the *Communist Manifesto* claimed that the advancing capitalist revolution must be followed by a transition to socialism, while Mill saw it as a far more open question:

> The question of Socialism is not, as generally stated by Socialists, a question of flying to the sole refuge against the evils which now bear down on humanity; but a mere question of comparative advantages which futurity must determine. We are too ignorant either of what individual agency in its best form or Socialism in its best form can accomplish to be qualified to decide which of the two will be the ultimate form of human society. (Mill, 1848/1900: 129)

Experiments designed to answer this 'mere' question of comparative advantage dominated the development debate and spilt rivers of blood for the next 140 years. A return to socialism cannot be ruled out, but it is unlikely to take the statist forms that dominated those years.

Yet the triumph of capitalism and the contingent and crisis-ridden nature of development processes do not disprove all the insights of alternative theoretical traditions. Demands for planning and social ownership had been sidelined before the onset of the global economic crisis in 2008, but this had not eliminated the exploitation, inequality and uneven development that led to the critiques of market theory outlined in Chapter 1 (Cowan and Shenton, 1996; Brett, 2000b; Wade, 2004). This crisis has produced an immediate return to levels of state intervention comparable to those experienced in the 1940s, with consequences that are too early to predict. Methodological individualism cannot explain the 'categorical inequality' created by institutionalized oppression and 'coercive exploitation' (Tilly, 1985: 169) that dominated DCs during their early transitions, and dominates LDCs now. These inequalities were a function of the different kinds of rules that governed their pre-capitalist class structures, which enabled elites to extract the large surpluses needed to finance the initial investments required to build modern economic systems. They demanded 'hard work for low pay, to say nothing of exploitation ... [by] compelling labor from people who cannot say no; from women and children, slaves and quasi-slaves' (Landes, 1999: 381–2). The result was political and economic authoritarianism, and, when favourable conditions emerged, countervailing demands for social democracy or revolutionary socialism.

Capitalism eventually created a more inclusive society by generating 'an overwhelming efficiency and an increased standard of living' that produced 'an overriding interest in the preservation and improvement of the status quo' by both capital and labour (Marcuse, 1968: 9, 11). But reform also depended on 'popular resistance' organized by socialist movements that forced the ruling political and economic class to impose 'protection and constraints on their own action' (Tilly, 1985: 169–70). Revolutionary socialism provided the basis for command economies in the east, while democratic socialism facilitated a historic compromise with capitalism in the west. In 1895, Engels (1895/1967: 288) argued that universal suffrage in Germany could become 'an instrument of emancipation' for the working class that would preclude the need for violent revolution, and reformists like Bernstein (1899/1961) and Crosland (1956) broke with revolutionary Marxism to produce the social democratic compromises between capitalism and socialism that had created the welfare state and humanized capitalism in the west by the second half of the 20th century.

The pluralistic reforms analysed in Part II are the most recent manifestation of this compromise, with 'path dependence and cumulative causation' creating 'distinct varieties of capitalism' by combining them in different ways (Hodgson, 1999: 151). These achievements are exerting a powerful influence on the political and economic struggles in LDCs, since they show how capitalism can create prosperity and freedom by transcending the repressive forms that characterized its early days. However, these reforms are being introduced in societies still characterized by levels of inequality, insecurity and political coercion, which are often worse than those that prevailed in the west in the 19th century. Crucially:

> poor countries now confront the strategic policy issues of development from an absolutely lower level of per capita income than did the presently developed countries ... [and] their relative positions

are also inferior compared to other countries – unlike the early comers ... [that began] from a position of superior per capita income relative to those countries. (Meier, 1976: 95)

The failures of statist socialism have removed it from the political agenda, but the need to deal with the market failures that turned it into a powerful political and social movement means that intense conflicts still continue over the institutional changes needed for progressive transitions in societies that lack the endowments needed to eliminate deprivation and exploitation, and the organizations needed to manage the conflicts they generate.

These issues – the kinds of rules that should govern relationships between governments and economic agents, between politicians and bureaucrats and citizens, between priests and their parishioners, men and women, and nation-states and their neighbours – have dominated development theory since the 19th century. The capitalist revolution is making dramatic strides, but is still incomplete in emerging LDCs like China, India and Brazil. However, they have institutionalized many of the processes and acquired many of the assets needed to sustain their transformations, but this is not so in the weakest LDCs, like those in Africa, where 'there is very little modern capitalism ... and most of the factors which facilitate its development remain weak or nonexistent' (Callaghy, 1988: 78). If we are to address these problems, we must first look more systematically at the relationship between competing models and developmental outcomes and how the resulting institutional changes are influenced by the political, economic and social conflicts generated by their cultural values and endowments.

Classifying and evaluating alternative politicoeconomic models

Societies change their 'politicoeconomic' models to improve the incentives and sanctions that motivate political and economic agents and the people they serve, focusing in particular on their tendency to centralize or decentralize decision-making. Economists emphasize shifts from central command to free markets, but recognize that virtually all economic systems operate as regulated markets (Wiles, 1962: 18). Political scientists focus on shifts from authoritarianism to democracy, but accept that all polities occupy intermediate positions between the two. Linz and Stepan (1996: 38) show that most LDCs have operated as authoritarian rather than totalitarian states, which involve 'limited degrees of pluralism, weak levels of social mobilization and ill-defined but predictable limits on the exercise of power'. These distinctions depend on the logical incompatibility between markets and centralized allocation systems:

> Resource allocation is either circumferential or central, either market or non-market. Indeed these last four words demonstrate that the dichotomy, command or market, is logically exhaustive. Either the enterprise receives orders from above as to where to obtain materials and transmit products or it does not. If it does not it must agree with those who deliver to it or to whom it delivers. But such a process of agreement is by definition a market, however imperfect. (Wiles, 1962: 57)

Societies combine political and economic authority systems in different ways. Authority is fused in feudal, command or segmentary societies, and separated in market societies, but the relationships between authoritarianism, democracy, planning and markets vary dramatically. Totalitarian regimes limit economic freedom to protect their political monopolies, and command economies are incompatible with liberal democracy; but right-wing corporatist regimes like Nazi Germany used controlled markets and private ownership, while Stalinist Russia suppressed them. Many different combinations are possible within these limits, as we see in Figure 9.1.

We can therefore classify societies along two dimensions – from democracy to totalitarianism, and from command planning to free market – with all societies exhibiting some degree of authoritarianism and economic regulation. Theorists make strong claims about the rela-

Figure 9.1 *Alternative politicoeconomic models*

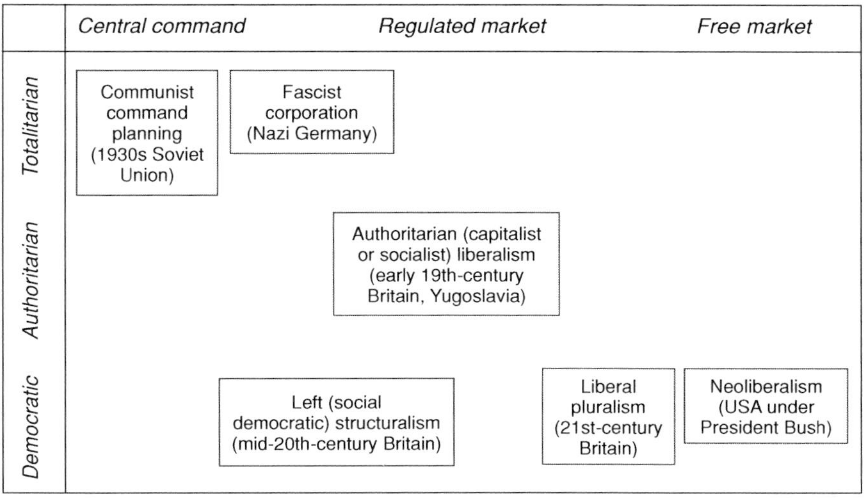

	Central command	Regulated market	Free market
Totalitarian	Communist command planning (1930s Soviet Union)	Fascist corporation (Nazi Germany)	
Authoritarian		Authoritarian (capitalist or socialist) liberalism (early 19th-century Britain, Yugoslavia)	
Democratic	Left (social democratic) structuralism (mid-20th-century Britain)	Liberal pluralism (21st-century Britain)	Neoliberalism (USA under President Bush)

tionship between particular positions along these two dimensions and developmental outcomes measured in terms of growth, state capacity and freedom:

- neoliberals believe in markets, so they gravitate to the bottom right-hand corner of Figure 9.1
- left-wing structuralists believe in democratic states and move towards the bottom left-hand corner
- liberal pluralists seek the centre ground by trying to combine strong state agencies with well-regulated markets
- authoritarian liberals favour the top right-hand corner, claiming that too much democracy will threaten economic discipline and property rights
- Communists who reject democracy and private enterprise, and Fascists who subordinate it to a monopolistic political party, favour the top left-hand corner.

Societies move along these continuums as supporters of particular positions capture power by claiming that doing so will increase growth or resolve crises, but the relationship between the adoption of particular models and developmental outcomes is highly uneven, as we see in Figure 9.2.[4]

Figure 9.2 shows a clear relationship between market economies, democracy and state capacity in DCs, but demonstrates that they use varied levels of state regulation. It also shows that successful and unsuccessful early transitions occurred in societies with authoritarian constitutions and heavily regulated markets, and that liberalism and structuralism can produce success or failure. This suggests that successful transitions do not just depend on formal institutional change, but on dialectical processes involving complex and contingent relationships between the demands imposed by new models, the characteristics of the models they are supposed to replace, and the willingness of different interests in the society to give them their support. This view was central to the theories of social, economic and political dualism created by classical development theorists, which we will review in Chapters 10 and 11. They argued that these processes rarely led to the substitution of one 'pure' model by another, but the production of new hybrids that are 'not a mere copy of either' (Malinowsky, 1945/1961: 10).[5] To understand these processes:

> We need dualistic models rather than monistic ones, and developmental as well as equilibrium models if we are to understand differences precisely and grapple effectively with the processes of political change. (Almond, 1960: 25)

Figure 9.2 *Politicoeconomic models and state performance*

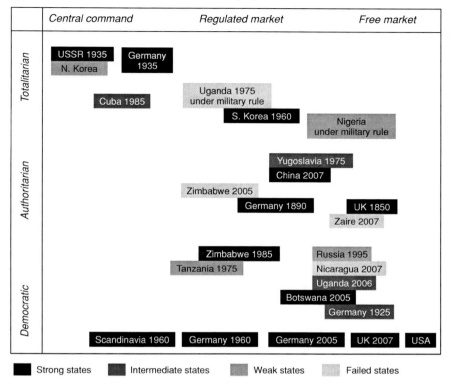

Hybridity means that societies can combine political and economic authority systems in many different ways. However, there is always 'some limit to the randomness of history' (Silverberg and Verspagen, 2005: 532), because almost all LDCs now operate within limits set by the need to create democratic capitalist states. Their ability to do this effectively depends on the existence of social and political movements with a vested interest in capitalism that can present themselves, as Marx and Engels argued (1845–6/1974: 66), 'as the representative of the whole of society' and persuade enough people to accept that their interests do actually represent 'the common interests of all the members of society'. To do this and give the liberal model the hegemonic status it has now achieved in DCs, their victory must also benefit 'many individuals of the other classes which are not winning a dominant position'.

Different kinds of movements have used different kinds of models to manage developmental transitions in the modern era:

- emergent national capitalists have used authoritarian states to build their firms, control labour and exclude their competitors

- liberal capitalists have used markets to replace centralized traditional, corporatist or socialist institutions
- the political and bureaucratic classes have used state power to control productive resources, and sustain their own kinship and political networks.

Capitalism has now marginalized most pre-capitalist ruling classes – feudal aristocracies, theocracies and coercive despotisms – and many subordinate classes too – independent peasants and artisans and the industrial working class in DCs. However, the consolidation of the ongoing transitions to capitalism in LDCs cannot be guaranteed, but depends on the ability of its supporters to create strong states capable of managing the destructive effects of these changes. As Stiglitz (2001, pp. xi–xii) says:

> Rapid transformation destroys old coping mechanisms, old safety nets, while it creates a new set of demands, before new coping mechanisms are developed. This lesson from the nineteenth century has, unfortunately, all too often been forgotten by the advocates of the Washington consensus, the modern-day version of liberal orthodoxy.

These states must protect property rights, encourage investment and extract enough taxes to provide the social protection and safety nets needed to maintain public order and social cohesion. This generates serious contradictions between the need for economic investment and labour discipline and the demand for freedom and private and collective consumption. These threaten the ability of governments to retain the political support they need to guarantee state power. Liberal theorists assume that democratic capitalist states can solve these problems by coordinating the interdependent activities of relatively autonomous political, economic and civic agencies, which will automatically generate socially optimal outcomes through 'mutually advantageous bargaining' and ensure that we all live in 'the most efficient of all possible worlds' (Olson, 2000: 39). However, as Olson also argues, the claim that individualized bargaining must produce optimal results is highly problematic in all societies, and we have just seen that creating these institutions is especially difficult in LLDCs where liberal reforms have often been followed by crisis and breakdown, and most successful transitions have been managed by authoritarian states. How should we respond to these anomalies?

Competing models, political competition and developmental transitions

Structuralists claimed that market failures in LDCs required strong and even authoritarian states, but the governments they advised sometimes used their power effectively, but more often abused it. Liberalization should have overcome these problems but often failed, because many state agents refused to give up their rents and implement the reforms, and, when they did, weak local firms could not compete effectively in open markets. Democracy was expected to overcome state failures but elections were often manipulated and/or led to populist or divisive economic policies that undermined economic discipline and intensified ethnic conflict. The result has been the policy impasse described in Chapter 1, which appears to have discredited both liberalism and structuralism.

There have therefore been powerful criticisms of both traditions that have discredited both. However, we cannot afford to ignore their insights, because they still provide us with the tools we need to understand these state and market failures. The liberal claim that structuralism in weak states creates economic distortions and rents has been vindicated in many contexts, as has the structuralist claim that new or 'infant' firms need politically managed transfers and protection from foreign competition in weak economies with poor infrastructure and limited human capital. The infant industry argument also explains state as well as economic failures, because strong democratic states depend on the existence of a developed capitalist and working class.

Thus we can only understand blocked development by accepting the critiques that liberals and structuralists make of each other's models, but doing this seems to rule out all the policy agendas that have dominated the modern era. Disastrous failures in many LLDCs force us to recognize the strength of this pessimistic conclusion, but many important successes also demonstrate that viable solutions can be found, although they have rarely followed the prescriptions of either tradition in a rigorous way. This obliges us to explain why simultaneous attempts to build new states and modern capitalist classes sometimes produced vicious circles and cumulative decline, and sometimes virtuous circles and sustained growth.

We saw in Part I that the uncertainty of the relationship between policy regimes and outcomes is a function of the substantive characteristics of existing cultural systems, economic capacities, and political processes and organizations. These issues are neglected in current orthodoxy, but in reality strong states and effective markets depend on the viability and diversity of the political and civic agencies that mediate the relationships between civil society and the state, and of the firms that generate the livelihoods and taxes that sustain the whole system. The history of modern China was determined by the interaction between the Kuomintang, the Communist Party, the Japanese invaders, and their relationships with the landlords and peasants; and that of South Africa by relationships between British imperialism, Afrikaner and African nationalist parties and their relationships with the mining industry, capitalist farmers and manufacturers. Thus competing ideologies and strategies drew on different theoretical traditions, but actual outcomes depended on highly contingent conditions and events that enabled particular groups to assume power, redistribute resources in new ways, and thus initiate the changes that had long-term structural effects.

Academic theorists often ignore these substantive issues but the 'practical theorists' involved in political and economic struggles have had to understand the links between theoretical models, the distribution of wealth and status, popular support, and the ability to capture and use power. They have drawn their historical understandings and theoretical insights from academia, but used them to rationalize and justify the actions of the political parties and social movements they created to promote their agendas:

- conservatives formed liberal parties, supported by business organizations, to promote market-based systems
- radicals formed corporatist or socialist parties, supported by trade unions, to promote state-led systems
- nationalists used ethnically based parties and/or rebel movements and traditional social organizations to organize the anticolonial struggle and manage postcolonial transitions.

These activists understood two things:

1 Structural change does not depend on spontaneous individual interactions, but, as Lenin (1902/1969: 79) put it, on organizations, leaders and intellectuals that represent and provide significant social interests with the theoretical insights they need to understand their own situations, and the nature of the 'relationships of all classes and strata to the state and the government'. Lenin famously argued that socialism had to be brought to the working class by 'the bourgeois intelligentsia ... from without' (pp. 31–2).

2 Successful transition not only depends on appropriate theoretical models, but also on the relative strength of their organizations and their ability to respond to contingent and often unanticipated events. The minority Bolshevik Party only captured state power in 1917 because of Russia's military defeat; the minority Nazi party did so in 1933 because of the world depression and the failure of the Communists and social democrats to cooperate; while Ghandi played a key role in the peaceful transition in India and Mandela in South Africa.

However, while contingency is important, these processes and outcomes were not random, but depended on:

- the nature of the relationship between different social classes and movements and the strength and orientation of the state
- the capacity, forms of ownership and distribution of property characterizing the economy
- the cultural systems that dominate society
- people's access to external ideas and financial resources.

The nature of these initial endowments generates many different possible transition paths, as Linz and Stepan's (1996, Ch. 3) seminal study of democratic transitions shows. They identify four different 'ideal typical non-democratic regimes', which are characterized by qualitatively different kinds of state–society relationships in terms of their pluralism, ideology, mobilization and leadership. These include authoritarianism, totalitarianism, post-totalitarianism and what they call 'Sultanism', but which we will call 'patrimonialism'. The first three are differentiated by the degree of autonomy allocated to or appropriated by civic organizations, and the extent of the constraints that can be imposed on the leadership. In the fourth:

> The private and the public are fused, there is a strong tendency toward familial power and dynastic succession, there is no distinction between a state career and personal service to the ruler, there is a lack of rationalized impersonal ideology, economic success depends on a personal relationship to the ruler, and, most of all, the ruler acts only according to his own unchallenged discretion, with no large impersonal goals. (Linz and Stepan: 1996: 52)

These different starting points determine the objective possibilities available to societies as they begin their developmental transitions, and explain many of the anomalies that we identified earlier. The lack of democratic competition and arbitrary exercise of authority in such states explains the inexperience of the political and social entrepreneurs who try to create new parties and civic organizations, and the inappropriate skills, authoritarian assumptions and lack of respect for the formal rules of the bureaucratic class; while the weakness of their capitalist classes explains the need for subsidies and rents (Khan, 2000). Successful democratization would eliminate these practices and rents and the patron–client ties that enable political, bureaucratic and economic elites to continue these practices, so they have strong incentives 'to block the very processes that promote [it]' (Tilly, 2000: 2).

Similar problems have confronted post-Communist societies. They had created powerful state apparatuses, but ignored the need for bureaucratic autonomy outlined in Part II, by fusing the authority of the party and the state and using command planning that divided society 'into two groups: those who give instructions and those who follow them' (Gorbachov, 1987: 29). The energy and ruthlessness that characterized these huge social projects were generated by external threats, not democratic elections, but they ultimately collapsed because governments could not deal with the social and technological complexities demanded by modern information-based systems, and the demands for greater freedom from subordinated groups. The shift to markets was sudden and dramatic, but dominated by antagonistic conflicts created by the legacies of their socialist pasts.

Kohli (2004) provides us with a systematic comparative analysis of the processes that produced both successful and weaker versions of the authoritarian states that have operated in the third world. He identifies three 'state types', which he calls cohesive capitalist, fragmented multiclass, and neopatrimonal states:

- *Cohesive capitalist states*, like South Korea, are strong states, but are based on a 'repressive and authoritarian' politics supported by nationalist 'ideological mobilization', which have generated rapid economic growth by maintaining 'a close alliance with producer or capitalist groups', and 'tight control over labor' (Kohli, 2004: 10).
- *Fragmented multiclass states*, like India and Brazil, maintain real but limited democratic accountability, but have had to make far more concessions to popular demands and have generated very mixed results.
- *Neopatrimonal states*, whether operating as dictatorships or 'nominal democracies' like Nigeria, are based on 'personalistic leaders unconstrained by norms or institutions, and bureaucracies of poor quality', office-holders who treat 'public resources as their personal patrimony', and 'state-led development ... [that] often resulted in disaster' (Kohli, 2004: 9–10).

Easy transitions to democracy, competitive markets and socially responsible capitalism are unlikely in such transitional societies and usually take generations to complete, because:

- their rulers use clientalism, corruption and force to retain power
- their new entrepreneurs rely on political contacts for handouts and monopoly privileges to build their assets
- their social and religious leaders depend on ethnic, theocratic and communal values to maintain their authority and status.

The result is contradictory demands and perverse incentives that produce unstable outcomes, which lead to vicious circles in the weakest states, but sometimes to virtuous ones in successful but usually authoritarian capitalist states, such as Britain in the 18th and early 19th centuries and South Korea and Taiwan in the late 20th.

Conclusions

Three key conclusions emerge from this analysis:

1 Institutions and policy regimes, and the theories that sustain them, do matter, but the way they influence performance depends on the nature of the substantive social contexts in which they operate.
2 The threats and opportunities that confront transitional societies can only be understood by combining the insights of all the apparently contradictory paradigms that have dominated the discipline since its inception.
3 Focusing on the processes that produce structural change generates more serious conflicts and crises than those addressed in the ortho-dox social sciences, which focus on the need to maintain equilibrium rather than manage change, and therefore ignore the tensions gener-ated by the juxtaposition of contradictory institutional systems during early transitions.

This tells us why attempts at institutional reform have produced such uneven results, and exposes the limitations of the theoretical assump-tions based on methodological individualism that still govern the current orthodoxy. It justifies Elias's call for a contextualized and collectivistic analysis based on a historical and 'process-sociological approach', which recognizes the limitations of western knowledge systems when they are transferred to non-western environments, as well as the rationality and viability of the normative principles and knowledge claims of pre-modern societies, in contexts where limited resources and external threats make it impossible for them to behave as western individualists would. This approach

> is based on the realization that on the plane of human groups, of relations between people, one cannot proceed with the aid of concepts, or a process of conceptualization, of the same kind as those used on the level of atoms or molecules and their relations to each other … whenever and wherever … [these] occur they are essentially identical in structure and dynamics. But this can no longer be said of the structure and dynamics of the groups formed by human beings,

nor, therefore, of language. These can change relatively quickly. They are different at different times and in different places. To orient oneself on this integration-plane of the universe it is of little help to look around for laws, or concepts functioning as laws, applicable to the human world in the same way in all times and places. The task to which this integration level sets human beings seeking orientation is to *discover the order of change in the course of time*. (Elias, 2001: 173–4, emphases added)[6]

We will now use this approach in order to review and reconstruct the classical developmental traditions. We will first contextualize these arguments with a short historical review of the modern development process and two case studies on the tensions created by the problems of dualism and structural change in Chapter 10, and then review their social, political, economic and practical implications in Chapters 11–14.

Notes

1 These assumptions underpinned colonial theory in the 19th and 20th centuries (see Brett, 1973: Chs 1–3). Kohli (2004) attributes much of the successes or failures of postcolonial states to the nature of their colonial regimes.

2 This analysis is an extension of that provided in Chapter 4 and systematized in Tables 4.1 and 4.2.

3 For an early review of these issues, see Brett (1969). For an account of the indispensable role of illegal informal markets in Soviet planning, see Nove (1964, 1983).

4 These judgements are based on general background information and do not establish a demonstrable correlation, but illustrate the complexity of the relationship between formal institutional rules and state and economic performance.

5 Malinowsky (1945/1961: 18) called this 'three-column anthropology'. We call it 'three-column political economy'.

6 This approach is consistent with Marxist theories of historical materialism.

Chapter 10

Learning from History

Market failures, start-up problems and state-led development

The crisis of structuralism in the late 1970s was used to justify the liberal claim that free trade would 'maximise world income' (Johnson, 1968: 88), that 'superior economic performance' depended on 'competitive markets, secure property and contract rights, stable macroeconomic conditions, and efficient government provision of public goods', and that 'democratic political institutions are the ones most conducive to human welfare' (Clague, 1997b: 368). Liberal pluralist theory is still dominated by these assumptions because it recognizes the need for strong state and civic institutions, but only to improve or supplement 'the functioning of the price mechanism' and not to 'supplant' it, as structuralist theorists did (Lal, 1996: 30).

We saw in Part II that institutional theorists have developed a comprehensive model of the relationship between markets, hierarchies and solidaristic systems that allows them to apply 'standard economics' rather than structuralism to 'address the problems of less-developed countries' (Clague, 1997a: 14). On the other hand, evolutionary economists, as we saw in Chapter 3, recognize that institutional choice and design cannot be separated from historically determined contextual conditions, as Lipsey et al. (2005: 49) point out:

> Understanding long-term growth in S-E [structuralist-evolutionary] rather than neoclassical terms matters in many ways, particularly as it relates to policy. An important debate relates to the conditions for creating growth in poorer countries. There is general agreement that a necessary condition is that the economy be market-oriented to a significant extent. Some in the neoclassical tradition argue that establishing completely free markets for goods, services, and capital flows is also sufficient ... Others in the S-E tradition argue that the evolutionary hand needs significant amounts of policy assistance. It received such assistance, they argue, in most of the older industrial economies, also in the Asian Tigers, and it is needed in other countries today.

Thus structuralists have argued that the need to build rather than simply sustain state, for-profit and non-profit institutions, together with the problems of social dualism identified in the next two chapters, generates additional problems of market failure in many LDCs, which disrupt liberal reforms and demand far more state intervention than is needed in DCs. They claim that liberals have forgotten that virtually all now developed countries used 'interventionist ... policies ... [to promote] infant industries during their catch-up periods' (Chang, 2002: 18), and that 'the role of the state has been decisive for patterns of industrialization in the developing world' (Kohli, 2004: 381). Most of them do not reject markets, but claim that these problems of late development mean that they will only operate effectively after the appropriate institutions have been created, so higher levels of collective intervention are needed to build market systems rather than sustain them.

Liberals contest these claims. They argue that 'non-market decision making' will usually produce 'inefficient political and economic structures' that are likely 'to persist for long periods of time' (North, 1981: 7). They argue that 'growth-retarding regimes, policies, and institutions are the rule rather than the exception, and the majority of the world's population lives in poverty' (Olson, 1982: 175), because most governments in LDCs have not been committed to development but to maintaining their own power and wealth. Their belief in economic competition is supported by Marx and Engels' (1848/1968: 40) claim that 'free competition, accompanied by a social and political constitution adapted to it ... has created more massive and more colossal productive forces than have all preceding generations together', and by Friedman's (1962: xx) claim that 'competitive capitalism also promotes political freedom because it separates economic power from political power and in this way enables the one to offset the other'.

Both these paradigms are therefore based on plausible theoretical claims and have informed policy programmes in many contexts. These can be treated as natural experiments whose results can be used to test these competing claims. We will do this now by identifying the 'empirical attributes and experiences' of successful and unsuccessful developmental experiments in the modern era, in order to use them 'as a means of generalizing about the deeper social and institutional dynamics' that produced them (Faguet, 2002: 193–3). They do not operate under controlled conditions and are affected by many path-dependent variables where even 'small events of a random character – especially those occurring early on the path – are likely to figure significantly in "selecting" one or others among the set of stable equilibria, or "attractors" for the system' (David, 2005: 151). This excludes the use of formal mathematical models based on 'tight logical propositions formulated as theorems, which are refuted by a single counter example' (Mokyr, 2005:

195). However, they 'do more than tell unverifiable stories to explain [these] historical events', because this approach recognizes that 'although every event is in some ways unique', they also share important 'commonalities' (Lipsey et al., 2005: 15), especially because practitioners have always relied on a limited range of policy regimes to achieve their objectives.

What concerns us now are the 'start-up problems' that confront societies undergoing early developmental transitions. These arise because the political and economic markets and rational bureaucracies needed to sustain liberal democratic capitalism only operate effectively where people already know how to manage them and have created the investments needed to run them, while they can only acquire the necessary knowledge and skills in societies where they already exist. This chicken or egg problem explains why humanity took millennia to build progressive modern systems, but their increasing dominance also suggests that these institutions are indeed 'valid in themselves, independently of their origin', as Jaspers (1963: 72) claimed, but our analysis of dualism will show that they are not 'identically transferable', as he suggests, without reference to local conditions or cultures.

We will address these issues by providing a brief review of the nature of the policy regimes and historical processes that facilitated developmental transitions in some places and blocked them in others, hoping that this will 'help us to pick and choose among them' (Mokyr, 2005: 196). We will show that outcomes have not only depended on the choice of liberal or structuralist policies by particular societies, but also on the strength of the social and political movements and the scale and distribution of the technological and organizational endowments. We look first at the creation of the modern world system, and then at the challenge to development theory posed by the LLDCs, focusing on two African cases.

States and markets in early capitalist development

The first and second industrial revolutions

Modern capitalist institutions were consolidated in Holland and Britain through the creation of secure property rights, freedom of scientific and technological experimentation, and state intervention to protect domestic agriculture and industry, expand markets and expropriate foreign assets through imperialistic expansion. In Britain, these policies embraced

> the colonies, the national debt, the modern mode of taxation, and the protectionist system. These methods depend in part on brute force, e.g., the colonial system. But they all employ the power of the

State, the concentrated and organised force of society, to hasten, hot-
house fashion, the process of transformation of the feudal mode of
production into the capitalist mode, and to shorten the transition.
Force is the midwife of every old society pregnant with a new one. It
is itself an economic power. (Marx, 1867/1974: 703)

Pomeranz (2000: 69–70) confirms the broad thrust of Marx's argument by
showing that the claim that 'western Europe grew fastest ... [in the 18th
century] because it had the most efficient markets ... is quite unconvincing',
because 'China (and perhaps Japan as well) actually came closer to resem-
bling the neoclassical ideal of a market economy'. Habib's (2005: Ch. 6)
description of capitalism in Mughal India and Rodney's (1973) of the
precolonial textile trade in northern Nigeria also confirm the extensiveness
of market-based systems in non-western societies. Instead, Pomeranz shows
that Britain depended on its ability to capture external resources to make
the first shift from 'proto-industrial to industrial' society, and on a set of
'institutions and conjunctures' that depended on centralized coercion rather
than 'market principles'. These included the slave trade and New World
mining labour systems, the modern corporation originally 'created for
extra-continental encounters' and used to underwrite 'the huge fixed costs
of violence' (Pomeranz, 2000: 296). Britain used protectionist trade policies
during its whole start-up period, and only abandoned them 'for free trade'
in the 1840s after it had 'achieved industrial leadership' (Landes, 1999:
375). But even this did not involve a genuine shift to laissez faire, because
'colonialism and overseas coercion ... continued to matter for many
decades, if not as much as before 1850' (Pomeranz, 2000: 284).

However, state intervention fostered rather than undermined capitalist
development in Holland and Britain because governments were
constrained by political institutions that enabled key social groups to
ensure that property rights were protected, taxation limited, and the
freedom to innovate guaranteed. North (1981: 153) shows that the Dutch
States-General (parliament) 'fostered the growth of trade ... and protection of the property rights that made such growth possible' and that an
assembly 'composed of merchants and landed gentry' retained the 'crucial
power to tax' in Britain (p. 156). Lipsey et al. show that the modern
science that created the basis for the Industrial Revolution depended on
the existence of political pluralism and university autonomy. These

were a part of European pluralism in which universities were to some
extent free from state and religious control. Another contributor to
the victory of science over religious repression was the pluralism of
political control. When Catholic countries turned against the new
science, some Protestant countries welcomed it, particularly the
Netherlands and England. (Lipsey et al., 2005: 238)

State power was not constrained in this way in France and Spain, so government 'was able to acquire control over the power to tax', and to create property rights that 'did not encourage efficiency' (North, 1981: 152). The Catholic Church 'managed to crush scientific enquiry in southern Europe within one generation after Galileo's condemnation', so that 'the centres of the new science migrated north, particularly to the Protestant countries' (Lipsey et al., 2005: 237). Thus what distinguished northern from southern Europe was not only the use of state power to manage economic change, but also the nature of the social forces that were involved in regulating the way it was exercised.

The first Industrial Revolution occurred in Holland and then in Britain, and was diffused to Europe a generation later 'by British technicians who took the technology to the Continent and made it work' (Lipsey et al., 2005: 263). 'Latecomers' in Europe and North America also adopted Listean state-led 'national' policies during their catch-up phase. They made concessions to free trade in the third quarter of the century, when their demands for British imports, 'especially of capital and capital goods, were virtually unlimited', but as they built their own industries, reciprocity gave way to rivalry 'between developed countries ... of whom only Britain had a built-in interest in total freedom of trade' (Hobsbawm, 1969: 139). Protectionism intensified in Germany, France and the USA after the depression in the 1870s, and 'these same protectionist countries ... [overtook] Britain' during these years (Kiely, 2007: 34). Their successes did not depend on interventionism or markets alone, but on a symbiotic relationship between the two. 'Economic growth accelerated in the period 1870–1913' (Desai, 2004: 85), because the emergent capitalist classes in Europe and the USA were able to build their new industries with active state support, and rely on the free access that Britain gave them to its commodity and capital markets.

The revolution in the north was followed by the forcible but partial transfer of capitalist institutions to the third world by colonial states who were not trying to export market institutions but to gain monopoly privileges for their own elites (Brett, 1973). This produced highly ambiguous results too complex to deal with here, but did begin to address the start-up problem involved in creating modern capitalist states by introducing Weberian bureaucracies, secure property rights and the rule of law, and eliminating some of the traditional obstacles to the creation of fully developed market societies. As Marx (1953/1973: 320) said, Britain fulfilled 'a double mission in India: one destructive, the other regenerating – the annihilation of old Asiatic society, and the laying of the material foundations of Western society in Asia'.

The capitalist transition initiated by colonialism did not follow liberal principles. It used force to impose its authority and often to transfer property rights to incomers, and governments 'that had to pave the way, by extensive public works and administrative services, not only for European settlement, but also for all modern activity' (Frankel, 1938: 256–7). Here:

> the Europeans' self-selection as full human beings gave them a free hand, as they saw it, to pillage everyone else – and to engage in the economic exploitation unparalleled in scale or form upon which Europe partly funded its modern wealth, and which made it within a few centuries the richest area of the planet. (Bessis, 2003: 20)

Local people were deprived of political and economic rights, while expatriate companies were given monopoly powers and coercive control over labour. Indirect rule partially reinforced traditional value systems and authority, but also reduced the accountability of traditional elites by eliminating earlier forms of resistance and protest. Societies were not allowed to protect infant industries, thus suppressing indigenous capitalist development (Brett, 1973; Kohli, 2004). Pomeranz (2000: 294–5) shows that Britain's desire to maintain 'a captive market for the mother country's industrial goods' contributed to deindustrialization in India. And Hobsbawm (1969: 139) claims that even non-colonies unable to defend themselves had to enter into 'unrestricted intercourse with the modern economies ... by gunboats and marines'. The result was dualism, discussed in Chapter 12, and blocked development, described in Chapter 11.

Protectionist rivalries, depression and war, 1919–45

The conflicts generated by great power rivalries culminated in the carnage of the First World War, which disrupted the relationships that had sustained growth in the late 19th century. The postwar settlement negotiated by the Allies at Versailles intensified inequalities and conflicts. According to Keynes:

> The Treaty [of Versailles] includes no provisions for the economic rehabilitation of Europe – nothing to make the defeated Central Empires into good neighbors, nothing to stabilize the new States of Europe, nothing to reclaim Russia; nor does it promote in any way a compact of economic solidarity amongst the Allies themselves; no arrangement was reached at Paris for restoring the disordered finances of France and Italy, or to adjust the systems of the Old World and the New. (Keynes, 1920/2005: Ch VI, para. 1)

Postwar chaos in Russia allowed the Bolsheviks to take power, suppress markets and create an autarchic command economy that transferred ownership to an autocratic bureaucratic class rather than the people. The peace treaty imposed on Germany stripped it of its shipping, its colonies, most of its coalfields and iron mines, imposed reparations that it could not pay, and limited its right to tariff protection (Keynes, 1920/2005). Britain could no longer finance international investments, and recession in all Europe's leading economies denied markets to producers in the rest of the world economy. The USA became the world's largest economy and should have opened its borders as Britain had done, but instead intensified its protectionist stance. The result was major depressions in 1919–21 and 1929–32 that produced 'four major trends away from liberal trading principles':

> Special treatment of international trade in agricultural products, private regulation of international trade through cartel agreements, the subordination of foreign trade policies to the requirements of domestic employment and development policies, and the intensification of regional trading arrangements. (Brown, 1950: 45)

The result was a highly interventionist global policy regime, but one that now constrained output rather than expanded it and intensified political conflict, as had been the case before the war. The result, according to Harry Dexter White, the chief American negotiator at Bretton Woods, was:

> a pattern of every country for itself, of inevitable depression, of possible widespread economic chaos, with the weaker countries succumbing first under the law of the jungle that characterised international economic policies of the pre-war decade. (White, 1943/1969: 38)

These economic failures had devastating political effects. Class conflict intensified. Divisions between democratic socialists and Communists loyal to the Soviet Union led to the triumph of militarism in Japan and Fascism in Italy, Germany, Spain and Portugal, and an intensification of pressure on and repression in the Soviet Union. The end result was 'wars within as well as among nations' (White, 1943/1969: 37) that culminated in the Second World War.

State-led reconstruction and recovery after 1945

The peace initiated another period of state-led development, one that provided for the economic rehabilitation of the war-damaged countries, through a compact of economic solidarity between the USA and the rest, mediated by the creation of the IFIs with limited but crucial power to regulate global economic relationships. This laid the foundations for liberal globalization, but it began as a system similar to that which had prevailed before 1914. Here liberalization and support from the strongest country was combined with structuralism in the weakest, as the USA allowed the war-damaged economies of Europe and East Asia greater market access, and used aid and military spending to help structuralist regimes in weaker economies rebuild their industrial capacity (Brett, 1983).

The IFIs were created in 1944 to regulate international monetary relationships and finance postwar reconstruction after negotiations between the USA, now the global economic power, and the rest of the war-damaged countries, as we saw in Chapter 5 (see Horsefield, 1969). Both strong and weak countries wanted a stable and integrated global economy that would eliminate the 'beggar-thy-neighbour' policies that had led to the war, but disagreed about the levels of state intervention and official aid that would be needed by Europe and Japan for economic reconstruction, and by the third world for early industrialization. The Americans wanted a system that would 'maintain international equilibrium at a high level of international trade', through commitments from members to sustain 'commercial polices designed to reduce trade barriers and to terminate discriminatory practices' (Morgenthau, 1943, cited in Horsefield, 1969, vol 3: 85).[1] The rest wanted US support for reconstruction and the right to control their borders and subsidize domestic industries until they had done so. Thus the French argued that a premature suppression of 'foreign trade and foreign exchange control ... after the end of hostilities ... would have ominous effects' (French Plan, cited in Horsefield, 1969: 97), and Keynes (cited in Horsefield, 1969: 27), representing Britain, wanted an agency that would automatically recycle resources from surplus to deficit countries and thus

> offset the contractionist pressure which might otherwise overwhelm in social disorder and disappointment the good hopes of our modern world. The substitution of a credit mechanism for hoarding would have repeated in the international field the same miracle already performed in the domestic field of turning stone into bread.

Keynes believed in free trade, but only if deficit countries could be helped to finance imports either through trade surpluses, commercial borrowing or aid. He had advocated protectionism in the early 1930s (Keynes, 1933), but the trade wars in the 1930s convinced him that it should and could be avoided if strong surplus economies would guarantee weaker ones access to the necessary credit. He saw the IFIs as agencies of global governance that could internationalize the state-led deficit financing that he had recommended for nation-states in *The General Theory of Employment, Interest and Money*, his major work (Keynes, 1936/1973).

The final Articles of Agreement of the IMF in 1944 were based on a compromise in which all countries made a låong-term commitment to liberalization, but retained the right to currency and other trade controls until they felt that they were strong enough to dispense with them. The IMF was given limited resources to provide (conditional) short-term support to countries confronting 'temporary' balance of payments problems, and the World Bank was set up to provide longer term developmental assistance (Brett, 1983, 1985). We saw in Chapter 5 that the Havana Charter for the creation of an International Trade Organization made so many concessions to interventionist demands that the US Congress refused to ratify it. It was replaced by the GATT, which was designed to systematically reduce tariffs on the basis of most favoured nation principles, and was succeeded by the WTO, where disputes between LDCs and DCs continue (Brown, 1950).

This settlement initiated a long period of postwar reconstruction in DCs and state-led development in LDCs based on protective tariffs, nonconvertible currencies and fixed exchange rates. The IFIs did not have the resources to fund these processes, but the USA assumed this role itself, and turned its balance of trade surplus into a deficit by financing the Marshall Plan and supporting large American garrisons across the world to control the Communist threat. This facilitated widespread growth, full employment and strong welfare systems in DCs, which reduced social exclusion and strengthened democratic institutions, (Brett, 1983: Part III) and enabled the East Asian tigers to begin their successful transitions, using strategies that shifted from import substitution to state-managed export promotion (Amsden, 1989; Wade, 1990; Chang, 2003b; Kohli, 2004). Structuralism also produced 'three decades of unprecedented growth' in Latin America between 1950 and 1981, but also rapidly 'growing inequalities' (Palma, 2003: 125). Thus different kinds of strategies combining strong state controls and private markets produced the postwar boom that rescued international capitalism from what had appeared to be a terminal threat at the beginning of the war. Its success then enabled the leading countries to liberalize in the 1970s and 80s, but only after their state-led recovery had enabled them to catch up with the USA.

The willingness of the USA to finance this global process was strongly influenced by Communist expansion in Eastern Europe, China, Korea, Vietnam and Cuba. These non-market economies also managed to sustain major industrial and social transformations, although at a terrible social and political cost. Once they had done this, they also found that they had created economic systems and social expectations that could no longer be managed effectively in the old way, producing the velvet revolutions in Eastern Europe and Russia, and partial liberalizations in China and Vietnam.

Growth was positive during the postwar boom. It increased by 3.6% in low-income countries and by 5.7% in middle-income countries between 1960 and 1970 (World Bank, 1978: 78), while industry, private foreign investment, aid and exports also grew (Morawetz, 1977). These results compared 'very favourably with the historical experience of both the LDCs and even of the DCs during their transition to industrialization' (Brett, 1985: 186). But these overall successes concealed significant inequalities in performance and emerging structural problems in the weaker countries, where regimes followed interventionist policies modelled on those being implemented in the developed world, but often produced poor results.

International inequalities between DCs and LDCs, and especially between the most successful and least successful LDCs increased dramatically, as did internal inequalities (Chenery et al., 1974; Morawetz, 1977). Countries following import substituting rather than export-oriented strategies suffered the major balance of payments and fiscal crises in the late 1970s that forced them to go to the IFIs for support. All these problems were exacerbated in the LLDCs by political and bureaucratic failures and crises, producing many disastrous reversals.

The need for special measures to deal with these problems was clear in the early 1970s:

> It has become more and more clear that measures designed to help developing countries as a group have not been effective for these least-developed countries. They face difficulties of a special kind and intensity: they need help specifically designed to deal with their problems. (OECD, 1972: 103)

But the response was not 'special measures' that took account of their structural weaknesses, but neoliberal orthodoxy exemplified by the World Bank's (1981: 3) seminal Berg Report in 1981, which attributed African failures to 'inappropriate state dominated policies', initiating the shift to neoliberalism of the 1980s (see also Bates, 1981; Lal, 1984). We will look at the theoretical and policy implications of this in later chapters, but first provide an empirical basis for that analysis by reviewing the complex history of two African states.

Structuralism, liberalization and crisis in postcolonial Africa

The 'new' states in Africa were given democratic constitutions and inherited structuralist economies at independence in the 1950s and 60s, but subsequent political and economic failures produced radical institutional change, involving shifts from democracy to authoritarianism and back again, and from structuralism to neoliberalism and then to attempts to build the pluralistic institutions described in Part II. We will review these contradictory and unstable processes in two states – Uganda and Zimbabwe – that have experimented with these options, producing very uneven outcomes where success or failure has depended on complex relationships between different kinds of structures and local political, economic and social variables at different stages. Before doing so, we will contextualize these cases by examining the major shifts in policy regimes that have taken place in postcolonial Africa. African history can be divided into three broad phases – the period from independence to the late 1970s, dominated by authoritarian structuralism; the neoliberal reforms between 1980 and the late 1990s; and the diverse attempts to build liberal pluralism that have been going on since then.

From colonialism to authoritarian structuralism

African societies operated at 'much lower levels of development' than those in South and East Asia when they were colonized, with 'a highly fragmented political structure, abysmally low levels of literacy, even among elites, and a simple agrarian technology' (Kohli, 2004: 291). Colonialism incorporated many existing political entities into larger territories, created modern administrations and communications networks, and built economies that exported raw materials in exchange for consumer goods. Administrators answered to metropolitan governments but could not impose tight controls over local people who retained control over smallholdings in peasant-based economies and answered to local chiefs. Colonial agendas were dominated by the need to maintain peace and order, and to create a primary producing economy where states gave monopoly power to expatriate firms and suppressed the growth of African capitalism (Brett, 1973; Mamdani, 1976; Campbell, 1979). South Africa, Zimbabwe, Kenya and Algeria were dominated by white settlers who initiated radical capitalist transformations but excluded Africans from political and economic power. Thus colonialism undermined but did not eliminate traditional institutions, and initiated partial and distorted transitions to capitalism that blocked further progress in most new states (Austen, 1987; Freund, 1998; Kohli, 2004).

Nationalist movements and political parties emerged in the 1940s in response to political and economic exclusion. They were given independence in the peasant-based colonies in the late 1950s and early 1960s, but only achieved it after liberation wars in the settler dominated states. Democratic constitutions shifted power to African elites who inherited structuralist economies that had enabled colonial administrators to privilege expatriate and state-owned firms, but now used them to transfer resources to African firms and managers. Rulers, not markets, allocated scarce resources, and this produced intense political competition for them in contexts that lacked the organizational systems needed to make the compromises necessary to manage it. The new political parties and civic groups were weak and dominated by 'sectional' rather than 'encompassing' interests, to use Olson's terms (1982). This intensified political conflict and led to a rapid shift to one-party or military rule. Inexperienced Africans replaced expatriate officials, expatriate firms were penalized, and ineffectual industrial strategies were initiated using heavily subsidized private sector or state-owned enterprises (SOEs). Donors encouraged this process by financing large-scale capital-intensive projects to support their home industries. As a result, resources were

> concentrated on large-scale urban-based enterprises, highly centralized systems of energy production and capital-intensive communications and transport systems, large-scale civil engineering projects and capital-intensive agriculture, all of which are inappropriate to the conditions prevailing in most Third World countries. (Burch, 1987: 179)

These policies suppressed exports, increased unproductive state spending, and led to unsustainable balance of payments, fiscal and debt crises that were exacerbated by the global recession in the late 1970s. Left-wing regimes like Tanzania and Ghana performed worse than right-wing ones like Kenya and the Ivory Coast (Austen, 1987), but the latter also suffered from growing conflict and inequality.

From authoritarian structuralism to liberalization and democratization

Governments then had to go to the IFIs for support and accept neoliberal structural adjustment policies in return. The IFIs attributed Africa's failures to 'inappropriate state dominated policies' that overloaded governments, distorted economic incentives, and generated unproductive monopoly rents (World Bank, 1981: 3; see also Bates, 1981; Lal, 1984). They demanded new policy regimes based on fiscal discipline, realistic exchange rates, the liberalization of foreign trade and domestic markets, and the privatization of SOEs, but their results were also disappointing. Sahn et al. (1997: 252) showed that liberalization produced some positive results when it was actually adopted, but that implementation was so poor that it had 'not generated rapid and sustainable economic growth'. The early liberalization programmes had been designed by economists, but governments had 'mostly refused to countenance real institutional reform', and often 'simply deceived ... [the IFIs], promising measures that they then failed to undertake or soon reversed' (van de Walle, 2001: 158; Sahn et al., 1997: 253ff.). According to the influential British Commission for Africa Report:

> As a barrage of problems struck Africa in the 1970s and 1980s, per-capita incomes declined sharply. That period was characterised by undemocratic governments, widespread corruption, and ineffectual states ... Africa has suffered from governments that have looted the resources of the state; that could not or would not deliver services to their people; that in many cases were predatory, corruptly extracting their countries' resources; that maintained control through violence and bribery; and that squandered or stole aid. (Commission for Africa, 2005: 107)

This shifted attention from economic policies to political mismanagement, so donors added 'good [democratic] governance' to their policy conditionalities. Their demands were reinforced by 'the emergence of a whole set of [domestic] social movements which are making demands on the political system that is unprecedented since the heyday of the struggle for independence' (Mkandawire, 1994: 156). Paradoxically, these demands were often driven by the spending cuts and liberalization imposed by structural adjustment itself, but they also legitimated donor demands for good governance, so many civic agencies received strong donor support. The result was a shift from neoliberalism to liberal pluralism in the 1990s, when governments were obliged to 'embark on the process of building institutions – in both government and civil society – that support economic development' (van de Walle, 1995: 154).

The successes and failures of liberal pluralism

The result has been some successes and many failures. Elections have forced regimes to respond to some domestic demands, and donor interventions have strengthened fiscal management and state capacity. Increases in raw material prices, now reversed as a result of the global crisis, increased growth in many countries, and better managed economies like Botswana, Uganda, Ghana and Mozambique have grown rapidly. Average growth rates for sub-Saharan Africa increased from 5.2% to an anticipated 5.8% between 2004 and 2008 (UNECA, 2007), while the 'number of civil wars dropped from fifteen to nine between 2002 and 2003' (Commission for Africa, 2005: 109). Further:

> more than two-thirds of the countries in sub-Saharan Africa have had multi-party elections, with a number of examples of peaceful,

democratic changes of government. Not all elections involved transfers of power and there are still a number of apparently immoveable presidents in office, but in terms of political freedoms, Africa has shown strong improvement in the last 20 years. (Commission for Africa, 2005: 107)

However, growth is still dominated by raw material exports, liberalization blocks industrial strategies to deal with cheap imports especially from China (UNECA, 2007), and the north still refuses to remove its own agricultural subsidies that block African exports. Rising food and fuel prices benefitted some countries but punished others, and the ongoing financial crisis is reducing raw material prices, intensifying competition and could also reduce access to aid. Many countries like Sudan, Chad, Ethiopia, Somalia, the DRC, Ivory Coast, Sierra Leone, Burundi and Zimbabwe are still dominated by economic failure, political instability and violence caused by multiple and interconnected crises.

Rulers have used the successes as evidence of an African renaissance, and donors have used them to justify increases in aid to build democratic capitalist societies (Commission for Africa, 2005). Left-wing pessimists use the failures as evidence of the destructive effects of Africa's deepening integration 'within the international [capitalist] division of labour' (Amin, 1994: 326), and of the need for 'social justice movements' led by progressive civic organizations representing poor and marginalized groups to conduct an anticapitalist struggle (Nabudere, 2000; Bond and Manyanya, 2002: Ch. 5). Right-wing pessimists attribute them to the failure to adopt market-based reforms because of the 'neopatrimonial' and predatory nature of African states.

Each of these claims explains some features of this conflicted and diverse landscape, but not others, while individual histories reveal more complex and contingent stories. Structuralist and liberal programmes have actually succeeded in some places and failed in others. Democratically elected regimes have sometimes managed progressive programmes that incorporated competing interests, and sometimes used state power to redistribute rents, destroy economic capacity and marginalize the majority of the population. Thus we cannot rely on one-sided theoretical and ideological claims of either neoliberal or structuralist paradigms to explain these contradictory processes. Instead, we need to develop 'more finely tuned analyses ... [that] probe actual state organizations in relation to one another, in relation to past policy initiatives, and in relation to the domestic and transnational contexts of state activity' (Evans et al., 1985: 353). We will do this now by reviewing the contrasting postcolonial experiences of Uganda and Zimbabwe.[2]

Uganda: from failed structuralism to successful liberalization

The first post-independence election in Uganda involved three parties based on ethnic and sectarian differences, but none achieved an overall majority. Milton Obote, the leader of the Uganda People's Congress (UPC), became prime minister in 1962. He bought off several opposition MPs, but responded to a constitutional attempt to unseat him by arresting key opponents in his Cabinet, suspending the constitution, and using the army to repress opposition. New elections were planned for 1971, but were pre-empted by a military coup led by Idi Amin, whose dictatorship suppressed all opposition and ruled by decree until it was defeated by a combination of the Tanzanian army and Ugandan guerrilla groups in 1979. Representatives of the major opposition movements then returned from exile and established a new democratic constitution and held an election in 1980, whose results were widely believed to be rigged. This returned Obote to power, but opposition groups went into the bush, conducted a successful civil war and took power in 1986 under the leadership of Yoweri Museveni, leader of the National Resistance Movement (NRM). It initially set up a 'broad-based government' with representatives of all the major political movements, including the UPC, and gradually introduced democratic elections. It started with indirect elections to local councils and then to the national Parliament, it then allowed 'non-party' elections using universal suffrage, and only adopted fully fledged multiparty democracy in 1995.[3]

These political changes were closely linked to changes in economic policy regimes. The British colonial regime had introduced export crop marketing and processing monopolies to protect expatriate producers, and land laws that favoured peasant over both settler and indigenous capitalist farmers. It adopted an industrial strategy in the 1950s based on SOEs and joint enterprises with private Asian firms, and transferred some marketing and processing monopolies from expatriate firms to African cooperatives. The new government continued these strategies in the 1960s and made new investments in infrastructure, education and health supported by significant inflows of aid. This structuralist strategy was relatively well managed until the late 1960s, and favourable world conditions and donor support produced annual per capita growth of about 1% over the decade.[4] However, it also created many of the problems identified by liberal theorists.

Inherited structuralist controls were used to maintain the political support of the emerging African middle class and the peasantry by Africanizing and expanding the civil service, the army and the parastatals (SOEs), transferring crop processing and marketing to African-owned cooperatives, and imposing controls over expatriate firms to improve opportunities for indigenous ones. However:

- Administrative reform produced a loss of valuable skills and increased unproductive administrative costs, constraints on expatriate firms reduced investment and efficiency, and officials and politicians were able to extract rents by exploiting their state-created monopoly powers, thereby increasing costs and reducing returns to small farmers.
- Import substitution led to state and donor subsidies to inefficient state, private and cooperative firms behind protective barriers that penalized export producers and the poor.
- Large tracts of land were allocated to absentee owners with political influence who made little use of them, and donor support to agriculture was based on inefficient investments in mechanical technology and exotic animals, which penalized small farmers, reduced exports, discouraged investment and increased inequalities.

The regime's dependence on state controls that enabled it to allocate resources to favoured clients explains its willingness to suppress democracy, and why it failed to win the support of an economically dominant southern elite that mainly supported opposition parties. Its failure to develop a poverty-focused strategy alienated the mass of the population.

At the end of the 1960s, the regime confronted balance of payments, fiscal and debt crises, and increased donor dependence. It then attempted to gain support prior to the forthcoming national elections by a 'move to the left' when it nationalized many foreign assets, but it lost donor support in the process. The resulting economic and political crisis ensured that Idi Amin was greeted with acclamation when he took power through a military coup in 1971.

However, his regime confronted even more difficult problems. It needed to build political support and finance the state and a seriously divided army,[5] but the investment, balance of payments and fiscal crises made it difficult for it to do so. It therefore responded to the demands of the African business community by expropriating Asian-owned firms, expelling most of the expatriate community and allocating their assets to African entrepreneurs. This intensified the economic and political crisis, and the regime responded with increasingly repressive and predatory policies that further undermined its ability to win political support, provide public services or rebuild the army (Brett, 1975; Campbell, 1979). As a result, the regime was easily defeated by the Tanzanian army and Ugandan guerrilla groups in 1979.

The UPC won a disputed election in 1980, and continued the corrupt structuralist policies of its predecessor. It reneged on undertakings to the

IFIs who attempted to introduce a structural adjustment programme in exchange for financial support. It politicized appointments to the army and civil service and excluded members of opposing political groups. It failed to defeat the NRM and other groups in the civil war that began in 1981, and this intensified the crisis. There was another military coup in 1985, and the NRM took over in 1986.

The NRM regime took power by force but created a 'broad-based government' incorporating opposition groups to end political conflict and rebuild the shattered economy. It initially adopted left-wing structuralist policies that the donors refused to fund, and its economic weakness soon forced it to accept a liberalization programme in return for their support. It did not comply with most of their demands until the end of the 1980s, but retained their support because they believed that the regime was committed to making a serious attempt to rebuild.

However, the regime had complied with virtually the whole programme by the middle of the 1990s. It had removed currency controls, balanced the budget, eliminated marketing monopolies, restored Asian property rights, and had started to privatize the large, corrupt and loss-making parastatal sector. It benefited from generous donor support that enabled it to balance the budget without cutting (very inadequate) social services, rebuild infrastructure, and finance imports. Uganda was the first country to qualify for debt relief from the IFIs, and the first to shift from a structural adjustment strategy to one based on a poverty reduction strategy (see Government of Uganda, 1997). The result has been growth rates of about 7% in the first decade, and almost 6% since then, mainly driven by growth in the private sector. The major benefits have been concentrated in the south, but without great increases in inequality (Appleton and Mackinnon, 1995).

Uganda is now seen as one of the major African success stories of the past 20 years and a model for the rest of Africa, but there is also a downside. The NRM victory was followed by civil war in the northern districts that had previously supported the UPC; political negotiations and an amnesty drew most of the guerrilla groups out of the bush at the end of the 1980s, but resistance from the millennial Lord's Resistance Army continues in one region, imposing heavy costs on the community and the society as a whole (Brett, 1995a, 1996a; Allen, 2006). Donor dependence continues, political conflict and patronage-based corruption are growing and increasingly coercive methods are being used to manipulate elections and retain support, so the risk of a reversion to the authoritarian and predatory habits of the past still exists (Barkan, 2005).

However, the achievements involved in making the transition from the political economy of predation and disorder to one characterized by rising per capita incomes, secure property rights, regular elections, and some limited improvements in state capacity cannot be denied. The political victory of the NRM has produced a shift from a vicious to a virtuous circle in Uganda. Economic growth increased political support for the regime, and political stability encouraged investment and donor support, showing that it is possible for failed African states to reconstruct themselves, given the right opportunities.

Zimbabwe: from successful structuralism to failed liberalization

Colonial Rhodesia was governed by an elected settler government that excluded the African population. It declared independence from Britain in 1965, was subjected to international sanctions and challenged by two African guerrilla groups in the 1970s. In 1979, a democratic constitution was negotiated and a government based on the Zimbabwe African National Union-Patriotic Front (ZANU-PF), led by Robert Mugabe, was elected in 1980 with a large majority. It was opposed by the Zimbabwe African People's Union (ZAPU), which represented the minority Ndabele tribe. There were regular elections, but dissent in Matebeleland, the ZAPU heartland, was violently suppressed in the late 1980s, when Nkomo's ZAPU joined the government in 1987, creating a de facto one-party state, governed by ZANU-PF.

Economic liberalization in the early 1990s increased political opposition, producing many civic organizations that united to form a new political party, the Movement for Democratic Change (MDC), in 1999. The regime lost a constitutional referendum in 2000, and resorted to populist economic policies and electoral manipulation and intimidation to win subsequent elections until the parliamentary and presidential elections in 2008. The MDC and an associated breakaway faction won the parliamentary elections and a majority in the first round of the presidential elections, but intense violence and intimidation orchestrated by the regime forced Morgan Tsvangirai, its presidential candidate, to withdraw from the second round. Mugabe returned to power and strongly resisted all attempts to produce the broad-based government pressed on it by regional leaders, and is now involved in an unstable coalition with the MDC.[6]

The settler regime had adopted a right-wing structuralist strategy to offset international economic sanctions in 1965, and had managed it very effectively, achieving almost 10 years of rapid industrialization and growth. ZANU-PF had used a socialist rhetoric during the civil war, but adopted a corporate capitalist strategy when it came to power. It allowed expatriate dominance of commercial farming and the formal urban economy to continue on a tightly regulated basis, and continued to run the existing parastatal sector well. It met its commitments to its African supporters by introducing a small land redistribution programme, limiting managerial controls over wages and working conditions, and improving conditions for more prosperous African farmers, and access to health, education and other social services. It retained a large proportion of senior white officials, but rapidly expanded the civil service to provide jobs for the growing number of well-trained Africans.

There was positive growth throughout the period, apart from drought-affected years, and significant improvements in African welfare. Policy was well managed and sustained by close relationships between officials and national producer associations inherited from the settler period, and by the willingness to retain most of the existing bureaucratic and capitalist classes and tax them to provide additional services to the regime's urban and rural constituencies. The regime was therefore able to retain political support without threatening economic stability or undermining the democratic process. However, structuralism had some negative long-term economic effects:

- socialist ideology led the regime to discourage new foreign investment and the emergence of a new African bourgeoisie[7]
- the capital-intensive nature of the economic system and labour controls suppressed employment and exports
- heavy taxation and credit controls maintained levels of state expenditure that crowded out new private investment
- the limited nature of the land reform programme did little to deal with rural overcrowding among communal farmers.

These constraints intensified economic and political stresses in the late 1980s. Shortages of foreign exchange (forex) and high taxation cut investment and increased unemployment among new secondary and university graduates. These problems could have been ameliorated without full-scale liberalization by encouraging small businesses and foreign investment and shifting to an East Asian-style export-oriented strategy, but pressure from the IFIs, domestic capitalists and the technocrats in the Ministry of Finance persuaded the regime to adopt a classical liberal economic structural adjustment programme (ESAP) in 1990. This had mixed results. Output initially fell because of drought and falling raw material prices, and investment was inhibited by increased demands for taxation and forex from the state. Competitive imports undermined domestic industry and increased unemployment, while attempts to reduce the fiscal deficit led to cuts in social services.

However, the programme was well managed, and had begun to resolve some earlier problems by the mid-1990s, when exports, employment and overall output began to grow rapidly. The IFIs and the private sector were optimistic, and negotiations began for a second phase of the ESAP programme. However, the reforms had heavy political costs –

trade unions were alienated by the loss of jobs and employment protection, civil servants by attempts to cut the fiscal deficit, and the mass of the population by cuts in social services. Support for ZANU-PF declined, new civic associations emerged to challenge these policies, and demands for land redistribution intensified. Political opposition grew, the MDC emerged as a real threat to ZANU-PF in 1999, and the regime lost a constitutional referendum in 2000.

So the regime reverted to structuralist policies to regain political support, but now operated them in populist and predatory ways, which destabilized the economic system. In 1998, it made large handouts to veterans of the liberation struggle and announced that it would redistribute commercial farms. This destabilized the budget, alienated the business class and the IFIs, provoked a run on the currency, and intensified inflation. It then:

- forcibly expropriated most commercial farms and redistributed the land to political cronies and small farmers, leading to a collapse in rural employment, food production and exports
- printed money to fund the state and produced hyperinflation
- used currency controls to reward supporters by allocating them heavily overvalued forex and destroyed the competitiveness of domestic industry
- introduced price controls to control inflation, but simply intensified shortages
- appointed army officers to manage parastatals, but they ran them into the ground
- destroyed the assets of tens of thousands of informal businesses in 2005, because they were seen as a political and economic threat to the system.

The result has been economic and political disorder, massive declines in output, employment, food production and exports, and a humanitarian crisis stemming from a combination of disease, hunger and dispossession, with life expectancy falling from more than 60 in 1990 to about 35 in 2008. Millions have migrated and many of those who remain depend on remittances and food aid for survival.

The IFIs withdrew support from the regime at the end of the 1990s, but donors have continued to provide humanitarian and food aid, mostly through NGOs. In 2007, the crisis forced the regime to enter into negotiations with the MDC in Johannesburg, brokered by the South African government. The MDC victory in the March elections of 2008 demonstrated that the regime had lost its political support and was entirely dependent on the waning power of the security services. The situation is now unstable and unpredictable – the economy is in ruins and can only be revived with donor support, which in turn depends on the ability of the contending factions to come to an acceptable political agreement that still eludes them at the start of 2009.

Conclusions

Two important conclusions can be drawn from this historical review:

1 Outcomes are not primarily determined by the technical aspects of policy regimes, but by the effectiveness of the governments that implement them. Strong governments have produced relatively successful structuralist as well as liberal programmes, while politically insecure and weak governments have failed.
2 Even the most repressive regimes cannot afford to ignore the need to impose economic discipline and maintain the support of key social groups if they are to survive over the long term, demonstrating the significance of political and contextual variables in the success or failure of developmental transitions.

These variables include the existence of local values, understandings and endowments, which often block the introduction of liberal institutions. Most countries have adopted structuralist policies to overcome the start-up problems created by late development during the modern era, but these policies, as well as liberal ones, only succeeded when governments were able to impose effective disciplines on managers, workers, consumers, and the political and bureaucratic classes themselves.

The successful early industrializers in northern Europe, Japan and East Asia used structuralist policies to create 'cohesive capitalist states'. Political systems denied political rights to the mass of the population, as in Britain and Holland in the 18th century, South Korea in the 1960s and 70s (Kohli, 2004: 84ff.) and Brazil between 1967 and 1973. Here repressive regimes were a 'central instrument for both the repression of subordinate classes and the reorientation of the process of industrial development' (Stepan, 1985: 317). However, they also collaborated with the business class and guaranteed their property rights, producing a symbiotic relationship between increasing state intervention and capitalist development rather than a mutually destructive one (see Evans et al., 1985: 353ff.).

All these regimes defended the property rights of the dominant classes, but also encouraged intense competition among them, and used state power to transfer assets to particular groups at the expense of others. They imposed heavy burdens on subordinated classes that involved 'hard work for low pay, to say nothing of exploitation ... of compelling labor from people who cannot say no' (Landes, 1999: 381). Authoritarianism helped to manage and contain the resulting conflicts and reduce the impact of what Olson (1982) calls 'particularistic distributional coalitions'. However, the state's need to meet the needs of the emerging capitalist and professional classes also facilitated the emergence of democratic institutions after the initial transition. Thus this account does not deny the need for economic and political liberalization as a long-term goal, but it does oblige us to recognize the contradictory nature of the choices that have to be made in transitional social situations.

Rapid non-authoritarian transitions have only occurred in favourable circumstances in certain states, such as the USA, Canada, Australia and New Zealand, dominated by European settlers who brought substantial resources of human capital with them and forcibly expropriated immense natural resources by 'destroying, expelling or subordinating indigenous populations' (Tilly, 2000: 13). The comparison between postwar reconstruction after the two world wars shows that the intense economic pressures imposed on countries like Germany and Russia in the 1920s and 30s led to authoritarianism, while access to US aid and markets after the Second World War facilitated rapid growth and democratic rule based on strong interventionist states. Foreign aid has also been crucial to the restoration of democracy and economic markets in Uganda and other African states.

Hence state-led development has succeeded, but it has also led to economic and political disaster, where ineffectual or predatory regimes suppressed innovation and transferred surpluses to parasitic classes in Spain and Portugal in the 17th and 18th centuries, in Uganda in the 1970s and Zimbabwe since 1998. So 'institutions ... that underpin property rights for all and broad-based investment ... have a causative influence on long-run development processes. And ... greater political equality can lay the basis for better economic institutions' (World Bank, 2006: 113). Some degree of political accountability and economic discipline is essential to avoid political breakdowns, but it is difficult to find cases that have managed this by depending solely on the orthodox teachings outlined in Part II.

The success or failure of the theoretical paradigms and policy regimes that have been used to manage developmental transition is influenced by the way they alter the rules that govern the terms on which political and economic elites exercise power, and that allow citizens to punish or reward them. However, the ability of both to exploit these rules depends on the substantive capacity of actually existing governments, capitalists and civic agencies in particular countries. These are still very weak in all LLDCs, and this is why societies governed by socially rational despots have often outperformed liberal ones during early transitions. However, as Buchanan and Tullock

(1962: 100) argue, this is only the case where 'some means ... [can] be taken to ensure that the dictator will remain benevolent'. The despots who succeeded in South Korea and China were indeed constrained by many factors – threats of invasion, the power of dominant elites, or donor conditionality. But these conditions are fortuitous and non-replicable, and despotism more often results in predation and waste. All this raises serious questions about the orthodox liberal demand for democracy and free markets and the strategies that the development community should pursue to strengthen local capacities to meet the substantive challenges that institutional restructuring always involves – questions that will be addressed in detail in the rest of Part III.

Further, outcomes have depended on the nature of the relationships between state agencies, the political demands of competing interests, and the ability of the actual firms operating in competitive economies to generate the surpluses needed to support them. It is not policy reforms alone that produce progressive change, but how regimes, firms, social and political movements, and external agencies respond to the contextually determined opportunities and threats they confront. Neither states nor economies can be isolated from the cleavages that rend civil society, create or destroy political and social movements, and generate the resources needed to reproduce them. The interdisciplinary analysis presented in Chapters 11–14 should help us to understand these processes better.

Notes

1   Morgenthau was secretary to the US Treasury and Keynes was the key economic adviser to the British Treasury.
2   These case studies are based on long-term research, most recently funded by the government's Department for International Development, carried out at the Institute for Development Studies, Sussex; Makerere University, Uganda; and more recently in the Crisis States Research Programme at the London School of Economics and the University of Witwatersrand, Johannesburg, reported in Brett (1992/3, 1998, 2005, 2008). I am greatly indebted to colleagues at all these universities for intellectual support.
3   See Appleton and Mackinnon (1995); Barkan (2005); Brett (1975, 1992/3, 1995b, 1998); Carboni (2008); Langseth et al. (1995); Mamdani (1976); Museveni (1992); Mutibwa (1992); Sathyamurthy (1991); and Carboni (2008).
4   Data from *Uganda: Second and Third Five Year Plans; Background to the Budget, 1970–71*, Statistical Abstract, 1971.
5   Personal communication, President Idi Amin, 1973.
6   See Botchwey et al. (1998); Brett (2005, 2008); Campbell (2003); Carmody (2001); Hammar (2003); Harold-Barry (2004); Herbst (1990); Jenkins and Knight (2002); Mumbengegwi (2002); Skálnes (1995); Stoneman (1988); Stoneman and Cliffe (1989); UN (2005); and Wild (1997). I owe a special debt to Sven Schwersensky, Andy Winter, Brian Raftopoulos and John Makumbe here.
7   This was a consequence of ZANU-PF's 'socialist' orientation; see Wild (1997) and Nicholas (1994); personal interviews in 2003 with Strive Masiyiwa, CEO Econet Wireless, and Jonathan Oppenheimer, CEO Anglo American Harare 1996–7.

Chapter 11

Explaining Blocked Development

The limits of liberal pluralism

Different versions of liberal pluralism are being used in DCs to manage the crises generated by structuralism and neoliberalism over the past 25 years. These reforms recognize the need for institutional change, but assume that its primary concern should be the need to maximize individual freedoms and defend rights, and they attribute poverty in LLDCs to the fact that the rules needed to do this are generally 'absent in developing countries' (Stiglitz, 2002: 73).[1] However, the assumption that these rules could be applied in the same way in weak states as in strong ones fails to recognize that their effective operation depends on the existence of demanding preconditions that are only now being developed in many LLDCs. Instead, it sees institutions as no more than 'the rules of the game in a society or, more formally ... the humanly devised constraints that shape human interaction' (North, 1990: 3), and assumes that social transformations require little more than a transition from policy regimes that undermine to those that safeguard individual property rights. If this were so, development could indeed take the form of the technical programmes promoted by the policy community that is now pressurizing LDCs to adopt these '"good institutions" ... with some minimal transition provisions (5–10 years) for the poorer countries' (Chang, 2003a: 503). These assumptions and the policy regimes based on them can, however, have very serious limitations.

The orthodox model attempts to:

- strengthen state capacity through democratic and civil service reforms
- create strong economic markets by consolidating property rights, privatizing state enterprises, encouraging small enterprises, and improving regulatory regimes and infrastructure
- strengthen civil society by building human and social capital, investing in pro-poor services and civic associations, and encouraging participatory management systems.

These reforms have produced important gains in many countries, but have also often been undermined by electoral manipulation, bureaucratic clientalism, institutionalized corruption, exploitative business practices, and sectarian and ethnic exclusiveness. These have subverted the operation of political, economic and social markets, generated perverse incentives, and undermined principles of rational management. For example:

- elections can sometimes inflame latent rivalries and lead to violence and political breakdown
- liberalization can sometimes lead to deindustrialization, unemployment and economic exclusion
- privatization can sometimes transfer resources to cronies or private sector monopolies and deny essential services to the poor
- participatory projects can sometimes reduce efficiency and increase inequalities.

These failures continue to threaten the modern development project, but they should not be used to devalue its emancipatory goals, or the enormous sacrifices made by millions of people who have struggled to achieve them since the start of the liberal enlightenment project in the 18th century. However, they call for a critical examination of the credibility of the empirical assumptions of liberal theory and its policy prescriptions in countries that are still acquiring the human and physical resources needed to sustain them. Classical development theorists also supported the enlightenment project, but recognized that the authoritarian institutions that actually governed the behaviour of people living in the third world rarely enabled them to behave, think or feel as though they actually were free individuals.

Pre-modern institutions in LLDCs varied from undifferentiated segmentary systems to complex empires, but were then subordinated to the needs and control of colonial powers, which applied liberal principles in their own societies but authoritarian ones in their 'dependencies' (Brett, 1973; Bessis, 2003). Colonialism often 'created a façade of a modern state that lacked scope or depth', which was then captured by indigenous elites who 'reduced it to a vehicle of personal and sectional aggrandizement' and were 'quite capable of destroying institutions they inherited', but not of 'constructing modern states anew' (Kohli, 2004: 395–6). Here the problem was not that political and economic markets failed, but that they were systematically suppressed, denying people the skills, experiences and assets needed to create them when the opportunity arose.

The political and economic markets created over the past 30 years are therefore far weaker than those in LDCs, so they demand much stronger forms of intervention and support than orthodox pluralism assumes. DCs also 'did not get where they are now through the [liberal] policies that they recommend to the developing countries today' (Chang, 2002: 2). Instead, early industrialization in the west and East Asia was based on authoritarian states, interventionist economies and ascribed and inherited status rather than individual freedom and choice. Indeed, the 'progressive' institutions that are now being exported to LLDCs typically took 'decades, if not generations to develop' in the countries where they originated (Chang, 2002: 116).

These conditions explain many developmental failures and the need for a distinct body of development theory and policy because:

1 The gap between actual capacities and the cultural and technical requirements of viable market- and science-based systems reduces efficiency and integrity.
2 The need to shift from old to new systems threatens existing interests and generates high contestation costs and social disruption.

This can lead to vicious circles and low-level equilibrium traps or actual breakdowns, as Myrdal recognized:

> With a low level of economic development follow low levels of social mobility, communications, popular education and national sharing in beliefs and valuations, which imply greater impediments to the spread effects of expansionary momentum; at the same time the poorer states have for much the same reasons and because of the very fact of existing internal inequalities often been less democratic and, in any case, they have, because they are poorer, been up against narrower financial and, at bottom, psychological limitations on policies seeking to equalise opportunity. Inequality of opportunities has, on the other hand, contributed to preserving the low 'quality' of their factors of production and a low 'effectiveness' in their production efforts. (Myrdal, 1956/1976: 689–90)

This generates start-up problems created by the need to find ways of building the social, political and economic capital required to eliminate the attitudes and power structures that sustain regressive institutions and reverse the vicious circles they generate. Only then can they institutionalize the progressive processes described by Rostow (1971) in his classic text.

Liberal pluralists are now attempting to resolve many of the apparently antagonistic conflicts between classical structuralism and neoliberalism, but have hardly addressed these historical and contextual issues at all. They assume that development can simply be induced by changing institutional rules, and so they 'collectively misrecognise'[2] the problematic nature of the contexts in which their reforms have to be implemented, their disruptive impact on local actors and existing structures, the political and social conflicts they will generate, and the scale and nature of the resources needed to facilitate them. Most importantly, they also fail to see that these conflicts and dislocations are a direct outcome of the institutional reforms that liberal theory prescribes.

These serious problems do not negate the need for free markets and science-based management systems discussed in Part II, but they do oblige us to recognize that those who hope to create them also need to return to the long-standing, but recently forgotten insights of the classical developmental traditions. Theorists concerned with the special problems of late development from the 18th century onwards have recognized that the institutions and policies that work in DCs can represent a long-term goal for all societies, but they need to be tailored to local cultures, capabilities and endowments, and that special interventions will be needed to compensate groups whose interests must be threatened by the resource transfers they entail. They saw that these reforms must involve long-term changes in social and economic structures, forms of political organization and the intervention of creative individual leadership.[3]

First we will consider the developmental problems generated by the existence of incompatible values and structures in LLDCs, and then we will look at the contestation costs generated by structural change. We will argue that these problems can only be overcome by supplementing individualistic liberal pluralism with a socially based analysis that recognizes the theoretical and practical consequences of the existence of multiple value systems, understandings and endowments in societies that are not simply trying to maintain existing liberal institutions but to build new ones.

Contradictory cultures, market failures and start-up problems

The pluralist project that sustains the post-Washington consensus is firmly anchored in methodological individualism and liberal capitalism, and ignores or rejects the socially oriented traditions that have sustained corporatist and socialist projects since the 19th century. It treats hierarchical and collective forms of organization as a necessary evil to be accepted when market-based exchanges would otherwise fail, as we saw in Part II. For the pluralist project:

- its primary normative goal is the creation of individual freedom

- its central empirical assumption is that societies are composed of people who actually see themselves as self-interested but socially responsible individuals
- its key operational assumption is that these individuals can be relied on to maximize their own utilities by bargaining freely and rationally with others, and that they will maximize social welfare by doing so.

Pluralists recognize the existence of market failures and the need for collective interventions to deal with opportunistic behaviour, informational asymmetries, externalities, open access resources, natural monopolies, and poverty and exclusion. Their analyses and prescriptions are fully compatible with an individualistic methodology and applied in different ways in all capitalist economies. Most people in DCs recognize that their right to freedom must be complemented by a duty not to threaten the liberties of others, and the need for public and private organizations to manage the conscious, collective and compulsory political and social interventions necessary to overcome market failures, although, even there, high levels of deprivation and individualization also lead to serious failures and breakdowns that we cannot address here.

However, liberal pluralists ignore the fact that people's ability to live lives based on these principles depends on the pre-existence of the appropriate institutional framework, and assume that even 'uneducated private agents' in LDCs will respond to market signals 'much as neoclassical theory would predict'. They do not recognize the existence of possible tensions between local and liberal institutions and values, but treat them as 'second best adaptations to the risks and uncertainties' in local environments and therefore as 'likely to enhance efficiency'. They also assume that political failures in weak states will generally produce worse outcomes than market failures (Lal, 1996: 30–1).

Unfortunately, their assumptions are only partially true, because individualism is not intrinsic to human nature, but is a socially constructed response to life in modern societies. Douglas (1986: 112) shows that successful institutions demand a close correlation between their conceptual apparatuses and authority systems, and the dispositions, aptitudes or 'self-knowledge and ... identities' of their members. Elias (2001) shows that the nature of the 'we-I' balance, which determines how people balance their rights as individuals against their obligations to society and the agencies that control it, has changed dramatically over time. In pre-modern societies, people lived in highly insecure environments and were utterly dependent on their kinship and community networks. This imposed powerful social constraints on what they could do or believe, constraints that only disappeared in modern societies after they had created virtual full employment and effective welfare systems.

People in transitional societies are often even more insecure than those in pre-modern ones because of the disruptive effects of structural change, so it is hardly surprising that they fail to turn themselves into liberal individualists when their governments introduce free markets and democratic elections, often at the behest of the donor community. Appropriate cultures can only be sustained in societies that have already created the organizations and practices on which they depend, because people are not born free, but only acquire freedom where the institutions on which freedom depends already exist. As Weber (1976: 24)[4] says:

> For though the development of economic rationalism is partly dependent on rational technique and law, it is at the same time determined by the ability and disposition of men to adopt certain types of practical rational conduct.

People in the poorest societies also desire individual autonomy, free markets and efficient and honest corporate structures,[5] but few can evade the contradictory demands imposed by traditional obligations to family, patrons, clan, tribe, sect, class, or party. Hence liberal institutions are essential for long-term development, but societies that wish to replace their existing non-liberal institutions with liberal ones, or, more realistically, to restructure them, confront serious start-up problems since they demand fundamental changes to deep-seated beliefs and expectations. These new values and models have been brought in from the outside, and were disseminated under colonialism by 'the European residents, the missionaries and the administrators, the settlers and the entrepreneurs' (Malinowsky, 1945/1961: 15), and now by the donor community, international NGOs, foreign firms, western-based education systems, and local elites who have assimilated the liberal paradigm.[6]

These models offer poor people the image of a future they would like to have, and exert a powerful influence over policies and behaviour, but the behavioural codes they require can only be fully consolidated and diffused where most people already understand them and can adopt them without threatening the social and economic networks that defend them from harm. Hence, as Oakeshott argues, the knowledge that a society requires in order to manage a given set of institutional arrangements

> is unavoidably knowledge of its detail: to know only the gist is to know nothing. What has to be learned is not an abstract idea, or a set of tricks, not even a ritual, but a concrete, coherent manner of living in all of its intricateness ... The politics of a community are not less individual (and not more so) than its language, and they are learned and practiced in the same manner. (Oakeshott, 1991: 62)

People in slave, feudal, theocratic, Communist or colonial societies could not learn how to be free to choose because they knew they would be severely punished if they did.[7]

The tension between the knowledge and resource endowments needed to sustain modern as opposed to pre-modern institutions takes many forms in LDCs:

- *Socially*, it is manifested in anti-individualistic value systems that support networks of trust focused on particular groups rather than on society as a whole, and in high levels of 'categorical inequality' (Tilly, 2003: 32) that consign certain groups to permanent subordination on the grounds of race, religion, caste or class.
- *Economically*, it is manifested in low levels of human, social and physical capital, an underdeveloped capitalist class, inadequate infrastructure and weak regulatory frameworks.
- *Politically*, it has been manifested in long traditions of authoritarian rule and the lack of a legitimate and competent state – its bureaucratic and judicial apparatuses, and the parties, interest groups, research institutes and media organizations required to sustain it.[8]

The result is insecure livelihoods, high levels of inequality and personal dependence, and weak states. These cannot guarantee peace, security or an adequate supply of public and merit goods because they are run by elites tied into systems of collective obligation to family, ethnic group or religion that impose heavy demands on even the richest of them, so they cannot survive on their official salaries. These obligations override those imposed by formal constitutional or bureaucratic rules to produce clientalistic systems that generate 'seemingly nonrational, inconsistent, and chaotic behavior' (Price, 1975: 12) involving 'a wide variety of practices involving the giving and receiving of favors, *almost invariably based on corruption*' (van der Walle, 2001: 51, emphases added). These traditional ties are reinforced by the perverse bureaucratic practices inherited from modern authoritarian statist systems where personal loyalty to rulers was more crucial than merit, and the ability to reward supporters with jobs and patronage was a crucial element in the struggle for power.

As a result, few people are able to live up to the demands of liberal 'best practice'. Elites and social groups who are threatened by its demands subvert its operation, and the performance of the new political, economic and social institutions is undermined by the perverse incentives generated by clientalistic relationships and rent-seeking behaviour.

Classical modernization and Marxist development theorists have always recognized the tensions that will be generated by attempts to transfer new institutions to societies where the 'relevant structures' do indeed 'vary beyond ... limits' that exceed 'the general limits of variability of social structures in the relevant spheres' (Parsons, 1951/1964: 178). Central to their work is the idea of 'dualism', which recognizes the negative and positive effects of the coexistence of modern and traditional cultures and institutions for developmental transitions, and the often non-liberal solutions required to overcome them.

Successful LDCs like Taiwan, Malaysia, China and South Vietnam have introduced markets and integrated themselves into the global system, disproving the pessimistic claims of dependency and third world theorists outlined in Chapter 1. However, they combined these with non-liberal interventionist strategies that owe much to the structuralist tradition. Equally, failed attempts to introduce liberal reforms in countries like post-Sandinista Nicaragua, Iraq and Zimbabwe have exposed the limits of liberalization, and the possibility that 'corrupt or degenerating societies' can survive for long periods because of the 'decay of political organization and the increasing dominance of disruptive social forces' (Huntingdon, 1968: 86). What, then, is dualism, and how can it block developmental transitions?

Dualism, contested transitions and blocked development

Social systems have been built on institutions with very different characteristics that depend on different and even contradictory rules, and on the dispositions and understandings needed to ensure that people are willing and able to follow them. Contact between different systems produces institutional adaptations and corresponding changes in value systems but these are internalized slowly and unevenly. The generalized and forcible contact between these contradictory systems generated by the expansion of capitalism and imposition of colonialism created new institutions in third world societies that supplanted and delegitimized their existing cultural and knowledge systems, but as Marx and Engels (1845–6/1974: 88) saw, 'the peculiar form of intercourse' that had 'been ousted by that belonging to a larger interest, remains for a long time afterwards in possession of a traditional power'. The interplay between imported and indigenous systems did not produce mere coexistence, but dualism – understood as the emergence of 'a new type of culture, related to both Europe and ... [the third world] yet not a mere copy of either' (Malinowsky, 1945/1961: 10).

Thus one of the most important distinctions between classical development theorists and orthodox social scientists has been their willingness to recognize the role of dualism in both transforming 'traditional' societies and blocking a full transition to 'modernity'. They recognized that competing value systems also exist in DCs, so that they are 'dualistic in this sense', but they also argued that these values have far more pervasive and contradictory effects in transitional societies undergoing fundamental structural change (Almond, 1960: 23). Thus Boeke saw dualism as a situation in which an external social system, most frequently 'high capitalism' but possibly also 'socialism or communism', led to a 'clash between an imported and an indigenous social system of a divergent character' and produced new hybrids. This demanded a new kind of approach based on

> three economic theories combined into one: the economic theory of a precapitalist society, usually called primitive economics, the economic theory of a developed capitalistic or socialistic society, usually termed general economic theory ... and the economic theory of the interaction of two distinct social systems within the borders of one society, which might be called dualistic economics, if this term had not better been reserved for the combined economic theory of a dual society as a whole. (Boeke, 1953/1976: 131)

The result has been societies characterized by partially assimilated and competing institutional systems based on contradictory values and principles, as Price argued:

> in traditional societies ... organizations whose formal aspects have been transplanted from highly industrial societies, and which therefore appear to the observer as 'modern' social structures, are in reality penetrated by aspects of the indigenous ('traditional') social system, and ... this produces hybrid institutions, many of whose features are dysfunctional to successful achievement of organizational goals. (Price, 1975: 11)

Eggertsson (2005), 50 years after Boeke, has now argued that this concept needs to be introduced into institutional economics, since its focus on exchanges between rational individuals means that it cannot otherwise explain the existence of perverse incentives and policy failures. He shows that where people have already internalized the appropriate values, changing the rules by creating secure property rights and open markets will indeed operate as 'a first-order policy instrument ... [that] will shape social norms, harmonize material interests, consolidate a weak and fragmented state or tame a predatory one, and launch economic growth' (Eggertsson, 2005: 182). However, for this to happen, they must have acquired these values, have access to the necessary technology and investments, and not have a vested interest in maintaining the old rules. Thus institutional change will fail in contexts where

> new rules clash with old and still prevalent institutions unless the reformers know how to solve the conflict and are able to do so.

Necessary tools for removing dysfunctional institutional elements (including social norms) are sometimes unavailable, or when they are available, the reformers, with their incomplete models, sometimes may not know how deep to dig until the new institutions take root. (Eggertsson, 2005: 30)[9]

Classical modernization, Marxist and third world theorists all accepted this idea, and provided different but not incompatible explanations for its continued existence. Modernization theorists argued that local value systems survived because they were functionally necessary to maintain local social systems that had little contact with modernity. Marxists argued that colonialism reinforced pre-capitalist structures and values, and allowed authoritarian traditional political and economic elites to block indigenous capitalist development and protect the interests of foreign political and economic elites. They argued that 'the modernity of one sector is a function of the backwardness of the other' (Laclau, 1971: 31; see also Brett, 1973; Bessis, 2003). Both assumed that local systems would eventually be assimilated by modern ones, as did indigenous nationalist elites who rejected 'traditionalism' and based their demand for independence on liberal principles of democracy and rational planning.[10] However, many modern multiculturalist theorists not only recognize traditional values and elites, which continue to exist, but believe that they can provide the basis for revolts against colonialism and European civilization, and for autonomous locally driven development strategies (Sachs, 1992; Escobar, 1995; Rahnema, 1997).

Classic versions of dualism dealt with the tensions generated by the imposition of modern institutions on pre-modern societies by capitalism and colonialism, but they have now been further complicated by recent transitions from statist to liberal capitalist systems. These involve new conflicts between the collectivistic principles and dependency relationships encouraged by statism, and the atomistic individualism required by market societies. These problems explain many of the crises involved in the liberal structural adjustment programmes being applied in former command and structuralist economies. Dualism has not disappeared but taken on new and more complex characteristics that can be subsumed under the idea of 'institutional multiplicity'. This relates to the complex and often contradictory interactions between traditional, corporatist and liberal value systems and the institutional arrangements they support.[11]

Dualistic theory was discredited in the 1960s and 70s because it had been used to justify racism and colonialism by attributing 'economic backwardness' to virtually immutable cultural values that caused local people to minimize their effort and income. Liberal critics like Higgins (1976) and Lipton (1968) showed that local people were indeed rational maximizers within the limits set by their assets and capabilities.[12] Dependency theorists claimed that dualism was used to explain away developmental failures that were actually caused by capitalism and imperialism. Thus Frank (1969: 62) argued that

> dualist theory and the diffusionist and other theses based on it are inadequate because the supposed structural duality is contrary to both historical and contemporary reality: the entire social fabric of the underdeveloped countries has long since been penetrated by, and integrated into, the world embracing system of which it is an integral part.

These critiques, and the poor performance of many state-led programmes designed to overcome problems created by dualism, then opened the way for the reassertion of orthodox liberal and liberal pluralist theory based on culture-free methodological individualism. It assumes that everyone is a rational individual, and all rational individuals will accept new market-based systems because of their manifest superiority to earlier systems based on different forms of traditionalism or collectivism. However, this is not the case where communities are still committed to racist, sectarian, familial, collectivistic or patriarchal value systems, which undermine the operation of liberal institutions and lead to political, economic and social oppression and blocked development.[13] This does not negate the normative goals or analytical principles of liberal pluralistic theory, but it does mean that most LDCs have to overcome deep-seated problems before they can adapt them to their own needs. DCs took centuries of often violent struggles to universalize these values, struggles that are now being replicated in most LDCs. They may produce similar results in the long term, but reformers cannot simply ignore the tensions and dislocations that dualism generates until they have done so. Dualistic arguments have now re-emerged to explain institutional failures in LLDCs, in the form of 'neopatrimonial theory',[14] in transitional economies and even in more successful 'fragmented-multiclass states', to use Kohli's terms,[15] like Brazil and India.

All societies contain multiple value and knowledge systems, but these only generate disruptive problems during periods of fundamental institutional change, because this not only introduces new rules, but also changes the allocation of power and wealth.[16] Shifting from closed to open markets, from collectivistic to individualistic moral codes, from patrimonial to science-based organizations, and from theocratic to contingent and experimentally based knowledge systems should produce long-term social gains but also threatens the assets and value systems of those with a vested interest in the existing order. Free elections threaten the power of corrupt dictators, free competition bankrupts inefficient firms, and equality and toleration are incompatible with the unquestioned authority of husbands, chiefs and religious or tribal leaders. And these threats are not just felt by elites, but by many social groups that depend on the security provided by their families, communities, tribes or religions. Thus, as Parsons argued:

> Change in the social system is possible only by the operation of mechanisms which overcome the resistance of vested interests. It is, therefore, always essential explicitly to analyze the structure of the relevant vested interest complex before coming to any judgment of the probable outcome of the incidence of forces making for change. These considerations will often yield the answer to the questions of why processes of change either fail to occur altogether or fail to have the outcomes which would be predicted on a common-sense basis. (Parsons, 1951/1964: 491–3)

Liberalization always threatens the privileges of the rich and powerful and the stability of the social networks, coping mechanisms, knowledge systems and cultural values that sustain whole communities. The demand for freedom and equal rights that has dominated world history since the start of the enlightenment has always led to antagonistic conflicts and imposed heavy contestation costs on the societies involved. According to Huntingdon (1968: 41):

> Modernity breeds stability, but modernization breeds instability ... It is not the absence of modernity but the efforts to achieve it which produce political disorder. If poor countries appear to be unstable, it is not because they are poor, but because they are trying to become rich.

Thus opposition to liberal reforms does not disappear when donors demand institutional change as the price for foreign aid, and these programmes may fail because of technical weaknesses, but more often because of political battles between stakeholders who use competing value systems to defend existing assets or claim new ones. Incumbent regimes appeal to traditional loyalties or the need for national unity to justify their hold on power, while opposition movements invoke liberal principles and demand democratic reforms. These struggles determine the success or failure of reform programmes, but cannot be explained by methodological individualism because they are rooted in collective and contradictory loyalties, are driven by social movements rather than individual agency, and motivated by what is often zero-sum competition for scarce resources.

Conclusions

Recognizing the effects of institutional multiplicity in LDCs obliges us to transcend the limits of liberal pluralism and recognize that the existence of many pre-modern values and practices are bound to block an immediate transition to modernity. Many third world critics use these failures to negate the whole enlightenment project, but the fact that liberal reforms challenge existing value systems and are resisted by vested interests does not reduce the potential benefits they might bring to exploited or excluded groups marginalized by the political and economic constraints imposed by pre-modern institutions. The latter subjugated slaves, lower castes, serfs, colonized subjects, collective farm workers, women and people of colour to control by repressive elites. It has been their demand for freedom, and not just the needs of their western advisers that has always justified the demand for liberal reforms. Thus the antagonistic conflicts and failures experienced by most LLDCs do not negate the validity of the normative claims of liberal pluralist theory, nor the coherence of its analytical framework. However, they do justify the need for a distinct body of development theory, which not only recognizes the universalistic claims embodied in the various UN charters, but also explains why progressive change has been blocked or reversed in so many contexts.

These insights, and the need to adapt liberal theory to take account of them, informed the structuralist tradition from Hegel, List and Marx in the first half of the 19th century to the modernization and dependency theory that emerged to deal with postwar and postcolonial reconstruction in the second half of the 20th. It recognized that creating liberal or socialist systems in contexts dominated by institutional dualism demanded forms of political intervention that would enable societies to develop forms of collective intervention that were more complex and far-reaching than those required in already developed societies.[17] Most structuralists failed to recognize the extent to which state intervention would also be compromised by the disruptive effects of dualism and the neopatrimonial politics associated with it, allowing their project to be challenged by liberalism in the 1980s and 90s. However, this does not negate the validity of the insights of the classical tradition, as the failure of so many liberal programmes shows.

We have stressed the negative implications of dualism to emphasize the relevance of the classical tradition to the crisis in development theory. However, we will also show that local institutions can play a positive as well as a negative role in developmental transitions, and create the basis for a synthesis between liberal pluralism and classical structuralism theory by moving from a theory based on methodological individualism to one based on hybridity and social institutionalism. This will show that the 'rationality' of local value systems has to be evaluated in relation to local contexts, these can often play progressive developmental roles, and they are never static, but change continuously in response to their interactions with external ones. This means that effective interventions will need to involve hybrid solutions that combine 'western' and 'traditional' institutions in new ways in order to accommodate themselves to local capacities, dispositions and endowments.[18] The struggle for development is now taking place in conditions that are very different from those that existed during the early phases of the postcolonial revolution. This does not mean that we should jettison old insights, but it does oblige us to combine them in new ways. Hence, the developmental challenge is not to eliminate non-western institutions, but to adapt them to modern needs and to manage the inevitable conflicts that this will generate better than we are doing now.

Notes

1   Fine et al. (2001) identify the limits of the market failure assumptions behind the 'new Washington consensus'.
2   Bourdieu (1992: 68) provides us with numerous examples of situations where 'collective misrecognitions ... are both the precondition and the product of the functioning of the field'.
3   For successful cases, see Linz and Stepan (1996: 92–3) on Spain, and Kohli (2004: 87ff.) on Korea.
4   Note the direct parallel here with Bourdieu (1992).
5   This claim is based on interviews with hundreds of highly marginalized people in Uganda between 1965 and 1998.
6   In recent years, 10% of US PhDs in economics have gone to Korean students (Ho-Joon Chang, personal communication).
7   At the end of the Spartacus revolt, 6,000 slaves were crucified along the Appian Way leading to Rome.
8   The majority of the national or foreign senior planners in LDCs that Ilchman (1969: 497–8) surveyed in the late 1960s were hostile to mass involvement in decision-making because they believed that 'the great majority of the population entertains traditional values and practices that are thought to be incompatible with economic development'.
9   Eggertsson (2005: 208) also notes that 'even when the demand for new institutions comes from below, there is no guarantee that the proposals are backed by a workable knowledge of the relevant social technologies'.
10 For example, Zolberg (1969: 294) noted that the new leaders of Ivory Coast believed that their transition from 'the status of subjects ... [to] that of citizens' required an end to the authority of 'traditional structures of authority' and traditional values that were 'usually designated as *racisme* by political leaders' and condemned in the constitution.
11 I am indebted to James Putzel and colleagues on the LSE Crisis States Programme for clarification of this point.
12 However, Putnam (1993: 183) echoed Boeke's pessimism 40 years later when he argued that the lack of 'norms and networks of civic engagement' meant that 'the outlook for collective action remains bleak' in southern Italy.

230 Reconstructing Development Theory

13 Here see Harrison and Huntingdon (2000), Allen and Skilton (1999) and Putzel (1997) on the 'dark side of social capital'. These problems are not confined to LDCs as the prewar history of Germany and the recent history of former Yugoslavia show.
14 See Bayart (1993); Bayart et al. (1998); Brett (2008): Callaghy (1984); Chabal and Daloz (1999); Hyden (2000); Joseph (1987); and van de Walle (2001).
15 See Kohli (2004: 8ff.) for a useful typology of effective as opposed to regressive states.
16 I owe this point to Jonathan Di John.
17 This literature is reviewed in Brett (1983, 1985).
18 I am indebted to Jo Beall (personal communication) and Inka Mathauer (2001) for clarifying this point.

Chapter 12

A Theory of Developmental Transformations

The ethnologist ... [must] describe and analyze one of the most significant phases in human history, that is, the present westernization of the world. Observations on culture change ... reveal to us also the general laws of diffusion: they provide the materials for the understanding of certain aspects of human culture: the tenacity of beliefs and traditional modes of life; the reasons why certain aspects of culture diffuse more rapidly than others – in short the dynamic character of the process.

As a humanist he ought to be aware that in this process there are involved human interests and passions that are still largely under the full control of agents of the active Western civilization. This control has not always been scientifically enlightened by a knowledge of all the facts at issue. Even now we must ask: are [these] changes ... such as to bring about a common existence of harmonious cooperation; or must they lead to temporarily suppressed but powerful forces of coming disruption, upheaval and historical catastrophe on an unprecedented scale? (Malinowsky, 1945/1961: 3)

Towards a sociology of developmental change

The start-up problems created by the existence of contradictory value systems and limited endowments, the contestation costs generated by 'the problem of order' identified in Chapter 4, and the problems of dualism discussed in Chapter 11 help to explain the failure of the liberal pluralist agenda in many LLDCs. They do not negate all its goals and policy prescriptions, but they do demand significant revisions of its reform agenda as these societies go through their developmental transitions. Identifying the nature of these revisions, and suggesting second-best policy solutions to problems of transition, has always been the primary concern of development theory and the reason why it has had to transcend methodological individualism and create a 'theory of the social' (Mouzelis, 1995: 42), which focuses on the role of structures rather than individual agency in institutional change in LDCs. Here decisions cannot simply be treated as a function of the choices of atomized individuals, but of 'the specific institutional contexts ... within which ... they operate'. Thus, the needs and interests that motivate different kinds of individuals, such as 'Peruvian peasants, United States farmers, Spartan helots, Roman slaves or medieval serfs', are

> socially constructed ... [so that] an adequate conceptualisation of the notion of interests must seriously examine context, both on the level of conceptual tools ... and on the level of first-order social phenomena (one has to relate interests to specific historical and socio-cultural contexts). (Mouzelis, 1995: 37–8)

The great figures in this long tradition – Burke, Hegel, Marx, Durkheim, Weber, Parsons, Malinowsky, Gramsci, Barrington Moore and Tilly – are concerned to explain both the necessary social conditions that liberal capitalism must sustain and the collective obligations it must enforce to enable its citizens to behave as if they were actually free to make autonomous choices about what to do or be, and also those processes involved in transitions to societies that sustain individual autonomy from those where they do not. Their work involves a shift from a formalistic and individualistic approach to institutions to a social approach, which, as Malinowsky (1944/1960: 46)[1] claimed, recognized that 'the individual can satisfy his interests or needs and carry out any or every effective action only through organized groups and through the organization of activities'. He argued that any attempt to describe individual existence in any civilization obliges us

> to link up its activities with the social scheme of organized life, that is, with the system of institutions prevailing in that culture. Again, the best description of any culture in terms of concrete reality would consist in the listing and analysis of all the institutions into which that culture is organised. (Malinowsky, 1944/1960: 48)

These theorists focus on the relationship between historically created cultural systems and institutional change. They not only provide a better understanding of the sociology of modern capitalism than methodological individualism and of the problems of social dualism and contested transitions outlined in Chapter 11, but also help to provide solutions to these problems by recognizing the positive contribution that local practices and knowledge systems can make to developmental change. We will first look at what they say about the role of socially imposed obligations and unconscious conditioning in creating social order in all social systems, including liberal capitalism. We will then examine the role of collectivistic value and knowledge systems in creating social order and providing services in LDCs and the tensions generated by attempts to replace them with market-based institutions based on possessive individualism. We will conclude by looking at the need to create hybrid institutions that will help to turn the adaptation of western models from 'an imitative and dependent activity' into 'a creative process which must ultimately result in the evolution of new social forms and autonomous modes of thought' (Brett, 1973: 16).

Collective values, social institutionalism and human agency

Individualists use what Granovetter (1992) calls an 'undersocialized conception of human action' that assumes that people exhibit 'rational, self-interested behavior affected minimally by social relations'. Classical development theorists, using the dualistic assumptions discussed in Chapter 11, believed that 'social relations' still dominated behaviour in pre-market societies, but that these 'became much more autonomous with modernization'. Liberals operating in the individualistic tradition treat these obligations 'as a frictional drag that impedes competitive markets' (Granovetter, 1992: 53–6). We saw in Chapter 11 that collective obligations to kinship networks, tribe, party or religion can indeed disrupt the 'mutually beneficial exchange and cooperation' between individuals generated by modern institutions (Weingast, cited in Moe, 2005: 217). However, the liberal assumption that collective values are inherently incompatible with rational market-based systems is highly problematic, because of the crucial role played by 'concrete personal relations and structures (or "networks") of such relations in generating trust and discouraging malfeasance' in all societies (Granovetter, 1992: 60).

If market societies did indeed always generate Pareto optimal solutions that gave everyone what they needed as well as what they were able to earn, people could be relied on to make individual choices that would also contribute to the general welfare. But we have already seen that competitive markets produce losers as well as winners. As Harriss-White (2003: 486) argues:

> Markets are not just socially embedded phenomena, they are sites of the exercise of power in ways which are not reducible either to the tool kit of the new institutional economics or to the norms of social embeddedness ... [instead] market power ... is situated in a structure of power which dominates the choices available to the participants.

These systems will only survive if losers as well as winners can be persuaded to accept their losses with good grace, and this in turn depends on the extent to which they have internalized value systems that induce them to do so. Thus market societies are not just places where atomized individuals interact, but are 'structures of power' that are socially constructed through state regulation, the activities of civic associations and large firms, and *'the expression of forms of social authority and status derived from outside the economy'*, for example those based on patriarchal or religious authority (Harriss-White, 2003: 486–90, emphases added). These can reinforce inequalities and exclusion, and block development as we know, but they can also guarantee contracts and maintain the trust required to sustain 'spontaneous exchanges' even in marginalized societies (Richards, 1985; Leach and Fairbairn, 1996; Jones, 2005). Thus the wrong kinds of collectivistic obligations are part of the problem, but the right kinds have to be part of the solution, because all societies depend on collective obligations to sustain the institutions and organizations that create the basis for cooperative interdependence.

Thus individual freedom is never absolute but constrained by the need to obey the rules and live by the unconsciously acquired knowledge and value systems that enable people to operate effectively in their social milieu. So, as Marx and Engels (1845–6/1974: 59) claim, what we call society is not an aggregation of atomized individuals but

> a material result: a sum of productive forces, an historically created relation of individuals to nature and to one another, which is handed down to each generation from its predecessor; a mass of productive forces, capital funds and conditions, which on the one hand, is indeed modified by the new generation, but also on the other hand prescribes for it its conditions of life and gives it a definite development, a special character. It shows that circumstances make men just as much as men make circumstances.

Hence individuals 'can attain their ends only insofar as they themselves determine their knowing, willing, and acting in a *universal* way and make themselves links in this chain of social connexions' that must exist 'not as freedom but as *necessity*' (Hegel, 1821/1967: 124, emphases added).[2] They therefore can only have 'rights insofar as ... [they have] duties and duties insofar as ... [they have] rights' (p. 109). Furthermore, Burke provided a powerful challenge to the atomistic and individualistic assumptions of neoliberal theory, when he argued that:

> Duties are not voluntary. Duty and will are even contradictory terms. Now though civil society might be at first a voluntary act (which in many cases it undoubtedly was) its continuance is under a permanent standing covenant, co-existing with the society; and it

attaches upon every individual of that society, without any formal act of his own ... Men without their choice derive benefits from that association; without their choice they are subjected to duties in consequence of these benefits; and without their choice they enter into a virtual obligation that is as binding as any that is actual. (Burke, 1791/1803: 204–5)

Rights and duties are formally specified and enforced by law at the macro-level, but created by the experience of living the informal relationships that sustain daily life at the micro-level. Bourdieu (1992) uses the concept of 'habitus' to describe how these apparently spontaneous experiences structure people's understandings, dispositions and opportunities. He sees it as a 'product of history' that produces 'structured, structuring dispositions'. These are generated by the way in which people's real activities create their 'practical relation to the world', and 'generate and organise practices and representations that can be objectively adapted to their outcomes without presupposing a conscious aiming at ends or an express mastery of the operations necessary in order to obtain them' (Bourdieu, 1992: 52–4). This is true of DCs and LDCs, but the dispositions that condition their responses and behaviour are very different in each. Few people have the right to make voluntary choices in the latter, but even in the former, their 'autonomous' choices must be compatible with the needs and expectations of everyone else. This therefore emphasizes the role of structure rather than individual agency, but, as Bourdieu also shows, these social constraints limit freedom but do not determine outcomes:

Through the *habitus*, the structure[,] of which it is the product[,] governs practice, not along the paths of a mechanical determinism, but within the constraints and limits initially set on its inventions. This infinite yet strictly limited generative capacity is difficult to understand only so long as one remains locked in the usual antimonies – which the concept of the *habitus* aims to transcend – of determinism and freedom, conditioning and creativity, consciousness and the unconscious or the individual and society. Because the *habitus* is an infinite capacity for generating products – thoughts, perceptions, expressions and actions – whose limits are set by the historically and socially situated conditions of its production, the conditioned and conditional freedom that it provides is as remote from creation of unpredictable novelty as it is from simple mechanical reproduction of the original conditioning. (Bourdieu, 1992: 55)

Individual freedom, and the capacity to operate as an autonomous agent, therefore depends on the demands of particular social systems that determine people's identities and capacities, and where they are located within them. Wage workers have more autonomy than slaves or serfs, but less than capitalists or managers; and citizens are more autonomous than subjects, but, as Scott (1987) shows, even subjects can find ways of asserting their autonomy, however limited they might be.

The critical role of social conditioning and obligation has now been rediscovered by the theorists who stress the importance of 'social capital' in modern capitalist societies. Thus Putnam (1993) and Fukuyama (1995) show that some collective values and social networks can have regressive effects, but that many others create the 'civic virtues' needed to sustain cooperative interdependence in 'high-trust' modern societies. They depend on 'spontaneous sociability and possess dense layers of intermediate associations' that need to be generated by 'traditional social and ethical habits',[3] and depend on collective obligations to ensure that individuals do not pursue their private interests in predatory ways, but

> pursue what Tocqueville termed 'self interest properly understood', that is, self-interest defined in the context of broader public needs, self-interest that is 'enlightened' rather than 'myopic', self-interest that is alive to the interests of others. (Putnam, 1993: 88)

Putnam showed that democratic reforms worked better in northern Italy where society had inherited traditions based on trust and diffuse reciprocity than in the south where traditions were based on distrust, 'vertical dependence and exploitation' (p. 181). This enabled him to avoid the pitfalls of both cultural relativism and dualism by showing that cultural values could be used to explain both successes and failures:

> Stocks of social capital such as trust, norms and networks … tend to be self-reinforcing and cumulative. Virtuous circles result in social equilibria with high levels of cooperation, trust, reciprocity, civic engagement, and collective well-being … Conversely the absence of these traits in the uncivic community is also self-reinforcing. Defection, distrust, shirking, exploitation, isolation, disorder, and stagnation intensify one another in a suffocating miasma of vicious circles. (Putnam, 1993: 177)

Weber (1976) also showed that the operation of progressive forms of capitalism depended on the emergence of a Protestant ethic and societies composed of the kinds of individuals whose rational attempts to maximize their own interests would be compatible with the kinds of socially responsible decisions required for its operation. These were 'individuals' who did not display 'absolute unscrupulousness in the pursuit of selfish interests in making money', but regarded 'the [legal] earning of money' as 'the expression of virtue and proficiency' and therefore as 'the expression of one's duty as a calling'. Weber (1976: 53–7) also showed that these dispositions were not inherent in human nature, but had been 'proscribed as the lowest form of avarice' in Europe in the Middle Ages, and differed from the antisocial 'selfishness' that characterized many European and Asiatic countries at the time 'whose bourgeois-capitalistic development ... has remained backward'.[4] Modern socialist theory and practice also uses a social theory based on collectivism and class solidarity rather than individualism to sustain the working-class parties and trade unions that have moderated the worst effects of capitalist competition and helped to build inclusive social order in DCs.[5]

Identifying the need for socially imposed obligations and social order in this way introduces a functionalist element into the analysis that seems to contradict the emphasis on structural change that drives this study. But the comparative analysis of evolutionary theory in Chapter 3 showed that structural change was inevitable in contexts where different social systems coexist in asymmetrical ways. Social order depends on inequalities in wealth, status and power as we have seen, so any set of institutional arrangements must be able to create rewards and punishments that will persuade the poor as well as the rich to consent to, or at least comply with, their demands. However, liberal theory ignores these problems by assuming that all contracts in market-based systems are based on voluntary choices between free individuals. This claim is not credible in dualistic LDCs where incomplete markets and authoritarian traditionalism create what Tilly (2003) calls systems of 'categorical inequality'. They assign people to high or low status positions not on the basis of 'individual-by-individual scrutiny of all possible candidates' as liberal theory assumes, 'but in response to organized social processes that do not themselves conform to the [individualistic] sorting model ... [so the] resulting differences do not vary continuously, but bunch categorically – by gender, nationality, ethnicity, race, religion, and so on' (Tilly, 2003: 32).

The rules that assign wealth or poverty differ from society to society, and grant different degrees of freedom to the 'individuals' who constitute them. Equality of opportunity exists as a formal right in DCs, although it is also highly constrained even there since long-term 'cycles of disadvantage' perpetuate immense and largely inherited inequalities.[6] However, the growth in absolute incomes and welfare provision does enable the idea of equality to operate as a socially useful myth for the majority of the population. But these rights were only achieved after often violent struggles by out-groups against their assignment to ascribed categories – slave, serf, subject, wage slave or outcast – that led to structural changes, which also benefited 'many individuals of the other classes that ... [were] not winning a dominant position' (Marx and Engels, 1845–6/1974: 66). It was these struggles that eliminated slavery, feudalism and medieval absolutism, and forced societies to universalize the principle of equal rights, and, however partially, to internalize the dispositions, social obligations and civic engagement needed to sustain them.[7]

Now, traditional categorical inequalities cannot simply be legislated away in LDCs because they still create the basis for a functioning social order and sustain the wealth and power of dominant elites. Yet they are also opposed by excluded local groups and social movements that campaign for the principles of freedom and scientific rationality, and often pay a high price for doing so. As Schuurman (1993: 27) says:

> Social movements (new and old) in the Third World are not expressions of resistance against modernity; rather they are demands for access to it. When those excluded unite in groups and forge ties of solidarity, this must not be seen as an embryonic form of a new society, but rather as a survival strategy. There are enough reasons to characterize many Third World countries as aborted modernity projects, if only because of the exclusion of large parts of the population. Citizenship and Participation (Enlightenment ideals!) are (directly or indirectly) highly regarded by these social movements; participants want access to welfare and wellbeing. They are no longer willing to be shifted to the sidelines.

Liberal models play a crucial role in progressive transitions, but liberal institutions can only be introduced without heavy social costs if former winners can be persuaded to give up their privileges and/or existing systems of social security, and the groups that replace them are willing to compensate them in some way for what they are bound to lose.[8] The idea of development depends on universal goals, but social change does not produce smooth transitions. Instead it involves often disruptive attempts to reconcile liberal and non-liberal value systems by producing new hybrids that constantly evolve in response to the tensions generated by the conflicting demands of competing social groups and value systems.

Dualism, historical relativism and institutional hybridity

People in modern societies with strong welfare systems and science-based cultures do not depend on traditional value and authority systems and social networks, but these created social order in pre-capitalist societies and still play a crucial role in LDCs where modern institutions are too weak to protect them all from harm. Fortes and Evans-Pritchard (1940/1970: 17) showed that 'innumerable ties' existed in African societies, 'backed by coercive sanctions, clanship, lineage and age-set ties, the fine-spun web of kinship', as well as 'myths, fictions, dogmas, ritual, sacred places and persons' that 'counteract the tendencies towards political fission arising out of the tensions and cleavages in the social structure'. They depended on collective obligations rather than individual rights, and traditional knowledge systems rather than modern science, but did enable people to access support mechanisms in contexts where formal political and economic systems could not protect them from crime or social insecurity or provide them with jobs.

Liberal reforms threaten deeply held beliefs, devalue traditional skills, and disrupt social relationships in these contexts, so even progressive change always involves 'a hard and obstinate struggle with itself' (Hegel, 1822–30/1975: 127), and it gives some cultural and knowledge systems precedence over others and undermines the cultural heritages and personal security of many groups and individuals.[9] This does not deny the need for development, but it does oblige us to recognize the enormity of the costs it imposes on many of those it is supposed to benefit. These conflicts and tensions have been generated for millennia by the clash between civilizations with unequal technological and military capacities, and usually led to the forcible subordination of the weak by the strong, and the disruptive change processes identified by Malinowsky in the opening quotation. Yet liberals now assume that different systems can interact on the basis of voluntary exchange, and the world can create unity out of diversity by promoting cultural pluralism rather than domination and forcible assimilation. Here the mutual recognition of 'the uniqueness and plurality of the identities of the groups and societies making up humankind'

> gives policy expression to the reality of cultural diversity. Indissolvable from a democratic framework, cultural pluralism is conducive to cultural exchange and to the flourishing of creative capacities that sustain public life. (UNESCO, 2001: Articles 1 and 2)

However, the positive benefits of 'cultural pluralism' are not self-evident nor universally accepted, despite the admirable but often ignored sentiments of the UNESCO declaration, because the demands of the dominant western culture are experienced by the weakest societies as a threat to their identities and self-respect, and because an unqualified commitment to pluralism ignores the 'dark side' of many traditional values and practices.

The need to resolve this tension between local autonomy and the demands of modernity has always been a defining feature of and the most difficult challenge confronted by development theorists. We will take it up here by outlining a theory of social change that retains a commitment to liberal and solidaristic values, but recognizes that the viability of any particular value and authority system depends on the capacities and dispositions and, therefore, the objective possibilities that exist in the societies concerned. This involves a shift from cultural to historical relativism, and shows why all societies must follow different routes to modernity. Cultural relativism involves an uncritical approach to local value systems and practices; historical relativism involves a critical approach that recognizes that liberal principles are based on universalizable values, but that they can only be fully realized in contexts where the social and economic preconditions needed to sustain them have already been created. This obliges us to search for ways of distinguishing between more and less progressive traditional value systems, and for ways to strengthen the former and weaken the latter while adapting them to modern requirements. The result will be new hybrids that combine external and internal models in different ways in response to local capacities and needs.

This approach also enables us to recognize the contribution of third world theorists who stress the positive role of traditional institutions, and the negative consequences of premature liberal transitions. It involves an attempt to find routes to modernity that are conditioned by the insights of orthodox theory, but must differ from earlier transitions because the structures generated by past histories 'have profound implications for the transition paths available and the tasks different countries face when they begin their struggles to develop consolidated democracies' (Linz and Stepan, 1996: 55). The long-term result will not be a 'convergence to a presumed unique "Western" model, but to historically located and specific varieties of capitalism in each country' (Hodgson, 1999: 151).

We will develop the argument in three stages:

1 We will first show that the value and knowledge systems that govern traditional institutions do not simply depend on abstract principles but on the actual conditions under which people live.
2 We then consider the developmental potential of new hybrids by recognizing that institutional dualism does not produce 'a mere fusion or mixing but something oriented on different lines' (Malinowsky, 1945/1961: 21).
3 Finally we will evaluate the potential of these adaptations by considering the effectiveness of the authority, incentive and accountability mechanisms they use.

The competing claims of liberal and traditional knowledge systems

The normative and truth claims of modern social sciences can only be shown to be superior to those of traditional knowledge systems when the means–ends relationships they postulate – for example that competitive markets maximize productive efficiency – can actually operate in real societies in the way their proponents claim. This depends on the extent to which the actors in any system actually have the personal characteristics imputed to them by the theorists, as we saw in Chapter 11. If everyone in pre-capitalist societies were indeed socially responsible possessive individualists, they would, like the Puritan settlers in North America, have already created market-based institutions and guaranteed their success by being willing and able to obey their rules and deploy the skills they demanded. This is not the case in most LDCs, so the credibility of the empirical assumptions underpinning the liberal paradigm has to be fundamentally reassessed.

The ability of any knowledge system to explain behaviour, and what could be done to change it, is therefore historically contingent because, as Hubner (1983: 108–9) showed, social scientific knowledge operates as a function of social structure so that 'it is a historical situation which decides what the scientific facts will be, and not vice versa'. Institutional structures, and not undersocialized individual preferences, determine how people understand who they are, what they prefer, how they should behave, as well as their capabilities and life chances. These not only specify the rules they must obey, but also teach them to think in ways that enable these institutions to survive in modern as well as pre-modern societies. What differentiates them are the kinds of personalities and knowledge systems that are required in market societies as opposed to those based on slavery, feudalism, ethnicity, caste, class or religion. According to Douglas (1986: 112):

Any institution that is going to keep its shape needs to gain legitimacy by distinctive grounding in nature and in reason: then it affords to its members a set of analogies with which to explore the world and with which to justify the naturalness and reasonableness of the instituted rules, and it can keep its identifiable continuing form.

Any institution then starts to control the memory of its members: it causes them to forget experiences incompatible with its righteous image, and it brings to their mind events which sustain the view of nature that is complementary to itself. It provides the categories of their thoughts, sets out the terms for self-knowledge, and fixes identities. All of this is not enough. It must secure the social edifice by sacralizing the principles of justice.

And as Foucault (1970: xx) shows, this means that all communities must operate within the constraints of codes that will – in 'governing its language, its schemas of perception, its exchanges, its techniques, its values, the hierarchy of its practices – establish for every man, from the very first, the empirical order with which he will be dealing and with which he will be at home'.

These codes may only be based on partial understandings, but they must be mutually intelligible and sufficiently consistent and 'true' to enable those who use them to solve the practical problems they confront. Once created and generalized, as Winch (1970b: 106) shows, they bring a unity to people's 'interests, activities and relationships with other men', which constitute the life of any individual and thus provide them with the categories through which they make sense of what they do as social beings. Contradictory codes will coexist and generate structural conflict in communities divided by ethnicity, religion or class, but they all still depend on a socially conditioned unconsciousness of people's sociohistorical and economic condition that governs the way they construct their realities and go about their business (Lukacs, 1971: 52).

So the viability of liberal democratic institutions depends on the empirical fact that most people have unconsciously internalized the appropriate 'codes' in DCs, but the fact that they have not yet fully done so in most LDCs seriously weakens the ability of liberal theorists to use methodological individualism to explain how these societies operate and how they could be transformed. Its claim to maximize freedom and productivity can be scientifically justified, but liberal institutions can only be fully actualized in particular historically created contexts, where the necessary codes have been generated by a long and still evolving process of social experimentation, scientific analysis and open competition, as we saw in Chapter 3. This is not the case in contexts where some people have acquired the necessary dispositions and understandings and others have not, creating, as Parsons says, conditions in one part of the social structure 'which are incompatible with the needs of the other'. He continues:

> We may say with considerable confidence to those whose values lead them to prefer for kinship organization the system of mediaeval Europe or of Classical China to our own that they must choose. It is possible to have either the latter type of kinship system or a highly industrialized economy, but not both in the same society. Either one requires conditions in the corresponding part of the social structure, which are incompatible with the needs of the other. In other words, *a given type of structure in any major part of the society imposes imperatives on the rest*, in the sense that given that structure, if it is to continue, other relevant structures in the same society cannot vary

beyond certain limits which are substantially narrower than are the general limits of variability of social structures in the relevant spheres. (Parsons, 1951/1964: 178, emphases added)

This takes us back to the methodological and practical implications of our analysis of dualism in the last chapter. We saw there that the intrusion of a more complex system of rules, values and practices may create new opportunities and freedoms, but even the most progressive alternatives will not displace existing systems until some demanding conditions can be met. According to Malinowsky (1945/1961: 53):

> A comprehensive institution endures because it is organically connected and satisfies an essential need of society. It can be suppressed, but it is then driven underground. It can be mutilated, deprived of this or that aspect or prerogative, but it disappears only with the destruction of the whole cultural identity of a people. Either this, or it can be replaced by a more adequate institution, fulfilling the same function, satisfying the same needs, and conforming, let us say, to the standards of Western civilisation.

In the real world, 'cultural identities' are rarely wholly destroyed, new systems are rarely 'more adequate' than old ones in all respects, and, as Malinowsky (1945/1961: 53) also says, the destruction of one system before replacing it with a better one 'would result in complete anarchy and disorganisation', as in 'sections of detribalised Africa where something like such a state as this already exists in some respects'. The levels of 'anarchy and disorder' that now prevail in many LLDCs confirm the accuracy of his analysis.

Members of the development community who are asking local communities to make an immediate transition to pluralistic institutions attribute these disorders to inappropriate local value systems and the corrupt or predatory behaviour to which they give rise.[10] What they often fail to acknowledge is that they are also a defensive reaction to the incompleteness of the transition to modern institutions, and to the corresponding failure to provide local people with the resources they need to live by the new rules they are introducing. Social and economic cohesion in DCs depends on their ability to satisfy people's 'essential needs' – for livelihoods, social security and collective representation. These, in turn, depend on the existence of strong capitalist firms, a well-managed welfare state, and highly articulated social and political organizations in civil societies.

These do not exist in most LLDCs, so liberal pluralism does not yet represent a 'more adequate' substitute for what they had before. So it is hardly surprising that people are not prepared to forego their commitments to their existing values that still meet many functional needs in LDCs because they are based on knowledge systems that work better in those contexts than liberal ones would. Their practices may contradict the principles set out in the UN and UNESCO charters, but cannot simply be disregarded because sustainable progress will only occur where new practices are at least partially compatible with local needs and capacities. This will involve the evolution of hybrids that can sometimes use market solutions,[11] or impose collectivistic or solidaristic solutions to overcome market failures.

These hybrids may not conform to all the normative principles outlined in Chapter 2, but their performance needs to be evaluated using a comparative institutional theory that recognizes the efficacy of their incentive and accountability mechanisms in the societies where they operate. To do this, we will first look at the way in which the complex interactions between modern and traditional institutions impact on the change process, and then at the nature of the incentive and accountability mechanisms governing the operation of different kinds of organizations.

Cultural contact, social change and institutional hybridity

Local traditions and codes are never entirely home-grown but have always been modified by forcible or voluntary processes that have transferred new practices from one society to another (Leach, 1970; Castells, 2001: 53). These processes now operate at 'unprecedented speed' as globalization increases access to external models, policies and programmes. However, successful change cannot be pushed through by visiting experts who substitute one set of rules for another but by the energy generated by the struggle for scarce resources between groups with contradictory interests and needs, which produce the evolutionary processes based on unconscious and competitive selection described in Chapter 3. These processes were once dominated by the encounter between colonial and traditional systems, but are now dominated by a multiplicity of contradictory demands from competing local elites, western political, economic and cultural agencies, and the 'multiple shifting identities ... mobilized in the postcolonial politics of everyday life', which can help to resist or connive with new systems of rule (Werbner, 1996: 1–2).

In these contexts, groups identify their goals, manage their internal and external relationships, and measure their successes or failures using their own constantly evolving theoretical models. Liberal theory specifies how political, economic and social elites *should* behave, but often do not, while most codes are embedded in practical knowledge and articulated by organic intellectuals and community leaders – chiefs, elders, priests, imams, spirit mediums, teachers and politicians. As Gramsci (1971: 326–7) says:

> Philosophy in general does not in fact exist. Various philosophies or conceptions of the world exist, and one always makes a choice between them ... What must next be explained is how it happens that in all periods there co-exist many systems and currents of philosophical thought, how these currents are born, how they are diffused, and why in the process of diffusion they fracture along certain lines and in certain directions.

These contested interactions generate transitions with contingent outcomes in response to the balance of local forces and unforeseen eventualities – droughts, changes in prices, new discoveries, the emergence of a new or death of an old leader, or regime change. Evolutionary optimists assume that 'fitter' movements will eventually triumph, just as capitalism displaced slavery, feudalism and the command economy. However, they ignore the ability of reactionary elites to use force to introduce or sustain '[in]appropriate social technologies' that are 'the main cause of relative economic backwardness' (Eggertsson, 2005: 11) and that these conflicts can lead to the cumulative disorder and breakdown that characterizes many weak or failed states, such as Rome under Nero or Zimbabwe under Mugabe. We identified the risks associated with these conflicts in Chapter 11, but are now concerned with the positive contributions that asymmetrical cultural contact can make to developmental transformations by integrating local and imported models to generate new syntheses that differ from both. Malinowsky noted that the colonial state banned traditional practices like warfare, slavery, genital mutilation and witchcraft, but not others like chieftainships, and produced new hybrids that were not

> a mere fusion or mixing, but something orientated on different lines with definite purposes, which are not quite integrated with each other, and which therefore do not act in any simple manner; above all, do not simply mix or fuse with African cultures, but modify them in a much more complicated and dynamic way. (Malinowsky, 1945/1961: 21)[12]

These dialectical and conflictual processes can produce highly ambiguous results. Colonial rulers selectively withheld 'the full benefits of the higher [western] culture' from the local population (p. 58). Nationalist elites justified their anticolonial struggle by demanding the liberal rights that their rulers espoused, but then often reinstated old forms of oppression. Subordinated groups responded to colonial oppression by subverting 'the process of [colonial] domination through disavowal' by acting in ways that led to 'the production of hybridization rather than the noisy command of colonialist authority or the silent repression of native traditions' (Bhabha, 1994: 121–2).[13]

They also use 'everyday forms of resistance' based on passive resistance and crime to oppose oppressive systems – 'slavery, serfdom, caste domination and in those peasant-landlord relations in which appropriation and status degradation are joined' (Scott, 1997: 319). In South Africa, both African elites and subordinated classes based their claim to freedom on liberal principles; in the Arab world, excluded groups have resorted to Islamic fundamentalism.

Oppressed people can therefore invoke either liberal principles to challenge autocracy, as the African National Congress did in apartheid South Africa, or traditional value systems, as Islamic fundamentalists do to protect themselves from dislocative change. These processes can be operationalized through formal social and political movements, or through the concrete personal relations and networks that structure the politics and economics of everyday life (Fuller and Harriss, 2006). The international development community plays a key role in these processes, but it operates as one political force among many and only achieves its goals if it can persuade significant local strata and movements that their models will significantly enhance their life chances.

Change in LDCs therefore follows complex and contradictory paths. External models can help to liberate some communities from the constraints they confront, but only if they are adapted to take account of local dispositions and capacities. This insight helps us to transcend the contradiction between universalism and localism, and some of the conflicts between third world and classical modernization theories by recognizing that new hybrids can produce 'new social forms and autonomous modes of thought' (Brett, 1973: 14–16). It also explains how informal institutions interact with the formal ones described in Part II and introduces an additional element into the conceptual apparatus of institutional pluralism.

In LDCs, formal liberal institutions often coexist within informal local ones, as we see in Table 12.1.

Table 12.1 *Parallel traditional and modern institutions*

Sector	State	Economy	Social
Modern	National parties Police	Capitalist firms Doctors	Priests Prenuptial contracts
Traditional	Patronage networks Vigilante groups	'Black' economy Traditional healers	Spirit mediums Bride price

Some traditional institutions are survivals from the past, others are new adaptations to the exigencies of modern life, but they all compete with, and are interpenetrated by, modern ones. Development practitioners often ignore or reject the former, but they are usually deeply entrenched and still perform important functions, so they need to make informed judgements about the interests they serve, those they negate, how fit they are for purpose, and how they can be adapted and helped to perform better.

Accountability and efficiency in hybrid systems

Hybrid institutions combine liberal with non-liberal institutions in order to achieve social order. Dispassionate judgements need to be made about the effectiveness of the latter as well as the former, and especially about the combinations they have produced in particular contexts. We know that autonomous individualism depends on well-regulated political, economic and social markets that enable citizens to act as principals and exert an appropriate influence over agents, but that these rights are systematically suppressed in autocratic, theocratic and command systems, and in illegal networks in DCs, where agents have almost full discretion over contracts with principals (see Coppola, 1972). Here:

> the state rules enfold the individual so tightly that the reciprocal control between rulers and ruled is so weak, the citizen's scope for decision, and thus the scope for individualization, is relatively limited. Especially in public life external control heavily outweighs the self-control of the individual, who is often thrown back on the private sphere. And even in this sphere the chances of individualization are further narrowed by the state monopoly of information, education, rights of association and assembly, etc. (Elias, 2001: 181)

Liberal principal–agent theory ignores such relationships, but it does alert us to the need to understand the mechanisms that govern institutions based on structural inequality and collectivistic or theocratic cultural systems. Understanding the principles on which such systems operate has always been a defining feature of development theory, which has had to understand the consequences of those interactions between institutions that have created social order by privileging the rights of agents over principals and those that are attempting to make agents accountable to their principals.

This tradition recognizes that pre-modern institutions must meet the same functional needs as modern ones – to maintain order, guarantee property rights, stabilize gender relationships, insure people against risk and enforce social discipline (Almond, 1960). It must also recognize that they operate within limits set by local capabilities and endowments and use value systems and rules that are generally understood and effectively, although often punitively, enforced. Power can be exercised through family dynasties, patron–client networks, chiefs or religious leaders whose authority depends on force, religion, ascription and/or charisma. It often cannot be formally challenged, creates dependency relationships among subordinate strata and permits an abusive use of power. However, while they do not involve the levels of accountability that modern market-based systems permit, they may impose significant limits on the ability of elites to operate in an entirely arbitrary way.

Thus even where authority depends on 'the command of organized force', it should be combined with 'a corresponding obligation to dispense justice, to protect ... [people] from enemies and safeguard their general welfare by ritual acts and observances'. But despotism is often checked by the possibility of 'movements of secession or revolt' and the 'ritual functions of chiefship' that operate as a real 'sanction against the abuse of political power and as a means of constraining political functionaries to perform their political obligations as well as their religious duties' (Fortes and Evans Pritchard, 1940/1970: 12–14, 19). Olson (1997: 39, 50) uses 'stationary bandit theory' to explain how these processes produced 'innumerable periods of economic progress under strong autocrats', and argues that secure warlords who 'use their power constructively to provide a peaceful order and other public goods', rather than for short-term predation, increase total output and guarantee themselves greater wealth and security in the long run. Here, as we will argue in Chapter 13, accountability does not depend on democratic controls, but on the effects of budget and other economic constraints that rulers ignore at their peril.

These mechanisms play a crucial role in dual societies, and still sustain social solidarity by creating what Tilly (2000: 11–12) calls 'networks of trust', or:

> interpersonal networks whose participants have strong incentives to meet their own commitments and encourage others to meet theirs. Such networks often pool risks and provide aid to unfortunate members. They commonly operate well, if and when they do, because their members share extensive information about each other and about their social environment because third parties monitor transactions among pairs of members and because exclusion from the network inflicts serious harm on members who fail to meet their commitments ... Trade diasporas, rotating credit circles, skilled crafts, professions, lineages, patron-client chains, and religious sects often exhibit these characteristics.

They also have a socially destructive side when they create the systems of 'categorical inequality', described in Chapter 9, which are used to sustain social movements that allow dominant groups to monopolize power and resist market-based reforms. Thus Afrikaners used racism to sustain their economic and political dominance in South Africa, Protestants and the Taliban used religion to do so in Northern Ireland and Afghanistan respectively, Brahmins used the caste system in India, and political elites use ethnic loyalties to do so in Africa. Yet they can also provide the building blocks for progressive hybrid solutions by providing the support networks needed to facilitate change in well-managed transitions, and by helping marginalized and excluded groups to respond to crises and breakdowns in weak or failed states.

Progressive developmental transitions in authoritarian systems can only occur where dominant groups can be persuaded to grant greater access to subordinated groups, who have acquired a sufficiently developed understanding of their own situation to extract the necessary concessions and where the transformation process does not generate unsustainable contestation costs.

Tilly (2000) shows that successful transitions of this kind have been rare. Linz and Stepan (1996) show that they are often blocked by adversarial conflicts between subnational groups with entrenched interests, and depend on the ability to ensure that 'almost all of the residents of a state identify with one subjective idea of the nation, and that the nation is virtually contiguous with the state'. But they also show that such conflicts need not be irredeemable, but can be resolved through 'complex negotiations, pacts, and possibly territorial realignments and consociational agreements' (Linz and Stepan, 1996: 23–7). They show that the transition to democracy in Spain was facilitated by a positive contribution from the leadership of the Catholic Church, and the ability to integrate 'peripheral nationalisms' into a pluralistic system which 'allowed complementary multiple identities ... [to] persist' (pp. 93, 102). The transition from apartheid to democracy and liberalization in South Africa involved low level insurgencies and international sanctions, but also the emergence of well-organized opposition parties and trade unions, and the intervention of churches, chiefs and other civic agencies. And both South Africa and India have used affirmative action programmes to sustain their transitions that favour historically disadvantaged racial groups or castes in order to create a more inclusive society.

Kohli (2004) shows that the economic transition in South Korea depended on a powerful alliance between a military regime and the capitalist class, where 'the fact that business was highly concentrated facilitated governmental control and collaboration', rule by a 'stationary bandit' minimized the transaction costs and populist concessions that disrupted many other transitions, and the forcible creation of 'top-down business associations' enhanced 'government's capacity to regulate the economy' (Kohli, 2004: 96). This repressive process did not produce disaster as liberal theory would predict, but a highly successful economic transformation that laid the foundations for a subsequent transition to democracy after a new 'cohesive capitalist state' had been created. Similar processes appear to be generating equally impressive results in China and Vietnam. Solidaristic traditional organizations have also made positive contributions to development in contexts with weak formal institutions or where crises and breakdowns have disrupted the performance of formal institutions and led to a retraditionalization of life. Thus Kaplan (1994) celebrates the role of Islam in creating order, dignity and personal security in the poorest slums in Turkey. Martinez Gonzalez (2006) shows that only traditional village-based gossip networks and local notables acting as 'development brokers' enabled local Mexican villagers to manage liberal participatory social development projects introduced by external agencies. And Faguet (2002: Ch. 6) showed that the performance of the best managed local authority in Bolivia depended on the existence of a traditional association based on a 'rebirth of Guarani consciousness and Guarani pride', which was able to pressurize the authorities into delivering the best services in the country. In Uganda, members of the local Baganda community where I was doing fieldwork reverted to precolonial practices by stoning armed robbers to death because they knew that the police were too corrupt to detain them (personal observation, 1991); while traditional vigilante groups re-emerged in Bugishu in response to the breakdown of formal judicial and police procedures (Heald, 1999). Heald also shows that 'Sungusungu groups' have emerged in Kenya and Tanzania to deal with the same problem, the most successful of which

> have been developed independently of the government and in opposition to both the police and the judiciary ... to protect local groups in an effort to prevent undue harassment by the police and courts. In such areas, local law has effectively taken over from national law with respect to significant offences, most notably theft. We have then a somewhat ironic situation with hybrid forms of organisation developing, which are, strictly speaking, illegal but officially authorised, neither part of the state nor totally rejected by it. [These] ... mobilised indigenous modes of governance and turned these to new ends, creating in so doing new forms of political unity and consciousness. (Heald, 2006: 2–3)

Jones (2005: 193) shows how a marginalized Ugandan community, recovering from an insurgency and with the virtual absence of state services, led people to turn to evangelical churches and burial societies to re-establish 'ideas of propriety and seniority, of living a respectable life, and of making younger men show due deference to the courts or churches ... to make a break with the memory of the insurgency, at a time when hierarchies were challenged and old certainties overturned'.

Informal, hidden and often illegal economies also can produce

> a highly organised system of income generating activities that are unrecorded in official figures and left out of official reports. The scale and extensiveness of these activities have profound implications for determining the real power of the state, for understanding the process of class formation and class struggle and for addressing Zaire's degree of economic development. (MacGaffey, 1987: 111)[14]

These enterprises operate outside formal legal systems, but generally 'have some physical artefact to substantiate their claim to property', because 'a specific group of people [have] reached a respected consensus as to who owns what property and what each owner may do with it' (De Soto, 2001: 195, 197). Networks built on religion, locality or ethnicity sustain the solidarities needed to support informal markets in Nigeria, however imperfectly (Meagher, 2006), while most microcredit institutions also depend on the existence of traditional and solidaristic norms and obligations in local communities.

Conclusions

Traditional institutions and value systems can sometimes block development, but can also contribute to progressive macro- and micro-developmental transitions by producing hybrid and path-dependent systems that generate new solutions to old problems. They combine different kinds of processes that depend on 'improvisation and innovation' where new institutions emerge as people borrow 'from the structures and practices already found in their own history', and what they have 'found in other institutional arrangements' (Jones, 2005: 195). They contribute to the organizational transformations involved in building new formal institutions and to local survival in societies experiencing the disruptions generated by fundamental structural change.

This chapter therefore provides a partial and conditional confirmation of the claims of third world theorists who believe that traditional institutions provide a viable alternative to modern ones, although it does not give them unconditional support. Traditional healing is a poor substitute for science-based medicine; vigilante groups for honest policing; informal contracting and solidaristic credit for modern property rights and financial institutions; and patrimonial patron–client networks for democratic parties and interest groups. However, they can contribute to progressive long-term transitions and cannot be dispensed with in LLDCs where the social and economic preconditions for the operation of successful liberal institutions are still being created. They need to be adapted and hopefully liberalized in the long run, but not simply suppressed in the short run.

We have argued here that the pluralistic orthodoxy that dominates the mainstream development community now recognizes the need for hierarchical and/or solidaristic organizations as well as market-based ones, and, indeed, is actively experimenting with community-based organizations to provide local services. However, pluralism is still deeply rooted in liberal individualism and thus often attempts to reject or marginalize forms of organization based on social, collective and ascribed rights and obligations. Some of these – command planning, dictatorship, theocracy, racism or patriarchy – are incompatible with principles laid out in the UN charters that legitimately claim to be based on a 'universally valid notion of progress' (Barry, 2001: 4). But these universalistic aspirations cannot usually be achieved overnight, while many solidaristic beliefs and practices, as Fukuyama and Putnam point out, are not only crucial to the maintenance of order and 'civilized life' in LDCs, but in DCs as well.

Thus, there is a need for a much broader and less individualistic version of pluralism that takes much greater account of local dispositions and capacities than the version that currently dominates the development community. Liberal democratic capitalism did not emerge full grown out of feudalism, but evolved in complex and disruptive ways by utilizing 'an immense variety of institutions and forms', and in conjunction with diverse non-capitalist elements, or 'impurities' (Hodgson, 1999: 148).[15] It was initially based on authoritarianism, imperialism and national monopolies in DCs, then on social democratic planning, and is now based on liberalization and globalization. These shifts at the centre have altered the goals and methodologies that are transferred to the periphery, and will continue to do so as new hybrids evolve in response to the conflicting demands generated by accelerating processes of technical and social innovation.[16] We will examine the political implications of these processes in Chapter 13 and their economic implications in Chapter 14.

Notes

1   And Marx (1858/1972: 18) argues that 'the [modern] period in which the view of the isolated individual becomes prevalent is the very one in which the interrelations of society ... have reached the highest state of development. Man is, in the most literal sense of the

word, a *zoon politicon*, not only a social animal, but an animal which can develop into an individual only in society. Production by isolated individuals outside society ... is as great an absurdity as the development of language without individuals living together and talking to one another. It would not be necessary to touch upon this point at all, had not this nonsense – which however was justified and made sense in the eighteenth century – been transplanted in all seriousness, into the field of political economy.'

2   And Burke (1791/1803: 202) was 'well aware that men love to hear of their power, but have an extreme disrelish to be told of their duty'.

3   Putnam (1993: 86ff.) outlines the history of the conflict between the individualistic and communitarian traditions in western political theory. The quotation is from Fukuyama (1995: 150).

4   For a complementary analysis, see Sen (1999: 121–3).

5   For an account of the development of class consciousness in Britain, see Thompson (1968).

6   For example, Rutter and Madge (1976: 302–3) reported that 'the gap between the social classes with respect to infant mortality, educational progress, economic resources, working conditions, and ill-health remains almost as wide as it had ever been' in Britain, despite economic growth and the welfare state.

7   Although, as Putnam (2000) shows, these commitments are being increasingly threatened by the growing atomization generated by the success of the neoliberal revolution.

8   A classic case would be the agreements that facilitated the final transition to liberal democratic capitalism in South Africa.

9   This is why Pareto optimality – the assumption that some people can gain without imposing losses on others – is incompatible with developmental change. Hence Cowan and Shenton's (1996: 7) claim that development theory emerged in the early 19th century in order to 'ameliorate the disordered faults of progress'.

10 See, for example, Bayart et al. (1998) and Chabal and Daloz (1999).

11 These would include the emergence of informal markets and associations governed by local solidaristic organizations. See De Soto (1989); MacGaffey (1987); and Meagher (2006).

12 These issues are dealt with in Brett (1973).

13 I am indebted to Jo Beall here.

14 On Africa, see also Meagher (1990), Brett (1993) and De Soto's (1989) study of 'the other path' in Peru.

15 'The impurity principle is ... a general idea applicable to all socio-economic systems ... [Every] system must rely on at least one structurally dissimilar sub-system to function. There must always be a coexistent plurality of modes of production, so that the social formation as a whole has the requisite structural variety to cope with change' (Hodgson, 1999: 126).

16 For example, liberalization, feminism, privatization and new public administration all began as critiques of current practices in DCs, and were then turned into policy conditionalities for LDCs.

Chapter 13

Building Strong States[1]

Social progress depends on the ability of states to defend borders, protect property rights, regulate markets, provide infrastructure and deliver social services. This, in turn, depends on the resources and motivation of the politicians and officials who provide them, and on their ability to support and tax the producers who generate the incomes to finance them. Effective states facilitate progressive change by encouraging economic investment, promoting social cohesion and providing efficient services, whereas weak ones block it by producing 'growth-retarding regimes, policies, and institutions' that 'prevent economic development' (Olson, 1982: 175). Liberal political theorists treat democracy as a defining feature of a developed society, so rapid democratization became a compulsory part of all liberal pluralist policy programmes in aid-dependent states. However, the last four chapters have suggested that democratic transitions are difficult to consolidate in societies confronted by the tensions generated by late-late development.

We saw in Chapter 10 that democracy and universal citizenship have been the exception rather than the rule in early developmental transitions, and that most elected postcolonial rulers soon responded to the political and economic crises they confronted by manipulating elections, suppressing opposition parties, or staging military coups. Authoritarian rulers often intensified economic failures and political disorder, but sometimes created successful capitalist states by ignoring the demands of special interests, building powerful bureaucracies and imposing economic and social discipline onto their societies. Thus we cannot simply assume that in strong states, 'democracy, equality, free markets and rapid economic growth can all be achieved simultaneously in the contemporary developing world' (Kohli, 2004: 422). Elections should enable citizens to replace incompetent or predatory rulers with 'growth-enhancing' ones, but they have often intensified social conflict, encouraged populist policies and produced political disorder in poor and highly fragmented societies with limited access to information and weak social capital.

Most people would prefer to live in strong democracies rather than weak dictatorships and many local social movements treat the struggle for democracy as their primary goal. However, autocracy or weak or pseudo-democracy prevails in most LLDCs, and people living in weak democracies with collapsing economies like Zimbabwe would almost certainly prefer to live in strong autocracies like China with full employment and social security. We therefore have to explain why successful democratic transitions are so rare in LLDCs, and also why authoritarian regimes often generate predation and disorder but sometimes facilitate rapid growth and social cohesion.

The relative success and sustainability of authoritarian and democratic institutions are not just a function of the rules that govern the political relationships between rulers and citizens, but also of those that govern the economic relationships between rulers and producers. The relationship between political and economic systems is a symbiotic one, as we saw in Chapter 9. Liberal theorists believe that democracy depends on free markets and vice versa, but structuralist postcolonial governments exercised direct control over the allocation of economic resources, and used the ability this gave them to extract economic rents to reinforce their hold on political power. Thus we can only explain the successes or failures of the different kinds of regimes that dominated the second half of the 20th century by analysing the effects of the shift from colonialism to independence based on authoritarian structuralist programmes in the first postcolonial period up to the 1980s, and the effects of the subsequent shift to liberalization.

The first transitions to authoritarian structuralism began in the late 1940s in Asia and in the late 1950s in Africa; the second transition, to political and economic liberalization, began in the 1980s, and was extended to the former Soviet Union after 1989. The results have been uneven, with some important successes, many false starts, and a great many disasters.[2] Explaining these mixed and often depressing results raises several difficult questions:

- What are the incentive and accountability mechanisms that influence the adoption and stability of successful or unsuccessful authoritarian projects?
- What substantive contextual variables facilitate or block democratic transitions?
- Why have both strong and weak authoritarian systems constantly given way to attempted democratization?
- What can be done to ensure that these experiments are more successful than their predecessors?

Chapters 9–12 showed that the challenges generated by dualism and the dislocations and conflicts involved in early transitions often undermined the ability of rulers to adopt and implement the political and economic institutions designed by their external advisers. We need to use these insights to explain the anomalous processes that produced the transitions between the four state types identified in Figures 9.1 and 9.2 – liberal democracies, statist social democracies, and authoritarian versions of left- and right-wing structuralism.

Problems of democratic consolidation in late development

The critical political problem confronting postcolonial societies has been their inability to create a stable and legitimated system for the exercise and transfer of political authority; a problem that manifested itself in the failure to consolidate the democratic transitions that were supposed to take place at independence. Democracy is certainly the least imperfect way of enforcing political accountability. It works relatively well in DCs, but only because they have built complex and costly organizational systems that mediate the contradictory relationships between rulers and ruled identified in Chapters 5 and 6. However, they only adopted democratic constitutions after excluded groups had had to force dominant ones to accept their claim to share power, and these constitutional changes had to be followed by long and difficult processes of democratic consolidation needed to build the civic and state organizations required by a competitive political system.[3]

We have seen that political markets are inherently oligopolistic even in DCs, and involve infrequent contests between the leaderships of a few parties who make non-enforceable promises to ill-informed voters, so they are even more vulnerable to opportunism and the disruptive effects of unforeseen consequences than economic markets. These problems are far more serious in LDCs that are usually characterized by non-negotiable ethnic, sectarian or class cleavages, limited access to human and social capital and information, weak political movements and state capacity, and many zero-sum conflicts over scarce resources. And they are most problematic in the earliest stages, when societies are being asked to make their initial transitions from authoritarian to democratic constitutions – the situation that confronted all postcolonial states at independence, and which has emerged again in most LDCs and post-socialist states over the past 20 years when they have also been asked to make equally disruptive transitions from structuralism to market economies.

Reformers assume that democracy and free markets are a universal good and will therefore be universally supported, but they ignore the fact that introducing them threatens existing allocations of power and wealth and therefore the willingness of rulers and citizens to adopt them. Authoritarian rulers used the control over credit, foreign exchange, subsidies and monopoly powers that structuralism gave them to privilege their supporters and punish their enemies, and did not have to face the electorate when their policies failed. Transferring their power over rents to the market robs them of their ability to buy political support, while making them stand for re-election threatens to deprive them, and the patron–client networks that depend on them, of their contracts, jobs and privileges. So it is not surprising that few authoritarian regimes have given up these privileges without a struggle, although their ability to retain them also intensifies resentment and the need for coercion.

The willingness of particular regimes to accept democratic transitions and the ability of particular societies to consolidate them therefore depends on many substantive variables rather than abstract theoretical principles. These variables include levels of social unity or fragmentation, the distribution of assets between classes, ethnic and sectarian groups and regions, and the nature of the property rights that structure economic relationships, levels of wealth or poverty, bureaucratic capacity, and external support or threats. Most LLDCs lack a strong sense of nationhood, are unwilling to recognize the obligations as well as rights associated with political freedom, and their governments are confronted by irreconcilable demands for very scarce resources. Their regimes have to satisfy enough of these demands in order to win elections, yet they are desperately poor and constantly forced to make zero-sum choices that reward one set of interests but destroy the life chances of another. In fragmented societies, losers rarely believe that they have been fairly treated, but attribute their failures to the class, ethnic or sectarian characteristics of the regime, and will therefore go to extreme lengths to keep their own groups in power or eliminate governments that are excluding them from a fair share of national resources.

The regimes that won the elections that initiated most transitions to independence were usually based on nationalist parties which involved broad coalitions of local interests united by their opposition to colonialism. But they then had to take direct responsibility for allocating scarce resources and could no longer simply blame inequality, inefficiency and poverty on their external rulers.[4] The need to win elections meant that they could not insulate themselves from the pressures and conflicts generated by non-negotiable class, ethnic or sectarian loyalties, patrimonial value systems, structural economic inequalities based on semi-feudal or other kinds of coercive pre-capitalistic relationships, and the weakness of local bureaucratic and capitalist classes. There was intense competition for political favours and the systematic exclusion of particular groups intensified opposition and the need for coercion. Rulers had to build autonomous economies, but could not allow free markets to operate because the economic elite did not take the form of a national bourgeoisie committed to progressive political change, but a petty bourgeoisie involved in primary accumulation based on rents that tended to generate 'wastage and theft' and 'political turmoil' (Khan, 2000: 25, 38).[5] These adversarial political processes resulted in populist attempts to pay off special interests and highly fragmented party systems; they also explain the prevalence of electoral manipulation, one-party rule or military coups. Thus democracy can also intensify the fragmentation and conflicts generated by the substantive historical and contextual conditions stemming from late development, generating the state failures that have dominated the postcolonial history of most LDCs and post-socialist countries. Hence:

> The failure of democratic consolidation is almost overdetermined for the foreseeable future. Ethnic civil wars and the economic chaos partially caused by the nearly stateless quality of some of the strife-torn polities make the creation of the rule of law, as well as democratic civil and political and economic societies, extremely difficult. (Linz and Stepan, 1996: 233)

Neoliberals assumed that the conflicts over politically allocated rents would disappear once rulers were forced to transfer resource allocation to economic markets, but failed to recognize that transferring ownership and economic rights from state to private agents was an inherently political process that would enrich some individuals, classes and regions and impoverish others. These processes generated different, but equally conflict-ridden and disruptive competition between claimants who were just as dependent on the need to acquire the political influence they needed in order to appropriate the property rights, contracts and open access resources as before.

These unavoidable conflicts explain the prevalence of aborted democratic transitions in the postcolonial world, and why contemporary rulers have systematically subverted the democratic reforms imposed by donors, despite opposition from many local pro-democracy movements. Most LLDCs are therefore still governed by hierarchical regimes ranging from fully fledged autocracies through a variety of authoritarian to proto-democratic systems that permit a limited degree of heavily controlled political competition.

Resolving these antagonistic conflicts and creating political mechanisms that enable societies to generate fair and generally accepted mechanisms for conflict resolution and the allocation of both benefits and losses are therefore crucial to their ability to overcome the political and economic crises that dominate all weak states.[6] We know that LDCs have followed many different transitional paths.[7] The most successful, such as Taiwan, South Korea and South Africa, first used authoritarianism to manage successful economic programmes that were followed by successful democratic transitions. Others, such as China and Vietnam still combine authoritarianism with successful and increasingly liberal economic policy regimes. But many more, such as Nicaragua and Malawi, have shifted from authoritarian to notionally democratic regimes and are still locked into vicious circles, while others, such as Uganda and Mozambique, appear to be combining partial democracy and managed liberalization, and making real, although uneven and uncertain, progress. Explaining these disparate histories obliges us to ask serious questions about the relationship between the constraints that govern the actions of rulers in democratic and non-democratic regimes, the contexts within which they operate, and the way the options and challenges are being reshaped by the success or failure of their policy programmes.

Authoritarianism, structuralism and democratic transitions or breakdowns

Liberal political theory deals with the rules and processes that govern relationships between elected politicians, officials, parties and interest groups and therefore assumes that democratic institutions already exist, so it cannot explain political behaviour and the way it influences structural change in authoritarian states. However, politics, understood as the struggle between contending interests to control or influence state power, is not confined to democracies but takes place everywhere. According to Clapham (1996: 8):

> Politics is about conflict, and about the ability of people to devise power structures which, on the one hand, may work to the overall benefit or disadvantage of the individuals who are affected by them, but which, on the other hand, will invariably confer considerably greater benefits and costs on some people than on others. Not only is politics itself a contest, but the words and ideas which are used to describe it are contested too.

Democratic constitutions seek to create inclusive processes that oblige the groups that capture power to use it to benefit society as a whole, and to enable citizens to punish them if they fail, but authoritarian regimes suppress opposition so that they can allocate resources to favoured groups without regard for the consequences. Such regimes could survive indefinitely if they were able to ignore the social and economic consequences of their actions, but managing state power forces them to meet a wide array of contradictory economic and administrative demands, which presents even the most repressive regimes with serious *political* challenges they have to overcome if they are to survive.

Despots need to maintain the capacity and loyalty of their security services, bureaucracies, the economic elites that generate their resources, and the political compliance of their subjects. They can only do this successfully when they are willing and able to act as 'rational despots', in Olson's terms (1997: Ch. 3), by managing the economic system well enough to sustain their ability to tax, maintain the infrastructure needed to meet their bureaucratic and economic needs, pay off their associates and supporters, and provide good enough livelihoods and services to subordinate classes to minimize social discontent, or punish them for noncompliance. Success enables them to strengthen their hold on power and their social support, but failure weakens the capacity of their state apparatuses and economies, and intensifies incompatible demands and scarcities.

However, we know that managing these complex processes is extraordinarily difficult in LLDCs characterized by categorical inequalities, antagonistic class, ethnic and sectarian tensions, and zero-sum conflicts over scarce resources. Here rulers are often forced to resort to counterproductive economic policies that buy short-term political support but intensify long-term economic and bureaucratic weaknesses. Their opponents can be suppressed for long periods but only by increasing unproductive expenditure on repressive apparatuses that further reduce economic output and undermine bureaucratic capacity, and by adopting oppressive policies that delegitimize the regime, reduce political support and sometimes lead to popular uprisings or rebellions that produce regime change. Explaining the behaviour of particular regimes, or the survival or decay of authoritarian state systems therefore requires an interdisciplinary and historical analysis that does not focus on the processes that enable functioning democracies to maintain themselves, but on the relationships between economic, social and political processes, and between domestic and international models and agencies that generate the evolutionary processes of competitive selection described in Chapter 3. These have sometimes allowed despots to die in office and authoritarian political systems to survive for long periods, and at other times have brought both down in a matter of months or years.

These problems explain the difficulties associated with the attempts to facilitate the transition from authoritarian structuralism to the liberal pluralist models described in Part II. Most of these attempted transitions were reluctantly initiated by authoritarian regimes in LLDCs in response to donor pressures because they were unable to sustain viable bureaucratic and economic systems; more successful transitions are taking place in thriving authoritarian states that have been able to create many of the preconditions for democratic consolidation we identified earlier. What we need to do now is examine the causes and consequences of these contrasting experiences by first examining the processes that sustain or undermine authoritarian regimes in unsuccessful LLDCs and successful LDCs, and then their implications for attempts at democratization and democratic consolidation.

Explaining successful authoritarian transitions to democracy

Democratic theorists assume that non-accountable rulers will behave in predatory and antisocial ways, because 'power tends to corrupt and absolute power to corrupt absolutely' (Acton, 1948). However, despots who wish to survive should nevertheless adopt rational growth-enhancing policies that give entrepreneurs enough incentives to persuade them to expand their output and therefore their capacity to pay taxes and enhance state power. We also know that many examples of such regimes have existed – England under the Tudors, Prussia under Frederick the Great, Germany under Bismarck, South Africa under apartheid, South Korea under Park Chung-hee, and China under the Communist Party. Most of them not only ignored democratic principles, but also imposed left- or right-wing structuralist policies that enabled their rulers to extract rents on a large scale. However, while corruption was certainly endemic in all these societies, it did not lead to breakdown but to the long-term development of a strong capitalist class. How, then, can we explain this apparent anomaly?

Theorists working on 'developmental states' in East Asia have attributed their successes to the fact that their regimes maintained a relatively autonomous relationship with the key interest groups in their societies. Here 'autonomy' from particularistic demands allowed them to impose the disciplines on their own officials, economic elites and subordinate classes needed to sustain their successful economic transitions, while the fact that their autonomy was relative and not absolute forced them to respond to the legitimate needs of key interest groups (Leftwich, 1994; Evans, 1995; Kohli, 2004).

However, while the idea of relative autonomy tells us why these states worked so well, it does not explain why these rulers chose to apply it when so many authoritarian rulers elsewhere failed to do so. These differences confirm our earlier claims that formal rule systems influence political behaviour, but that outcomes are always determined by the substantive and contextual variables that influence the way they are implemented. Thus we can only explain the extraordinary differences between the successful East Asian and weak African nation-states by identifying the local variables that induced some rulers to behave as rational despots while others did not. Olson (1997) argued that despots will only minimize their exactions when they are secure enough to be able to assume that they will reap the long-term benefits of their actions. This may be true in some cases, but secure despots have also been known to overexploit their subjects. Instead, it seems more probable that their performance is likely to depend on two variables – the threat of invasion or domestic unrest, and the scale of the political and economic capital they could draw on to overcome it.

The absolute rulers of Western Europe were constantly at war or threatened by war, and only retained their autonomy by building enough military capacity to defend themselves. This, in turn, depended on their ability to sustain the industrial and financial capacity needed to pay for their armies, and to maintain the good health and compliance, if not the consent, of their people, so war-making and state-making were closely linked (Tilly, 1985). The East Asian NICs and Malaysia in the 1950s and 60s were threatened by Communist insurgencies and/or invasion, which not only motivated their leaders to impose disciplined economic policy regimes on their societies, but also persuaded the USA, Japan and Britain to support their efforts. The Communist parties in China and Vietnam, and the nationalist regime in South Africa also confronted major threats from hostile states and/or internal opposition movements that led them to discipline their own officials and producers, and improve economic and social provision for at least some of the poor.

However, these threats alone do not explain success, since other insecure regimes have tried but failed to emulate them. Exceptional leaders usually played a critical role, but the historical record suggests that their ability to do so also depended on earlier social transformations, which had created enough human capital, as well as the state and economic capacity to defend frontiers, control dissent, consolidate a capitalist revolution, and create some degree of nationalist solidarity, as we saw in Chapter 10.[8] These successful (but rarely benevolent) despots were able to build strong states and capitalist economies by using authoritarian controls to generate virtuous circles, in which state power was used to enable their embryonic capitalist classes to become internationally competitive and their successes strengthened the capacity of their states to increase taxes and spending on infrastructure and social services.

Thus authoritarian regimes with a commitment to development have been able to build successful 'cohesive capitalist states', as Kohli shows (2004: 381). However, most of them then did make transitions to democracy, but only after their economic transitions had been completed. A critical factor here has been the emergence of an internationally competitive capitalist class that could finance itself out of profits rather than state-generated rents, as we will see in Chapter 14. During early transitions, many embryonic capitalists have a vested interest in the existence of corruption, but once the class has matured, they need a state that will enforce property rights and provide good services, in other words, a liberal democratic state. Thus, as Moore (1967: 418) said, 'a vigorous and independent class of town dwellers has been an indispensable element in the growth of parliamentary democracy. No bourgeois, no democracy.'

Hence democracy has emerged in Europe and Japan, in the stronger states of Latin America, in South Africa and in the post-Communist states of the former Soviet Union. It has yet to do so in China and Vietnam, but the immense social changes induced by the emergence of a dynamic capitalist and professional class are intensifying similar demands there.[9] White (1993b: 244) argued that an immediate shift to liberal democracy in China would mainly advantage local economic elites and 'foreigners', while marginalizing the majority of the population. But he felt that limited forms of local democratization were feasable 'in the short term', and would 'become more meaningful as socioeconomic development proceeds'. So these stable transitions to democracy can be explained by their large investments in human capital, the need for open and accountable institutional arrangements to sustain modern economic and information systems, and the ability of the mature capitalist and working classes to force regimes to recognize their demand for full political rights.

These authoritarian transitions to democracy support the liberal claim that democratization is teleologically linked to modernization and the social and economic relationships created by mature capitalism. However, it also confirms the claims of classical development theorists, who argue that very different social and political dynamics are at play in early transitions than in mature capitalist or socialist democracies, and it is therefore mistaken to expect the former to adopt fully fledged liberal political or economic models until they have generated the political, economic and social capital needed to do so. However, very different principles apply in the underperforming LLDCs that are the primary focus of this chapter.

Explaining authoritarian crises and breakdowns

Democracy was replaced by authoritarianism in most postcolonial states, but the new rulers did not operate as rational despots but adopted predatory policies that locked them into long-term vicious circles that perpetuated economic and political disorder. Yet this also had paradoxical results, because these weaknesses destabilized these regimes and generated domestic demands for democratization, which forced them to turn to a donor community committed to political and economic liberalization. Thus weak as well as strong authoritarian states find it hard to resist demands for democratic transitions, but the former find it much harder to manage them effectively.

We showed that democratic institutions failed in LLDCs because they were introduced into societies characterized by dualistic value systems and embryonic capitalist economies that generated antagonistic and non-negotiable class, ethnic and/or sectarian conflicts. The strong autonomous authoritarian rulers in East Asia used their authority to manage these tensions and promote viable development, but weak regimes in fragmented and impoverished societies confronted unsustainable demands from officials, supporters and clients and depended on embryonic capitalist firms that were often owned by relatives or political cronies to whom they were politically beholden. These regimes did not confront major external threats that forced them to build strong states, and lacked the bureaucratic skills and capital required to build modern states and capitalist firms. In the early structuralist postcolonial period, they were often assisted by donors who wanted to suppress left-wing opposition movements, and funded inappropriate capital-intensive projects that marginalized small farmers, entrepreneurs and workers (Burch, 1987).

The colonial authorities blocked the development of an autonomous capitalist class and autonomous political and social movements, and decolonization took place so quickly in the 1950s and 60s that political parties and interest groups were weak, and usually based on divisive ethnic or sectarian loyalties. Once they had taken power, these weaknesses grew, since 'governing parties atrophied' and 'leaders sought to entrench themselves in power by using the machinery of the state to suppress or co-opt any rival organisation – be it an opposition political party, a trades union, or even a major corporation' (Clapham, 1996: 56–7). In some cases, easy access to resource rents derived from oil or other minerals compounded these problems. The result was bad governance and economic decline. Corrupt politicians and officials transferred resources to inefficient political cronies, not efficient firms, supported oppressive landlords or parasitic managers of state-owned or state-subsidized enterprises, maintained costly military apparatuses at the expense of social services, eliminated freedom of expression and investigation, and systematically excluded potential opponents from economic opportunities.

This led to a system based on political and economic monopolies, which generated perverse incentives that not only reduced services to the public, but also the state's capacity to maintain public order and sustain state power and the loyalty of its supporters. Corrupt politicians and officials took bribes rather than collect taxes, enforce foreign exchange regulations or control borders, and they transferred their gains to foreign accounts. Corrupt contractors failed to build or maintain essential infrastructure; while corrupt and incompetent political cronies ran inefficient state enterprises or non-viable private firms. These policies were not only supported by the officials who took the bribes, but also by the emerging capitalist entrepreneurs whose survival depended on their access to the rents they received in exchange – as our analysis of primitive accumulation in Chapter 14 will show.

All this reduced exports and economic output, and generated fiscal and balance of payments crises. As a result, governments had to intensify their use of perverse policy instruments – deficit financing, overvalued exchange rates, irrational credit controls, regressive taxation and corrupt privatization programmes – to finance their activities and reward supporters. These further distorted economic incentives and intensified shortages and threats to excluded groups, thus increasing opposition and the need for even further counterproductive expedients. The system eliminated formal political opposition, but also undermined the political parties and social movements that leaders could rely on for 'organised political support' (Clapham, 1996: 59). The result was a series of vicious circles, where bad governance led to economic decline that reduced state capacity and intensified competition for political and economic support and favours, which then strengthened the need for the destructive policies that had created the original problem (see Brett, 2008).

The unsustainable and illegitimate nature of these processes generated chronic political instability and demands for political change. Regimes can suppress opposition for long periods by eliminating or intimidating opponents, marginalizing autonomous political and social movements, and forcibly suppressing popular protests. However, these expedients are costly because they produce a 'general political economy of disorder' and declining state capacity (Chabal and Daloz, 1999: xix). In viable democracies, these failures should lead to electoral defeat; while in autocracies and pseudo-democracies, they intensify mass discontent as well as factional conflicts within the ruling coalition, and between significant social groups based on class, ethnic or sectarian loyalties. Factional conflicts can produce destabilizing threats to leaders and their clients; while exclusion, oppression or impoverishment can produce popular uprisings or insurgencies that lead to regime change, as in Uganda, or chronic civil war, as in Somalia and the Democratic Republic of the Congo (DRC). Where states can suppress resistance, people move into informal markets and create relatively autonomous local enclaves – subject to the authority of local patrons or reconstructed traditional systems (MacGaffey, 1987; De Soto, 1989).

Perhaps most significantly in the modern period, these crises bankrupted regimes and forced them to go to the donor community for support and thus lose their autonomous control over policy (Clapham, 1996, esp. Part III). So most weak authoritarian regimes are now locked into asymmetrical relationships with the donor community, and are being obliged to at least pay lip service to the liberal pluralist policy programmes associated with the post-Washington consensus. How effective is this relationship likely to be?

Donors, governments and the politics of noncompliance

Aid dependency gives the donor community a crucial political role in institutional reform, policy formulation and implementation in LLDCs, because regimes find it easier to ignore local opponents than their paymasters. Donor demands relate to the major issues contested by political movements in DCs – constitutional and administrative systems, macro- and microeconomic policy decisions, and the level and distribution of social services. However, while donors can oblige rulers to accept new policies, international law forces them to rely on formally sovereign local governments to allow them to actually implement them. This also stops them from engaging in 'partisan' politics by supporting opposition movements that might be more willing to support their policies than incumbent regimes.[10]

Aid dependence therefore has critical implications for the autonomy and policy choices available to local regimes, but the relationships involved generate serious conflicts of interest and perverse incentives, but have not produced the political and administrative structures needed to manage them successfully. Donors promote pro-poor policies in response to the demands of their political constituencies in their home countries, but they have to rely on host governments to implement them. These have different and often contradictory agendas, since they are primarily concerned with their own political survival and, therefore, promoting the welfare of the often unproductive special interest groups on which they rely for support rather than maximizing the welfare of the poor.

This tension explains many of the failures that have dominated the aid relationship since the start of the structural adjustment programmes managed by the IFIs in the 1980s. These programmes were designed to reduce official privileges and rents, impose cuts in social services, and threaten unviable but protected local firms.[11] They have now been replaced by poverty reduction programmes that are designed to shift resources to poverty-focused social services and small businesses and therefore to shift resources from the patron–client networks, narrow ethnic or sectarian political constituencies and ineffectual neopatrimonial bureaucracies on which most regimes rely for support. Democracy should allow the poor to force their rulers to support these policies, but their traditional social organizations lack the financial or social leverage needed to operate autonomously, while most poor people depend on vertical patron–client networks that silence their voices and reinforce their dependence.[12]

Furthermore, donors' interventions can also be subverted by rent-seeking behaviour and the exercise of non-accountable power in the foreign community. International firms use their economic power to dominate local markets, and their political links to secure contracts for inappropriate high-cost projects (Burch, 1987). Donors also use aid to buy political support from corrupt regimes and to give their own staff privileged lives, while weak accountability allows them to conceal often spectacular failures (Nicholls, 1998; Folster, 2001).

So aid programmes have unavoidable political implications and are subject to significant levels of conflict and malfeasance. Yet this does not in itself threaten their legitimacy, since that depends on whether they are likely to have progressive outcomes. What is crucial, however, is the efficacy of the political processes involved in the aid relationship – the dependence on programmes formulated by foreign advisers that have to be presented as apolitical solutions to technical problems rather than the outcome of political negotiations between competing interests. These programmes are supposed to benefit society as a whole, but they involve shifts in wealth and power that produce major contradictions and perverse incentives, which turn implementation into a political contest between agents with very different agendas (see Ferguson, 1996).

Donors design pro-poor programmes that local governments are obliged to accept. In functioning democracies, choosing between pro-poor and pro-rich policies would be negotiated through open political debate between radical and conservative parties and civic organizations. Winning coalitions would have to mobilize the necessary support and manage the compromises needed to compensate potential losers who are often the most powerful economic and political players in these societies. Yet donors cannot do either of these things in LLDCs, given the supposedly apolitical nature of the aid relationship. The broad thrust of their policies is determined in their home countries, while detailed programmes are formulated in host countries using 'technical' missions that recognize the existence of, but do not enter into, formal negotiations with competing interests. Instead, they interview 'opinion leaders', run focus groups and workshops, and conduct surveys and participatory learning exercises that culminate in general, sectoral and project agreements. These may be debated in local parliaments, but the need for donor approval limits their influence, and final agreements emerge from closed meetings between ministers, officials and donor representatives. They are then implemented by state bureaucracies, consultancy firms or NGOs heavily influenced by foreign technical advisers and consultants.[13]

As a result, the aid relationship, like all gift economies, operates on 'the sincere fiction of a disinterested exchange' that enables 'relations of dependence that have an economic basis ... [to be] disguised under a veil of moral relations' (Bourdieu, 1992: 113, 123). This requires a shared 'misrecognition' of how the exchange works – caused by the gap between the formal sovereignty allocated to weak states and their substantive inability to meet the demands of 'empirical' statehood, which requires the capacity to exercise effective power within their own territories' (Clapham, 1996: 21). The result is the politics of noncompliance and hidden transfers, where regimes make promises they do not plan to keep and donors attempt to bypass regimes they do not trust by using NGOs or for-profit firms. Many of the players understand the unspoken rules of this game, but most prefer not 'to look the truth of politics in the face', but deceive themselves 'about the nature of politics and the role ... [they] play on the political scene' (Morgenthau, 1943/1969: 13).

The politics of noncompliance produces a gap between the promises that donors and host governments make and what they are actually willing to do. Donors expect host governments to introduce institutional and policy reforms that will increase their accountability and reduce their rents; while governments respond by foot-dragging or the corrupt deals that subverted structuralist programmes in the first postcolonial period and liberal ones in the second. Ignoring the need to come to terms with the many vested interests opposed to their policies enables donors to push through what may well be progressive pro-poor programmes, but this only drives their opponents underground and forces them to subvert the formal policy process and generate the 'political disorder' that exists in many weak states.

The resulting impasse explains the widespread pessimism that dominates the aid industry,[14] which cannot be resolved by ignoring these conflicts of interest, making normative appeals to actors to behave better, or looking for new paradigms that will overcome them, because they 'are not a sign of the imperfect understanding of society, on the contrary they belong to the nature of reality itself' (Lukacs, 1971: 10). The conflicts that generate this impasse stem from real inequalities and economic transfers that are directly affected by the changes in the institutional reforms and policy paradigms adopted by donors and the governments they interact with. How, then, could rulers, political and social movements, and donors interact more effectively?

Managing political and policy processes in weak states

Aid dependence gives donors a significant but not deterministic influence over institutional and policy reform in weak states, so we need to develop a realistic assessment of the objectives and the leverage they can exercise. Donors may well be motivated by self-interest rather than altruism, but this, in itself, tells us little about the effects of their actions. During the cold war, they often supported oppressive regimes or destabilized opposition movements, but the destruction of 'the ideologies of single-party statehood and statist economic management' at the end of the 1980s meant that:

> Western liberal political models could be regarded not as the imposition of values derived from one culture or stage of development on other cultures or developmental trajectories to which they were fundamentally unsuited, but rather as the transfer of political technologies of universal validity. (Clapham, 1996: 193)

This liberal donor project now not only involves democratization, but the attempt to combine economic liberalization with poverty reduction programmes based on small business development programmes and improvements in social services for the poor. Some donors undoubtedly allow their own strategic and economic interests to influence their choice of countries and projects, usually with poor results (Burnside and Dollar, 1998: 31, 28). However, all the aid-dependent countries are poor and in desperate need of support. Thus what is really at issue is not whether donors also make gains out of the aid relationship but why the politics of the aid relationship often produces such uneven results?

Donor interventions have significant political implications. These include democratization to create the political space for opposition movements to organize and compete for power, changes in economic policy regimes that alter the ability of governments to allocate rents, and aid rationing that strengthens the regimes they support and weakens those they do not. Let us consider the impact of their actions in two areas – first, on the processes of democratization, and, second, on the problems of policy management as a whole.

First, the need for democratization is widely accepted, and supported by local social movements, but we saw earlier that it can have ambiguous effects in societies characterized by high levels of social and economic fragmentation, intense poverty and weak political and civic organizations. It should eliminate the extreme abuses of power of dictators like Mobutu, Idi Amin and Saddam Hussein, and enable opposition movements to challenge weak regimes by exploiting the anger generated by oppression, waste and exclusion.

However, while oppression intensifies resentment and the possible emergence of opposition movements, it only leads to effective political action when it can actually be channelled into effective organizational systems.[15] The poor usually lack the skills and resources to involve themselves in anything but localized resistance to oppression (Scott, 1987), or can be mobilized to support dominant elites through patron–client networks.[16] Pro-poor political movements can also have populist, ethnic or sectarian rather than progressive agendas,[17] or be marginalized through electoral manipulation. The collapse of socialism has recently weakened political movements based on horizontal class-based loyalties, and strengthened ethnic and sectarian movements based on vertical ties, so reducing the range of organizations that previously enabled the poor to make their voices heard. Thus democratization is often as likely to reinforce the influence of elites rather than the poor, as White suggests (1993b: 244), while donors are quite capable of subverting its results as they did in Palestine when Hamas won its majority. Consequently, its outcomes are highly contingent, and their effect on poverty reduction severely constrained by the limited ability of local groups to find effective leaders, finance their organizations, maintain the discipline needed for unified political action, and find viable economic policies that actually produce better results, given the failure of state socialism to do so.

These problems explain the enormous difficulties that all modern states have confronted during their democratic transitions, and the temptation to use the successes of the authoritarian 'cohesive capitalist states' to hold back political reforms in weak states. This, as Kohli (2004: 421) concedes, 'raises serious normative dilemmas', since his analysis of strong states, and ours of the problems created by neopatrimonialism and dualism in weak states, raises serious questions about the current commitment to immediate democratization in societies that lack the capacity to manage it effectively.

These contradictions between democratic freedoms and effective governance confront the whole development community – local rulers and activists, as well as their foreign advisers – with their most difficult choices. Democratization can lead to populism and corruption, while authoritarianism in weak states is more likely to consolidate the power of predatory rulers than to produce East Asian-style good governance based on relative autonomy. Equally important, societies can only learn how to manage democratic systems after they have actually introduced them – so the critical issue confronting the development community is not to reverse their commitment to democracy, but to take the challenges involved in consolidating democratic systems more seriously than they do.

Democratic consolidation demands:

- strong political parties to articulate interests and develop encompassing political programmes
- a dense array of civic organizations to represent particular interests
- research institutions and media that can subject public policy to informed criticism
- high general levels of literacy in the society.

Donors can play a large role in strengthening such agencies, although they are precluded from giving direct support to particular parties, and often ignore 'traditional' groups that play a key role in local organizational life. Donors can provide them with useful support, but they can also subvert the integrity of organizational systems by supporting favoured agencies and individuals and marginalizing others.[18] They also play a less controversial but crucial role in building human capital by financing educational systems – they have recently focused heavily on the value of primary and female education, but neglected the secondary and especially the tertiary education necessary to produce the local elites needed to assume the key leadership positions in political, economic and social life.

Second, donors exercise a decisive influence over policies, programmes and projects by giving or withholding aid and providing the technical advice needed to implement them. During the structuralist period, a great deal of aid was wasted on inappropriate capital-intensive infrastructure, industry and agriculture, not least because of the benefits it generated in home countries (Burch, 1987; Folster, 2001). Liberalization has therefore had major political implications, since it has changed the ability of regimes to buy political support by allocating rents, and it has been accompanied by a shift from investment in infrastructure and production into providing social services and building social capital. This avoids some of the distortions created by the provision of technologically inappropriate projects, but it pays too little attention to the need to increase employment and output.[19] These choices are driven by theoretical and political changes in home countries – notably the critique of state-led industrialization and the growing influence of developmental NGOs with a heavy emphasis on social provision and human rights. They are not set in stone, but subject to serious debate and continuous revision.

However, the greatest threat to aid relationships is the problem of noncompliance, identified in the last section. Donors attempted to impose strong conditionality in the 1980s and 90s, which came to include virtually every aspect of economic policy and governance, but this often failed.[20] In the early 2000s, they therefore shifted from conditionality to aid rationing, based on good policy performance This was justified by research demonstrating that aid reduced poverty where countries followed 'good fiscal, monetary and trade policies', but failed where they did not. Supporting good performers was expected to 'have a large, positive effect on developing countries' growth rates' (Burnside and Dollar, 1998: 1, 34),[21] and to eliminate noncompliance by giving them unconditional support, and withdrawing it from bad performers. Donors would still have to make difficult choices about priorities, policy and conflict management, but would be able to negotiate these on relatively equal terms with good governments that did represent the interests of the poor.

These strategies may work in strong states, but they ignore the needs of the poorest people in the weakest states, where bad policies stem from the contradictory pressures created by neopatrimonialism and weak endowments, as we know. So the greatest challenge to donors is to find strategies that enable them to support the poor in societies where aid to ineffective or predatory governments will increase waste and strengthen their hold on power.

Perhaps the most sophisticated response to this problem is provided in the World Bank's *World Development Report 2004*, discussed in Chapter 6. This developed a politically sophisticated model based on new public management theory that identified alternative ways to generate effective accountability and incentives in LDCs. The primary concern of these mechanisms is to put 'poor people at the centre of service provision: by enabling them to monitor and discipline service providers, by amplifying their voice in policymaking, and by strengthening the incentives for providers to serve the poor' (World Bank, 2004: 1). The report defines accountability as the ability of users to oblige providers to deliver good services. It then shows that accountability can either operate indirectly, following a 'long route' where users persuade state agents to oblige public or private providers to give them what they need, or a 'short route', usually involving some form of market-based exchange where they pay private providers for services and exit if they are dissatisfied.

This model is built on Hirschmann's and Paul's analysis of exit and voice, competitive markets and democratic states outlined in Chapter 4.[22] It follows standard pluralist theory in arguing that both routes

Figure 13.1 *Direct and indirect accountability mechanisms for service delivery systems*

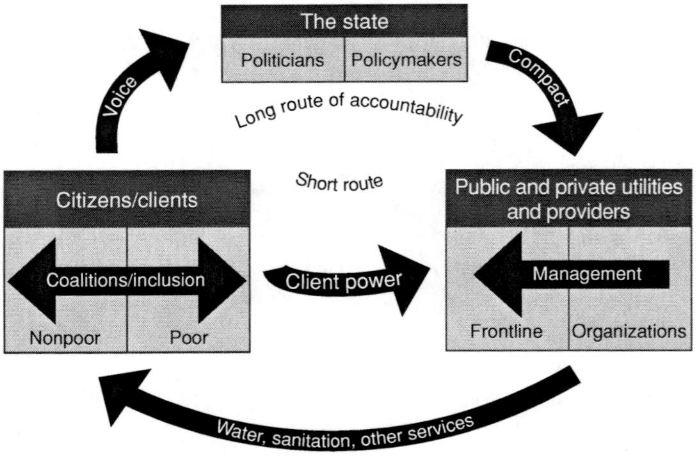

Source: World Bank, 2004: 162

should coexist. It assumes that the long route depends on democracy, although we noted earlier that access to political influence in authoritarian states can be mediated by many different variables – personal networks, corruption, ethnic loyalties and so on. But the report does recognize that political monopolies often block the long route and exclude the poor and it provides a wide range of alternative mechanisms that practitioners could use to overcome this problem by strengthening the short route. These include the use of private firms, NGOs, community-based agencies, and introducing markets and user representation into the state apparatus itself. It identifies eight organizational models that could be used to do this, and relates them to the local conditions that should influence choices between them (World Bank, 2004: 106–8). Most do not involve fundamental institutional change, but the need for

> pragmatic incremental reforms that are not likely to fully address service delivery problems but can alleviate acute service problems while … creating the conditions for deeper and more favourable change – say building capacity that can respond to service delivery challenges. This can be contrasted with … 'incremental incrementalism' that merely solves one set of immediate problems but creates others. For example, working around existing government and governance structures with no strategy for how these temporary measures will affect the long term. (World Bank, 2004: 48)

These changes would not produce revolutionary shifts in the distribution of wealth and power, but they would involve small steps in the right direction that are preferable to noncompliance and stalled development. They can be facilitated by external donors, but will only survive if they also strengthen the organizational capacity of the poor and increase their ability to unblock the long route to genuine democratic accountability in the future.

This analysis can be used to justify a wide range of options. These include bypassing governments by using NGOs or for-profit firms to deliver services in the weakest states. Some do excellent work, others are wasteful and ineffectual; they are accountable to donors rather than beneficiaries, and attempts to evaluate their performance are costly and often ineffective, as we saw in Chapter 8. However, this strategy should be seen as an unavoidable, but least-worst solution. Bypassing the states that should provide overall policy guidance and manage conflicting interests will produce coordination problems, overlapping jurisdictions, perverse incentives, duplication in some areas and neglect in others. When donors go 'straight to provider organizations … [they] sidestep the policymaker as well as the compact' between policy-makers and beneficiaries and therefore undermine 'local accountability relationships'

(World Bank, 2004: 204). These strategies must therefore be combined with continuous efforts to strengthen state capacity by improving public services, and the political and social movements that actually make it possible for both elites and the poor to articulate their interests, oblige governments to take account of their demands, and negotiate viable compromises to their often apparently incompatible demands.

Conclusions

This chapter suggests that simply shifting from authoritarianism and traditional bureaucracies to democracy and pluralistic service delivery systems will not guarantee effective long-term developmental transitions, since the effectiveness depends on local conditions and capacities. Changing institutional rules affects behaviour, but not necessarily in the way that reformers expect, because enforcing them depends on the existence of appropriate values, understandings and endowments that can only be generalized through practice. Theory-based reforms play a significant role in these processes – few people still support systems based on theocracy, racism, command planning, or pure laissez faire. We also know that societies that have ignored the technical demands required to create effective political and economic markets, rational bureaucracies and solidaristic institutions, described in Part II, also pay a heavy price for doing so. These pluralistic solutions enable reformers to make use of a far wider range of organizational alternatives than were available to their structuralist or neoliberal predecessors, but they also have to respect the need for social and economic discipline if they are not to produce poor results.[23]

The development community, national actors as well as the donor community are attempting to introduce liberal pluralistic models – democratic states, rational bureaucracies, effectively regulated markets, strong capitalist firms and small businesses, and strong solidaristic civic organizations. We have seen that these have often failed either because of the absence of the necessary capacities and endowments, or because of the threat they pose to reactionary local or foreign regimes or social movements. However, this does not discredit their normative goals or technical claims because we have yet to discover more effective ways of generating freedom, cooperative interdependence and equitable growth. These models are therefore critical to all attempts at social and political emancipation, but institutionalizing them is bound to be a long-term process. It will only succeed if development practitioners respect the organizational principles summarized in Part II, but also if they can overcome the political challenges that this project generates in LDCs, where it will not only alter the distribution of wealth and power, but also threaten existing values, identities and demand skills and endowments that are in short supply.

The result will not be linear transitions to a uniform system of liberal democratic capitalism specified in the often identical templates that development consultants use to transform institutions in counties whose histories they know nothing about. Instead, they will produce new hybrids that will be influenced by these external models, but only be created and consolidated by the political energy of local social movements and their external advisers, and often in direct opposition to the dominant political, economic and social elites. Understanding and intervening effectively in these processes demands a credible theory of political agency and practice that will have to manifest itself in the creation and maintenance of political parties and social movements that represent the interests of subordinated classes as well as dominant elites, and will have to operate at macro- and micro-levels. We do not have the space to take up these problems of political organization and mobilization in detail here, only to emphasize their critical importance in the long-term management of emancipatory change.

The processes that make international headlines relate to the national and international struggles associated with regime change, but these always fail unless they are combined with an increase in the organizational capacities needed to sustain genuinely accountable institutions at every level from the household to the global system. They depend on the ability to combine local and imported models in creative ways, as we saw in Chapter 12. Malinowsky and other classical development theorists recognized the need for a dual approach to the problems of late development many years ago, and, in doing so, provided practitioners with a flexible and potentially creative agenda. Both local activists and outsiders can always find some 'room for manoeuvre' at international and local levels, even in hostile environments.

This analysis has demonstrated that political processes always involve a complex array of highly contingent interventions by multiple players with different and usually conflicting agendas and resources. These processes operate in authoritarian as well as democratic states, although the constraints that bind rulers and citizens are different in each. But there will always be some room for manoeuvre, whether for donors to use their leverage to make major changes in total systems, businessmen to buy political support or create parallel markets and evade state controls, or the poor to use foot-dragging and evasion to subvert the authority of the rich. The critical fact about political systems is that they are constructed and constantly reconstructed by human intervention. As Gramsci (1971: 172) said:

[The active politician] bases himself on effective reality, but what is this effective reality? Is it something static and immobile, or is it not a relation of forces in continuous motion and shift of equilibrium? If one applies one's will to the creation of a new equilibrium among the forces which really exist and are operative – basing oneself on the particular force which one believes to be progressive and strengthening it to help it to victory – one still moves on the terrain of effective reality, but one does so in order to dominate or transcend it (or to contribute to this). What 'ought to be' is therefore concrete; indeed it is the only realistic and historical interpretation of reality; it alone is history in the making and philosophy in the making, it alone is politics [and, we would add, 'development'].

Thus, as Murray (1992: 79) argues, paraphrasing Schaffer:

We should start always from where we are, with what we have in hand, and not from some abstract model of where we would like to be. The study of organization is not at all the Leninist question of what is to be done, but the more complicated and less certain question of what can be done.

Notes

1 I am grateful to Colin Leys for helpful comments on this and the next two chapters.
2 See footnote 15, Chapter 1.
3 Linz and Stepan (1996: 4–15) provide the seminal analysis of these processes.
4 Failed rulers and radical movements still blame the colonial legacy and imperialism for uneven development. These claims cannot be dismissed, but international inequalities are a fact of life that limit but do not determine the ability of regimes to solve their problems. Many poor postcolonial states have now succeeded, but only by accepting responsibility for their own failures as well as their successes.
5 I owe this insight to Horace Campbell.
6 The analysis in this chapter is heavily indebted to the work of the Crisis States Research Programme at the London School of Economics.
7 For a useful review, see White and Luckham (1996).
8 See North (1981) on Britain and Holland; Landes (1999) on Japan; Tilly (1997a) on France; and Kohli (2004) on South Korea.
9 On the other hand, Hutton (2006) emphasizes the costs associated with the limitations imposed by the authoritarian nature of the Chinese state.
10 This may be why the recent British Commission for Africa report failed to ask 'why African politicians are so little interested in building capable states' (Booth, 2005: 494). The World Bank is not permitted to 'interfere in the political affairs of any member; nor shall they be influenced in their decisions by the political character of the member [state] ... concerned', but must base their decisions on 'economic considerations' alone (Articles of Agreement, IV (10)). An exception here are the German political foundations that have played a key role in supporting patricular parties and social movements in many countries.
11 See, for example, Killick et al. (1998); Mosley et al. (1991); and Sahn et al. (1997).
12 I am indebted to discussions with Kate Meagher here.
13 This analysis is based on personl experience as a policy adviser in the UK, Uganda, Zimbabwe and Somalia.
14 See, for example, Bauer (1981); Boone and Faguet (1998); Easterly (2006); Ferguson (1996).

15 See Tilly (1997c) for an anlaysis of the relationship between disruptive social change and political revolutions.

16 For classic texts, see Bailey (1965); Lipset (1963); Lemarchand (1972); Powell (1970); and Scott (1972).

17 See Mann's (2005) analysis of how the democratization of politics can produce regimes that engage in extreme forms of racist oppression.

18 I owe this point to Kate Meagher.

19 The UN's Millenium Development Goals (UNDP, 2003: 1–3), adopted by 189 countries in 2000, include the eradication of extreme poverty, inequality, ignorance and disease, environmental sustainability and the need for a 'global partnership for development', but ignore the need for major investments in structural economic changes. I owe this point to Robert Wade.

20 For a discussion, see Campbell (2001); Mosley et al. (1991); Ranis (1997); and Sachs (1988).

21 This influential paper was widely criticized but its findings were robustly defended in Burnside and Dollar (2004).

22 For further key texts, see Hirschman (1970) and Paul (1992).

23 See, for example, my analyses of the weaknesses of many participatory and cooperative programmes (Brett, 1996b, 2003).

Chapter 14

Building Capitalist Economies

Liberal economists attribute developmental failures to the politically generated price distortions, perverse incentives and unproductive rents, which are created by structuralist programmes and which stop market forces from maximizing efficiency and equity. They believe that subjecting local producers to local and international competition will not only generate economic growth, but also good governance by eliminating the political rents that make corruption possible. We set out the liberal case for market systems in Chapter 4, and in Part III have shown why structuralists believe that free markets will benefit poor countries as well as rich ones only when they have all attained 'nearly the same degree as possible of industry and civilisation, political cultivation and power'. They believe that 'under the existing conditions of the world, the result of general free trade would not be a universal republic, but … a universal subjection of the less advanced nations to the supremacy of the predominant manufacturing, commercial, and naval power' (List, 1841/1904): 103).[1]

This debate has dominated development theory and practice in the modern era and obliges us to review the case for and against free trade and liberalized markets in weakest LDCs, and also to examine the nature and effects of the alternative kinds of policy regimes that structuralists have adopted to overcome the problems of market failure they identified. We will first make the case for free markets and free trade in situations characterized by late development, and then look at the variety of strategies that have been adopted by regimes that have rejected it.

Maximizing comparative advantage and eliminating political rents

Liberals claim that free markets will maximize world income because, all else being equal, LDCs not only share the advantages of comparative advantage, outlined in Chapter 4, with DCs, but should gain *more* from trade than them for four reasons:

1 Lower wage costs in LDCs than in DCs will encourage investors to move from high- to low-wage economies and from rich to poor countries.

2 LDCs make larger gains than DCs from trade because it enables them to replace their own inefficient technologies with far more efficient machinery and production processes without having to meet the costs of developing them.
3 Trade enables them to exploit the scale economies generated by modern technology by accessing global as well as domestic markets.
4 Access to global capital markets enables them to invest far more rapidly than would be possible using their limited domestic savings.

The 7–10% growth rates experienced by the export-intensive Asian success stories have strongly reinforced these claims.

Liberal trade theory was a response to the mercantilist theories that dominated the 16th and 17th centuries, which assumed that nations could best enrich themselves 'if they ever observed this rule; to sell more to strangers yearly than we consume of theirs in value', and thereby prevent 'the importation of Hemp, Flax, Cordage, Tobacco and divers other things which we fetch from strangers to our great impoverishing' (Mun, 1664/1928: 5, 7). They saw trade as a zero-sum game in which countries could only enrich themselves at their neighbour's expense. However, Hume (1752/1955) demonstrated that countries could not run a continuous trade surplus without worsening their own terms of trade and eventually impoverishing themselves, while Ricardo's analysis of comparative advantage showed that all countries would benefit from trade even where the absolute costs of production were higher in all sectors in one country than the other.[2] This turned trade into a positive-sum game that should maximize productivity, benefit weak countries more than strong ones, and become 'the principal guarantee of the peace of the world' (Mill, 1848/1900: 352).[3]

Economists used these arguments from the 19th century onwards to expose 'the errors of protectionism and the advantages of free trade', but, as Emmanuel (1972: xiv) said, 'the normal practice of the world ... has been and still remains protectionism'. Liberals responded to this paradox with an analysis of the effects of protectionism in DCs and inappropriate import substitution policies in LDCs, which demonstrated that the balance of payments and wider economic crises that afflicted most LDCs were not the outcome of the use of free markets, but a failure to actually implement them, and that state-led policies would rarely produce the desired results.

First, LDCs initially assumed that the superiority of western industry meant that local firms could only produce successfully for protected domestic markets, so their policies were based on import substituting industrialization (ISI) in response to 'export pessimism' (Little, 1982: 51–2). Most theorists, myself included (Brett, 1983), did not see that this had less to do with their own weaknesses than with the high tariffs and subsidies used by DCs to exclude low-wage manufactures and agricultural products. By the 1970s, tariff reductions and the expansion and liberalization of international credit markets had already reduced these barriers and enabled industrial exports from the East Asian NICs based on imported capital goods and low-wage labour to begin to penetrate western markets. The result has been a major relocation of labour-intensive industry from DCs to LDCs, and, more recently, of knowledge-based and capital-intensive industry producing for growing local and mature DC markets.[4]

This shift has validated liberal theory and strengthened the political position of liberalizing governments in successful LDCs like China, India, Brazil and South Africa. They are now asking DCs to complete the free trade revolution by eliminating their remaining tariffs and subsidies, so recent failures in WTO negotiations have had more to do with protectionism in DCs than LDCs. The US government has 'actually increased government assistance to business' so that smaller manufacturers are 'eligible to receive loans at about 50% of prime rate, subsidized by the federal government', and in 1999, 'there were 821 different income tax credit schemes promoting investment in the real economy in the 50 states of the US' (Reinert, 2000: 18–19). LDCs still control their borders, but they can invoke free trade theory to justify their refusal to reduce their own controls until the DCs reduce theirs.

Second, many ISI programmes were badly executed and based on several dubious assumptions:

- that LDCs should shift production from raw materials to manufactures because inelastic demand for the former must worsen their terms of trade[5]
- that they could never compete effectively in domestic and export markets without protection or subsidies
- that they should maintain fixed exchange rate regimes and not use devaluation rather than tariffs and subsidies to increase their economic competitiveness
- that Keynesian theories justified the use of deficit spending to provide public services and subsidize unprofitable new ventures.

These policies increased industrialization in many countries, but were unsustainable in the long run.

ISI used the foreign exchange and taxes generated by internationally competitive primary exporters to buy capital equipment and spare parts and subsidize uncompetitive manufacturers whose products were far more expensive than the imports they displaced. This reduced investment in the export sector, which led to a balance of payments crisis that reduced their capacity to import capital equipment and spare parts and repay foreign debts. Subsidizing loss-making firms at the expense of profitable ones reduced taxation and produced a fiscal crisis that threatened the states' capacity to finance infrastructure and welfare services. Forcing consumers to buy expensive domestic rather than cheap imported goods increased inequalities, while domestic markets were too small for local industries to take advantage of economies of scale. Further, most protected industries used capital-intensive imported rather than 'appropriate' local equipment, especially those supported by official aid, which destroyed jobs, depressed demand, and increased inequality and exclusion.

Most societies used fixed exchange rates, and maintained overvalued currencies that reduced competitiveness, exacerbated balance of payments and financial crises, and increased the need for tariffs and quotas, international borrowing and, ultimately, public spending cuts. This confirmed Friedman's (1953: 196) claim that fixed rates were incompatible 'with unrestricted multilateral trade', as did the fact that the political costs of managing these economic crises declined significantly when market-based exchange rates were introduced in the late 20th century.[6] Finally, governments that used deficit spending to increase demand and sustain local employment generated inflation rather than growth, because of poor investment opportunities stemming from the absence of effectively functioning credit, community and labour markets.

By the 1980s, the economic case against structuralism seemed to be overwhelming and was used to justify the structural adjustment programmes that made LDCs liberalize trade and exchange rates, prioritize exports, and balance their budgets.

Liberals also attributed the political failures discussed in Chapter 13 to the problems inherent in all political attempts to ignore markets, control investment and set 'administered' prices that structuralist economic programmes involved. They claimed that giving rulers monopoly powers over resource allocation enabled them to extract rents from producers or consumers, which they would use to enrich themselves and their cronies, and to buy political support. These rents would sustain what Bhagwhati (2002: 36–41) calls 'directly unproductive profit-seeking activities' that reduce welfare by rewarding people for 'chasing rents instead of producing goods and services that would add to national income' (p. 36, citing Krueger, 1974).[7] Hence rent-seeking behaviour depends on the perverse incentives generated by non-market social and political interventions – the ability of politically connected elites, feudal lords, party cadres, licensing officials, Mafiosi, ethnic elites – to use force to exclude a rival producer from a market or a consumer from seeking a cheaper supplier. This is confirmed by our analysis of the economic distortions generated by weak and/or authoritarian governments in Chapter 13.

This liberal analysis rehabilitated liberal market theory by producing a compelling critique of the failings of the structuralist programmes followed by most LDCs. However, its assumptions that emerging firms in weak states should be able to compete effectively with strong ones, that classical ISI is the only viable approach to state-managed development, and 'that the removal of institutions and rights that protect rents is always desirable as a way of moving towards greater efficiency and better economic performance' can also be questioned (Khan, 2000: 21).[8] Most of its criticisms of old-style ISI are certainly valid, but we will now question their tendency to identify gains from trade with those from free trade, show that state-led export-oriented industrialization (EOI) has overcome many of the failings of ISI, and that some kinds of rents are crucial to late-late development.

Infant economies and states, primary accumulation and managed markets

The gains from trade are incontrovertible, and almost certainly could bring greater benefits to LDCs than to DCs, since the most successful NICs would not have enjoyed unprecedented growth over the past 30 years without it. However, the fact that poor countries can benefit from trade does not prove that they would not benefit more by shifting from free to managed trade if their governments could do this effectively. The NICs now compete effectively on global markets, but this is only after long-term industrialization programmes based on interventionist policies, while neither structuralism nor liberalization has solved the problems of the weakest LLDCs. To explain these anomalies, we need to return to the market failure arguments in classical development theory, and then to the ongoing debate over the role of the state in export-oriented development.[9]

Scale economies, liberalization and uneven development

Ricardian comparative advantage theory depends on a number of basic assumptions, most critically, the existence of constant or diminishing returns to scale, and full employment. When these exist, both high-cost and low-cost countries will benefit from trade, even where all the producers in the latter can outcompete those in the former. This is because the most efficient producers in the low-cost economies will make greater profits by increasing production and exporting to higher cost economies, but will only be able to do so by attracting resources from less efficient home producers whose production must fall, creating a compensating demand for imports from high-cost economies. In these countries, unemployment will rise in the industries that are affected by additional imports, but it will be absorbed by those that are now able to export to high-cost countries. Total costs of production will decline, benefiting both low- and high-cost economies.

However, pure Ricardian theory ignores the economic and political consequences of technological progress in DCs that reduces the costs of production by exploiting scarce information and economies of scale. Where low-cost firms expand output by substituting capital-intensive for labour-intensive technology, they reduce prices and employment by exploiting economies of scale, but need not attract labour from less successful domestic firms and increase the need for imports. Instead, expanding exports enables them to reduce unit costs, offset the low wage rates that prevail in LDCs and reap most of the gains from trade. This gives first-comers a major and often decisive advantage over latecomers, which is compounded by the existence of location-specific external economies that reduce the costs of production of all firms and encourage them to 'cluster' in particular environments. These include well-developed physical infrastructure, human capital, professional and technological networks, strong state regulation, and high levels of social cohesion.

The cumulative benefits and costs generated by these processes explain the existence of combined and uneven development.[10] Access to state-of-the-art technology, inputs from neighbouring firms, and the social and physical infrastructure needed to sustain it depend on pre-existing investments, which give firms investing in first-comers a strong competitive advantage over those operating in other locations who have not been able to afford to make them. These advantages are also cumulative – the increased taxes generated in areas of concentration enable governments to continually improve services and thus reduce everyone's costs, while each additional investment increases the advantages of existing players.

As a result, liberalization alone does not remove the structural advantages that first-comers in DCs retain over latecomers in LDCs, and explains why 'the distribution of national economic performance measured by average output per person has become more unequal [in the twentieth century] than at any previous time in history' (Eggertsson, 2005: 9). Continuous technological progress and diminishing costs in DCs are driven by market competition, and confirm Marx's (1894/1972: 58) claim that 'the normal case of modern industry ... [involves] an increasing productivity of labour and the operation of a larger quantity of means of production by fewer labourers', and the analysis of the modern evolutionary economists reviewed in Chapter 3. It also explains the preponderance of interventionism rather than free trade in early industrialization, described in Chapter 10.

Dependency theorists used this tendency towards uneven development to justify their claim that capitalism was incompatible with industrialization and development in LDCs (Thomas, 1974; Wallerstein, 1998). However, the ongoing shift of industry from DCs to the most successful NICs has seriously undermined this claim, as we know, but the results have not been universally beneficial. These shifts have indeed lifted millions out of poverty in a few high-growth regions, but they have also marginalized millions more and destroyed industrial jobs in less successful centres. Thus neither liberal nor old-style dependency theorists can account for the complex and contradictory processes that have restructured the world economy since the 1980s. We can only make sense of these processes by developing a far more nuanced explanation that recognizes the existence of different kinds of scale economies, and the significance of political as well as economic variables. These create different kinds of options for countries at different levels of development, and are strongly conditioned by contextual and historical variables.

The costs incurred by any firm depend on its access to technology, managerial and workforce skills, wage rates, and external services and markets. In most sectors, least cost technology and quality controls impose a minimum scale of operation that creates high barriers to entry in poor environments that lack the necessary skills and services, so they can rarely break through these barriers without external support. As Mill said:

> It cannot be expected that individuals should, at their own risk, or rather to their certain loss, introduce a new manufacture and bear the burden of carrying it on until the producers have been educated up to the level of those with whom the processes are traditional. (Mill, 1848/1900: 556)[11]

And these inequalities are wider now than in the 19th century:

> The wide and absolute gap in income and technology between today's industrialized and developing countries ... created a powerful and continuous tension between the almost unlimited number of internationally produced goods, which (apart from the ability to pay) the underdeveloped countries would find more useful and desirable than domestically produced goods, and, conversely, the small and restricted number of their domestically produced goods which can be sold on the international market. Indeed this tension is such a dominant characteristic of modern underdevelopment that the way in which a country seeks to deal with it must be regarded as a central feature of its development. (Bienefeld and Godfrey, 1982: 44–5)

These barriers cannot be overcome by low wages alone because competitiveness also depends on access to workforces with adequate levels of skill, easy access to inputs and professional services, good infrastructure and large markets. Trade and financial liberalization over the past 30 years has enabled LDCs to exploit economies of scale by accessing global markets, and allowed the subsidiaries of transnational corporations (TNCs) or strong national firms to generate high profits by combining imported technology and low wages to produce the unprecedented growth rates that have characterized the successful NICs and discredited export pessimism. However, this has not reduced global inequalities but redistributed them in increasingly complex and contradictory ways that are not eliminating the structural obstacles to industrialization in the poorest countries.[12] There are two key reasons for this:

1   Scale economies operate not only at the level of an actual production facility, but also at the level of multiplant firms, states and regions. Large firms have better access to credit, research and development, and marketing and advertising, making it impossible for small producers to challenge the global dominance of Coca-Cola, Microsoft or GlaxoSmithKline, for example. Recent WTO agreements on intellectual property rights reinforce these inequalities.
2   Even small firms in DCs benefit from the positive externalities generated by access to better human and physical capital, infrastructure and public services:

The circulation of value through social infrastructure can produce geographical concentration of high quality conditions. Such regions then appear 'naturally' advantaged for accumulation by virtue of the 'human and social resources' that have been built up there. Production capital will likely be attracted to these regions on such a basis. (Harvey, 2006: 403)

This produces economies of agglomeration or 'clustering' because 'the likelihood of finding the right kind of labour power, raw materials, replacement parts, etc., improves the more individual capitalists and labourers cluster together – substitutions minimize the possibility of breakdowns in the circulation processes of individual capitalists' (Harvey, 2006: 406).

Creating these 'externalities' is only possible in societies that can sustain the effective state and civic institutions described in Part II. However, we have also shown that most LLDCs are governed by weak 'neopatrimonial states' and subject to high levels of mistrust and social insecurity, so foreign investors avoid them, and their domestic firms do not share a level playing field with their better endowed competitors in the west and the emerging NICs. Thus LLDCs confront two major sources of market failure that they do not share with their first world competitors. First, an 'infant economy' rather than an 'infant industry' problem, created by low levels of economic and human capital, and second, the 'infant state' problem, examined in Chapter 13.

This analysis of scale economies and positive externalities explains why successful countries, such as Japan and Germany from the 1950s to the 1980s and the Asian NICs now, have been able to run long-term trade surpluses and impose serious deflationary pressures on their less successful neighbours, and why liberalization alone will not solve the problems of weak states with embryonic capitalist economies. Thus the world economy is indeed characterized by structural inequalities, although these inequalities are not immutable, as most dependency theorists assumed.

As a result, most DCs are now richer than they were a century ago and still dominate the global economy, and a few LDCs and transitional economies have made rapid progress. However, most of the LLDCs with embryonic capitalist classes and weak states have fallen back since they cannot compete successfully with the new NICs with strong states, access to modern technology and virtually unlimited supplies of low-cost labour.[13] This has also had regressive effects in semi-industrialized LLDCs with relatively high wages. The result in South Africa, for example, has been multiple trajectories that have produced significant levels of instability and intensified inequalities:

> There are those workers benefiting from the opportunities of liberalization, such as BMWSA's employees and, to some extent, the Zambian workers who get better jobs through South African investment [there]. Then there are those workers, such as those in casual and outsourced work, as in the domestic appliance sector ... who are forced to accept worse working conditions because of intensified competition [from South Korea]. Lastly there are those in sectors such as footwear whose jobs have disappeared altogether [due to Chinese competition] and who are forced to survive through informal activities. (Webster, 2005: 65)[14]

These effects are much worse in LLDCs where low-cost Chinese competition has forced them to revert to low-value-added raw material production, which initially improved their raw materials prices, although these are now threatened (yet again) by the latest global capitalist crisis. Only the stronger LDCs are able to strengthen their industrial capacity, and even there deindustrialization is generating intense social and economic dislocations.[15]

State power, primitive accumulation and capitalist development

This analysis of the economics of uneven development can be complemented by Marxist theories of primitive (or primary) accumulation,
which focus on the characteristics of the capitalist class itself, and the
distinctive kinds of economic and political relationships that emerge at
different stages of capitalist development. These are historically and
therefore path determined in any society, and create its ability to compete
in open markets, interact with the state and civil society, and the nature
of its interventions in processes of institutional reform. Neoclassical
economists do not address these issues, since they treat both giant
corporations and microentrepreneurs as individuals with equal access
to markets. However, development/evolutionary theorists recognize that
their assumptions simply ignore most of the key analytical and policy
problems generated by the historically and path-determined processes
that have produced concentrations of powerful capitalist firms in the
north, and a predominance of semi-feudal, petty capitalist and peasant
producers in most LLDCs.

Marx's theory of primary accumulation represents an essential
complement to Listean structuralist theory, because it shows why
managing early capitalist development generates qualitatively different
demands from those involved in regulating mature capitalist systems.
He shows that mature capitalist firms reproduce themselves by investing
profits (or surplus value), but this is not possible for emergent firms,
producing a fundamental contradiction:

> The accumulation of capital pre-supposes surplus-value: surplus-
> value presupposes capitalistic production: capitalistic production
> presupposes the pre-existence of considerable masses of capital and
> of labour-power in the hands of producers of commodities. The
> whole movement, therefore seems to turn in a vicious circle, out of
> which we can only get by supposing a primitive accumulation (previ-
> ous accumulation of Adam Smith) preceding capitalistic accumula-
> tion; an accumulation not the result of the capitalist mode of
> production, but its starting point. (Marx, 1867/1974: 667)

Thus 'infant' firms need to fund their initial investments from external transfers until they can generate the profits needed for investment or
to underwrite commercial loans. Historically, this has required positive
intervention by the state. So emerging capitalist classes:

> all employ the power of the State, the concentrated and organised
> force of society, to hasten hot-house fashion, the process of transfor-
> mation of the feudal mode of production into the capitalist mode,

and to shorten the transition. Force is the midwife of every old society pregnant with a new one. It is itself an economic power. (Marx, 1867/1974: 703)

This process depends on the ability of the emerging capitalist class to persuade states to use their coercive power to extract the rents they need to finance their initial investments in modern enterprises, and provide them with the infrastructure and protection they need.

Khan (2000: 23) has provided us with a rigorous analysis of the contradictory implications of this process. He shows that state-generated rents are required to create the wider organizational framework needed to 'ensure that markets work', and then distinguishes between inefficient and efficient rents. He accepts that rent-seeking processes are intensely competitive and often generate 'wastage and theft' (p. 25) and 'political turmoil' (p. 38). However, he also follows Marx by arguing that state power has had to be used to create 'new property rights, and often entirely new economic classes ... [through a] process of seizure or transfer of assets', a process that must continue until private firms can finance themselves out of profits (p. 25). This means that rents are needed to provide 'the resources necessary for accumulation', and it also has crucial implications for 'the role of politics and power', and 'the ways in which class conflicts might determine the overall magnitude of the surplus and its allocation'. He contrasts this with the neoclassical tradition that treats rents as mechanisms 'that provide incentives for innovation, learning, information generation or efficient monitoring', and 'does not look at rents as having a political determinant' (p. 66).

In Europe, primary accumulation involved the dispossession of the peasantry, the dissolution of feudal or religious estates,[16] the creation of a credit system and national debt, and the extraction of surpluses from colonies. In the former command economies in the east, it involved the transfer of state assets to former political or bureaucratic elites, followed by legal and illegal transfers from the state and the financial sectors.[17] LLDCs face the most intractable problem of all because 'very little modern capitalism' exists there 'and most of the factors which facilitate its development remain weak or nonexistent' (Callaghy, 1988: 78). Here, legitimate rents are generally provided by donors, and illegitimate ones are the result of political corruption. All these processes therefore involve forms of state intervention as well as transfers based on access to social and political networks that are not based on the orthodox individual property rights central to neoclassical theory. However, they are needed to build capitalist enterprises, but their existence does not in any way guarantee a viable transition to what Weber (1920/1983: Ch. 2) calls 'modern' capitalism based on rational calculation and ethical obligation rather than predation and 'avarice'. The struggle for rents in poor societies intensifies political, economic and social conflict, and often produces economic decline, political despotism, predation and breakdown rather than long-term growth, as we saw in Chapter 13. Thus it is the need and struggle for political rents that helps to explain the weakness of most states in LLDCs, and their ability to meet the conditions that govern the pluralistic post-Washington model that donors are attempting to impose on them.

So emerging capitalist economies cannot be consolidated without access to rents, and although both legitimate and illegal rents can facilitate long-term capitalist transitions, they can also, and perhaps more frequently, generate the perverse incentives and destructive conflicts that can ultimately lead to the crises and breakdowns described in Chapter 10.

Economic policy regimes and late-late development

This analysis of scale economies and primitive accumulation has important and highly ambiguous policy implications. It validates the liberal case for trade and its critique of old-style ISI managed by weak authoritarian states, but it also demonstrates that free markets alone are unlikely to produce a developmental transformation in weak states. The East Asian NICs accepted both of these insights and shifted from ISI to EOI when their local markets were saturated, and used well-managed credit controls, targeted subsidies and lower but significant tariffs to benefit particular firms, control imports and encourage manufactured exports. Their states were strong enough to guarantee property rights, encourage foreign investment, enforce fiscal and labour discipline, and invest heavily in infrastructure, education and social security. This enabled new firms to overcome their start-up problems and compete successfully on world markets, eliminating the balance of payments and fiscal constraints, and creating full employment and better services that guaranteed social inclusion and cohesion, as we saw in Chapter 10 (Amsden, 1989; Wade, 1990; Kohli, 2004).

South Korea and Taiwan are now liberalizing their political and economic institutions, but only after making the transition to developed country status. Other intermediate states like China, India and South Africa are following differing versions of this 'governed market model', and are having to deal with the serious tensions this always generates. These include conflicts between:

- demands for democracy and the need for an autonomous and authoritative state
- access to export markets and protection for firms threatened by cheap imports

- the rights of capitalists and labour
- the need for taxes, investment and savings as opposed to higher consumption, better welfare services and greater equality.

These contradictory demands always generate political and economic tensions that could destabilize people's willingness to accept the inevitable compromises and pay-offs on which social cohesion depends:

- China has to defend a political monopoly and balance the contradictory demands of a statist and socialist past with the demands of a dramatically expanding capitalist class.
- India has to deal with the immense problems of economic and social marginalization, and a structuralist economic past.
- South Africa has to incorporate the historically excluded black majority into an open society, and retain the support of white capitalists and professionals and black unions as it dismantles the protectionist barriers and state control that guaranteed jobs and social order (see, for example, Standing et al., 1996; Marais, 1998).

These successful regimes have experimented with a wide array of policies that have involved a combination of market liberalization as well as tight regulation and controls and subsidies designed to allow high-cost producers who would otherwise be destroyed by competition to survive by getting the prices wrong, in order to overcome the start-up problems discussed earlier. This has increased growth and sometimes equity, but also involved asset transfers that have generated serious tensions and imposed heavy demands on the state. Their programmes represent creative solutions that have combined state and market-based approaches in ways that reflect local conditions and respond to the constraints generated by the problems of late development and structural change. They are achieving real successes, although at the expense of new inequalities and environmental degradation. Their achievements have been a major factor in challenging the one-sided claims of neoliberal theory, and provide LLDCs with possible models that may be far more relevant than what is happening in DCs in the north.

However, the infant state and economy problems discussed earlier make it hard for LLDCs to emulate them. Social and economic conflict, patrimonial bureaucracies and weak civic institutions reduce the state's capacity to enforce social cohesion and regulate economic interests. Their infrastructure is rudimentary, as are their capitalist classes, while dualistic value systems and high levels of scarcity, insecurity and mistrust intensify ethnic or sectarian rivalries. Their formal economies were dominated by loss-making state and private companies dependent on monopoly rights, subsidies or protection that collapsed when exposed to competition. Their 'real' economies are informal, largely illegal and invisible, in order to evade regressive taxes and repressive state controls (MacGaffey, 1987; De Soto, 1989; Meagher, 2006). Weak exports, rents and tax evasion generate chronic foreign exchange and fiscal crises and sustain a culture of corruption and moonlighting that is a rational response to the state's inability to pay a living wage (Munene, 1995). Rapid population growth makes it virtually impossible to increase per capita incomes among the poor or provide adequate education, health and other services. Secondary and tertiary education is scarce and skill shortages are exacerbated by migration and endemic diseases.

These weaknesses have been compounded by the partial implementation of policy reforms as a result of the extreme levels of aid dependence and perverse and conflict-ridden relationships that often prevail between national states and the donor community, examined in Chapter 13. This community is led by the IFIs, but composed of many multilaterals, bilaterals and international NGOs with limited local knowledge, distinct agendas and few incentives to coordinate their activities, provide comprehensive services and avoid duplication and weak accountability to their own electorates.

Many local regimes would like to implement old-style import substitution programmes that enable them to appropriate rents and allocate political favours, but they cannot finance them alone, and donors refuse to help them. Yet they also lack the resources to shift from ISI to EOI as the NICs have done. This also requires a capacity to tax, manage formal state agencies, and provide genuine incentives for, and impose effective sanctions on, officials, so it will be unlikely to work until the local capitalist class is strong and socially responsible enough to pay its taxes, generate the jobs and output needed to satisfy basic social needs, and oblige the regime to behave in appropriate ways.

Conclusions

Few of these states have been able to resolve many of the start-up problems identified earlier, nor will they be able to do so if they have to have adopted all the 'good policies' embodied in the liberal pluralist package before they receive significant amounts of donor support. This is because LLDCs confront a chicken and egg problem, which ensures that they will only be able to improve their capacity to exercise state power after they have increased the capacity and morality of their firms and civic institutions, and they will only be able to do this after they have built strong states. This problem confirms Kohli's (2004: 421) proposition that we cannot expect 'all good things', like democracy, free markets and open civic institutions, 'to go together' in these fragmented and underendowed societies. However, we cannot give up attempts to introduce more effective institutions into specific contexts where they do fit, and especially to find ways of adapting them to local capacities and value systems in order to do so. This raises issues of sequencing and adaptation that will ultimately depend on the ability of practitioners to tailor them to the particular needs of specific societies. All we can do here and in the concluding chapter is to identify some of the general principles that they should take into account.

Paradoxically, the neoliberal case for the use of markets rather than state controls is probably strongest in LLDCs where state capacity is weakest. Markets cut demands on the state apparatus, and reduce perverse incentives and rents by removing the monopoly controls and irrational prices that facilitate official corruption and obstructionism. Thus, although well-managed administrative interventions would probably expedite growth, state controls only intensify predation in patrimonial states where they are always abused. As a result, moving from controlled to market-based exchange rates to balance exports and imports, liberalizing credit allocations, and privatizing loss-making state enterprises should produce better results than structuralism, despite the difficulties identified earlier. The rapid growth of informal firms in parallel markets in weak and centralized states demonstrates the benefits of liberalization where the political preconditions for effective regulation are absent (see De Soto, 2001). What we are suggesting here, therefore, is that pure market solutions should be treated as a second-best alternative to effective state intervention in weak or failed states.

However, we have also seen that these solutions will not enable infant economies to generate the resources they need to achieve take-off, and that this imposes major obligations on donors to transfer the necessary surpluses to them and ensure that they will be effectively used. Many influential interests have opposed these shifts, arguing that encouraging foreign investment and liberalizing credit markets will solve their foreign exchange, fiscal and investment crises (US Congress, 2000). But the deep crisis in the global economy makes this proposition even less plausible than before, so this forces us to reconsider the political economy of aid dependence identified in Chapter 13.

This challenge raises many difficult issues:

- Liberalization and Asian competition have destroyed local firms and pushed people into low-cost primary production, subsistence-based informal activities, crime and prostitution.
- Raw material prices were rising but are now falling as the depression intensifies, so returning to primary exports does not represent a viable long-term solution for a world in which agriculture is increasingly mechanized and most poor people live in cities.

- Devaluation might work better than tariffs and quotas to defend local productive capacity, but not in countries that made windfall gains from mineral exports or large aid flows.
- Old-style ISI and even South Korean-style large-scale EOI are probably impossible in societies with infant economies and infant states, so they need active programmes of small, medium and large-scale business creation based on secure property rights, subsidies, micro-credit, tax-raising import duties, training and research programmes, well-regulated capital–labour relationships, and major investments in basic infrastructure.

These are the sorts of firms that enable the poor to survive in marginalized environments; the crucial problem now is for governments, with or without donor support, to find better ways of supporting them through the elimination of repressive regulations, better infrastructure and social services, and direct transfers. 'Rents' are essential in capitalist development – the problem is to shift from the illegitimate transfers endemic in patrimonial states to legitimate ones that increase efficiency and equity.

These policies are not controversial. However, their success in strengthening the economic capacity of these societies also depends on necessarily simultaneous attempts to eliminate predation and rebuild state capacity in LLDCs. In the last analysis, therefore, successful development depends on the ability to solve the problems of political and economic transition, so this chapter and Chapter 13 have demonstrated the interdisciplinary nature of the challenges involved in creating and implementing policy agendas that can address both aspects of this problem at the same time. We will take up these issues in our final chapter.

Notes

1 List (1841/1904: 111) is credited with inventing the infant industry argument, but his analysis goes further, recognizing that development is also dependent on the capacity of the state, 'science and arts' and 'morality and intelligence'.
2 For a summary of Ricardo's classic two commodity, two country model, see Haberler (1961).
3 Bhagwati (2002) and Krugman (1997) provide rigorous but accessible defences of free trade.
4 BMW 3 Series cars are now produced in South Africa and exported to the north (Masondo, 2003; Webster, 2005: 58).
5 This is the Singer-Prebisch hypothesis (see Prebish, 1959); for a critique, see Bauer (1971).
6 Several of the financial crises that have affected both DCs and LDCs – Britain in 1967 and 1976, Mexico in 1994, East Asian economies in 1997, and Argentina in the period 1999–2002 – would have been less destructive had their currencies been allowed to depreciate. According to Polak (1977: 45), 'any regime under which the balance of payments adjusts itself automatically throughout changes in the [exchange] rate excludes the possibility of a balance of payments deficit by assumption'.

7   Rents can be defined as an income that exceeds the market-based return from an activity, and are therefore excluded by fully competitive markets.

8   Khan himself rejects this proposition.

9   This analysis is drawn from Brett (1983: Chs 2 and 3, 1985: Ch. 2).

10 Or why 'to them that have shall be given, from them that have not shall be taken away, even that which they have', or what Wade (2004) calls the 'Matthew effect'.

11 However, post-Washington consensus theorists ignore the fact that 'productivity-enhancing knowledge is developed through production-based learning, and that such learning may be curtailed if the intense competitive pressures associated with liberalization have a negative effect on production' (Deraniyangala, 2001: 95).

12 These shifts have also increased structural inequalities and created serious social dislocations in DCs that are increasing demands for protection against low-cost imports, but this issue will not be addressed here.

13 The Lewis (1954) model of 'development with unlimited supplies of labour' tells us that rising wage costs need not reduce China's competitiveness in the forseeable future. This problem is compounded for LLDCs by rapid improvements in human capital stemming from the success of China's educational and population control programmes.

14 These insights are based on the collaborative research carried out by the Sociology of Work Unit at Witwatersrand Univeristy and the Crisis States Programme at the LSE between 2002 and 2005.

15 Trevour Manuel, then minister of finance in South Africa, noted that trade with China was having these effects in South Africa (interview, 2004).

16 See Sansom (2004) for a fictional account of the transfer of monastic properties to the emergent bourgeoisie in 16th-century England.

17 Information from students from the former Soviet bloc.

Theory, Agency and Developmental Transitions

Beyond the impasse in development theory

This book seeks to produce a credible theory of development that takes the needs, capacities and limitations of the poorest rather than richest people and societies as its starting point. The idea of development still exercises a powerful influence on theory and practice in both DCs and LDCs, where it operates as a set of normative goals, policy programmes and teleological expectations. These have generated processes of institutional and policy reform designed to maximize freedom, prosperity, equity and cooperative interdependence by creating open science-based institutional systems since the start of the modern era.

We have argued that this idea has universal relevance, but that the emerging discipline of development studies is primarily concerned with structural changes in LDCs, which create problems that are not confronted in DCs, and therefore demand more complex theoretical constructs and policy programmes than are needed by the latter, and which are addressed by orthodox liberal theorists. We identified the methodological issues that confront the theorists who have been addressing these problems in Part I, the principles that govern institutional best practice in DCs that serve as models for LDCs in Part II, and showed why problems of late development block their adoption in LDCs and require alternative hybrid solutions in Part III.

This approach has been designed to construct a coherent theory of emancipatory institutional transitions by identifying the positive contributions that apparently contending paradigms have made to this crucial enterprise. The conflicts between socialist and liberal conservative agendas that were reproduced in debates between dependency and neoliberal theories in LDCs are now giving way to liberal pluralistic initiatives in both, which recognize that strong states, markets and solidaristic organizations need to coexist in order to create interdependent global, national and local agencies that respect each other's autonomy, service each other's needs, and resolve conflicting demands without resorting to coercion and command. These models have displaced those of the classical development theorists who recommended far more centralized and even authoritarian solutions in LDCs.

These demands for democracy, competitive economies and open social systems are not only made by the international donor community, but also by local people who want to share the freedom and prosperity that only these institutions can bring. Attempts to satisfy them depend on the adequacy of the liberal pluralist model that informs the 'post-Washington consensus', described in Part II, which transcends many of the one-sided assumptions imposed by structuralist or liberal fundamentalists. However, while the mainstream development community sees it as the final solution to the problem of late development, we have shown that recent attempts to operationalize it in the weakest LLDCs have failed, because those societies lack the dispositions, understandings and endowments needed to sustain it. The need for a distinctive theory of development that treats the liberal pluralist model as a long-term goal, but recognizes that this must be combined with an understanding of the need for collective responses and constraints based on different analytical assumptions and practices in LLDCs is therefore as urgent as ever.

This claim that development studies still offers us potentially viable solutions is not just a matter of faith, but a response to the ability of many societies to make successful transitions to liberal democratic capitalism by modifying orthodox theoretical principles, as we saw in Chapter 10. Countries that were once almost as poor, oppressed and insecure as the LLDCs have transformed themselves into mature social democracies over the past 200 years, rapid growth is lifting millions out of poverty in Asia, democratization is occurring in most of the south and east, and halting but significant improvements are taking place in some weak states, while DCs are more aware of their need to contribute more to the emancipation of the poorest people in the poorest countries than ever before.

However, these successes have also been used to justify unrealistic claims that the decline of right- and left-wing corporatism has completed the enlightenment project, and ended the Hegelian notion of history understood as the processes of structural change that have concerned us here (Fukuyama, 1992: xii–xiii). These claims ignore the environmental, economic and political crises that confront an increasingly integrated, productive, but unequal and insecure global system. Unprecedented growth now threatens the earth's capacity to sustain civilized life, and yet another financial and economic crisis is now destabilizing the basic institutions of capitalism itself; while economic and political failures in LLDCs still trap billions in conditions of extreme deprivation and insecurity. These failures threaten the global system as well as the analytical models and institutional systems that sustain it. We can therefore conclude by identifying the key features of the three crises we have just identified and make some general comments about the role of comparative institutional theory in addressing them.

Institutions, agency and the development crisis

Markets, market failures and the environmental crisis

We have virtually ignored the environmental consequences of economic growth in LDCs, despite their crucial and contradictory institutional and political implications. We accept that there is a real conflict between market-driven economic growth, poverty alleviation and environmental sustainability that now confronts humanity with its greatest challenge. However, we have failed to address it here for three reasons:

1 The problem has been created by the overconsumption of the rich, who cannot expect the poor to limit their right to growth to help them solve it. Our main concern has been with the challenges confronting LLDCs whose poverty minimizes their contribution to the problem rather than those of successful LDCs and DCs who are primarily responsible for the crisis.

2 But extreme poverty does have serious environmental consequences, since it encourages unsustainable population growth, the overexploitation of essential natural resources, and the use of inefficient and destructive technologies. Thus growth in LLDCs could actually reduce environmental degradation if it were combined with a major shift to low-impact technologies[1] and effective population controls, while failure to adopt sustainable social and economic programmes will not only exacerbate their own problems, but intensify the destructive use of global resources.

3 So the critical issue is not to eliminate growth there, but to introduce more effective institutions based on the incentive and accountability mechanisms that encourage both producers and consumers to shift from high-impact to low-impact technologies.

However, the global problems of resource depletion and waste disposal raise deeply challenging problems of market failure for activists in both DCs and LDCs, since these threats stem from the failure of societies to deal effectively with the externality and non-excludability problems identified in Chapter 4. Market competition forces all producers to expand using least cost production methods, or face extinction. Our tendency to exhaust open-access resources like forests and fisheries, and our inability to limit emissions into sinks for waste products – the air, seas, rivers and lakes – has produced overexploitation and a 'tragedy of the commons' (Hardin, 1968; Ostrom, 1990). While alternative technologies often do exist that would reduce these pressures, we cannot assume that they will always reduce costs, so even well-intentioned producers will be unable to adopt them as long as free markets prevail, thus challenging the technological optimism of many neoliberal theorists. Instead, national and global governance structures are needed to impose far stronger limits on the ability of producers to use least cost but environmentally damaging technologies than now exist, although this will often increase prices, reduce consumption and is likely to have highly disruptive effects on the viability of the economic system as a whole. This will, of course, also generate intense conflict among and strong opposition from both producers and consumers.

Thus the failure of the voluntary limits set by the Kyoto Protocol in the 1990s to reduce emissions was entirely predictable,[2] so we clearly cannot survive without a pluralistic solution involving far higher levels of state regulation than now prevail. These would need to include green taxes, subsidies and managed markets, with far more demanding targets than the ones that already exist for carbon emissions at the very least.[3] However, the willingness to impose these controls will inevitably involve many sacrifices, and this raises even more serious questions about the ability of democratically elected governments to invoke them.

There is overwhelming scientific evidence for the dangers we face, and many interest groups and media outlets are actively promoting this message. Unfortunately, however, there is a clear political contradiction between the demand for growth and environmental sustainability. Democratic governments cannot question the need for growth because voters would remove them if they did. The energy-intensive industries use their huge resources to challenge attempts to reduce emissions, and few citizens are willing to actually change their increasingly energy-intensive lifestyles. Thus governments are doing very little to reduce emissions and a great deal to promote growth and full employment, while these national political failures are compounded by the fact that pollution is a global problem, where the highest gains accrue to the most powerful societies, and the heaviest costs are being carried by the poorest ones. The most critical problem, therefore, is for the leading polluters – both producers and consumers – to be made to change their behaviour. But the global agencies that have to address this problem do not have the powers and resources needed to negotiate a just distribution of the costs and benefits of these changes or to enforce the resulting agreements, as we saw in Chapter 5.

Regulatory failures and the crises in global capitalism

The dominance of neoliberal theory at the global level was sustained by the long boom that began in the 1980s, which encouraged neoliberals to reduce levels of state regulation in global and national financial and credit markets, notably, but not exclusively, in the USA. The result was speculative activity driven by perverse incentives that removed virtually all controls over risk. This produced unsustainable levels of debt and unpredictable shifts in prices, which confirmed Keynes' (1936/1973: 159) claim that 'when the capital development of a country becomes a by-product of the activities of a casino the job is likely to be ill-done'. This has produced a number of relatively localized crises and speculative bubbles that finally burst in 2008, threatening the survival of the global credit and monetary system and a classic Keynesian deflation comparable to the great crash of the early 1930s (Galbraith, 1954/1992). Here, banks cannot lend, demand declines, companies are bankrupted and new investment becomes increasingly difficult, leading to yet further falls in demand, investment and employment. In the early 1930s, public spending cuts and protectionism intensified the problem (Friedman and Schwartz, 1963).

This crisis also stems from the tendency of neoliberal theorists to ignore the problems of market failure identified in Chapters 4 and 7, and the corresponding need for state regulation at both national and global levels. Credit markets are highly competitive, so even large banks found it hard to adopt prudent banking procedures when their competitors did not. Imperfect information made it impossible for depositors, investors and borrowers to understand the risks created by the complex and virtually unregulated financial instruments created over the past 20 years, so they were not able to make rational choices about their investments. The immense pay-offs for key traders and agencies, and the benefits offered to investors and borrowers in good times, as well as the assumption that governments could not allow the biggest players to fail intensified the problems of market failure stemming from bounded rationality, opportunism, moral hazard and adverse selection.[4] Bankers made immense profits, their depositors and borrowers also benefited but carried the heaviest risks, and responsible bankers were marginalized. However, the interdependent nature of the whole system based on interbank lending ensured that everyone has had to pay a heavy price once these perverse incentives pushed the system beyond sustainable limits.

Thus national and especially global credit and financial markets suffer from particularly acute problems of market failure, and should therefore be subjected to far closer regulation and controls than many other industries. However, democratic governments have failed to adopt or enforce these measures[5] because of political pressures from powerful banking lobbies, and demands for cheap credit from voters. These problems have been compounded by the weaknesses of the international regulatory agencies, because globalization stops national governments from imposing greater controls on their own banks than those that exist elsewhere.[6] These risks have now led to the forced nationalization of many banks and calls for tighter regulation and large subsidies to key industries – a repetition of the last great crash in the 1930s. Thus the demand for regulation constantly emerges after a crisis, and diminishes once it seems to be over. As I argued 26 years ago during an earlier banking crisis created by uncontrolled lending to national governments:

> In favourable conditions banks, like other capitalist enterprises, find little use for state regulation or state intervention and assume that market competition will guarantee the efficiency, stability and legitimacy of their operations. Thus Citibank in 1978 attacked the 'fairness and relevance' of the laws and regulations controlling their domestic activities and called for 'a sharp turn towards truly liberal [that is, neoliberal] ideals in which government is a silent partner in the relationship among individuals' [Annual Report, 1978]. Once equilibrium is threatened, however, only the adequacy of the state structures supporting the whole system can save it from collapse ... and the whole capitalist class will expect them to provide both the resources and guarantees necessary to solve the problems which they have created. (Brett, 1983: 226, see also, 1985: Ch. 9)

This passage was part of a broader analysis (pp. 222–9) that argued that the asymmetrical and underregulated nature of the global capitalist economy, and the privileged position occupied by the USA in it, was unsustainable in the long term. The subsequent boom encouraged governments to become 'silent partners in the relationship among individuals' during the neoliberal revolution, but the inevitable collapse has forced even the neoliberal fundamentalists in the late Bush administration to nationalize the commanding heights of the US credit industry and force its citizens to carry the costs of its bad debts, in order to avert an otherwise catastrophic collapse of global capitalism. This apparently paradoxical outcome simply confirms Polanyi's (1944/2001: 151/2) claim that 'collectivist' attempts to control markets have not been the outcome of 'anti-liberal' political conspiracies, but to protect 'vital social interests' from 'the weaknesses and perils inherent in the self-regualting market system'.

The political implications of the environmental and capitalist crises

The current environmental and credit crises can therefore be attributed to the market failures generated by externalities, imperfect information, opportunism and malfeasance, identified in Chapters 4 and 7. We argued there that many theorists and policy-makers have recognized the need for strong states and effective regulation to overcome them, and that this has produced a partial retreat from neoliberal fundamentalism to more viable pluralistic programmes that should have had the capacity to address these crises. Unfortunately, the intensity of the current crises stems from the fact that few governments, and especially the late Bush administration in the USA, have been willing to go far enough down this road. On the other hand, we can already see that the credit crisis, like the great depression in the 1930s, has produced a rapid change in attitudes and a generalized, although often unconscious, reversion to the Keynesian interventionist policies that prevailed in the third quarter of the 20th century, and far more tentative attempts to respond to the environmental crisis.

Yet radicals can legitimately claim that these responses have been too limited and have come too late. However, we saw above that democratic processes generally encouraged rather than inhibited the excesses that have precipitated these crises, while major sacrifices will be necessary if we are to resolve them. This forces us to ask whether the combination of democratic states, new public management systems and free economic markets, outlined in Part II, will guarantee us a secure future. The mass unemployment and intensification of economic competition created by the interwar crises persuaded many serious theorists to support right- or left-wing authoritarian solutions, so we cannot ignore the possibility that a failure to control the current global crises will threaten the hegemony of the liberal institutions that seemed to have been completed by the ending of the cold war.

Although we cannot rule out a resurgence of authoritarian ideologies, the left- and right-wing regimes that emerged in the interwar period clearly have little to teach us about responsible forms of environmental and economic management. Liberal pluralism therefore remains our best option, but its recent failures also demonstrate that we have to radically change the relationship between collective interventions and the right of individual firms to make free market choices if we are to control the inherent tendency of capitalism to generate uneven development, destructive externalities and unmanageable economic and social crises.

However, the actual policies that have produced these crises were not only a function of the inherent tendency for uncontrolled markets to produce these negative effects, but of the failure of the citizens living in DCs to use their political and economic freedoms to build the social and political movements needed to enable politicians committed to necessary but unpalatable policies to be elected.[7] During the long boom, which ended in 2008, politicians had to respond to demands from voters with unrealistic expectations about the possibility of maximizing both growth and environmental sustainability, and they will only be able to prioritize the latter rather than the former if their supporters make it possible for them to do so. As a result, we are now being forced to confront the most paradoxical market failure of all. The success of free economic and political markets has enabled billions to live prosperous lives, although they have yet to provide billions more with even the rudiments of a civilized life. However, they have also generated production processes that now turn out to be ecologically and economically unsustainable, which threaten present and especially coming generations with economic instability, drought, floods and plagues.

This does not eliminate the case for markets, but it does demand a major shift to far more rigorous forms of state and social regulation and intervention that prioritize equity and environmental sustainability over the maximization of individual consumption and choice. Powerful social and political movements have supported and still support policies of this kind. Thus democracy has produced very different outcomes in the USA, dominated by socially irresponsible neoconservatives for the past eight years, than in countries like Canada or Sweden where social obligation imposed much stronger limits on the right of individuals to behave in ways that seriously threaten social cohesion and environmental sustainability. Here, an informed and active citizenry has built organizations that promote responsible behaviour even when it imposes serious constraints on their right to pursue 'courses of their own' that generate negative externalities for others (Bunting, 2008). Command planning systems did not solve these problems, since they produced poor environmental and economic results, punished critics and reformers, and created a dependent and passive, not active citizenry. This generation faces much greater dangers than past ones, but has more resources to deal with them. It will have to impose tight controls on the tendency for free markets to generate unsustainable levels of consumption, waste and risk, or pay a high price for its failure to do so in the not too distant future.

Managing the crisis of late-late development

The primary concern of this book has been to identify and remove the obstacles to the emancipation of people living in the poorest societies in the world. Their fate is directly linked to the ability of the rich to solve the problems of overconsumption, inequality and instability that we have just identified, but we have not been able to address the cultural and organizational challenges that doing this raise here. What has concerned us are the very different challenges that confront the LLDCs whose people have been excluded from both the benefits and challenges of modernity because they have yet to consolidate the market and science-based institutions, which have already transformed the north and are rapidly transforming the most successful LDCs. There is no guarantee that their transitions will ever be completed, given the opposition they generate from powerful groups with a vested interest in non-liberal institutions, and the fact that past failures to overcome these problems still threaten development studies with the 'stigma of disillusion' and represent the main challenge to the analysis presented here.

We saw in Chapter 1 that conservative and radical development theorists have tried to overcome the problems of transition by using a variety of competing policy-oriented models during the modern era:

- structuralists used state-led institutions to impose new cultures and institutions on recalcitrant societies
- neoliberals tried to remove the perverse incentives created by these controls by introducing free markets
- third world theorists responded to the tensions generated by both approaches by asking communities to delink from global capitalism and return to their traditional values and institutions.

We have argued that all these paradigms have identified some of the real difficulties that confront transitional societies but ignored others, and that the most significant debates in the discipline are no longer over the merits of one of these paradigms or the other, but over the value of different kinds of pluralistic solutions that combine market, state and community-based institutions in different ways in different kinds of situations. However, we also argued that the orthodox liberal pluralism that dominates the official discourse of the development community still ignores many of the most serious challenges that these countries face, and have therefore called for a far more complex and flexible response to the crisis than the post-Washington consensus currently recommends.

Liberal pluralism demands the immediate adoption of

- democratic constitutions that assume that citizens will be free to choose their rulers
- impersonal bureaucracies that will provide effective and equitable services
- free markets that will not be 'distorted' by politically or socially generated controls and/or rents
- egalitarian social arrangements that guarantee equal rights and maximize individual freedom.

However, local political identities and people's capacity to organize in LLDCs still depend on a variety of collective ethnic or sectarian obligations, patriarchal gender relationships, and vertical patron–client authority systems, which are incompatible with the individualistic principles of liberal democracy and open social institutions, while local firms also depend on traditional linkages with social and political networks as well as external subsidies to survive international competition.

We have argued that progressive national governments and donors need to be far more open to hybrid solutions that might conflict with their liberal principles by allowing local people to use the codes and normative principles they understand best. These principles could confirm the authority of traditional rulers and elites that limit individual freedom, equalities and rights, as we saw in Chapter 11, but they can also sustain practices that incorporate effective accountability mechanisms and generate economic efficiency, as we saw in Chapter 12.[8] Thus hybridity can sustain practices that we disapprove of, but successful adaptations of this kind, combined with support for dispossessed groups resisting oppression, will not produce stagnation but generate evolutionary transformations by enabling people to combine external insights and their local knowledge systems and increase their capacity to solve problems incrementally, as they learn by doing.

We saw in Chapter 13 that the *World Development Report 2004* (World Bank, 2004) lays out a wide range of alternative organizational systems that create direct and indirect solutions to the accountability problem. These are fully consistent with the analytical and normative propositions that have motivated this study. We have argued that the crisis of uneven development can only be overcome by creating diverse service delivery organizations that provide elites with adequate incentives but also enable their beneficiaries to make them promote the social interest rather than their own. Beneficiaries can do this when they are able to enter into spot market transactions with suppliers to meet their particularistic needs. However, they cannot exercise effective controls over the collective problems mediated by the state or the general rules that govern their social and economic lives as atomized individuals, but only as members of solidaristic agencies.

SOs and social movements operate at all levels. They include 'informal' local structures like household and friendship networks, as well as national, regional and global networks, associations and political parties. This is true in DCs, where they are often based on democratic principles and formal bureaucracies, as we saw in Chapter 8, but they are equally crucial in LDCs where formalized agencies coexist with informal institutions and organizations based on informal kinship, class, ethnic and religious ties that are even more important there than they are in DCs. They not only mediate relationships between people, firms and the state, but also operate as small enterprises to sustain livelihoods, insure against risk, and maintain social cohesion.

The vicious circles and political problems of noncompliance that dominate life in LLDCs, identified in Chapter 13, survive where predatory elites can use ethnic or sectarian values and patron–client ties to resist attempts by the poor to build autonomous organizations based on horizontal linkages. Democratization and liberalization make it harder for elites to suppress demands from the poor by strengthening their potential ability to exercise exit and voice, but too little has been done to strengthen their substantive ability to build autonomous organizations, despite participatory and 'capacity-building' projects of many kinds. This is an intrinsically difficult problem for two reasons:

- human and social capital is scarce in these environments and outsiders find it hard to operate in local organizations without reducing their autonomy
- building 'progressive' organizations will always be resisted by reactionary elites.

If change agents are to unblock the development process, they need to strengthen the organizational capacity of the local political and economic elites who play an indispensable role in the development process, but also that of the poor whose voices they can now usually ignore with impunity. Many theorists argue that external interventions must always distort the efforts of local communities to solve their own problems, but this ignores the limited resources at the disposal of the local intellectuals and leaders, who should organize these processes, and their ignorance of potentially better solutions. It also underestimates the willingness and ability of dominant elites to intimidate or exclude them. Donors should not pre-empt the role of local agencies and can easily undermine what they do. Donors have limited information about local conditions, have to confine their support to particular organizations, and can strengthen reactionary organizations, intensify conflicts between groups, and undermine internal accountability mechanisms by favouring particular groups or leaders and excluding others (Meagher, personal communication; World Bank, 2004: Ch. 11). However, they cannot afford to ignore the need to help to build local institutional capacity, and have given NGOs primary responsibility for this role. They have made many errors, but are constantly looking for more effective ways of performing it.

Formal shifts to democracy and competitive markets are therefore a necessary condition for further progress, but they only succeed when all the economic, social and political agencies needed to operationalize them can be strengthened, and when modern institutions can be complemented by traditional practices that can strengthen accountability and make use of useful local skills, solidarities and value systems. Thus practitioners need to make qualitative judgements about the regimes and policies they support or oppose, and not simply impose standardized rules, while liberal pluralist theory should set ultimate goals, but not overdetermine short-term interventions. There are no universal blueprints for action, so best practice depends on the capacity to make the best use of existing social and human capital.

LLDCs depend on donors for aid, institutional models and technical advice, and their commitment to liberal principles is shared by local westernized elites who are equally committed to democracy, economic freedom and science-based knowledge systems. These reforms have been opposed by major groups, and often exceed the technical capacities of their societies. At the same time, an underfinanced donor community has demanded changes that can produce costly and destabilizing results without providing the support needed to overcome the start-up problems they create. Thus the liberal development community as a whole has also failed to acknowledge the political implications of their poverty reduction programmes. There is a corresponding need to strengthen the capacity of potential winners to support their programmes, compensate losers, and finance the real costs involved in funding the shift from pro-rich to pro-poor policy agendas that they now demand.

Open, pluralistic and science-based institutions are difficult to create, but their limitations and short-term failures do not discredit their normative goals or technical claims, because their failures often stem from the resistance of reactionary regimes or social movements. Hence liberal models are crucial to all attempts at social and political emancipation, but institutionalizing them is not just a technical problem but generates practical challenges that demand a credible theory of political agency and practice that has to operate at both macro- and micro-levels. Major public debates over development issues generally focus on major changes in institutional arrangements, conflicts over changes of regime, and national policy agendas, and often ignore positive achievements and local level struggles. However, we have shown that new institutions or governments will fail unless they are accompanied by improvements in the human and organizational capital needed to sustain genuinely accountable institutions at every level from the household upwards. Recognizing that the capacity for effective development is a function of continuous improvements in existing capacities and the development of new hybrids at all levels of society offers practitioners major opportunities and a viable agenda, because it enables both local activists and outsiders to always find some 'room for manoeuvre', even in hostile environments:

> For most of them, most of the time, the opportunities are for small steps and little pushes. To the individual these may seem insignificant, but the sum of these small actions makes great movements. (Chambers, 1983: 192)

These actions will always be constrained by local circumstances. They will be informed by 'organic intellectuals' – teachers, priests, traditional leaders and local activists – and their results will depend on their ability to understand local dispositions and capacities and relate to local power structures. But successful transitions also depend on leaderships with access to the 'most advanced thought in the world' (Gramsci, 1971: 325), that are not only able to operate at local but also at national and international levels. They have to be able to build political support, understand the need for open institutions and democratic contestation, and manage the complex technical programmes involved in building and sustaining state capacity and poverty-focused economic change.

Development theory is based on a commitment to freedom, equity and cooperative interdependence, and is the repository for all we know about how to improve the lot of the poorest as well as the wealthiest societies in the world. It offers a wide range of alternative paradigms and prescriptions, but change agents in particular societies can only make effective use of them by adapting them to meet the objective possibilities generated by local cultures and capabilities. They need to understand the theoretical principles synthesized in this book, but also how to make contextually informed judgements about where to intervene and who to support or oppose in order to generate progressive social transitions. These interventions will generate unavoidable conflict and crises, since developmental transitions not only produce losses and reversals, but also the openings that enable excluded groups to challenge ongoing injustices and the institutional arrangements that sustain them, and create the possibility of 'emancipation through social conflict' (Sklar, 1967: 1).

Notes

1   For examples of environmentally sustainable technologies, visit the website of the Ashden Awards (www.ashdenawards.org).
2   Gwyn Prinz, presentation at LSE.
3   The official Stern Review (2006: Chs 14 and 15), sponsored by the UK Treasury, probably provides an overoptimistic review of these options.
4   Many bankers may be utterly responsible, but regulatory regimes, like policemen, are essential to deal with the minorities whose irresponsibility threatens the survival of the rest.
5   As I write, the financial press is asking why Bernard Madoff was allowed to run a fraudulent investment agency in the USA that lost more than $50bn over a 10-year period.
6   This point was emphasized in a BBC TV interview (21/9/2008) by Gordon Brown, British prime minister and former chancellor of the exchequer, as the scale of the credit crisis became evident. However, neither he nor the Conservative opposition attempted to addrss the problem until they were forced to do so by the credit crunch.
7   I owe this point to Deborah Doane at the World Wildlife Fund.
8   As T.S. Eliot (1939/1951: 58) said: 'the best government must be relative to the character and the stage of intelligence of a particular people in a particular place at a particular time'.

References

Acton, J. (1948) *Essays on Freedom and Power*, Glencoe, Free Press.

Alchain, A.A. and Demsetz, H. (1972) 'Production, information costs and economic organisation', *American Economic Review*, 62(5): 777–95.

Allen, T. (1996) 'A flight from refuge', in T. Allen, *In Search of Cool Ground: War, Flight and Homecoming in Northeast Africa*, London, James Curry.

Allen, T. (2000) 'Taking culture seriously', in T. Allen and A. Thomas, *Poverty and Development in the 20th Century*, Oxford, Oxford Universtiy Press.

Allen, T. (2006) *Trial Justice: The International Criminal Court and the Lord's Resistance Army*, London, Zed Books.

Allen, T. and Skelton, T. (1999) *Culture and Global Change*, London, Routledge.

Almond, G. (1960) 'Introduction: a functional approach to comparative politics', in G. Almond and J. Coleman (eds) *The Politics of the Developing Areas*, Princeton, Princeton University Press.

Alter, C. and Hage, J. (1993) *Organizations Working Together*, Newbury Park, Sage.

Amin, S. (1994) 'The issue of democracy in the contemporary world', in U. Himmelstrand, K. Kinyanjui and E. Mburugu (eds) *African Perspectives on Development*, London, James Curry.

Amsden, A. (1989) *Asia's Next Giant: South Korea and Late Industrialization*, New York, Oxford University Press.

Appleton, S. and Mackinnon, J. (1995) *Poverty in Uganda: Characteristics, Causes and Constraints*, Oxford, Oxford Centre for the Study of African Economies.

Arrow, K.J. (1963) *Social Choice and Individual Values*, New Haven, Yale University Press.

Arrow, K.J. (1985) 'The economics of agency', in J.W. Pratt, and R.J. Zeckhauser, *Principals and Agents: The Structure of Business*, Boston, Harvard Business School Press.

Austen, R. (1987) *African Economic History: Internal Development and External Dependency*, London, James Curry.

Ayer, A.J. (1948) 'The principle of utility', in G.W. Keeton and G. Schwartzenberger, *Jeremy Bentham and the Law*, London, Stevens.

Bachrach, P. and Baratz, M. (1962) 'Two faces of power', *American Political Science Review*, 56(4): 947–52.

Bacon, R. and Eltis, W. (1978) *Britain's Economic Problem*, 2nd edn, London, Macmillan.

Bailey, F. (1965) *Politics and Social Change*, Berkeley, University of California Press.

Bain, J. (1962) *Barriers to New Competition*, Boston, Harvard University Press.

Banfield, E. (1975) 'Corruption as a feature of governmental organization', *Journal of Law and Economics*, 18(3): 587–605.

Baran, P. (1957/1962) *The Political Economy of Growth*, New York, Monthly Review Press.

Barkan, J. (2005) 'An African "success" past its prime', in *Challenge and Change in Uganda*, Washington, Woodrow Wilson International Center.

Barry, B. (2001) *Culture and Equality: An Egalitarian Critique of Multiculturalism*, Cambridge, Polity Press.

Bates, R. (1981) *Markets and States in Tropical Africa: The Political Basis of Agricultural Policies*, Berkley, California University Press.

Bauer, P. (1972) *Dissent on Development*, London, Weidenfeld & Nicolson.

Bauer, P. (1981) *Equality, the Third World, and Economic Delusion*, London, Weidenfeld & Nicolson.

Bayart, J.-F. (1993) *The State in Africa: The Politics of the Belly*, London, Longman.

Bayart, J.-F., Ellis, S. and Hibou, B. (1998) *The Criminalisation of the State in Africa*, Oxford, James Curry.

Becker, G. (1981) *A Treatise on the Family*, Cambridge, Harvard University Press.

Bentley, A. (1908) *The Process of Government*, Chicago, University of Chicago Press.

Berle, A. and Means, G. (1932) *The Modern Corporation and Private Property*, New York, Macmillan.

Bernstein, E. (1961/1989) *Evolutionary Socialism: A Criticism and Affirmation*, New York, Random House.

Bessis, S. (2003) *Western Supremacy: The Triumph of an Idea?*, London, Zed Books.

Bhabha, H. (1994) *The Location of Culture*, London, Routledge.

Bhagwati, J. (2002) *Free Trade Today*, Princeton, Princeton University Press.

Bhaskar, R. (1979) *The Possibility of Naturalism*, Brighton, Harvester.

Bienefeld, M. and Godfrey, M. (1982) *The Struggle for Development*, New York, Wiley.

Blair, J. (1972) *Economic Concentration*, New York, Harcourt Brace.

Boeke, J. (1953/1976) 'Dualistic economics', reprinted in G. Meier (1976) *Leading Issues in Economic Development*, 3rd edn, New York, Oxford University Press.

Bond, P. and Manyaya, M. (2002) *Zimbabwe's Plunge: Exhausted Nationalism, Neoliberalism and the Search for Social Justice*, London, Merlin.

Bonin, J., Jones, D. and Putterman, L. (1993) 'Theoretical and empirical studies of producer cooperatives', *Journal of Economic Literature*, 31(3).

Boone, P. and Faguet, J.P. (1998) 'Multilateral aid, politics and poverty: past failures and future challenges', in R. Grant and J. Nijman (eds) *The Global Crisis in Foreign Aid*, New York, Syracuse University Press.

Booth, D. (1993) 'Development research: from impasse to new agenda', in F. Schuurman, *Beyond the Impasse: New Directions in Development Theory*, London, Zed Books.

Booth, D. (2005) 'The Africa Commission Report: what about the politics?', *Development Policy Review*, 23(4): 493–8.

Botchwey, K., Collier, P., Gunning, J. and Hamada, K. (1998) *Report from a Group of Independent Persons Appointed to Conduct and Evaluate Certain Aspects of the Enhanced Structural Adjustment Facility*, Washington, IMF.

Bourdieu, P. (1992) *The Logic of Practice*, Cambridge, Polity Press.

Bower, J. (1977) 'Effective public management', *Harvard Business Review*, 55(2): 124–30.

Bowles, S. (1985) 'The production process in a competitive economy', *American Economic Review*, 75(1): 16–36.

Bowles, S. and Gintis, H. (1996)' Is the demand for workplace democracy redundant in a liberal democracy?', in U. Pagano and R. Rowthorn, *Democracy and Efficiency in the Democratic Enterprise*, London, Routledge.

Bradley, K. and Gelb, A. (1983) *Cooperation at Work: The Mondragon Experience*, London, Heinemann.

Braverman, H. (1971) *Labor and Monopoly Capitalism*, New York, Monthly Review Press.

Brenner, R. (1977) 'The origins of capitalist development', *New Left Review*, 104: 25–93.

Brett, E. (1969) 'Politics, economic and rationality', *Social Science Information*, **8**(2): 49–66.

Brett, E. (1970) 'Cooperatives and rural development in Uganda', in R. Apthorpe (ed.) *Rural Cooperatives and Planned Change in Africa*, Geneva, UNRIST.

Brett, E. (1973) *Colonialism and Underdevelopment in East Africa: The Politics of Economic Change*, London, Heinemann.

Brett, E. (1975) 'The political economy of General Amin', *IDS Bulletin*, **7**(1): 15–22.

Brett, E. (1983) *International Money and Capitalist Crisis: The Anatomy of Global Disintegration*, London, Heinemann.

Brett, E. (1985) *The World Economy Since the War*, London, Macmillan.

Brett, E. (1988) 'Adjustment and the state, the problem of administrative reform', *IDS Bulletin*, **19**(4): 4–11.

Brett, E. (1992/3) *Providing for the Rural Poor: Institutional Decay and Transformation in Uganda*, Brighton, IDS & Kampala, Fountain Press.

Brett, E. (1993) 'Voluntary agencies as development organisations: theorizing the problem of efficiency and accountability', *Development and Change*, **24**(2): 269–303.

Brett, E. (1995a) 'Institutional theory and social change in Uganda', in J. Harriss, J. Hunter and C.M. Lewis (eds) *The New Institutional Economics and Third World Development*, London, Routledge.

Brett, E. (1995b) 'Neutralising the use of force in Uganda: the role of the military in politics', *Journal of Modern African Studies*, **33**(1): 129–52.

Brett, E. (1996a) 'Rebuilding war-damaged communities in Uganda', in T. Allen, *In Search of Cool Ground: War, Flight and Homecoming in Northeast Africa*, London, James Curry.

Brett, E. (1996b) 'The participatory principle in development projects: the costs and benefits of cooperation', *Public Administration and Development*, **16**(1): 5–20.

Brett, E. (1998) 'Responding to poverty in Uganda: structures, policies and prospects', *Journal of International Affairs*, **52**(1): 313–27.

Brett, E. (2000a) 'Understanding organizations and institutions', in D. Robinson, T. Hewitt, and J. Harriss (eds) *Managing Development: Understanding Inter-organisational Relationships*, London, Sage.

Brett, E. (2000b) 'Development theory in a post-socialist era: competing capitalisms and emancipatory alternatives', *Journal of International Development*, **12**: 728–802.

Brett, E. (2003) 'Participation and accountability in development management', *Journal of Development Studies*, **40**(2): 1–29.

Brett, E. (2005) 'From corporatism to liberalisation in Zimbabwe: economic policy regimes and political crisis 1980–1997', *International Political Science Review*, **26**(1): 93–106.

Brett, E. (2008) 'State failure and success in Zimbabwe and Uganda: the logic of political decay and reconstruction in Africa', *Journal of Development Studies*, **44**(3): 339–67.

Brown, W.A. (1950) *The United States and the Restoration of World Trade*, Washington, Brookings Institution.

Buchanan, J. (1987) 'Forward', in G. Tullock, *The Politics of Bureaucracy*, New York, University Press of America.

Buchanan, J. and Tullock, G. (1962) *The Calculus of Consent*, Ann Arbour, University of Michigan Press.

Bull, H. (1977) *The Anarchical Society*, London, Macmillan.

Bunker, S.G. (1985) 'Peasant responses to a dependent state: Uganda', *Canadian Journal of African Studies*, 19(2): 371–86.

Bunting, M. (2008) 'Lessons from the Nordic model', *Guardian*, 18 August.

Burch, D. (1987) *Overseas Aid and the Transfer of Technology: The Political Economy of Agricultural Mechanisation in the Third World*, Aldershot, Avebury.

Burke, E. (1790/1971) 'Reflections on the revolution in France', in A. Arblaster and S. Lukes, *The Good Society*, London, Methuen.

Burke, E. (1790/1803) 'Reflections on the revolution in France', in *The Works of the Right Honourable Edmunde Burke*, vol. 5, London, Rivington.

Burke, E. (1791/1803) 'An appeal from the old to the new Whigs', in *The Works of the Right Honourable Edmund Burke*, vol. 6, London, Rivington.

Burkie, S. (1993) *People First: A Guide to Self-Reliant, Participatory Rural Development*, London, Zed Books.

Burnside, C. and Dollar, D. (1998) *Aid Policies and Growth*, Working Paper 1777, Washington, World Bank.

Callaghy, T. (1984) *The State-Society Struggle: Zaire in Comparative Perspective*, New York, Colombia University Press.

Callaghy, T. (1988) 'The state and the development of capitalism in Africa: theoretical, historical and comparative reflections', in D. Rothchild and N. Chazan, *The Precarious Balance: State and Society in Africa*, Boulder, Westview.

Campbell, B. (2001) 'Governance, institutional reform and the state: international financial institutions and political transition in Africa', *Review of African Political Economy*, 88: 155–76.

Campbell, H. (1979) The Commandist State in Uganda, DPhil, Sussex University, Brighton.

Campbell, H. (2003) *Reclaiming Zimbabwe: The Exhaustion of the Patriarchal Mode of Liberation*, Trenton NJ, Africa World Press.

Carboni, G. (2008) *No-party Democracy? Ugandan Politics in Comparative Perspective*, Boulder, Lynne Rienner.

Carmody, P. (2001) *Tearing The Social Fabric: Neo-liberalism, De-industrialisation, and the Crisis of Governance in Zimbabwe*, Portsmouth, NH, Heinemann.

Castells, M. (2000a) 'The rise of the fourth world', in D. Held and A. McGrew, *The Global Transformations Reader*, Cambridge, Polity Press.

Castells, M. (2000b) *End of Millennium. The Information Age: Economy Society and Culture*, vol. 3, 2nd edn, Oxford, Blackwell.

Castells, M. (2001) 'Information technology and global capitalism', in W. Hutton and A. Giddens, *On the Edge: Living with Global Capitalism*, London, Vintage.

Chabal, P. and Daloz, J.-P. (1999) *Africa Works: Disorder as a Political Instrument*, Oxford, James Curry.

Chambers, R. (1983) *Rural Development: Putting the Last First*, Harlow, Longman.

Chandler, A. (1980/1990) 'The United States: seedbed of managerial capitalism', in A. Chandler and H. Deams (eds) *Managerial Hierarchies: Comparative Perspectives on the Rise of Modern Industrial Enterprises*, Boston, Harvard University Press, reprinted in D. Pug (1990) *Organization Theory: Selected Readings*, 3rd edn, Harmondsworth, Penguin.

Chang, H.-J. (2002) *Kicking Away the Ladder*, London, Anthem Press.

Chang, H.-J. (2003a) 'Institutional development in historical perspective', in H.-J. Chang (ed.) *Rethinking Development Economics*, London, Anthem Press.

Chang, H.-J. (2003b) 'The East Asian development experience', in H.-J. Chang (ed.) *Rethinking Development Economics*, London, Anthem Press.

Chenery, H., Ahluwalia, M., Bell, C., Duloy J. and Jolly R. (1974) *Redistribution with Growth*, London, Oxford University Press.

Chomsky, N. (1970) 'Introduction', in D. Guerin, *Anarchism*, New York, Monthly Review Press.

Clague, C. (1997a) 'The new institutional economics and economic development', in C. Clague (ed.) *Institutions and Economic Development: Growth and Governance In Less-developed and Post-socialist Countries*, Baltimore, Johns Hopkins University Press.

Clague, C. (1997b) 'The new institutional economics and institutional reform', in C. Clague (ed.) *Institutions and Economic Development: Growth and Governance In Less-developed and Post-socialist Countries*, Baltimore, Johns Hopkins University Press.

Clapham, C. (1996) *Africa and the International System: The Politics of State Survival*, Cambridge, Cambridge University Press.

Clarke, P. and Wilson, J. (1961) 'Incentive systems: a theory of organisation', *Administrative Science Quarterly*, 6(2):129–166.

Coase, R. (1937) 'The theory of the firm', *Economica*, 4: 386–405.

Coase, R. (1960) 'The problem of social cost', *Journal of Law and Economics*, 3(1): 1–44.

Coates, D. (1975) *The Labour Party and the Struggle for Socialism*, Cambridge, Cambridge University Press.

Coleman, J. (1960) 'Conclusion', in G. Almond and J. Coleman, *The Politics of the Developing Areas*, Princeton, Princeton University Press.

Commission for Africa (2005) *Our Common Interest: Report of the Commission for Africa*, London, HMSO.

Coppola, F.F. (1972) *The Godfather*, Los Angeles.

Cowan, M. and Shenton, R. (1996) *Doctrines of Development*, London, Routledge.

Crosland, C. (1956) *The Future of Socialism*, London, Cape.

Crozier, M. (1967) *The Bureaucratic Phenomenon*, Chicago, University of Chicago Press.

Dahrendorf, R. (1959) *Class and Class Conflict in Industrial Society*, London, Routledge & Kegan Paul.

Darwin, C. (1859/1872) *The Origin of Species*, 6th edn, London, John Murray.

David, P. (2005) 'Path dependence in economic processes: implications for policy analysis in dynamical system contexts', in K. Dopfer (ed.) *The Evolutionary Foundations of Economics*, Cambridge, Cambridge University Press.

Dawkins, R. (1988) *The Blind Watchmaker*, Harmondsworth, Penguin.

Dawkins, R. (1989) *The Selfish Gene*, 2nd edn, Oxford, Oxford University Press.

Deraniyangala, S. (2001) 'From Washington to post-Washington: does it matter for industrial policy?', in B. Fine, C. Lapavitsas and J. Pincus (eds) *Development Policy in the Twenty-first Century: Beyond the post-Washington Consensus*, London, Routledge.

Desai, M. (2004) *Marx's Revenge: The Resurgence of Capitalism and the Death of Statist Socialism*, London, Verso.

De Soto, H. (1989) *The Other Path: The Invisible Revolution in the Third World*, New York, Harper & Row.

De Soto, H. (2001) *The Mystery of Capital: Why Capitalism Triumphs in the West and Fails Everywhere Else*, London, Black Swan.

Deutsch, M. (1985) *Distributive Justice: A Social Psychological Perspective*, New Haven, Yale University Press.

Dias, C. and Vaughn, M. (2006) 'Bureaucracy, managerial disorganization, and administrative breakdown in criminal justice agencies', *Journal of Criminal Justice*, 34(5); 543–55.

Dobb, M. (1976) 'A further comment', in R. Hilton (ed.) *The Transition from Feudalism to Capitalism*, London, New Left Books.

Dopfer, K. (2005) 'Evolutionary economics: a theoretical framework', in K. Dopfer (ed.) *The Evolutionary Foundations of Economics*, Cambridge, Cambridge University Press.

Douglas, M. (1986) *How Institutions Think*, New York, Syracuse University Press.

Downs, A. (1957) *An Economic Theory of Democracy*, New York, Harper & Brothers.

Downs, A. (1967) *Inside Bureaucracy*, Boston, Little, Brown.

Drucker, P. (1990) *The New Realities*, London, Mandarin.

Dudintsev, V. (1957) *Not by Bread Alone*, London, Hutchison.

Dunleavy, P. (1991) *Democracy, Bureaucracy and Public Choice: Economic Explanations in Political Science*, Hemel Hempstead, Harvester Wheatsheaf.

Durkheim, E. (1893/1964) *The Division of Labour in Society*, New York, Free Press.

Duverger, M. (1954) *Political Parties, their Organisation and Activity in the Modern State*, London, Methuen.

Easterly, W. (2006) *The White Man's Burden: Why the West's Efforts to Aid the Rest Have Done So Much Ill and So Little Good*, Oxford, Oxford University Press.

Eaton, J. and Lipsey, R. (1978) 'Freedom of entry and the existence of pure profit', *Economic Journal*, 88: 455–69.

Ebrahim, A. (2003) 'Accountability in practice: mechanisms for NGO's', *World Development*, 31(5): 813–29.

Edwards, M. (1989) 'The irrelevance of development studies', *Third World Quarterly*, 11(1): 116–36.

Edwards, M. and Hulme, D. (1995) *Non-governmental Organisations – Performance and Accountability: Beyond the Magic Bullet*, London, Earthscan.

Eggertsson, T. (2005) *Imperfect Institutions: Possibilities and Limits of Reform*, Michigan, University of Michigan Press.

Eisenstadt, S. (1963) *The Political Systems of Empires*, New York, Free Press.

Eisenstadt, S. (1966) *Modernization, Protest and Change*, Englewood Cliffs, Prentice Hall.

Elias, N. (2001) *The Society of Individuals*, ed. M. Schroter, London, Continuum.

Eliot, T.S. (1939/1951) *The Idea of a Christian Society*, London, Faber.

Emmanuel, A. (1972) *Unequal Exchange*, London, New Left Books.

Engels, F. (1895/1967) 'Introduction to The class struggles in France', in *Engels: Selected Writings*, ed. W. Henderson, Harmondsworth, Penguin.

Escobar A. (1995) *Encountering Development: The Making and Unmaking of the Third World*, Princeton, Princeton University Press.

Esteva, G. (1992) 'Development,' in W. Sachs (ed.) *The Development Dictionary*, London, Zed Books.

Evans, P. (1995) *Embedded Autonomy: States And Industrial Transformation*, Princeton, Princeton University Press.

Evans, P., Reuschemeyer, D. and Skocpol, T. (1985) 'On the road to a more adequate understanding of the state', in P. Evans, D. Reuschemeyer and T. Skocpol, *Bringing the State Back In*, Cambridge, Cambridge University Press.

Faguet, J.-P. (2002) Decentralizing the Provision of Public Services in Bolivia: Institutions, Political Competition and the Effectiveness of Local Government, PhD, London School of Economics.

Fals Borda, O. (1992) 'Social movements and political power in Latin America', in A. Escobar and S. Alvarez, *The Making of Social Movements in Latin America: Identity, Strategy, and Democracy*, Boulder, CO, Westview Press.

Fals Borda, O. (1998) *People's Participation: Challenges Ahead*, London, Intermediate Technology.

Fanon, F. (1967) *The Wretched of the Earth*, Harmondsworth, Penguin.

Ferguson, J. (1996) *The Anti-politics Machine: 'Development', Depoliticization and Bureaucratic State Power in Lesotho*, Cambridge, Cambridge University Press.

Fine, B., Lapavitsas, C. and Pincus, J. (eds) (2003) *Development Policy in the Twenty-first Century: Beyond the post-Washington Consensus*, London, Routledge.

Fine, R. (2001) *Political Investigations: Hegel, Marx, Arndt*, London, Routledge.

Finer, S. (1958) *Anonymous Empire*, London, Pall Mall.

Folbre, N. (1994) *Who Pays for the Kids? Gender and the Structure of Constraint*, London, Routledge.

Folster, N. (2001) Systemic Constraints and Aid Outcomes: The History of Canadian Official Development Assistance to Tanzania, PhD, London School of Economics.

Fortes, M. and Evans-Pritchard, E.E. (1940/1970) *African Political Systems*, London, Oxford University Press.

Foster, J. (2005) 'The self-organizational perspective on economic evolution: a unifying perspective', in K. Dopfer (ed.) *The Evolutionary Foundations of Economics*, Cambridge, Cambridge University Press.

Foucault, M. (1970) *The Order of Things*, London, Tavistock.

Foucault, M. (1980) *Power/Knowledge: Selected Interviews and Other Writings 1972–1977*, ed. M. Gordon, Hemel Hempstead, Harvester Press.

Foweraker, J. (1995) *Theorizing Social Movements*, London, Pluto Press.

Foweraker, J. (1998) 'Review article: institutional design, part systems and governability: differentiating the presidential regimes of Latin America', *British Journal of Political Science*, 28(4): 651–76.

Frank, A. (1969) 'Sociology of development and underdevelopment of sociology', and 'Dialectic, not dual society,' in A. Frank, *Latin America: Underdevelopment or Revolution*, New York, Monthly Review Press.

Frankel, S.H. (1938) *Capital Investment in Africa*, London, Oxford University Press.

Freund, B. (1998) *The Making of Contemporary Africa: The Development of African Society since 1800*, 2nd edn, Boulder, Lynne Rienner.

Friedman, M. (1953) 'The case for flexible exchange rates', in M. Friedman, *Essays in Positive Economics*, Chicago, Chicago University Press.

Friedman, M. (1962) *Capitalism and Freedom*, Chicago, Chicago University Press.

Friedman, M. and Schwartz, A. (1963) *A Monetary History of the United States*, Princeton, Princeton University Press.

Fukuyama, F. (1992) *The End of History and the First Man*, London, Penguin.

Fukuyama, F. (1995) *Trust: The Social Virtues and the Creation of Prosperity*, London, Penguin.

Fuller, C. and Harriss, J. (2006) 'For an anthropology of the modern Indian state', in J. Harriss, *Power Matters: Essays on Institutions, Politics and Society in India*, Delhi, OUP.

Galbraith, J. (1954/1992) *The Great Crash 1929*, Harmondsworth, Penguin.

Gerschenkron, A. (1962/1976) 'Economic backwardness in historical perspective', in G. Meier, *Leading Issues in Economic Development*, 3rd edn, New York, Oxford University Press.

Geyer, M. and Bright, C. (2000) 'World history in a global age', in D. Held and A. McGrew, *The Global Transformations Reader*, Cambridge, Polity Press.

Giddens, A. (1991) *The Consequences of Modernity*, Cambridge, Polity Press.

Gintis, H. (1976) 'The nature of the labor exchange', *Review of Radical Political Economics*, 8: 36–54.

Glyn, A. and Sutcliffe, B. (1972) *British Capitalism, Workers and the Profits Squeeze*, Harmondsworth, Penguin.

Gorbachev, M. (1987) *Perestroika: New Thinking for our Country and the World*, London, Collins.

Gorz, A. (1982) *Farewell to the Working Class: An Essay on Post-industrial Socialism*, London, Pluto.

Government of Uganda (1997) *Poverty Eradication Action Plan*, Kampala, Ministry of Planning and Economic Development.

Gramsci, A. (1971) *Selections from the Prison Notebooks of Antonio Gramsci*, ed. and trans. by Q. Hoare and G. Nowell Smith, London, Lawrence & Wishart.

Granovetter, M. (1992) 'Economic action and social structure: the problem of embeddedness', in M. Granovetter and R. Swedberg, *The Sociology of Economic Life*, Boulder, Westview.

Greer, G. (1971) *The Female Eunuch*, London, Paladin.

Gruber, L. (2000) *Ruling the World: Power Politics and the Rise of Supranational Institutions*, Princeton, Princeton University Press.

Guerin, D. (1970) *Anarchism: From Theory to Practice*, New York, Monthly Review Press.

Habermas, J. (1971) *Toward a Rational Society*, London, Heinemann.

Habermas, J. (1976) *Legitimation Crisis*, London, Heinemann.

Habermas, J. (1979) *Communication and the Evolution of Society*, London, Heinemann Educational Books.

Habib, I. (2005) 'Potentialities of capitalist development in the economy of Mughal India', in I. Habib, *Essays in Indian History: Towards a Marxist Perception*, New Delhi, Tulika Books.

Hager, W. (1980) 'Germany as an extraordinary trader', in W. Kohl and G. Basevi, *West Germany: A European and Global Power*, Toronto, Lexington.

Halpern, M. (1971) 'A redefinition of the revolutionary situation', in N. Miller and R. Ayer (eds) *National Liberation: Revolution in the Third World*, New York, Free Press.

Hammar, A. (2003) *Zimbabwe's Unfinished Business: Rethinking the Land, State and Nation in the Context of Crisis*, Harare, Weaver Press.

Harberler, G. (1961) *A Survey of International Trade Theory*, Princeton, Princeton University Press.

Hardin, G. (1968) 'The tragedy of the commons', *Science*, 162: 1243–8.

Hardin, R. (1982) *Collective Action*, Baltimore, Johns Hopkins University Press.

Harris, N. (1972) *Competition and the Corporate Society: British Conservatives, the State and Industry*, London, Methuen.

Harrison, L. and Huntindon, S. (2000) *Culture Matters: How Values Shape Human Progress*, New York, Basic Books.

Harrison, W. (1960) *The Government of Britain*, 6th edn, London, Hutchinson.

Harriss, J. (2002) *Depoliticizing Development: The World Bank and Social Capital*, London, Anthem Press.

316 *References*

Harriss-White, B. (2003) 'On understanding markets as social and political institutions in developing economies', in H.-J. Chang, *Rethinking Development Economics*, London, Anthem.

Harold-Barry, D. (2004) *Zimbabwe: The Past is the Future*, Harare, Weaver Press.

Harvey, D. (2006) *The Limits to Capital*, new edn, London, Verso.

Hayek, F.A. (1944/1994) *The Road to Serfdom*, Chicago, University of Chicago Press.

Hayek, F.A. (1955/1964) *The Counter-revolution of Science: Studies on the Abuse of Reason*, New York, Free Press.

Heald, S. (1999) *Controlling Anger: The Anatomy of Gisu Violence*, London, James Curry.

Heald, S. (2006) Making law in rural East Africa: Sungusungu in Kenya, Crisis States Working Paper, London School of Economics.

Hegel, G.W. (1802/1964) 'The German constitution', in *Hegel's Political Writings*, Oxford, Clarendon Press.

Hegel, G.W. (1821/1967) *The Philosophy of Right*, London, Oxford University Press.

Hegel, G.W. (1822–30/1975) *Lectures in the Philosophy of World History*, Cambridge, Cambridge University Press.

Held, D. (1987) *Models of Democracy*, Cambridge, Polity Press.

Herbst, J. (1990) *State Politics in Zimbabwe*, Berkeley, University of California Press.

Higgins, B. (1956/1976) 'The dualistic theory of underdeveloped areas', in G. Meier (ed.) *Leading Issues in Economic Development*, 3rd edn, New York, Oxford University Press.

Hirschmann, A. (1970) *Exit, Voice and Loyalty: Responses to Decline in Firms, Organizations and States*, Cambridge, Harvard University Press.

Hobbes, T. (1651/1968) *Leviathan*, Harmondsworth, Penguin.

Hobsbawm, E. (1969) *Industry and Empire*, Harmondsworth, Penguin.

Hobsbawm, E. (1976) 'From feudalism to capitalism', in R. Hilton, *The Transition from Feudalism to Capitalism*, London, New Left Books.

Hobson, J. (1902) *Imperialism: A Study*, London, Allen & Unwin.

Hodgson, G. (1999) *Economics and Utopia: Why the Learning Economy is not the End of History*, London, Routledge.

Hodgson, G. (2005) 'Decomposition and growth: biological metaphors in economics from the 1880s to the 1980s', in K. Dopfer (ed.) *The Evolutionary Foundations of Economics*, Cambridge, Cambridge University Press.

Holland, S. (1976) *The Socialist Challenge*, London, Quartet Books.

Holloway, J. and Picciotto, S. (1978) *State and Capital: A Marxist Debate*, London, Arnold.

Hood, C. (1991) 'A public management for all seasons?', *Public Administration*, 69(1): 3–19.

Hoogvelt, A. (2001) *Globalization and the Postcolonial World: The New Political Economy of Development*, Basingstoke, Palgrave – now Palgrave Macmillan.

Horsefield, J.K. (1969) *The International Monetary Fund*, 3 vols, Washington, IMF.

Hubner, K. (1983) *Critique of Scientific Reason*, Chicago, University of Chicago Press.

Hughes, O. (1994) *Public Management and Administration*, Basingstoke, Macmillan – now Palgrave Macmillan.

Hume, D. (1752/1955) 'On the balance of trade', in D. Hume, ed. E. Rotwein, *Writings in Economics*, London, Nelson.

Huntingdon, S. (1968) *Political Order in Changing Societies*, New Haven, Yale University Press.

Huntingdon, S. (1997) *The Clash of Civilizations and the Remaking of the World Order*, London, Touchstone.

Hutton, W. (2006) *The Writing on the Wall: China and the West in the 21st Century*, New York, Free Press.

Hyden, G. (2000) 'The governance challenge in Africa', in G. Hyden, D. Olowu and H. Okoth Ogendo, *African Perspectives on Governance*, Trenton, NJ, Africa World Press.

Ilchman, W. (1969) 'Productivity, administrative reform and antipolitics: dilemmas for developing states', in R. Braibanti, *Political and Administrative Development*, Durham, Duke University Press.

Islam, T. and Jackson, K. (2001) 'Microcredit and poverty alleviation: smooth talking on a rough road', *Discourse*, 4(1): 43–59.

Jain, P.S. (1995) 'Managing credit for the rural poor: lessons from the Grameen Bank', *World Development*, 24(1): 79–89.

Jaques, E. (1976/1990) 'The stratified depth-structure of bureaucracy', in D. Pugh, *Organization Theory: Selected Readings*, Harmondsworth, Penguin.

Jaques, E. (1990) 'In praise of hierarchy', *Harvard Business Review*, 68(1): 127–33.

Jaspers, K. (1963) *The Future of Mankind*, Chicago, Chicago University Press.

Jenkins, C. and Knight, J. (2002) *The Economic Decline of Zimbabwe: Neither Growth nor Equity*, Basingstoke, Palgrave – now Palgrave Macmillan.

Jensen, M. and Meckling, W. (1976) 'Theory of the firm: managerial behavior, agency costs and ownership structure', *Journal of Financial Economics*, 3(4): 305–60.

Jensen, M. and Meckling, W. (1979) 'Rights and production functions: an application to labour managed firms and codetermination', *Journal of Business*, 52(4): 469–506.

Jessop, B. (2003) *The Future of the Capitalist State*, Cambridge, Polity Press.

Johnson, H. (1968) 'International trade: theory', in D. Stills (ed.) *International Encyclopedia of the Social Sciences*, New York, Free Press, vol. 8.

Jones, B. (2005) Local-level Politics in Uganda: Landscapes at the Margins of the State, PhD, London School of Economics.

Joseph, R. (1987) *Democracy and Prebendial Politics in Nigeria*, New York, Cambridge University Press.

Kaplan, R. (1994) 'The coming anarchy', *Atlantic Monthly*, 273(2): 44–76.

Kant, I. (1784/1991a) 'Idea for a universal history with a cosmopolitical purpose', in H. Reiss (ed.) *Kant: Political Writings*, 2nd edn, Cambridge, Cambridge University Press.

Kant, I. (1784/1991b) 'An answer to the question: what is enlightenment?', in H. Reiss (ed.) *Kant: Political Writings*, 2nd edn, Cambridge, Cambridge University Press.

Kant, I. (1795/1991c) 'Perpetual peace: a philosophical sketch', in H. Reiss (ed.) *Kant: Political Writings*, 2nd edn, Cambridge, Cambridge University Press.

Kanter, R. (1972) *Commitment and Community: Communes and Utopias in Sociological Perspective*, Cambridge MA, Harvard University Press.

Kanter, R. (1985) *The Change Masters: Corporate Entrepreneurs at Work*, London, Routledge.

Kaplan, A. (1964) 'Some limitations on rationality', in C.J. Fredrich (ed.) *Rational Decisions*, New York, Atherton Press.

Kelly, P. (ed.) (2002) *Multiculturalism Reconsidered: Culture and Equality and its Critics*, Cambridge, Polity Press.

Keohane, R. (2000) 'Sovereignty in international society', in D. Held and A. McGrew, *The Global Transformations Reader: An Introduction to the Globalization Debate*, Cambridge, Polity Press.

Keohane, R. (2002) 'Commentary on the democratic accountability of non-governmental organizations', *Chicago Journal of International Law*, 3(2): 477–9.

Key, V. (1952) *Politics, Parties and Pressure Groups*, 3rd edn, New York, Crowell.

Keynes, J.M. (1920/2005) *The Economic Consequences of the Peace*, The Project Gutenberg eBook.

Keynes, J.M. (1933) 'National self-sufficiency', *New Statesman and Nation*, 6: 124–5.

Keynes, J.M. (1936/1973) *The General Theory of Employment, Interest and Money*, London, Macmillan.

Keynes, J.M. (1943/1969) 'Proposals for an International Clearing Union', in J.K. Horsefield (1969) *The International Monetary Fund*, vol. 3, Washington, IMF.

Khan, M. (2000) 'Rents, efficiency and growth', in M. Khan and J. Sundaram, *Rents, Rent Seeking and Economic Development*, Cambridge, Cambridge University Press.

Khan, M. (2003) 'The new political economy of corruption', in B. Fine, C. Lapavitsas and J. Pincus (eds) *Development Policy in the Twenty-first Century: Beyond the post-Washington Consensus*, London, Routledge.

Kickert, J.M., Klijn, E.-H. and Koppenjan, J. (1997) *Managing Complex Networks: Strategies for the Public Sector*, London, Sage.

Kiely, R. (2007) *The New Political Economy of Development: Globalization, Imperialism, Hegemony*, Basingstoke, Palgrave Macmillan.

Kilby, P. (2006) 'Accountability for empowerment: dilemmas facing non-governmental organizations', *World Development*, 34(6): 951–63.

Killick, T. with Gunatilaka, R. and Mar, A. (1998) *Aid and the Political Economy of Policy Change*, London, Taylor & Francis.

Kingsbury, B. (2002) 'The democratic accountability of non-governmental organizations: first amendment liberalism as global legal architecture: ascriptive groups and the problems of liberal models of international civil society', *Chicago Journal of International Law*, 3(1): 183–9.

Knight, J. (1992) *Institutions and Social Conflict*, Cambridge, Cambridge University Press.

Kohli, A. (2004) *State-directed Development: Political Power and Industrialization in the Global Periphery*, Cambridge, Cambridge University Press.

Korten, D. (1989) 'The US voluntary sector and global realities: issues for the 1990s', mimeo.

Kropotkin, P. (1910/1971) 'Anarchism', reprinted in A. Arlbaster and S. Lukes (1971) *The Good Society*, London, Methuen.

Krugman, P. (n.d.) *In Praise of Cheap Labor*, http//web.mit.edu/krugman/www/smokey.htm/.

Krugman, P. (1997) *Pop Internationalism*, Cambridge, MA, MIT Press.

Kuhn, T. (1964) *The Structure of Scientific Revolutions*, Chicago, University of Chicago Press.

Laclau, E. (1971) 'Feudalism and capitalism in Latin America', *New Left Review*, 67: 19–55.

Lal, D. (1984) *The Poverty of Development Economics*, London, Institute of Economic Affairs.

Lal, D. (1985/1996) 'The misconceptions of 'development economics', in K. Jameson and C. Wilbur, *The Political Economy of Development and Underdevelopment*, 6th edn, New York, McGraw Hill.

Landes, D. (1999) *The Wealth and Poverty of Nations: Why Some are so Rich and Some so Poor*, London, Abacus.

Langseth, P., Katorobo, J., Brett, E. and Munene J. (1995) *Uganda: Landmarks in Rebuilding a Nation*, Kampala, Fountain Press.

Laski, H. (1938) *A Grammar of Politics*, 4th edn, London, Allen & Unwin.

Leach, E. (1970) *Political Systems of Highland Burmah: A Study of Kachin Social Structure*, London, Athlone Press.

Leach, M. and Fairbairn, J. (1996) *Misreading the African Landscape: Society and Ecology in the Forest-Savanna Mosaic*, Cambridge, Cambridge University Press.

Leftwich, A. (1994) 'Governance, the state and the politics of development', *Development and Change*, 25(2): 363–86.

LeGrand, J. and Robinson, R. (1984) *Privatizing the Welfare State*, London, Allen & Unwin.

Lemarchand, R. (1972) 'Political clientalism and ethnicity in tropical Africa, *American Political Science Review*, 66(1): 68–90.

Lenin, V. (1902/1969) *What is to be Done? Burning Questions of Our Movement*, Moscow, Progress Publishers.

Lenin, V. (1916/1970) *Imperialism*, Moscow, Progress Publishers.

Leontief, W. (1966a) 'Postulates: Keynes's *General Theory* and the classicists', in W. Leontief, *Essays in Economics*, New York, Oxford University Press.

Leontief, W. (1966b) 'Modern techniques for economic planning and projection', in W. Leontief, *Essays in Economics*, New York, Oxford University Press.

Lester, J. (2000) *Escape from Leviathan: Liberty, Welfare and Anarchy Reconciled*, Basingstoke, Macmillan – now Palgrave Macmillan.

Lewis, A. (1954) 'Economic development with unlimited supply of labour', *The Manchester School*, May.

Lewis, D. (1999) *International Perspectives on Voluntary Action: Reshaping the Third Sector*, London, Earthscan.

Leys, C. (1983) *Politics in Britain: An Introduction*, London, Heinemann.

Leys, C. (1996) *The Rise and Fall of Development Theory*, London, James Curry.

Linz, J. and Stepan, A. (1996) *Problems of Democratic Transition: Southern Europe, South America, and Post-Communist Europe*, Baltimore, Johns Hopkins University Press.

Lipset, S. (1962) 'Introduction', in R. Michels, *Political Parties: A Sociological Study of the Oligarchical Tendencies of Modern Democracy*, Springfield, Cromwell-Collier.

Lipset, S. (1963) *Poltitical Man*, London, Mercury Books.

Lipsey, R., Carlaw, K. and Bekar, C. (2005) *Economic Transformations: General Purpose Technologies and Long Term Economic Growth*, Oxford, Oxford University Press.

Lipton, M. (1968) 'The theory of the optimising peasant', *Journal of Development Studies*, 4(3): 327–51.

List, F. (1841/1904) *The National System of Political Economy*, London, Longman, Green.

Little, I. (1982) *Economic Development: Theory, Policy and International Relations*, New York, Basic Books.

London Edinburgh Weekend Return Group (1980) *In and Against the State*, London, Pluto.

Lorenz, E. (1991) 'Neither friends nor strangers: informal networks of subcontracting in French industry', in G. Thompson, J. Frances, R. Levacic and J. Mitchell (eds) *Markets Hierarchies and Networks: The Coordination of Social Life*, London, Sage.

Lukacs, G. (1971) *History and Class Consciousness: Studies in Marxist Dialectics*, London, Merlin.

Luxemburg, R. (1818/1972) 'Socialism and war', in *Selected Political Writings*, ed. R. Looker, London, Jonathan Cape.

Luxemburg, R. (1913/1963) *The Accumulation of Capital*, London, Routledge Kegan & Paul.

MacGaffey, J. (1987) *Entrepreneurs and Parasites: The Struggle for Indigenous Capitalism in Zaire*, Cambridge, Cambridge University Press.

McGregor, D. (1990) 'Theory X and theory Y', in D. Pugh (ed.) *Organization Theory: Selected Readings*, 3rd edn, Harmondsworth, Penguin.

McGuire, M. and Troisi, A. (1997) 'Evolutionary biology: a basic science for psychology?', in S. Baron-Cohen (ed.) *The Maladapted Mind: Classic Readings in Evolutionary Psychopathology*, Hove, Psychology Press.

MacIntyre, A. (1988/1998) *The MacIntyre Reader*, ed. K. Knight, Cambridge, Polity Press.

MacPherson, C. (1962) *The Political Theory of Possessive Individualism: Hobbes to Locke*, London, Oxford University Press.

Malinowsky, B. (1944/1960) *A Scientific Theory of Culture and Other Essays*, New York, Oxford University Press.

Malinowsky, B. (1945/1961) *The Dynamics of Culture Change: An Enquiry into Race Relations in Africa*, New Haven, Yale University Press.

Mamdani, M. (1976) *Politics and Class Formation in Uganda*, London, Heinemann.

Mandel, E. (1992) *Power and Money: A Marxist Theory of Bureaucracy*, London, Verso.

Mann, M. (2005) *The Dark Side of Democracy: Explaining Ethnic Cleansing*, Cambridge, Cambridge University Press.

Manning, N. (2002) 'The new public management in developing countries', in C. Kirkpatrick, R. Clarke and C. Polidano (eds) *Handbook on Development Policy and Management*, Cheltenham, Edward Elgar.

Mao Tse-tung (1937/1954) 'On contradiction', in *Selected Works*, vol. 2, New York, International Publishers.

Mao Tse-tung (1939/1954) 'The Chinese Communist Party and the Chinese revolution', in *Selected Works*, vol. 3, New York, International Publishers.

Marais, H. (1998) *South Africa, Limits to Change: The Political Economy of Transition*, London, Zed Books.

Marcuse, H. (1968) *One Dimensional Man: The Ideology of an Industrial Society*, London, Sphere Books.

Margolis, J. (1975) 'Bureaucrats and politicians: comment', *Journal of Law and Economics*, 18(3): 645–59.

Mars, T. (1974) 'The National Academy of Administration: normative vocabularies and organisational reality', in B. Schaffer (ed.) *Administrative Training and Development: A Comparative Study of East Africa, Zambia, Pakistan and India*, New York, Praeger.

Mars, T. (1992) 'Public sector organization: where next?', *IDS Bulletin, New Forms of Public Administration*, 23(4): 18–30.

Marshall, T. (1964) *Class, Citizenship, and Social Development*, New York, Doubleday.

Martinez Gonzalez, A. (2006) A Transaction Cost Approach to Community Participatory Development: Orthodox Theory vs Reality in Traditional Communities in Mexico, PhD, London School of Economics.

Marx, K. (1847/1968) 'Wage labour and capital', in K. Marx and F. Engels, *Selected Works*, London, Lawrence & Wishart.

Marx, K. (1852/1968) 'The eighteenth Brumaire of Louis Bonapart', in K. Marx and F. Engels, *Selected Works*, London, Lawrence & Wishart.

Marx, K. (1853/1973) 'Articles on India and China', in *Surveys from Exile: Political Writings*, vol. 2, Harmondsworth, Penguin.

Marx, K. (1858/1972) *The Grundrisse*, ed. D. McLellan, New York, Harper & Row.

Marx, K. (1858/1973) *The Grundrisse*, Harmondsworth, Penguin.

Marx, K. (1859/1968) 'Preface to a contribution to the critique of political economy', in K. Marx and F. Engels, *Selected Works*, London, Lawrence & Wishart.

Marx, K. (1862/1977) 'Letters to Lasalle and Engels', in D. McLellan, *Karl Marx: Selected Writings*, Oxford, Oxford University Press.

Marx, K. (1867/1974) *Capital: A Critical Analysis of Capitalist Production*, vol. 1, London, Lawrence & Wishart.

Marx, K. (1894/1972) *Capital: A Critique of Political Economy*, vol. 3, London, Lawrence & Wishart.

Marx, K. and Engels, F. (1845–6/1974) *The German Ideology*, ed. C.J. Arthur, London, Lawrence & Wishart.

Marx, K. and Engels, F. (1848/1968) 'Manifesto of the Communist Party', in *Selected Works*, London, Lawrence & Wishart.

Masondo, D. (2003) 'Trade liberalisation and the restructuring of work in post-apartheid South Africa', *Society in Transition*, 34(2): 295–319.

Mathauer, I. (2001) Institutional Pluralism and Inter-Organisational Relations in Local Health Care Provision in Uganda: Institutionalised Pathologies or Healing Organisations?, PhD, London School of Economics.

Meagher, K. (1990) 'The hidden economy: informal and parallel trade in north-western Uganda', *Review of African Political Economy*, 47.

Meagher, K. (2006) 'Social capital, social liabilities and political capital: social networks and informal manufacturing in Nigeria', *African Affairs*, 105(421): 553–82.

Meier, G. (ed.) (1976) *Leading Issues in Economic Development*, 3rd edn, New York, Oxford University Press.

Metcalf, J. (2005) 'Evolutionary concepts in relation to evolutionary economics', in K. Dopfer (ed.) *The Evolutionary Foundations of Economics*, Cambridge, Cambridge University Press.

Michels, R. (1911/1962) *Political Parties: A Sociological Study of the Oligarchical Tendencies of Modern Democracy*, Springfield, Cromwell-Collier.

Miliband, R. (1973) *The State in Capitalist Society: The Analysis of the Western Power System*, London, Quartet Books.

Mill, J.S. (1848/1900) *Principles of Political Economy*, 6th edn, London, Longmans Green.

Mill, J.S. (1859/1910) 'On liberty', in *Utilitarianism, Liberty, Representative Government*, London, Dent.

Mill, J.S. (1861/1910) 'Considerations on representative government', in *Utilitarianism, Liberty, Representative Government*, London, Dent.

Mill, J.S. (1869/1985) *The Subjugation of Women*, London, Dent.

Miller, G. (1992) *Managerial Dilemmas: The Political Economy of Hierarchy*, Cambridge, Cambridge University Press.

Mkandawire, T. (1994) 'Adjustment, political conditionality and democratisation in Africa', in G.A. Cornia and G.K. Helleiner, *From Adjustment to Development in Africa: Conflict, Controversy, Convergence, Consensus?*, Basingstoke, Macmillan – now Palgrave Macmillan.

Moe, T. (1984) 'The new economics of organisation', *American Journal of Political Science*, 28(4): 739–77.

Moe, T. (1995) 'Toward a theory of public bureaucracy', in O. Williamson, *Organisation Theory: From Chester Barnard to the Present*, expanded edn, Oxford, Oxford University Press.

Moe, T. (2005) 'Power and political institutions', *Perspectives on Politics*, 3(2): 215–33.

Mokyr, J. (2005) 'Is there a theory of economic history?', in K. Dopfer (ed.) *The Evolutionary Foundations of Economics*, Cambridge, Cambridge University Press.

Moore, B. (1967) *Social Origins of Democracy and Dictatorship: Lord and Peasant in the Making of the Modern World*, Harmondsworth, Penguin.

Morawetz, D. (1977) *Twenty-five Years of Economic Development*, Washington, World Bank.

Morgenthau, H. (1943/1969) 'Foreword to US government preliminary draft outline of a proposal for an international stabilisation fund of the united and associated nations', in J.K. Horsefield (ed.) *The International Monetary Fund, 1945–1965*, vol. 3, Documents, Washington, IMF.

Morgenthau, H.J. (1954) *Politics among Nations: The Struggle for Power and Peace*, 2nd edn, New York, Knopf.

Mosher, F. (1978) 'Public administration', in F. Lane (ed.) *Current Issues in Public Administration*, New York, St. Martin's Press.

Mosley, P., Harrigan, J. and Toye, J. (1991) *Aid and Power: The World Bank and Policy-based Lending*, vol. 1, London, Routledge.

Mouzelis, N. (1995) *Sociological Theory: What Went Wrong? Diagnosis and Remedies*, London, Routledge.

Mumbengegwi, C. (ed.) (2002) *Macroeconomic and Structural Adjustment Policies in Zimbabwe*, Basingstoke, Palgrave – now Palgrave Macmillan.

Mun, T. (1664/1928) *England's Treasure by Foreign Trade*, Oxford, Blackwell for the Economic History Society.

Munene, J. (1995) 'Organizational pathology and accountability in health and education in rural Uganda', in P. Langseth, J. Katorobo, E. Brett and J. Munene, *Uganda: Landmarks in Rebuilding a Nation*, Kampala, Fountain Press.

Murray, R. (1981) *Transfer Pricing and the State*, Brighton, Harvester.

Murray, R. (1992) 'Towards a flexible state', *IDS Bulletin, New Forms of Public Administration*, 23(4): 78–88.

Museveni, Y. (1992) *Sowing the Mustard Seed: The Struggle for Freedom and Democracy in Africa*, Basingstoke, Macmillan – now Palgrave Macmillan.

Mutibwa, P. (1992) *Uganda since Independence: A Story of Unfulfilled Hopes*, Kampala, Fountain Press.

Myrdal, G. (1953) *The Political Element in the Development of Economic Theory*, London, Routledge.

Myrdal, G. (1956/1976) 'Development and underdevelopment', in G. Meier (ed.) *Leading Issues in Economic Development*, 3rd edn, New York, Oxford University Press.

Nabudere, D. (2000) *Globalisation and the Post-colonial State*, Harare, AAPS Books.

Nash, M. (1963) 'Approaches to the study of economic growth', *Journal of Social Issues*, 29(1): 1–5.

Nelson, R. and Winter, S. (1982) *An Evolutionary Theory of Economic Change*, Cambridge, MA, Harvard University Press.

Neumann, F. (1937/1957) 'The changes in the function of law in modern society', in F. Neumann, *The Democratic and the Authoritarian State: Essays in Political and Legal Theory*, London, Collier-Macmillan.

Neumann, F. (1942) *Behemoth*, London, Gollancz.

Nicholas, S. (1994) 'The state and the development of African capitalism in Zimbabwe', in C. Leys and B. Berman (eds) *African Capitalism in African Development*, Boulder, Lynne Rienner.

Nicholls, L. (1998) From Paradigm to Practice: The Politics and Implementation of Sustainable Human Development in Uganda, PhD, London School of Economics.

Niskanen, W. (1971) *Bureaucracy and Representative Government*, Chicago, Aldine-Atherton.

Niskanen, W. (1973) *Bureaucracy: Servant or Master?*, London, Institute of Economic Affairs.

Niskanen, W. (1975) 'Bureaucrats and politicians', *Journal of Law and Economics*, 18(3): 617–43.

Nolan, P. (1988) *The Political Economy of Collective Farms: An Analysis of Post-Mao Rural Reforms*, Cambridge, Polity Press.

North, D. (1981) *Structure and Change in Economic History*, New York, Norton.

North, D. (1990) *Institutions, Institutional Change and Economic Performance*, Cambridge, Cambridge University Press.

North, D. (1995) 'The new institutional economics and third world development', in J. Harriss, J. Hunter and C.M. Lewis (eds) *The New Institutional Economics and Third World Development*, London, Routledge.

Nove, A. (1964) *Was Stalin Really Necessary?*, London, Allen & Unwin.

Nove, A. (1983) *The Economics of Feasible Socialism*, London, Allen & Unwin.

Oakeshott, M. (1971) 'On being conservative', in A. Arblaster and S. Lukes (eds) *The Good Society: A Book of Readings*, London, Methuen.

Oakeshott, M. (1991) 'Political education', in M. Oakeshott, *Rationalism in Politics and Other Essays*, new edn, Indiannapolis, Liberty Fund.

OECD (Organization for Economic Cooperation and Development) (1972) *Development Cooperation, 1972 Review*, Paris, OECD.

Offe, C. (1985) *Disorganized Capitalism: Contemporary Transformations of Work and Politics*, Cambridge, Polity Press.

Olson, M. (1965) *The Logic of Collective Action*, Cambridge, Harvard University Press.

Olson, M. (1982) *The Rise and Decline of Nations: Economic Growth, Stagflation, and Social Rigidities*, New Haven, Yale University Press.

Olson, M. (1997) 'The new institutional economics: the collective choice approach to economic development', in C. Clague, *Institutions and Economic Development: Growth and Governance in Less-developed and Post-socialist Countries*, Baltimore, Johns Hopkins University Press.

Olson, M. (2000) 'Big bills left on the sidewalk: why some nations are rich, and others poor', in M. Olson and S. Kahkonen (eds) *A Not-so-dismal Science: A Broader View of Economies and Societies*, Oxford, Oxford University Press.

Ostrom, E. (1990) *Governing the Commons: The Evolution of Institutions for Collective Action*, Cambridge, Cambridge University Press.

Ostrom, E., Schroeder, L. and Wynne, S. (1993) *Institutional Incentives and Sustainable Development: Infrastructure Policies in Perspective*, Boulder, Westview.

Ostrom, V. (1974) *The Intellectual Crisis in American Public Administration*, Alabama, Alabama University Press.

Ouchi, W. (1980) 'Markets, bureaucracies and clans', *Administrative Science Quarterly*, 25(1): 129–141.

Palma, G. (2003) 'The Latin American economies during the second half of the 20th century – from the age of "ISI" to the age of "the end of history"', in H.-J. Chang (ed.) *Rethinking Development Economics*, London, Anthem Press.

Parsons, T. (1937/1968) *The Structure of Social Action: A Study in Social Theory with Special Reference to a Group of Recent European Writers*, 2 vols, New York, Free Press.

Parsons, T. (1951/1964) *The Social System*, New York, Free Press.

Parsons, T. (1954) 'The present position and prospects of systematic theory in sociology', in T. Parsons, *Essays in Sociological Theory*, rev. edn, Glencoe, Free Press.

Paul, S. (1992) 'Accountability in public services: exit, voice and control', *World Development*, 20(7): 1047–60.

Picciotto, R. (1997) 'Putting institutional economics to work: from participation to governance', in C. Clague (ed.) *Institutions and Economic Development: Growth and Governance in Less-developed and Post-socialist Countries*, Baltimore, Johns Hopkins University Press.

Piore, S. and Sable, C. (1984) *The Second Industrial Divide*, New York, Basic Books.

Polak, J. (1977) 'Monetary analysis of income formation and payment problems', in IMF, *The Monetary Approach to the Balance of Payments*, Washington, IMF.

Polanyi, K. (1944/2001) *The Great Transformation: The Political and Social Origins of our Time*, 2nd edn, Boston, Beacon Press.

Pollak, R. (1985) 'A transaction cost approach to families and households', *Journal of Economic Literature*, 23(2): 581–608.

Pomeranz, K. (2000) *The Great Divergence: China, Europe, and the Making of the Modern World Economy*, Princeton, Princeton University Press.

Poulantzas, N. (1980) *State, Power, Socialism*, London, Verso.

Powell, J. (1970) 'Peasant society and clientalist politics', *American Political Science Review*, 64(2): 411–25.

Pratt, J. and Zeckhauser, R. (1985) 'Principals and agents: an overview', in J.W. Pratt, and R.J. Zeckhauser, *Principals and Agents: The Structure of Business*, Boston, Harvard Business School Press.

Prebisch, R. (1959) 'Commercial policy in the underdeveloped countries', *American Economic Review*, 49(2): 251–73.

Price, R. (1975) *Society and Bureaucracy in Contemporary Ghana*, Berkeley, University of California Press.

Prigogine, I. (2005) 'The rediscovery of value and the opening of economics', in K. Dopfer (ed.) *The Evolutionary Foundations of Economics*, Cambridge, Cambridge University Press.

Putnam, R. (1993) *Making Democracy Work: Civic Traditions in Modern Italy*, Princeton, Princeton University Press.

Putnam, R. (2000) *Bowling Alone: The Collapse and Revival of American Community*, New York, Simon & Schuster.

Putterman, L. (1986) *Peasants, Collectives and Choice: Economic Theory and Tanzania's Villages*, London, Jai.

Putzel, J. (1997) 'Accounting for the dark side of social capital: reading Robert Putnam on democracy', *Journal of International Development*, 9(7): 939–49.

Rahnema, M. (1997) 'Towards post-development: searching for signposts', in M. Rahnema and V. Bawtree, *The Post-development Reader*, London, Zed Books.

Ranis, G. (1997) 'The World Bank near the turn of the century', in R. Culpeper, A. Berry and F. Stewart (eds) *Global Development Fifty Years After Bretton Woods*, Basingstoke, Macmillan – now Palgrave Macmillan.

Ranson, S. and Stewart, J. (1994) *Management for the Public Domain: Enabling the Learning Society*, Basingstoke, Macmillan – now Palgrave Macmillan.

Rawls, J. (1973) *A Theory of Justice*, Oxford, Oxford University Press.

Reinert, F. (2000) *The Other Cannon: The Other Cannon and the History of Economic Policy*, Norsk Investor Forum and SVN Oslo, University of Oslo, Centre for Development and Environment.

Reinke, J. (1998) 'Does solidarity pay? The case of the small enterprise foundation, South Africa', *Development and Change*, 29(3): 553–76.

Richards, P. (1985) *Indigenous Agricultural Revolution: Ecology and Food Production in West Africa*, London, Hutchinson.

Rima, I. (1978) *Development of Economic Analysis*, 3rd edn, Homewood, IL, Irwin.

Rodgers, D. (2006) 'Living in the shadow of death: gangs, violence, and social order in urban Nicaragua, 1996–2002', *Journal of Latin American Studies*, 38(2): 267–92.

Rodney, W. (1973) *How Europe Underdeveloped Africa*, London, Bogle-L'Overture.

Roemer, J. (1979) 'Divide and conquer: micro foundations of the Marxist theory of discrimination', *Bell Journal of Economics*, 10: 695–705.

Rostow, W. (1971) *The Stages of Economic Growth: A Non-Communist Manifesto*, 2nd edn, Cambridge, Cambridge University Press.

Rousseau, J.-J. (1758/1973) 'A discourse on political economy', in J.-J. Rousseau, *The Social Contract and Discourses*, London, Dent.

Rowbotham, S., Segal, L. and Wainwright, H. (1979) *Beyond the Fragments: Feminism and the Making of Socialism*, London, Merlin.

Rueschmeyer, D. and Evans, P. (1985) 'The state and economic transformation: towards an analysis of the conditions underlying successful intervention', in P. Evans, D. Reuschemeyer and T. Skocpol, *Bringing the State Back In*, Cambridge, Cambridge University Press.

Rutter, M. and Madge, N. (1976) *Cycles of Disadvantage: A Review of Research*, London, Heinemann.

Sachs, J. (1988) 'Conditionality, debt relief, and the developing country debt crisis', in J. Sachs (ed.) *Developing Country Debt and Economic Performance*, vol. 1, London, University of Chicago.

Sachs, W. (ed.) (1992) *The Development Dictionary: A Guide to Knowledge and Power*, London, Zed Books.

Sahn, D., Dorosch, P.A. and Younger, S.D. (1997) *Structural Adjustment Reconsidered: Economic Policy and Poverty in Africa*, Cambridge, Cambridge University Press.

Samuleson, P. (1956) 'Social indifference curves', *Quarterly Journal of Economics*, 30(1): 1–22.

Sansom, C. (2004) *Dissolution*, London, Pan.

Sartori, G. (1976) *Parties and Party Systems*, Cambridge, Cambridge University Press.

Sathyamurthy, T. (1991) *The Political Development of Uganda, 1900–86*, London, Gower.

Schaffer, B. (1969) 'The deadlock in development administration', in C. Leys, *Politics and Change in Developing Countries: Studies in the Theory and Practice of Development*, Cambridge, Cambridge University Press.

Schumpeter, J.A. (1943) *Capitalism, Socialism and Democracy*, London, Unwin.

Schumpeter, J.A. (1964) *Business Cycles*, New York, McGraw Hill.

Schuurman, F. (ed.) (1993) *Beyond the Impasse: New Directions in Development Theory*, London, Zed Books.

Scott, J. (1972) 'Patron-client politics and political change in South East Asia', *American Political Science Review*, 66(1): 91–113.

Scott, J. (1987) *Weapons of the Weak: Everyday Forms of Peasant Resistance*, New Haven, Yale University Press.

Scott, J. (1997) 'Domination and the arts of resistance', in M. Rahnema and V. Bawtree (eds) *The Post-development Reader*, London, Zed Books.

Semmler, R. (1989) 'Managing without managers', *Harvard Business Review*, 67(5): 76–84.

Sen, A. (1990) 'Gender and cooperative conflicts', in I. Tinker (ed.) *Persistent Inequalities: Women in World Development*, New York, Oxford University Press.

Sen, A. (1999) *Development as Freedom*, Oxford, Oxford University Press.

Sen, A. (2006) 'Opinion: continuing the conversation [on gender and cooperative conflicts]', *The Hindu*, 3 February, www.hindu.com/2006/02/03/stories/2006020305661100.htm.

Shepsle, K. and Bonchek, M. (1997) *Analyzing Politics: Rationality, Behavior, and Institutions*, New York, Norton.

Siffin, W. (1957) *Toward a Comparative Study of Public Administration*, Bloomington, Indiana University Press.

Silverberg, G. and Verspagen, B. (2005) 'Evolutionary theorizing on economic growth', in K. Dopfer (ed.) *The Evolutionary Foundations of Economics*, Cambridge, Cambridge University Press.

Simon, H. (1957) *Administrative Behaviour*, 2nd edn, New York, Macmillan.

Skálnes, T. (1995) *The Politics of Economic Reform in Zimbabwe: Continuity and Change in Development*, Basingstoke, Macmillan – now Palgrave Macmillan.

Sklar, R. (1967) 'Political science and national integration', *Journal of Modern African Studies*, 5(1): 1–11.

Slater, D. and Tonkiss, F. (2001) *Market Society: Markets and Modern Social Theory*, Cambridge, Polity Press.

Smith, A. (1776/1991) *The Wealth of Nations*, New York, Knopf.

Social Research (1985) New social movements, special issue, 52(4).

Spencer, H. (1850/1971) 'Social statics', in A. Arlbaster and S. Lukes, *The Good Society: A Book of Readings*, London, Methuen.

Spiro, P. (2002) 'The democratic accountability of non-governmental organizations', *Chicago Journal of International Law*, 3(1): 161–9.

Standing, G., Sender, J. and Weeks, J. (1996) *Restructuring the Labour Market: The South African Challenge*, Geneva, International Labour Office.

Stepan, A. (1985) 'State power and the strength of civil society in southern cone of Latin America', in P. Evans, D. Reuschemeyer and T. Skocpol, *Bringing the State Back In*, Cambridge, Cambridge University Press.

Stern, N. (2006) *The Economics of Climate Change: The Stern Review*, Cambridge, Cambridge University Press.

Stiglitz, J. (2001) 'Foreword', in K. Polanyi, *The Great Transformation: The Political and Social Origins of our Time*, 2nd edn, Boston, Beacon Press.

Stiglitz, J. (2002) *Globalization and its Discontents*, London, Allen Lane.

Stiglitz, J. (2008) 'Turn left for sustainable growth', *The Economist's Voice*, 5(4): 1–3.

Stinchcombe, A. (1997) 'Tilly on the past as a sequence of futures', in C. Tilly, *Roads from Past to Future*, Lanham, Rowman & Littlefield.

Stoneman, C. (ed.) (1988) *Zimbabwe's Prospects: Issues of Race, Class, State, and Capital in Southern Africa*, London, Macmillan.

Stoneman, C. and Cliffe, L. (1989) *Zimbabwe: Politics, Economics and Society*, London, Pinter.

Streek, W. and Schmitter, P. (1991) 'Community, market, state – and associations?', in G. Thompson, J. Frances, R. Levacic and J. Mitchell (eds) *Markets, Hierarchies and Networks: The Coordination of Social Life*, London, Sage.

Suleiman, E. (2003) *Dismantling Democratic States*, Princeton, Princeton University Press.

Sweezy, P. (1970) *The Theory of Capitalist Development*, New York, Monthly Review Press.

Taylor, F. (1912/1990) 'Scientific management', in D. Pugh, *Organization Theory: Selected Readings*, Harmondsworth, Penguin.

Thomas, C. (1974) *Dependence and Transformation*, New York: Monthly Review Press.

Thompson, E. (1968) *The Making of the English Working Class*, Harmondsworth, Penguin.

Tilly, C. (1985) 'War making and state making as organized crime', in P. Evans, D. Reuschemeyer and T. Skocpol, *Bringing the State Back In*, Cambridge, Cambridge University Press.

Tilly, C. (1997a) *Roads from Past to Future*, Lanham, Rowman & Littlefield.

Tilly, C. (1997b) 'The modernization of political conflict in France', in C. Tilly, *Roads from Past to Future*, Lanham, Rowman & Littlefield.

Tilly, C. (1997c) 'Cities, bourgeois, and revolution in France', in C. Tilly, *Roads from Past to Future*, Lanham, Rowman & Littlefield.

Tilly, C. (1997d) 'Does modernization breed revolution?', in C. Tilly, *Roads from Past to Future*, Lanham, Rowman & Littlefield.

Tilly, C. (1997e) 'Future social science', in C. Tilly, *Roads from Past to Future*, Lanham, Rowman & Littlefield.

Tilly, C. (2000) 'Processes and mechanisms of democratisation', *Sociological Theory*, 18(1): 1–16.

Tilly, C. (2003) 'Changing forms of inequality', *Sociological Theory*, 21(1): 31–6.

Todaro, M. (1997) *Economic Development*, 6th edn, London, Longman.

Trotsky, L. (1930/2000) *The History of the Russian Revolution*, trans, C. Russell, www.marxists.org/archive/trotsky/works/download/hrr-vol1.pdf.

Trueman, D. (1951) *The Governmental Process*, New York, Knopf.

Tullock, G. (1965) *The Politics of Bureaucracy*, Washington, Public Affairs Press.

Tullock, G. (1987) *The Politics of Bureaucracy*, New York, University Press of America.

Turner, H., Clack, G. and Roberts, G. (1967) *Labour Relations in the Motor Industry: A Study of Industrial Unrest and an International Comparison*, London, Allen & Unwin.

UN (United Nations) (2005) *Report of the Fact-finding Mission to Zimbabwe to Assess the Scope and Impact of Operation Murambatsvina by the UN Special Envoy ... Mrs Anna Kajumulo Tibaijuka*, New York, UN.

UNDP (UN Development Programme) (2003) *Human Development Report: A Compact among Nations to End Human Poverty*, New York, Oxford University Press.

UNECA (UN Economic Commission for Africa) (2007) *Economic Report on Africa, 2007*, Adis Ababa, UNECA.

UNESCO (2001) *Universal Declaration of Cultural Diversity*, Paris, UNESCO.

United States Congress (2000) *Report of the International Financial Institutions Advisory Commission*, the Meltzer Commission, Washington DC.

Uphof, N. (1995) 'Why NGOs are not a third sector: a sectoral analysis with some thoughts on accountability, sustainability and evaluation', in M. Edwards and D. Hulme, *Non-governmental Organisations – Performance and Accountability: Beyond the Magic Bullet*, London, Earthscan.

Vaitsos, C. (1974) *Intercountry Income Distribution and Transnational Enterprises*, Oxford, Clarendon Press.

Van de Walle, N. (1995) 'Crisis and opportunity in Africa', in L. Diamond and M. Plattner (eds) *Economic Reform and Democracy*, Baltimore, MD, Johns Hopkins University Press.

Van de Walle, N. (2001) *African Economies and the Politics of Permanent Crisis*, Cambridge, Cambridge University Press.

Vanek, J. (1973) 'The Yugoslav economy viewed through the theory of labour management', *World Development*, 1(9): 39–56.

Vasilash, G. (1997) 'The human touch', *Automotive Design and Production*, October, www.autofieldguide.com/issues/1097.html.

Wade, R. (1988) *Village Republics: Economic Conditions for Collective Action in South India*, Cambridge, Cambridge University Press.

Wade, R. (1990) *Governing the Market, Economic Theory and the Role of Government in East Asian Industrialisation*, Princeton, Princeton University Press.

Wade, R. (2004) 'On the causes of increasing poverty and inequality, or why the Matthew effect prevails', *New Political Economy*, 9(2): 163–88.

Wallerstein, I. (1998) 'The present state of the debate on world inequality', in M. Seligson and J. Passe-Smith, *Development and Under-development*, 2nd edn, Boulder, Lynne Rienner.

Weber, M. (1920/1983) 'The Protestant ethic and the spirit of capitalism', in S. Andreski, *Max Weber on Capitalism, Bureaucracy and Religion*, London, Allen & Unwin.

Weber, M. (1922/1968) *Economy and Society*, Berkeley, University of California Press.

Weber, M. (1976) *The Protestant Ethic and the Spirit of Capitalism*, London, Allen & Unwin.

Webster, E. (2005) 'Making a living, earning a living: work and employment in Southern Africa', *International Political Science Review*, 26(10): 55–71.

Werbner, R. (1996) 'Introduction: multiple identities, plural areas', in R. Werbner and T. Ranger, *Postcolonial Identities in Africa*, London, Zed Books.

White, G. (1993a) 'Towards a political analysis of markets', *IDS Bulletin: The Political Analysis of Markets*, 24(3): 1–11.

White, G. (1993b) *Riding the Tiger: The Politics of Economic Reform in Post-Mao China*, Stanford, Stanford University Press.

White, G. and Luckham, R. (1996) *Democratization in the South: The Jagged Wave*, Manchester, Manchester University Press.

White, H. (1943/1969) 'Preliminary draft proposal for a United Nations Stabilisation Fund', in J.K. Horsefield, *The International Monetary Fund, 1945–1965*, vol. 3, *Documents*, Washington, IMF.

Wignaraja, P. (1991) *Participatory Development: Learning from South Asia*, Karachi, Oxford University Press.

Wild, V. (1997) *Profit not for Profit's Sake: History and Business Culture of African Entrepreneurs in Zimbabwe*, Harare, Baobab Books.

Wiles, P. (1962) *The Political Economy of Communism*, Oxford, Blackwell.

Williamson, J. (1990) 'What Washington means by policy reform', in J. Williamson (ed.) *Latin American Adjustment: How Much Has Happened?*, Washington, Institute of International Economics.

Williamson, O.E. (1975) *Markets and Hierarchies: Analysis and Anti-trust Implications*, New York, Free Press.

Williamson, O.E. (1987) *The Economic Institutions of Capitalism*, New York, Free Press.

Williamson, O.E. (2000) 'Economic institutions and development: a view from the bottom', in M. Olson and S. Kahkonen, *A Not-so-dismal Science: A Broader View of Economies and Societies*, Oxford, Oxford University Press.

Winch, P. (1970a) 'The idea of a social science', in B. Wilson (ed.) *Rationality*, Oxford, Blackwell.

Winch, P. (1970b) 'Understanding a primitive society', in B. Wilson (ed.) *Rationality*, Oxford, Blackwell.

Witt, U. (2005) 'The evolutionary perspective on organizational change and the theory of the firm', in K. Dopfer (ed.) *The Evolutionary Foundations of Economics*, Cambridge, Cambridge University Press.

Wolf, E. (1971) 'Introduction', in N. Miller and R. Ayer (ed.) *National Liberation: Revolution in the Third World*, New York, Free Press.

Wolin, S. (1960) *Politics and Vision: Continuity and Innovation in Western Political Thought*, London, Allen & Unwin.

Womack, J., Jones, D. and Roos, D. (1990) *The Machine that Changed the World*, New York, Rawson.

World Bank (1978) *World Development Report 1978*, Washington, World Bank.

World Bank (1981) *Accelerated Development in Sub-Saharan Africa: An Agenda for Action*, Washington, World Bank.

World Bank (1997) *World Development Report 1997: The State in a Changing World*, Washington, World Bank.

World Bank (2004) *World Development Report 2004: Making Service Theory of the Market Economy Work for Poor People*, Washington, World Bank.

World Bank (2006) *Annual Report, Africa*, www.worldbank.org/.

Young, C., Sherman, N.P. and Rose, T.H. (1981) *Cooperatives and Development: Agricultural Politics in Ghana and Uganda*, Madison, University of Wisconsin Press.

Zolberg, A. (1969) *One-party Government in the Ivory Coast*, rev. edn, Princeton, Princeton University Press.

Zusman, P. (1988) *Individual Behavior and Social Choice in a Cooperative Settlement*, Jerusalem, Magnes Press.

Index